The Rise of the Gunbelt

THE RISE
OF THE
GUNBELT

The Military Remapping of
Industrial America

ANN MARKUSEN PETER HALL
SCOTT CAMPBELL SABINA DEITRICK

New York Oxford
OXFORD UNIVERSITY PRESS
1991

Oxford University Press

Oxford   New York   Toronto
Delhi   Bombay   Calcutta   Madras   Karachi
Petaling Jaya   Singapore   Hong Kong   Tokyo
Nairobi   Dar es Salaam   Cape Town
Melbourne   Auckland

and associated companies in
Berlin   Ibadan

Copyright © 1991 by Ann Markusen, Peter Hall,
Scott Campbell, Sabina Deitrick.

Published by Oxford University Press, Inc.,
200 Madison Avenue, New York, New York 10016

Oxford is a registered trademark of Oxford University Press

Library of Congress Cataloging-in-Publication Data
The rise of the gunbelt : the military remapping of
industrial America / Ann Markusen . . . [et al.].
p. cm. Includes bibliographical references (p.) and index.
ISBN 0-19-506648-0
1. Defense industries—United States.
2. Military–industrial complex—United States.
3. Defense contracts—United States.
4. United States—Economic conditions—1945– —Regional disparities.
I. Markusen, Ann R. HD9743.U6R57 1991
338.4'76233'0973—dc20 90-7417

2 4 6 8 9 7 5 3 1

Printed in the United States of America
on acid-free paper

for Michael Teitz

Acknowledgments

Our first debt is to the National Science Foundation for the two grants that made possible the research on which this book is based. We are particularly indebted to the then-director of NSF's Geography and Regional Science Program, Dr. Ronald Abler, for his encouragement and support.

We also want to thank the officials of the many companies we interviewed in the course of the project. Since many would wish to remain anonymous, we have treated them all in this way. This does not reduce our indebtedness to them for being so generous of their time, both during the interviews and during the subsequent checking of our interview records. Those quoted in the book have given their permission. We want specifically to acknowledge Lee Atwood of North American Rockwell, who emerged from retirement to share his recollections with us. We would also like to thank Theron Rinehart of Fairchild, Dr. David Burgess-Wise of Ford Motor Company, Pat Stone of Allied-Signal, Dr. Morton Klein of the Illinois Institute of Technology's Research Institute, John Riggin of Hewlett Packard, Dr. Ted Bettway of TRW, Dr. Albert Bridges of Kaman Sciences, Joe Reich, Dan Lindheim of Congressman Ronald Dellums's office, Mark Hardesty and Mark Baldwin of the United Auto Workers, Captain David Larivee and Colonel Ken Fleming of the United States Air Force Academy, Lieutenant-Colonel Robert Swedenburg, and General Robert Herres of the United States Air Force for help in finding the right people, for sharing written materials, and for comments on our earlier drafts.

Many individuals at the University of California at Berkeley and at Northwestern University made particular contributions. At Berkeley, the Institute of Urban and Regional Development provided both a home and staff support for the project over many years, including editing by David Van Arnam and Marie Floyd. Liz Mueller and Mark Goldman worked as research assistants; Anneke Vonk drew the computer maps. At Northwestern, Janet Soule completed the near-final text. Tom Intorcio, Ben Wedge, Vickie Gwiasda, Jim Day, Karen McCurdy, RuthAnn Markusen, and Helzi Noponen contributed to the research effort at Northwestern, and Margo Gordon deserves special thanks for creating a second home for the project at Northwestern's Center for Urban Affairs and Policy Research. In our third home at Rutgers, Kim Smith deserves praise for her staff support.

We also want to thank Niles Hansen, as well as anonymous referees, for their comments on the first version of the manuscript, which have been invaluable in revising it for publication.

We are grateful to Sage Publications for permission to reprint portions of Ann Markusen, with Karen McCurdy, "Chicago's Defense-Based High Technology: A Case Study of the 'Seedbeds of Innovation' Hypothesis," *Economic Development Quarterly* 3, no. 1, pp. 15–31, copyright 1989, by Sage Publications, which are incorporated in Chapter 4.

A number of colleagues have shared their ideas, read portions of the manuscript, and given us excellent feedback. We would like to thank in particular Roger Montgomery, Bennett Harrison, Annalee Saxenian, Robin Bloch, Martin Schiesl, Erica Schoenberger, Amy Glasmeier, Al Rubenstein, Mark Goldman, Anthony Roso, Jay Stowsky, Michael Shuman, Roger Lotchin, and Michael Storper.

Finally, although he will probably be surprised, we want to recognize the support of Michael Teitz, a colleague at Berkeley. During the years of this research, our conversations with him have been stimulating and helpful, and have fed in no small way into our own thought. In partial recognition of his contribution, we dedicate this book to him.

Contents

Figures

Tables

The Rise of the Gunbelt

1

Introduction:
The Rise of the Gunbelt

Over the half-century since World War II, a profound change has come over the economic landscape of America—a change so obvious that it is the staple fare of newspapers and newscasts. It is summarized by media neologisms: Sunbelt, Frostbelt, and Rustbowl. Its essence is the relative decline of the old industrial heartland, the resurgence of New England, and the rise of new industrial regions on the nation's southern and western perimeter. It is symbolized by the decay of steel in Pittsburgh, engineering in Cleveland, and autos in Detroit, and by the emergence of new high-tech industrial complexes in California, Texas, Massachusetts, and Florida.

Millions of words have been written trying to explain it. And, indeed, the causes are neither few nor simple. But one factor has been overwhelmingly important, yet strangely neglected: the rise of what Dwight D. Eisenhower called the military–industrial complex. During and after World War II, in a way that was never before true, defense spending became a major determinant of economic prosperity or decay. Whole new industries, and a set of predominantly defense-dependent firms, were bred in lock step with the new, permanent bureau in charge of military matters—the Department of Defense. Pentagon dollars created industrial complexes in California orchards, in Arizona and New Mexico deserts, on Utah salt flats, in the Rocky Mountains of Colorado, and in Florida swamps. The lack of these dollars helped create industrial wastelands in cities that had once been the industrial core of America.

In this process, over the past half-century, defense contracting has produced a new economic map of the United States. The regions and metropolitan areas that have disproportionately gained are strung unevenly around America's perimeter, from the state of Washington through California to the desert states of the Southwest, on through Texas and the Great Plains, across to Florida, and discontinuously up the East Coast to New England.

Seeking an appropriate metaphor, we toyed with terms like "defense perimeter" and "defense crescent." We finally settled on the "gunbelt." For in their general shape, superimposed on the map of America, these new

3

military–industrial regions do indeed resemble the belt around the hips of the solitary sheriff in pursuit of the bad guys in an old western movie. The southwestern states, Texas, and the Great Plains make up the holster; Florida represents the handcuffs ready to be slipped on the wrists of the villains; New England is the bullet clip.

In contrast, Pentagon contracts have scarcely touched the broad interior of the country. This is particularly true of the northern Plains and Mountain states from Idaho to the Dakotas, and a wide strip of North Central and southeastern states from Wisconsin to Ohio to Tennessee. Although places here have benefited from the location of defense bases, the industrial impact has been minimal. Some defense money has made its way to plants in the Midwest, America's industrial heartland—but nowhere near as much as the area's industrial traditions and capacity would seem to warrant. And the historic evidence shows that during the 1950s—a key decade in the story that follows—the Midwest's share fell catastrophically, never again to recover. States like Michigan and Illinois may carry the sheriff's star, the badge of their honorable role in producing the flood of mass-produced capital goods and consumer goods that first made America prosperous and proud and permitted the Allied victory in World War II. But they are no longer where the military muscle is. They do not tote the gun or harvest the receipts from its manufacture.

This book explores two main questions about the gunbelt. First, exactly what is it, where is it, and what does it do? We answer these questions in Chapter 2, by summarizing the facts of defense contracting and the employment it generates. We present the data in maps and charts that give a graphic, almost animated, picture of the rise of the gunbelt and the decline of the industrial heartland.

Second, why did this momentous change occur? This is not nearly as straightforward a question as some might think. The main theme of this book is that the rise of the gunbelt has no one simple cause. Many elements enter in, but none dominates. True, the story does hinge on a few key founding fathers who either were born in California or settled there; true, they enjoyed flying in California's sunny skies. But there were also successful flyer-entrepreneurs who located under the gray skies of the Midwest and the East Coast, and there is not much evidence that climate proved a key factor for the Californians. True again, in the heat of World War II, factories were deliberately located in places thought to be strategically safe from enemy attack; but many of these plants were mothballed at war's end, and since then atomic weaponry has made no place really safe. True too, defense dollars have become the object of a huge lobbying effort that involves contractors, states, and localities and their political representatives. Doubtless, at the margin, such pressures have influenced key decisions. But overall, researchers agree that this process has done relatively little to affect the overall shape of the defense map. Like the advertising of commercial products, everyone has to join in but the market shares remain about the same as they were before.

True again, in much of the gunbelt, the frontier remained open until a late date. It would be foolish to suggest any facile association between the nineteenth-century frontier mentality and a twentieth-century enthusiasm for winning military contracts. Yet there may be a more subtle link. Long after the closing of the agrarian-settlement frontier in 1890, the expansive "can do," tall tale–telling western culture engendered a continuing frontier of urban-real-estate development, coupled with intense civic boosterism, that has provided a welcome to all kinds of new activities, including military installations and defense industries.

The military remapping of the United States results from a complex chain of structural causes and choices made by various public- and private-sector parties. Like an evolving highway system for which early decisions on road placement affected the further branching of routes, it arose from a series of locational choices embedded in a trio of strategic and political contexts. First, during and after World War II, America's changing military mission powerfully affected the role of the three armed services. Particularly, it created a new phenomenon: high-technology cold war, which depended on massive technological advance and boosted the Air Force and certain segments of the Navy into strategic prominence. Second, while military contracting is different in many ways from producing for the commercial market, this difference was underlined by the injection of the new technologies. Much of our story hinges on the success of certain military personnel and individual firms, in particular regions, in embracing and developing technological advance. Third, the three services had and have very different traditions, including different relationships with industrial contractors. These connections work themselves out in complex ways across the geographical space of America and across time.

Our story moves back and forth among historical events, institutions, and actors. Chapter 3 offers a preliminary sketch of a theory of location for the defense industries—a theory that captures the dynamism of the historical context. It encompasses the rise of cold war, with its new high-tech demands on manufacturing, and the behavior of company founders, military men, members of Congress, managers, workers, and civic boosters, and compares regions for their relative attractiveness to the new military–industrial complex. We outline five paths to the military–industrial city.

Having provided a set of road maps, we then go on tour. In turn, we visit each of the crucial sections of the gunbelt, showing how, at critical points in time, the interaction of key structural forces affected each area's power to generate or attract defense industries, or to lose them. Our sequence is both geographical and chronological. We range from the birth and early demise of the defense industry in the heartland (Chapter 4), through the rise of Los Angeles in the 1920s and 1930s (Chapter 5), the industrial renaissance of New England in the 1950s (Chapter 6), the story of Seattle, the "solitary survivor" (Chapter 7), to the recent development of new defense complexes in Colorado (Chapter 8) and the nation's capital (Chapter 9).

In each chapter, we argue that a unique concatenation of circumstances— shifting national military mission, changing service roles, rapidly evolving technology, the adaptive capacities of local entrepreneurs in industry, science, and civic boosterism—altered the balance of forces that helped shape the competitive power of one region, or one city, against another. This, then, is the central theme. We do not argue for a theory of historic inevitability: time and chance happeneth to places as to people. We do argue that powerful historic forces have greatly affected the ability of places to compete as well as the leadership powers of certain key people in the military–industrial complex.

Finally, in Chapter 10, we speculate more widely about the significance of the gunbelt. The rise of the gunbelt has been an expensive proposition for the United States, not just because of trillions of dollars spent but because of where those dollars have been spent. In many ways, cold war procurement has served as a very powerful regional policy. And while it may have helped the Old South to rebound from relative poverty, it provided a generous largesse to two areas that have always had high per capita regional incomes: New England and the Pacific coast. It has played an ambiguous role, therefore, in promoting regional equality.

Furthermore, the rise of the gunbelt has contributed to the overspecialization of many subregional economies, rendering those on both the losing and winning ends much more vulnerable to shocks associated with shifts in defense spending. Military spending cuts, such as those in full swing in the early 1990s, threaten to severely depress the economies of regions heavily favored in previous defense booms. Los Angeles, Boston, and Seattle face local difficulties as major weapons-systems funding and research-and-development efforts are scaled back.

The gunbelt has, we conclude, engendered new "seedbeds of innovation"—centers where a very distinctive business culture has thrived. This culture, marked by positive attitudes toward selling to the military, an emphasis on innovation and small-batch production instead of standardization and mass production, and meritocracy in place of traditional labor-relations systems, differs dramatically from that which characterizes the old industrial heartland, stretching from the Appalachians to the Mississippi and south to the Ohio.

The mounting of these new seedbeds has been extraordinarily expensive. Taxpayers have paid for the erection of whole new plant complexes and the infrastructure, schools, and even housing that accompany them. Since excess capacity has simultaneously developed in older heartland cities, this can be viewed as a wasteful duplication of public-sector investment. Furthermore, through the Pentagon patronage of the gunbelt, taxpayers have unintentionally financed a spectacular for-profit population-resettlement program. Several generations of scientists and engineers have been recruited from public universities in the industrial heartland to form new labor pools in the major gunbelt cities, and defense contracts have paid for their moves. Or they have been recruited as students by schools like MIT and Caltech, where their educations have been taxpayer-financed through research grants. In this fashion, taxpayers have paid for the formation of highly technical labor pools in selected military-oriented cities.

The gunbelt has had troubling socioeconomic consequences too. It has contributed to the segregation of Americans by class and race. In the increasingly high-tech business of outfitting the services, military contractors hire a disproportionate number of well-educated white men. And as cities in the industrial heartland are excluded from the military largesse and their traditionally strong industries are weakened by the absence of a more even-handed industrial policy, large pools of an urban underclass as well as displaced blue-collar workers are left with shrinking or inferior local employment prospects.

Furthermore, the rise of the gunbelt has been a major factor in the political realignment of the nation. As enclaves of defense-dependent activity have grown in the gunbelt, they have contributed to a notable geopolitical shift—more congressional seats in the South and West, and more Republicans and hawkish Democrats occupying those seats. We speculate that this has had a strong positive-feedback effect on military procurement per se, as certain congressional delegations push for the continuation of weapons programs that are essential to their local economies. In other words, the uneven geographical distribution of military business may have contributed to the boosting of military expenditures far beyond what purely strategic concerns called for.

All these issues we explore in our final chapter. We also speculate on what the United States would look like if defense production was concentrated in the same cities where cars, machine tools, and steel are made. The poor performance of the industrial heartland in recent years, especially with the challenge from European and Japanese competitors, may in part result from the geophysical isolation of high-tech military production from commercially oriented industries. What, then, of the future? We end our study by noting that the military–industrial frontier is now closed, at least geographically, and that other cities can not expect to win much of a share of high-tech military business. In large part, the future of the gunbelt, and its neglected counterparts, will depend on the course that the federal government takes to keep the nation competitive. And we argue that the recent initiatives toward peace and disarmament, while raising concerns among military contractors, offer a substantial opportunity to rebuild the economy and to eliminate the worst features of the gunbelt.

2

The Military Remapping of America

The gunbelt is a major—*the* major—phenomenon in the contemporary economic map of America. It consists of a new set of industrial locales that contain a wholly new set of industries and firms whose major preoccupation has been producing high-tech weaponry for the cold war. It is unprecedented in modern world history; no other Western industrial nation has seen so much of its leading-edge industrial capacity located, in so extraordinarily short a time, so far from the original centers of commerce and production.

In turn, the gunbelt has engendered cultures significantly different from the adversarial, bipartisan, and cosmopolitan culture associated with older industrial cities. Over the post–World War II decades, the special economy and business preoccupations of the gunbelt have become deeply rooted in its host communities, stimulating the growth of a new business and community culture around them. Gunbelt cities are by now a permanent phenomenon. By this final decade of the twentieth century, entire urban economies depend on the aerospace complex, which, in turn, relies on continued government spending.

In 1952, the nadir of American fortunes in the Korean War, few observers would have predicted the rise of the gunbelt or the slump of the industrial heartland. World War II had seen a phenomenal increase in military production across the United States, above all in the Pacific states of Washington and California. It had also prompted the opening of huge production complexes in interior states like Kansas and southern states like Georgia. But at that war's end, production was abruptly truncated, busy plants were put on a care-and-maintenance basis, and many wartime factories were mothballed. The start of the cold war and the Berlin airlift of 1948 to 1949 brought rearmament back on to the national agenda. The outbreak of hostilities in Korea in June 1950 made it a reality. But that war did not fundamentally affect the geography of production.

Up through the early postwar period, the industrial heartland was the locus of production of military hardware as well as producer and consumer durables. By 1990, all this had changed. The industrial heartland's share of military receipts had plummeted. Concurrently, its manufacturing capacity had grown more slowly than that of the rest of the nation. Beginning in the final years of the Vietnam War, from 1972 on, the Midwest posted significant manufacturing job losses, while states like California, Florida, and those in the Intermountain West enjoyed hefty gains. From 1982 to 1983, 242,000 defense jobs were added to the economy, chiefly in the gunbelt, while the net loss of 436,000 manufacturing jobs fell heaviest on the Midwest. In the Reagan buildup of the 1980s, defense spending accounted for nearly 1 million new jobs, 17 percent of all growth in private-sector employment between 1981 and 1985. These jobs, too, went lopsidedly to the gunbelt.

Accompanying these shifts were notable changes in the distribution of regional income. Per capita incomes rose in the gunbelt states and fell in the industrial heartland. In large part, these differential growth rates and income effects were the result of military-spending differentials and the construction of high-tech industrial complexes.

The production geography of 1952, and its subsequent transformation, can be appreciated by looking at two basic measures. One is an *input* measure: the dollar volume of defense contracts that each state and region received. The other is an *output* measure: the resulting employment generation in these places. Both show a remarkable net dispersion of military-oriented production out of the heartland and toward the gunbelt over the ensuing three decades. In what follows, we show how these shifts are associated with weapons systems, military clients, and lopsidedness in research spending.

The Shift in Defense Contracting

Defense contracting has been literally a multi-billion-dollar business. In the nearly four decades since the Korean conflict, total American defense spending has never sunk below $150 billion a year in terms of 1982 dollars (Fig. 2.1), or roughly 5 percent of total GNP (Fig. 2.2). Even before Korea, at the start of the cold war, the Truman Doctrine initiated a quasi-permanent defense industry to meet military needs in a civilian economy, thus creating what one analyst has called the "permanent war economy."[1] Although peaks occurred—during the Korean War, the early 1960s post-*Sputnik*/Cuban missile crisis era, the Vietnam War, and the buildup of the 1980s—even in the interludes between these bursts, spending never fell to the demobilization levels of the immediate post–World War II era, let alone the interwar years.

Peaks and troughs are important in one respect, though. In the peaks, procurement takes the lion's share of the increase (Fig. 2.3). But during the post–World War II era, there have been two different kinds of peaks. In "hot war" peaks—Korea, Vietnam—the demand for basic armaments diverted defense contracts to already equipped plants in the industrial heartland. During the "cold war" peaks—the missile buildup of the mid–1950s, the Strategic Defense Initiative of the 1980s—there was a marked shift to the gunbelt (Fig. 2.4).[2]

Prime contracts—which represent the largest single chunk of defense spending—capture the money that the Department of Defense pays for pri-

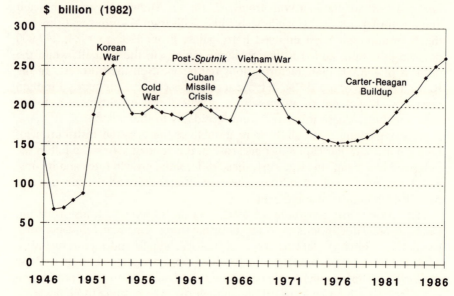

FIGURE 2.1. Real defense spending, 1946–1987 (in billions of 1982 dollars). (Council of Economic Advisors, annual)

FIGURE 2.2. Defense spending as percentage of GNP, 1946–1987. (Council of Economic Advisors, annual)

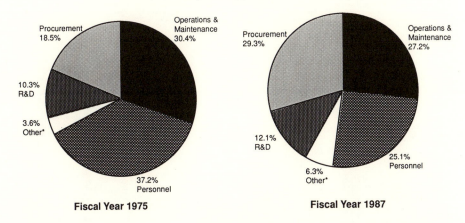

Fiscal Year 1975   Fiscal Year 1987

*Includes military construction, family housing, and non-DoD defense activities.

FIGURE 2.3. National defense outlays, by function, FY 1975 and FY 1987. (Office of Management and Budget)

vately produced supplies, services, and facilities that range from airframes and aircraft engines, to clothing, housing, and food. In 1952, the East North Central division—in popular language, the Midwest—received nearly 31 percent of total primes, with the Mid-Atlantic states getting the next biggest share, over 26 percent. By 1984, that combined 57 percent share had fallen

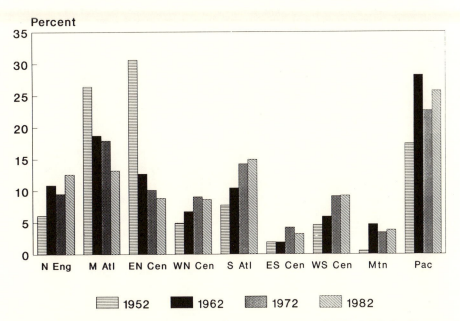

FIGURE 2.4. Major prime-contract awards, as percentage of U.S. total, by Census division, FY 1952–1982. (Department of Defense, annual)

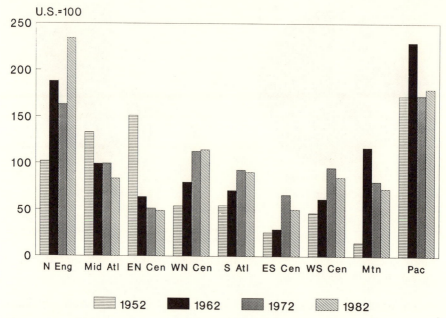

FIGURE 2.5. Prime contracts per capita, by Census division, 1952, 1962, 1972, and 1982. (Department of Defense, prime-contract awards)

to a mere 21 percent. Over that period, the gunbelt—which, in Census Bureau terms, consists of the New England, South Atlantic, East and West South Central, Mountain, and Pacific divisions—increased its share of prime from 38 to nearly 70 percent.[3]

This shift is even more dramatic when expressed in per capita terms (Fig. 2.5).[4] Over the entire thirty-year period from 1952 to 1982, the Pacific and New England divisions showed consistently greater-than-average per capita procurement, with all other divisions either oscillating above or below the average line or remaining well below it. Here, the contrast between the resurgent New England and the excluded industrial heartland is striking. Comparing 1952 with 1982, New England more than doubled its per capita share, while the East North Central division fell to one-third of its 1952 per capita share, and the Mid-Atlantic share fell as well. All the Sunbelt divisions increased their share, although the Mountain division lost after a spectacular buildup during the 1950s. By the 1980s, only three regions exceeded the national average, and two of them—New England and the Pacific—spectacularly so.

The Gunbelt Emerges

At the regional level, then, the picture has an almost cartoonlike clarity: a pronounced bicoastal bias in the pattern of procurement, in which the interior

TABLE 2.1.   Prime Contracts: Top Ten States, 1945–1982 (percent of total)

World War II to June 1945		Korean War 1952		Cold War 1958		Post-Sputnik/ Cuban Missile Crisis 1962	
New York	11.0	New York	16.3	California	21.4	California	23.9
Michigan	10.9	Michigan	13.7	New York	11.6	New York	10.7
California	8.7	California	12.8	Texas	6.9	Massachusetts	5.2
Ohio	8.4	Ohio	6.2	Washington	5.8	Connecticut	4.8
New Jersey	6.8	New Jersey	5.1	Kansas	5.6	Ohio	4.5
Top 5	45.8		54.1		51.3		49.1
Pennsylvania	6.6	Pennsylvania	5.0	Ohio	4.8	New Jersey	4.2
Illinois	6.1	Illinois	4.5	Connecticut	4.3	Texas	4.0
Indiana	4.5	Washington	4.3	New Jersey	4.2	Pennsylvania	3.8
Connecticut	4.1	Indiana	4.1	Massachusetts	3.5	Washington	3.7
Massachusetts	3.4	Texas	3.3	Pennsylvania	3.4	Michigan	2.7
Top 10	70.5		75.3		71.5		67.5

Vietnam War 1967		End Vietnam 1972		Begin Buildup 1977		Reagan Buildup 1982	
California	17.9	California	18.7	California	22.1	California	21.8
Texas	9.5	New York	11.0	New York	9.5	New York	7.5
New York	8.7	Texas	7.7	Texas	6.1	Texas	6.6
Missouri	6.1	Missouri	5.4	Massachusetts	5.3	Connecticut	5.7
Connecticut	5.2	Massachusetts	4.5	Missouri	5.2	Missouri	5.2
Top 5	47.4		47.3		48.2		46.8
Pennsylvania	4.4	Connecticut	4.0	Virginia	4.5	Massachusetts	5.1
Ohio	4.3	Florida	3.6	Connecticut	4.3	Florida	4.0
Massachusetts	3.8	Pennsylvania	3.5	Washington	3.8	Virginia	3.9
New Jersey	3.3	New Jersey	3.5	Pennsylvania	3.6	Ohio	3.2
Georgia	3.1	Virginia	3.2	Michigan	2.7	Maryland	3.0
Top 10	66.3		65.1		67.1		66.0

Sources: Clayton, 1970: 31, Table 4. U.S. Department of Defense, *Prime Contract Awards by Region and State* (Annual).

of the nation gets less than its share, and a secular shift, not always completely regular, away from the industrial heartland and toward the Sunbelt. But, like all such cartoons, this conceals a more subtle picture of military-production geography, clearer if we shift our focus to the states.[5]

In 1952, in the midst of the Korean War, a mere ten states (plus the District of Columbia) exceeded the per capita average in procurement. They were heavily concentrated in the industrial, densely populated Midwest, with subsidiary concentrations in southern New England, the adjacent Mid-Atlantic states, Texas, and the Pacific West. Michigan and Ohio then had a total of almost 20 percent of all primes; New York, 16 percent; California, nearly 13 percent. Overall, ten states accounted for over 75 percent of national prime spending—a higher degree of concentration, on this measure, than was ever subsequently recorded (Table 2.1).

By 1958, and even more clearly by 1962, defense-production geography was already transformed. The midwestern states were no longer in the top quartile of per capita spending. The states in the top group were clustered on the nation's periphery—in New England, California, and Washington— and also in the Plains, Rocky Mountain, and desert areas. California already enjoyed by far the biggest share of prime contracts, over 21 percent in 1958 and nearly 24 percent in 1962. Massachusetts had over 5 percent and Connecticut just under 5 percent of the total. These findings corroborate the earlier work of Roger Bolton, who showed that defense spending between 1952 and 1962 greatly stimulated income growth in the Pacific and Mountain states, moderately stimulated growth in the Atlantic (except New York) and Gulf Coast states, as well as in the interior states of Kansas and Missouri, and depressed growth in the East North Central region of the country.[6]

Vietnam, unlike Korea, did not reverse this shift in the center of gravity. The year 1967 marked the peak of the Vietnam War, as 1952 had for the Korean conflict. Yet with only small differences, such as the rise of Missouri and Georgia, the procurement map remained almost identical to that of 1962. California's share of total primes fell below 18 percent, while Texas sharply increased its share to nearly 10 percent. Although the midwestern states recorded above-average levels, they did not return to the predominance of the early 1950s. Ohio's share of primes declined steadily beginning in 1952. Michigan, and its midwestern neighbors Illinois and Indiana, no longer appeared in the top-ten list.

After Vietnam, the cold war gunbelt reverted to its position of prominence; the 1972 pattern of defense spending was similar to that of 1967, or indeed 1962. And so were the patterns of 1977, 1982, and 1984. Individual states slipped up or down, but overall there was great stability in the geographical distribution. In both 1977 and 1982, California retained its long lead over every other state, with about 22 percent of primes. Massachusetts, Connecticut, and New York together accounted for about 18 percent; Texas recorded 6 to 7 percent; Virginia and Missouri made respectable showings. By the time of the Carter–Reagan buildup, then, the new defense geography was largely in place; new programs merely reinforced the distribution pattern established during the crucial years of the cold war during the 1950s and early 1960s.

Trickling Down the Benefits: The Geography of Subcontracting

One might argue that just as auto production is concentrated in and around Detroit but car manufacturers buy parts from all over the nation, so defense subcontracting should help spread the defense dollars around. Any single weapons system has hundreds of subcontracts associated with it—the engines, radio equipment, guidance systems, and myriad other parts of a bomber are all subjects of separate bids. Good data on subcontracting, unfortunately, do not exist.[7] But the fragmentary research on the subject indicates that far from redistributing defense dollars, subcontracting tends to favor prime-contract locales.

TABLE 2.2.   Shipments of Defense-Oriented Industries, Prime Contracts and
Subcontracts, 1965, 1983

	Prime Contracts	
Subcontracts	*Greater than* *U.S. Average*	*Less than* *U.S. Average*
1983		
Greater than U.S. average	Connecticut	Vermont
	Massachusetts	Pennsylvania
	New Hampshire	Ohio
	Maryland	Indiana
	Utah	New Mexico
	Arizona	
	California	
Less than U.S. average	Maine	All other states
	Rhode Island	
	Virginia	
	Minnesota	
	Missouri	
	Kansas	
	Texas	
	Colorado	
	Washington	
1965		
Greater than U.S. average	Connecticut	New Hampshire
	Massachusetts	Vermont
	New York	New Jersey
	Utah	Ohio
	California	Minnesota
		Iowa
		Kansas
		Arizona
		New Mexico
Less than U.S. average	Georgia	All other states
	Missouri	
	Louisiana	
	Washington	

Source: U.S. Bureau of the Census, *Shipments of Defense-Oriented Industries, Current Industrial Reports.*

But that does not mean that firms subcontract locally. For defense contractors, space and distance are not constraints. Our own work confirms that
of Gerald Karaska, who concluded that there was a "free flow" of subcontracts
across the nation.[8] But it also demonstrates that some of the biggest prime-
contracting states are also strong subcontractors. Only five states in 1965 and
seven states in 1983—among which California, Utah, and three states in New
England were prominent—recorded above-average per capita figures for both
primes and subcontracts. Conspicuously missing are Michigan, Illinois, and
Wisconsin, although Ohio appears at both dates as a prominent subcontractor
(Table 2.2). Thus although subcontracts bring a small return flow to the
industrial heartland, most of the money remains in the gunbelt.

Percent of total awards

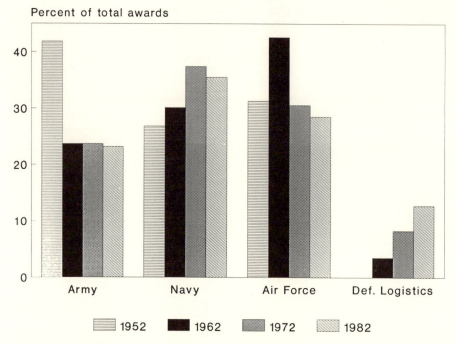

FIGURE 2.6. Military prime-contract awards by purchasing department, 1952, 1962, 1972, and 1982. (Department of Defense, prime-contract awards)

The Differing Geographies of Weapons Systems

Corresponding to the shift to the gunbelt are changes in the status of individual service arms and in priorities for different kinds of weapons. Korea, with the Army in the lead, was a conventional war fought with conventional equipment, perhaps the last of its kind. The 1950s were years of massive buildup of missile and space systems, catapulting the Air Force to a prominence it never subsequently lost. In the 1980s, with the emphasis on the Strategic Defense Initiative, the Air Force pulled further ahead, favoring electronic radar-type defensive shields. Since these different weapons systems are likely to be produced by different firms in different places, the argument would run, changes in the composition of procurement and the lead service would spell the rise or decline of states and regions.

The relative powers of the three main service arms do wax and wane, carrying certain regions with them (Fig. 2.6). The Army's share has always increased in times of combat wars. The Air Force, by contrast, commanded the largest proportion of service contracts during the cold war and missile buildup of the late 1950s and early 1960s; thereafter, its share has fallen off. In the 1980s, the Navy benefited from the Reagan administration's priorities for nuclear submarines.

Over the thirty-year period from 1952 to 1982, both Army and Air Force

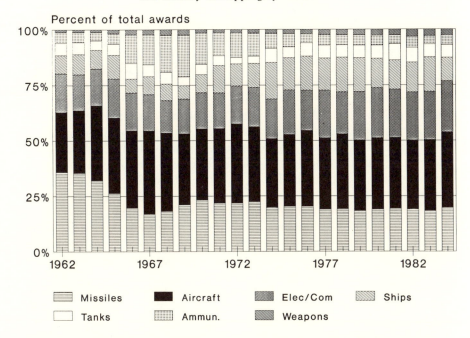

FIGURE 2.7. Prime-contract awards by major weapon system, 1962–1984. (Department of Defense, prime-contract awards)

purchases showed a pronounced southern and westward tilt (Appendix, Fig. A.2). After World War II, but before the missile buildup, both services' orders were concentrated in the Midwest and Northeast, although the Pacific expansion during World War II was well established. The southeastern and Mountain states were not yet important for defense-related production. Cold war policies of the 1950s changed that geography, however. By 1962, both Army and Air Force prime contracts revealed the opening of the South and West, relative to other parts of the nation. For the Air Force, this expansion was even more pronounced. By 1982, the Air Force was solidly a western service, awarding contracts there and along the north Atlantic seaboard. The Army, by contrast, consolidated somewhat and exhibited a southern tilt by 1982. The Navy, concentrated along the three coastal areas, is more geographically constrained than the other services, although contracting did become more spread out within regions, rather than across regions (as with the Army and Air Force).

These shifts become clearer when broken down by weapons system. No less than 75 percent of all prime contracts, in the past thirty years, have been in only seven broad weapons categories.[9] But there have been big shifts from one category to another (Fig. 2.7). Particularly notable is the decline in the importance of missiles after the massive buildup of the 1950s through the early 1960s. Aircraft had an increasing share in the early 1960s, reaching and remaining at about 35 percent of the total. Electronics and communication equipment showed the most spectacular rise in share, from about 15 percent at the start of the period to around 20 percent by the end. Each weapons category has its own unique geography (Appendix, Fig. A.3–A.9).

In aircraft, by far the largest category, contracting is extraordinarily concentrated (Appendix, Fig. A.3). The top five states received 86 percent of primes in 1984. The Pacific region recorded the largest share of contracts, about one-quarter. But in per capita terms, this area was overshadowed entirely by New England, and its shares have actually declined, while Missouri and Kansas have registered increases. The geography of missilery closely resembles that of aircraft, for the same companies—Boeing in Washington; General Dynamics, Douglas, Lockheed, Rockwell, and Hughes in California—dominate it (Appendix, Fig. A.4). No less than 42 percent of all missile primes in 1982 went to California contractors, while the Pacific division received over three times the national average per capita. The Mountain states also did well, but—like the Pacific—their share dropped somewhat over the period. As was the case with aircraft, the New England states showed the fastest growth. The Midwest, in contrast, recorded per capita procurement levels that were a fraction of the national average.

In contrast to aerospace, shipbuilding has been an industry in decline. During World War II, shipbuilding captured no less than 26 percent of military hard-good purchases; but that share had dropped to less than 7 percent by 1953, and it fell even further in the 1960s.[10] By the mid-1970s, of over 400 shipyards in the United States, only 11 privately owned yards were building new Navy ships. And even under the Reagan buildup, closures increased: 25 out of 110 in the four years to 1985 alone.[11] These yards were concentrated in a few coastal divisions, which have experienced mixed fortunes. New England has been the dominant partner and the overall beneficiary in per capita terms (Appendix, Fig. A.5).

Tanks and automotive vehicles are the Midwest's only strong defense card. Manufacture of both combat and noncombat vehicles remains concentrated in three East North Central states: Michigan, Ohio, and Indiana. But in per capita terms, California and Connecticut have pushed the Pacific and New England divisions above the national average, with New England demonstrating the greatest gains after 1972 (Appendix, Fig. A.6). Since the cold war has favored atmospheric over land-based weapons systems, the Midwest has stagnated—its comparative advantage waning in overall importance.

Weapons and ammunition reflect the gunbelt shift as well. Weapons production, the smallest category, was earlier concentrated in the Northeast and Midwest, but is increasingly dominated by California, whose share rose from 13 to 57 percent between 1962 and 1982 (Appendix, Fig. A.7). New England's per capita procurements plummeted in the decade from 1972 to 1982, but remained above average, while most of the heartland states lost shares of the weapons pie. Of all categories, ammunition shows the greatest volatility in procurement, peaking during the Vietnam War. Although companies in California and Minnesota are the leading producers, ammunition is the most spatially dispersed of all the weapons groups (Appendix, Fig. A.8). It is also the only weapons-system category where New England's per capita spending (in 1982) was below the national average.

The electronics and communications-equipment group shows a slow but steady rise in its share of all prime contracts—although here, it should be stressed, subcontracting plays a relatively big part. In 1962, the Mid-Atlantic and East North Central divisions had between them 55 percent of all prime contracts (Appendix, Fig. A.9). By 1982, that figure was down to 24 percent. The Pacific division, in contrast, sharply increased its share. In per capita terms, it was the same story. Because airframe manufacturers developed their own electronics capacities in the 1950s, military electronics concentrations have paralleled those of aircraft.

The Location of R&D

Contracts for research, development, test, and evaluation (RDT&E) form a critical part of the total defense budget. They go to businesses, educational institutions, government agencies, and other nonprofit organizations to conduct research. Of total federal R&D spending—nearly 50 percent of all R&D expenditure in the mid–1980s—national defense consumed 69 percent: a figure greater than the combined budgets of the Departments of Commerce, Education, Housing and Urban Development, and Interior. These contracts are very heavily concentrated among a few commercial firms, which have shown remarkable stability since the early 1960s.[12] As a result, R&D spending is even more concentrated geographically than prime contracts. This, too, has been consistent over a twenty-year period, with above-average R&D spending in the Mid-Atlantic and lower New England regions, across the central states, and into the Mountain region and Pacific coast (Appendix, Fig. A.10).

This is even truer when R&D is broken into its component parts: business firms, educational institutions, and other nonprofit organizations. In total awards to business firms, California leads all states, with 41 percent of business contracts in both 1962 and 1982, while New York has shown a marked decline since 1972. In per capita terms, Washington State leads, reflecting large Boeing R&D contracts; California is second. In awards to educational institutions, which totaled $850 million, Maryland and Massachusetts led all states in both absolute and per capita spending levels in 1982, reflecting the dominance of Johns Hopkins' Applied Physics Laboratory and MIT's Lincoln Laboratory. R&D contracts to nonprofit organizations are even more concentrated: California and Massachusetts received over 75 percent of awards in 1982, most going to Draper Lab in Cambridge and Aerospace Labs in California.

The Changing Geography of Defense Employment

These billions of defense dollars generate millions of defense jobs. But estimating their precise numbers is hard, mainly because most defense companies also produce nondefense goods and services. James L. Clayton has estimated that defense-generated employment totaled some 2.4 million jobs,

TABLE 2.3.   Defense Jobs, 1977, 1980, 1985

	1977 (000s)	1980 (000s)	1985 (000s)	1977–80		1980–85	
				(000s)	% Change	(000s)	% Change
Total defense jobs	5309	5498	6680	+189	3.6	+1182	21.5
Armed forces	2133	2041	2151	−92	−4.3	+110	5.4
Federal civilian	1263	1243	1322	−20	−1.6	+79	6.4
Private	1913	2214	3207	+301	15.7	+993	44.9
Primary	53	58	72	+5	9.6	+14	23.1
Manufacturing	1038	1200	1812	+162	15.6	+613	51.1
Services/construction	822	956	1323	+135	16.4	+366	38.3

Source: Henry and Oliver, 1987.

or 3 percent of the national total, in 1966.[13] More recent estimates by the Department of Commerce show 903,000 defense-related jobs nationally in 1965, rising to a peak of 1,251,000 in 1967, falling to a low of 675,000 in 1975, and then rising again to 948,000 in 1983.[14] The net increase of 242,000 defense jobs between 1972, as the Vietnam War was winding down, and 1983 contrasts sharply with a net loss of 436,000 manufacturing jobs in the same period.

Estimates of defense employment by sector have been generated from the federal government's 1977 input–output table. They show that defense-related private employment grew by an estimated 68 percent, from 1.9 to 3.2 million, between the beginning of the buildup in 1977 and 1985 (Table 2.3).[15] From 1980 to 1985, there was a net increase in private-sector jobs of 5.8 million, of which defense-related jobs accounted for nearly 1 million, or 17 percent. In contrast, direct government military jobs, both civilian and uniformed, grew much more modestly. The 1977 to 1985 buildup was principally a matter of hardware, not manpower.

Private-sector defense work partially compensated for massive losses in American manufacturing during the early years of the 1980s: while manufacturing industries lost almost 1 million jobs overall between 1980 and 1985, over 600,000 defense-related manufacturing jobs were added—an increase of more than 50 percent.[16] Defense accounted for some 5 percent of all manufacturing jobs in 1977, 6 percent in 1980, and about 9 percent in 1985. In durable manufacturing, more than 8 percent of all jobs were generated by defense in 1980 and no less than 14 percent in 1985. In the aircraft industry, defense employment increased as a share of total industry employment from 43 percent in 1977 to 62 percent in 1985; in shipbuilding, from only 31 percent in 1977 to 85 percent in 1985 (Table 2.4).[17]

Like the procurement contracts that generated them, these jobs were unevenly distributed across the nation. Clayton estimated that in 1966, "defense dependency" ranged from 9.7 percent of all employment in Alaska and 9.1 percent in Utah, to as little as 0.3 percent in Idaho. California, where 5.4 percent of all employment was defense-related, had 405,000 such jobs, just under 17 percent of the national total.[18] The Commerce/Census Bureau figures released in 1983—which are almost certainly underestimates—can be compared with total estimates of manufacturing employment for the same years, to produce location quotients. A location quotient of 1.00 or above means

TABLE 2.4.   Defense Employment Shares and Growth, Major Industries, 1977–1985

Major Industries	Defense Employment % Total			Employment Change			
	1977	1980	1985	1977–80		1980–85	
				(000s)	%	(000s)	%
Ordnance	44.8	59.9	70.5	13.4	43.4	24.8	56.0
Missiles, space	67.3	68.7	84.2	16.0	36.0	52.5	86.9
Communications equipment	35.2	41.8	49.6	47.1	42.5	96.7	61.2
Aircraft	43.0	37.2	62.0	36.6	17.0	167.8	66.7
Shipbuilding	30.7	49.3	85.3	39.4	55.8	53.0	48.2

Source: Henry and Oliver, 1987.

that defense industries are relatively more concentrated in that particular state than they are nationally.

The resulting maps (Fig. 2.8) show a relatively consistent pattern: New England, New York, the Washington, D.C., area, Florida, the central states from Missouri to Utah, Texas, Arizona, California, and Washington form the gunbelt, where employment is especially defense-dependent. Growth in defense jobs was concentrated in just a few states: California, as ever the leader, had nearly 17 percent of new defense jobs during 1967 to 1977 and over 36 percent from 1977 to 1983; Massachusetts had over 5 percent in the first period and 7.6 percent in the second; Florida and Texas had around 7 percent each in the latter period (Table 2.5). The gunbelt is a strong and persistent reality.

As well-paid engineering and scientific jobs gravitated toward gunbelt centers, the distribution of regional income shifted as well. Defense-related activity shored up the personal incomes of residents of gunbelt states and contributed overall to regional growth in the regions of the gunbelt.[19] In general over the postwar period, interregional per capita incomes have converged, with spectacular gains by the southern states and a fall toward the national norm on the part of the northern states. However, military receipts contributed to the maintenance of high per capita incomes in New England and the Pacific states, preventing a decline that might otherwise have mirrored the Midwest.

Military spending in the 1980s furthered these trends. New England, a major beneficiary and the top-earning region at the beginning of the decade, increased its per capita income from 9 percent above the national norm in 1982 to 20 percent above by 1987. The West maintained its 11 percent edge over the rest of the country, while the Great Lakes region continued to lag at 2 percent below the national average. In an econometric study of the states, William Warren found that higher per capita incomes were correlated with high per capita defense spending over the period from 1981 to 1985.[20] As the *New York Times* put it in an article entitled "Coastal States Widen Economic Lead," defense spending is a major element in the growing disparity between the nation's coasts and heartland.[21]

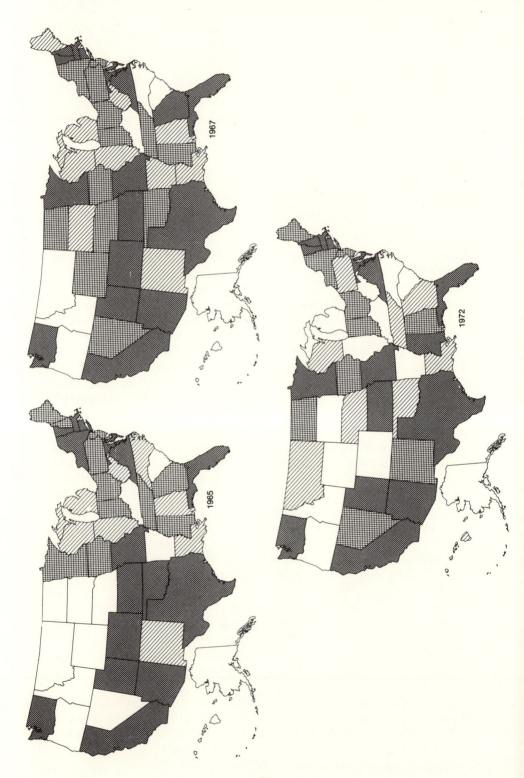

22

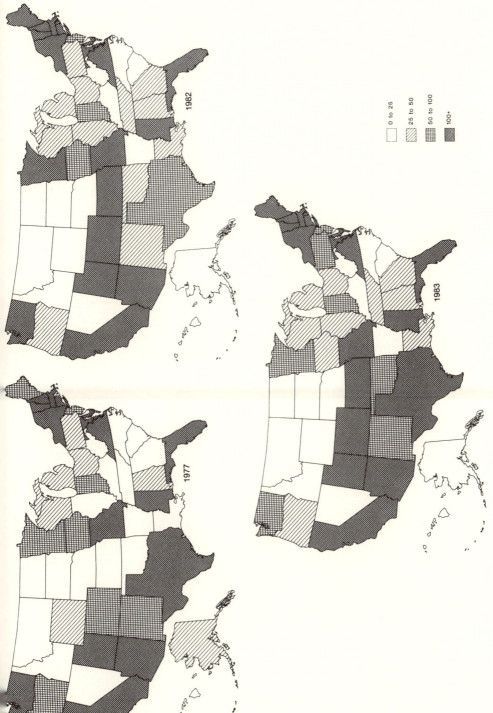

FIGURE 2.8. Location quotients: defense-manufacturing to total manufacturing employment, by state, 1965–1983.

0 to 25
25 to 50
50 to 100
100+

1982

1983

1977

23

TABLE 2.5.   Defense Employment and Manufacturing Employment, 1967, 1977, 1983

	Defense Employment Change (000s)		% National Defense Employment Change	
	1967–1977	1977–1983	1967–1977	1977–1983
Maine	−0.5	5.5	0.1	2.4
New Hampshire	−3.0	9.6	0.6	4.1
Vermont	0.2	1.3	0.0	0.6
Massachusetts	−27.7	17.6	5.2	7.6
Rhode Island	−1.6	6.1	0.3	2.6
Connecticut	−27.9	−6.6	5.2	−2.8
New York	−57.5	9.7	10.7	4.2
New Jersey	−25.1	4.7	4.7	2.0
Pennsylvania	−36.4	12.2	6.8	5.2
Ohio	−36.0	2.6	6.7	1.1
Indiana	−20.1	4.6	3.7	2.0
Illinois	−29.3	6.8	5.5	2.9
Michigan	−11.9	2.4	2.2	1.0
Wisconsin	−9.2	2.2	1.7	0.9
Minnesota	−15.0	6.4	2.8	2.8
Iowa	−6.1	−2.6	1.1	−1.1
Missouri	−23.6	0.1	4.4	0.0
North Dakota	−0.2	0.0	0.0	0.0
South Dakota	−0.2	0.0	0.0	0.0
Nebraska	−4.2	0.8	0.8	0.3
Kansas	−19.6	13.0	3.7	5.6
Delaware	−0.7	0.0	0.1	0.0
Maryland	−13.1	8.0	2.4	3.4
District of Columbia	0.1	0.0	0.0	0.0
Virginia	−3.8	11.5	0.7	4.9
West Virginia	−3.0	−0.4	0.6	−0.2
North Carolina	−8.0	1.6	1.5	0.7
South Carolina	0.3	0.5	−0.1	0.2
Georgia	−31.6	7.5	5.9	3.2
Florida	−2.8	17.0	0.5	7.3
Kentucky	−0.4	0.2	0.1	0.1
Tennessee	−14.6	4.5	2.7	1.9
Alabama	−2.0	2.1	0.4	0.9
Mississippi	17.7	−14.6	−3.3	−6.3
Arkansas	−2.4	1.0	0.4	0.4
Louisiana	−2.3	1.5	0.4	0.6
Oklahoma	−4.3	5.7	0.8	2.5
Texas	−33.8	15.5	6.3	6.7
Montana	−0.2	−0.1	0.0	0.0
Idaho	0.0	0.1	0.0	0.0
Wyoming	−0.2	−0.1	0.0	0.0
Colorado	−3.6	6.5	0.7	2.8
New Mexico	0.5	0.3	−0.1	0.1
Arizona	0.0	4.0	0.0	1.7
Utah	−3.5	3.0	0.7	1.3
Nevada	0.3	0.0	0.1	0.0

TABLE 2.5 (*cont.*)

	Defense Employment Change (000s)		% National Defense Employment Change	
	1967–1977	*1977–1983*	*1967–1977*	*1977–1983*
Washington	−3.2	−13.5	0.6	−5.8
Oregon	1.8	−0.2	−0.3	−0.1
California	−89.9	84.9	16.8	36.5
Alaska	0.1	0.0	0.0	0.0
Hawaii	−0.2	0.0	0.0	0.0
United States	−536.5	232.6	100.0	100.0

*Cannot be calculated.

Source: U.S. Bureau of the Census, *Current Industrial Reports.*

Conclusion

The 1950s represented a crucial turning point for American defense and for American defense industries. During the cold war, the United States assumed new global responsibilities. To uphold them, it created what came to be called the military–industrial complex: an interwoven system of production comprising the Pentagon, the armed services, private firms, and political players. Its geographical manifestation was the meteoric rise and sustained dominance of the gunbelt—the stretch from New England down the Atlantic seaboard, across the central states, and into the lower Mountain and Pacific regions. For forty years, albeit with large perturbations, the growth of manufacturing production and employment in these regions has been strongly and heavily defense-induced. Conversely, the industrial heartland never captured a sufficient share of cold war aerospace defense contracts, a fact that proved a significant element in its decline after 1970.

This remarkable industrial metamorphosis is the phenomenon, the mystery, that this study seeks to explain. A crucial set of factors converged to produce the gunbelt in the 1950s, that decade of maximum change. But it would be a mistake to start the story there, as though the transformation occurred on a blank map. Our search for clues begins with forces and circumstances that go well back into the early decades of this century. We start with the polar cases—the heartland, which began to yield its position as industrial center after World War II; and Los Angeles, the upstart that became and remains the aerospace capital of the nation.

3

Reading the Map: A Theory of Military–Industrial Places

Why did this dramatic regional shift in military production occur? To track the development of the gunbelt and its constituent parts, we invite you on an odyssey through geographical space and historical time. As a guide for this journey, we need a road map. Geographers, like other travelers, use ordinary maps to find which highway to drive. But they also use an array of more specialized material that allows them to anticipate and interpret the landscape before them. Geologic and topographic maps tell them that the going may get rough and the stopping places may be few; population-density maps will confirm the facts. To understand the gunbelt as it unfolds before us, we shall use a similar kind of composite map.

The map must convey some rather esoteric information. By using only the obvious sources, we run the risk of drawing the wrong inferences—like poor Inspector Lestrade, before Sherlock Holmes arrived on the scene and put him right. Climate maps show that Los Angeles enjoys plenty of sun; therefore, pilots found it easy to fly, and airplane manufacturers located around their needs. The map of education shows that universities cluster in New England; therefore, science begat advanced technology there. Both these conclusions contain a small grain of truth and a huge accretion of untruth. Other parts of America have sun, but attracted no early aircraft industry; snow-flecked Buffalo and rain-soaked Seattle did. Other parts of the country have good universities, yet few developed schools of aeronautical engineering and even fewer generated an advanced avionics industry. And some that did begat no aircraft industry.

So old-fashioned geographical location theory, the kind that still shows up in some textbooks, will not get us far. The truth, as usual, is more complex. Like Holmes, we must start our investigation in more obscure places.

The right place proves to be at the stratospheric level: the United States' mission, the vision the president and Pentagon top brass share about the nation's global role. As this vision has changed—from isolationism to global conflict to cold war—so has the basic philosophy of the right strategic response. The defense of the coasts was replaced by strategic bombing, then by intercontinental missilery, and finally by Star Wars. From that overarching imperative derive certain interlocking structures of defense production: the roles and powers of the different armed services; the demands of each service for military procurement; and, finally, the evolution of the military–industrial complex, a feature of the post–world war era that is unique in strategic history.

This maze of structural features affords space to a set of diverse actors—ranging from generals to university presidents, civic boosters to congressmen, heroic entrepreneurs to bureaucratic managers—each with individual preferences and perspectives. Then, coming right down to the ground, there are the places, each with its attributes—sometimes present and evident, sometimes latent and awaiting exploitation by local boosters—that present themselves to the locational actors as they traverse the landscape in search of possible production sites. Together they shape the historical growth trajectories of new military–industrial centers, which—quite unlike the machines they turn out—follow no simple parabolic course; instead, they exhibit multistage paths, with many slippages and even catastrophes en route.

Of course, this way of approaching the gunbelt suggests that it, in turn, plays no causal role in encouraging interservice rivalries or in shaping military appropriations or strategic policy. That is highly unlikely. Later in the book, we speculate on the possibility that the rise of the gunbelt itself has been a major factor in prolonging the cold war. But for now, we treat it as a derivative.

Strategic Missions, Service Roles

During this century, the United States' strategic role has gone through at least six main phases: dominant isolationism almost to the eve of World War II; active involvement in global conflict, followed by a brief period of disarmament; a long period of cold war marked by America's assumption of a global strategic role; a time of doubts and reversals broken by intense local conflict in Vietnam; the dismantling of some defense systems during the 1970s; and the development of the Strategic Defense Initiative in the 1980s.[1]

Prehistory, 1918–1941: Isolationism and the Fight for the Air Force

In the prehistory of the gunbelt, the period between the two world wars, the United States was still committed to its historic doctrine of isolationism, albeit inconsistently. The armed forces were seen as having purely defensive roles as guardians of America's coasts. This reinforced the conservatism of the two established service arms, the Army and the Navy, and made them resistant to the arguments of the fledgling airmen for an air force with an independent attack capacity. Major General William "Billy" Mitchell, assistant chief of the Army Air Service, argued that in future wars airplanes would attack far behind enemy lines, destroying the enemy's industrial capacity and sapping the morale of the civilian population. But Mitchell's strident campaign led to his court-martial in 1925 and resignation in 1926.[2]

In that year came a small concession: Congress accepted the 1925 report of the independent Morrow Board and created the semi-independent Air Corps headed by an Army major general; it was planned to have an eventual complement of 1,650 officers, 15,000 men, and 1,800 aircraft by 1932. But the funds were never forthcoming, and the goal was never achieved.[3] Another inquiry, carried out by the Baker Board of 1934, led to yet another compromise: the establishment in 1935 of an independent air force general headquarters, which resulted in perversely divided responsibilities—air-strike capacity, on one side, supply and training, on the other. Not until June 1941 did an Army regulation create the Army Air Forces under a chief who was also Deputy Chief of Staff for Air; not until March 1942 did the AAF gain virtually complete autonomy under a single chief, General H. H. "Hap" Arnold.[4]

Until 1938, even Arnold was committed to the limited doctrine of defense of the shores. So throughout the interwar period, the infant aircraft manufacturers, still dominated by founder engineer-entrepreneurs and by former wartime flyers, struggled to survive, often solely on small military infusions. To defend their position and argue their case before Congress and the Army, the airplane makers formed a manufacturers' association, but at first it enjoyed little success. A boom came in the late 1920s, with expansion of the commercial airline business; during 1927 to 1929, there was a fevered series of takeovers and mergers. With the Depression came collapse. Dependent both on a depressed commercial sector and on savagely reduced congressional Air Corps appropriations, many firms faced bankruptcy.[5]

Looming war in Europe brought only limited relief, although orders from future belligerents were helpful. As late as 1937 and 1938, obsessed by the notion of the Air Corps's subordinate defensive role, Army chiefs refused to concede the case for the B-17 bomber, and the Navy strongly opposed it. At the start of 1936, the Army Air Corps had a mere 1,100 planes, 300 of which were front-line combat aircraft; the Navy, 800. Well might Billy Mitchell rail, in 1935:

> We have subsidized an aircraft monopoly which is arming our potential enemies because we refuse to buy enough of its products to keep it going. ...When war comes we will have to take what the manufacturer happens to have on the market. We will spend billions of dollars until we have something workable. And we will encourage the growth of the most dangerous monopoly in the world.[6]

So as late as 1939, deprived of a mass market, the industry was innocent of mass-production techniques: "One typical aircraft manufacturer, and a highly efficient one too, turned out only two or three units a day in comparison with Detroit's production of two or three automobiles per minute."[7] And until the 1938 buildup, the industry was regarded as financially shaky.[8]

In September 1938, President Roosevelt reversed policy: he announced a program to build 10,000 planes, more than the Air Corps had requested. Arnold later wrote that this was the most important event in his career, and in the history of the service.[9] The beneficiaries were the pioneer airframe firms that had survived the Depression—Lockheed, Douglas, North American, Grumman, Curtiss-Wright, and Boeing—and the areas where these firms clustered: Los Angeles, Seattle, Buffalo, Long Island, and New England.

Global Conflict, 1941–1945

Thus the threat of war, followed by real war, gave the airmen what they had so long wanted: autonomy and a strategic offensive role. World War II showed that the airmen had been right: indeed, one nation could inflict huge damage on another nation's productive capacity and will to fight. Bombing extended the battle past the front lines and deep into enemy territory, destroying factories, transportation lines, cities, and civilians with frightening efficiency and rapidity.[10] The atomic bomb and its progeny, the hydrogen bomb, were the ultimate steps in the evolution of air warfare.

The major instruments of military power consequently became the bombers that could wreak such havoc. With strategic warfare's eclipse of the Army's machine guns, artillery, and tanks, and the Navy's battleships and submarines, the role of these services paled in comparison with that of the new Air Force, which emerged during World War II to play the leading role in cold war technology. And the Strategic Air Command was elevated from junior to senior military partner.

In parallel, the aircraft manufacturers played a heroic role, developing within a few years from a cottage industry to mass production. FDR's 1940 goal, 50,000 planes a year, was 100 times the output of the industry in the late 1930s; yet it was reached by 1942, and doubled by 1944.[11] North American, the most spectacular case, expanded from 6,000 employees in one plant in the summer of 1940 to 92,000 in five plants by 1943. Between January 1939 and September 1945, it produced over 42,000 planes, 10 percent more than its rival Convair and 14 percent of American World War II production.[12] Lockhead produced over 19,000 planes and expanded from 2,500 workers in late 1938 to 60,000 by early 1945, when it was the biggest American aircraft company. Douglas made 10,000 military versions of its famous DC-3.[13]

The message was not lost. Air power now dominated, and a new service emerged to manage it. In December 1945, President Truman was calling for a Department of National Defense, in which the Air Force would have full parity. The National Security Act of 1947 finally established the post of Secretary of Defense, a national military establishment in the Pentagon, and separate departments of the Army, Navy, and Air Force.[14]

At war's end, the war machine was brought to a shuddering halt. The services were demobilized. Plants were closed and mothballed. Many military producers, above all the aircraft manufacturers, struggled to survive. The

American leadership and the American people shared a notion that life would return to normal—that is, to minimal military involvement in world affairs. The wartime alliance, and the resulting victory, gave rise to hopes of an epoch of global peace.

The Cold War, 1948–1980

The uneasy peace lasted a scant three years. With the onset of the cold war, the Berlin blockade and airlift of 1948, and the Truman Doctrine of 1949, the United States was back on the world stage for good. Then came the Korean War and the report of Soviet parity in atom-bomb production. In 1953, the United States exploded a "dry" H-bomb, capable of being carried as a lightweight warhead.[15] The result, in January 1954, was the "doctrine of massive retaliation," backed by an armory of sophisticated new weapons with unparalleled destructive force.[16] Then, in 1957, came the Soviet *Sputnik* and the race into space. Together, these events brought about the aerospace revolution.

The essential feature of the mid-century military–political landscape was the cold war—a type of strife radically unlike any other in history. Weapons for the first time were designed not to be used; they were sought for their preemptive value. Each combatant had to continually improve its arsenal, so as to deter the other from using its arms. Fewer and fewer units of each successive weapon were made, but each was much more technically sophisticated than the last. A process of institutionalized innovation was set in motion. The new form of warfare, atmospheric rather than ground or sea, radically altered both the conduct of war-making and the production complex that fashioned the weapons and support equipment.[17]

Now, another ideological fight broke out—this time, within the newly independent Air Force. An older generation of wartime "flying generals," committed to the doctrine of strategic bombing, lacked enthusiasm for becoming "silent silo-sitters."[18] They were challenged by a group of Young Turks who were committed to space warfare through guided missiles: a war without soldiers. Triggered by a technological breakthrough—the lightweight H-bomb—these space warriors achieved a major shift in strategic planning: from the mid–1950s, Air Force strategy was based on a combination of intercontinental missiles, highly sophisticated fighters and reconnaissance planes, and a radar shield backed by defensive cruise missiles.

In turn, this brought a shift in procurement: within a few years, the call was no longer for conventional aircraft, but for craft—whether manned or unmanned—stuffed with complex electronic guidance and sensing equipment. The Atlas inter-continental ballistic missile (ICBM) received top-priority status from the Air Force in May 1954 and top national status in the summer of 1955.[19] In November 1955, an intermediate range missile received joint top priority. The IRBM, the Thor, was launched in 1957; the Atlas ICBM, a year later.[20] The industry faced a sudden challenge of reorientation as it labored to create completely new products requiring new components, skills, and a commitment to scientific research and development. The military–industrial complex was born, and it was not a child of the heartland.

With the arrival of President Kennedy in the White House and Ford Motors' Robert McNamara at the Pentagon, a new era began. Although the nation's broad military objectives remained the same, the means radically altered. Planning, programming, and budgeting promised to produce a new, rational, highly economic system of procurement.[21] Before the promise could be realized, however, the escalating Vietnam War upset everyone's assumptions: here again was hot war, but of a new kind, requiring that the Army learn the enemy's guerrilla tactics. The end of that war was followed by the defense contraction of the mid- to late 1970s. But as we have seen, these events had little effect on where military production took place.

The 1980s Peacetime Buildup

President Reagan's bold defense initiatives marked a partial return to the 1950s, with a boom in spending on major new weapons systems, an emphasis on aerospace, and growing expenditure on R&D, particularly in the fields of advanced radar devices, surveillance, communications systems, and information processing. New firms offering systems engineering and technical assistance (SETA) came to the fore, many of them spin-offs from aerospace companies under conflict-of-interest rules. They tended to concentrate in new centers like Washington, D.C., the military command-and-control headquarters; Colorado Springs, the nerve center for strategic defense and test bed for SDI; Huntsville, Alabama, and Titusville–Melbourne, Florida, both dedicated to military space activity; and, of course, aerospace industry headquarters in southern California.

Service Traditions and Service Rivalries

Central to the rise of the gunbelt was the victory of the Air Force's strategy for outsourcing to private firms over the Army's preferred strategy of in-house design and development. Ever since the earliest days of the republic, the Army had been wedded to the arsenal system, by which research, prototype development, and sometimes even production of weapons were conducted in government-owned and -run plants. The navy yard system, which dates back to the original Washington Navy Yard of 1790, was based on the same practice. For the young airmen of the 1920s, who tried the system at Wright Field in Dayton, it was an anachronism that did not work. But neither did the alternative of going to established automobile manufacturers, which had proved an expensive fiasco during World War I. This convinced Arnold and his fellow officers that the only way to get planes built was to go to their equally young and struggling colleagues in the infant aircraft industry. During the lean years of the 1920s and 1930s, the airmen did their best to supply the industry with small-scale orders. In 1938, when mass production became the order of the day, they logically went back to their industry colleagues.

In the aerospace revolution of the 1950s, the same tension between the Army and the Air Force reappeared. General Bernard Schriever, chief architect of the ICBM program, was fully committed to the Air Force doctrine of "going to industry and having industry develop and produce for us." Air Force's competitors were Wernher von Braun and his former German colleagues, brought to America at war's end to work at the Army's Redstone Arsenal at Huntsville, Alabama. They preferred to develop their missiles in-house, contracting out to the Army's old friend, the auto industry, for fabrication. In this battle, the Air Force won. By eschewing any in-house capacity, the Air Force commanded a big, well-heeled constituency of scientists, organized labor, and industry. Its impeccable free-enterprise viewpoint removed most of the stigma from the surge in public spending that the arms revolution entailed.

Later, in 1960, von Braun had his moment of triumph when his team became a critical nucleus of the new National Aeronautics and Space Administration (NASA). From then on, there were effectively two major sources of R&D and of procurement in the closely related missile and space fields: one, defense-based, under the control of the Air Force; the other, space-related, under the control of an ex-Army team in an ex-Army arsenal. But, final irony, the Army group found that it could not produce such complex equipment single-handily; it had to go to the same contractors the Air Force used. Private-sector, for-profit contracting had won out over the old in-house arsenal system.

The Military–Industrial Complex

The military–industrial complex has certain goals and characteristics that make it quite unlike any business cluster that has ever existed in the world, let alone the capitalist production system. Over the postwar period, its mandate has been the cold war imperative to keep in the technical lead. With less manpower and more highly developed science than the Soviet Union, the United States chose to fight the cold war by continually creating new and more terrible weapons that would deter. As a result the R&D component of the defense effort has risen dramatically over the postwar period, accelerating in the Star Wars era.[22] With this heavy commitment to publicly financed research and development has come an expansion in the ranks of the electrical and aeronautical engineers, nuclear physicists, mathematicians, systems analysts, and computer programmers required to design, develop, test, and evaluate high-tech weaponry. Airplanes that will flip over faster, fly a few hundred feet above the ground, and be less easily detected; radar that will more rapidly and accurately sense and identify the advance of an aggressive bomber or missiles; computers that can cope with a great mass and diversity of data piped in from satellites, radars, ships, and aircraft sensors—all of these must be designed and developed by highly skilled professionals and technicians.[23]

This process of defense-led innovation, which often produces economy-altering spin-offs, is different from all previous innovation in capitalist history. Whatever their different theoretical perspectives, economic historians have regarded innovation as an individual or a corporate entrepreneurial act whose risk and financing are assumed by the innovator in the hope of superprofitable returns.[24] But once the state steps in and sponsors nonstop research and innovation for narrow military ends, the nature of innovation changes. In the United States, where the national government now underwrites 70 percent of all R&D—almost three-quarters of which is military-related—innovation has become institutionalized, accelerated, and less sensitive to business cycles (although quite vulnerable to political cycles). The military–industrial complex is a new form of continual industrial innovation, even if its market spin-offs may be minimal.

A second feature of the military–industrial complex is its preoccupation with automated warfare. In addition to the aircraft and missile "frames," or "bodies," the "payload" they carry has become more significant and more sophisticated. Pilots and remote operators have come to rely increasingly on radar, guidance systems, communications equipment, and cybernetics to tell them where to fly, where to aim, what to dodge, and how to make decisions under conditions of uncertainty and rapid change. Strategic warfare has moved from bombers to missiles, becoming ever more capital- and technology-intensive. Electronic components, for instance, account for a larger share of value-added in each successive generation of weapons system. By the 1960s, electronics composed 13 to 20 percent of an airplane's value, and 50 percent of that of a missile.[25]

The aerospace giants and their communications and electronics suppliers broke ranks with industrial leaders of the mechanical era. Indeed, they are almost entirely a new breed. Firms like Hughes, McDonnell-Douglas, Rockwell, Grumman, General Dynamics, United Technologies, TRW, Litton, and Lear-Siegler were not major players before World War II. They not only are preoccupied with defense work, but have two other unusual features: a high degree of concentrated market power and extraordinary dependence on one buyer, the federal government.

Concentration among military contractors has been a feature, and a worry, since the very beginning of the aerospace industry. In early years, scale economies seemingly favored concentration, although some analysts believe that the government wanted few competitors, in part to ensure secrecy in bomber development. In 1930, forty-one aircraft models were manufactured by eighteen companies; by 1935, the number fell to twenty-six models by twelve companies. Thereafter, as aircraft-development financing by government ballooned from 45 percent to 67 percent in 1939 and 92 percent during World War II, the number of big contract winners declined precipitously, and companies divided into predominantly commercial and military camps.[26]

This concentration has been maintained throughout the postwar period,

TABLE 3.1.   Top 20 Prime-Contracting Firms, 1958 and 1984

	1958		1984	
Rank	Company	Value (millions of dollars)	Company	Value (millions of dollars)
1	Boeing	2,131.0	McDonnell-Douglas	7,684.2
2	General Dynamics	1,383.2	Rockwell–North American	6,219.3
3	General Electric	783.4	General Dynamics	5,951.5
4	Lockheed Aircraft	755.1	Lockheed Corp.	4,967.5
5	United Aircraft	661.1	Boeing	4,563.8
6	AT&T	659.8	General Electric	4,514.5
7	North American	647.7	Hughes Medical	3,230.5
8	Douglas Aircraft	513.4	United Technologies	3,206.8
9	Hughes Aircraft	472.6	Raytheon	3,093.0
10	Martin Co.	400.2	Litton	2,440.7
11	Sperry-Rand	370.1	Grumman Corp.	2,419.0
12	Chance Vought	360.4	Martin-Marietta	2,260.7
13	McDonnell	352.0	Westinghouse	1,943.5
14	IBM	316.5	LTV Corp.	1,655.3
15	RCA	288.3	Sperry Corp.	1,615.2
16	Northrop Aircraft	283.5	IBM	1,571.6
17	General Motors	280.9	Honeywell	1,354.4
18	Westinghouse	269.3	FMC Corp.	1,156.8
19	Republic Aviation	264.7	ITT Corp.	1,139.7
20	Chrysler Corp.	58.6	Ford Motor Co.	1,124.1
Cumulative share				
	Top 20 companies	52.6%		46.5%

Source: Aviation Week and Space Technology.

despite decades of government commitment to small business set-asides. By the mid–1980s, the top 100 companies accounted for 70 percent of total defense business, the top 20 for nearly 50 percent, and the top 5 for 20 percent (Table 3.1). At the level of individual weapons systems or parts, firms generally compete with only one or two others for an initial contract and, after winning it, exercise a virtual monopoly. Concentration has also evolved in supplier sectors. Most large aerospace firms have developed long-term relationships with one or a few highly reliable and responsive firms for each component. Many subcontractors have survived by occupying market niches and monopolizing the production of certain specialized parts.[27]

The aerospace industry and its suppliers, the communications-equipment and electronics/instrumentation industries, are heavily dependent on defense spending. According to the Department of Commerce's input–output model, the more traditional weapons industries—tanks, ammunition, ordnance, and shipbuilding—are highly defense-dependent; but so are missiles, aircraft, and communications.[28] Furthermore, individual firms and their divisions tend to serve just one master, either commercial markets or the military.[29]

This unusual fact of government-as-monopsonistic-buyer makes the aerospace marketplace different from other manufacturing concerns. To confound the picture even further, the government does not behave the way a textbook private monopsonist would. The latter strives to maximize profits by squeezing the seller; the former is obsessed by a search for technical perfection. In contrast to practice in commercial factories, where a certain percentage of output is expected to be faulty, the Pentagon is concerned primarily with precision and performance on the part of the aircraft: because of the obvious dangers of combat flying, safety and quality have always been high priorities. As one contractor told us, "You face demands for time, performance, and cost. You can have two, but not three. When selling to the Pentagon, its the time and performance that matters, and cost goes out the window."[30]

As a result of these peculiar market features, workers in defense firms operate in a paradoxical environment: although the new cold warfare is extremely capital-intensive, the equipment that delivers it is made by very labor-intensive methods. Aircraft and missiles do not lend themselves to the assembly-line techniques so fashionable in twentieth-century consumer-goods industries. Rather, they depend on a tremendous amount of teamwork, as well as highly specialized individual contributions to handle specific production problems. Cold warfare paraphernalia is produced in small batches, often to unique design specifications and with experimentation embedded in the construction itself. Often, too, defense-plant work is highly sensitive and classified, because the product is valuable only as long as the other side cannot replicate it.

Thus as early as 1947, 46 percent of Lockheed's costs consisted of labor inputs, compared with 34 percent in materials.[31] Parts production—whether in engines, fueling systems, or communications equipment—was also highly labor-intensive. Over time, this labor component has grown more and more sophisticated, and the share of high-tech labor—scientists, engineers, technicians—in strategic weaponry has risen as the share of materials and semi- and unskilled labor declined.

A New Locational Logic

All these features have generated a locational calculus that is quite different from the traditional one in the economic-geography textbooks. First, the new weapons systems created the possibility of new production complexes far from traditional centers. The technologies and production processes for aircraft are quite different from those for metals, autos, and other consumer goods.[32] Certain aspects of airframes, in particular, favored locations with a climate and topography that differed from that of the industrial heartland.[33] In addition, the peculiarities of military production—the need for secrecy and small-batch production, the emphasis on teamwork and experimental fabrication, the attitudes consonant with a career in designing ever-more-destructive weaponry—favored new centers outside the traditional heartland.

Second, the continual pressure to innovate has engendered and reinforced a tendency toward agglomeration and clustering on the part of the aerospace industry and its suppliers. In this, they are no different from other innovative industries, with their proclivity to concentrate in a few geographical arenas.[34] What distinguishes cold war military-production complexes from their commercial counterparts, however, is the continual nature of the innovative process. In these industries, products never reach the point of mass production. Manufacturers thus avoid the pressure to disperse to lower-cost production sites. Instead, the conditions of a youthful, innovative industry are perpetuated by Pentagon demand and dollars. Industries get stuck in the superprofit stage; with only a few conspicuous exceptions, they stay in the centers where they first emerged.[35]

These features are accentuated and complicated by other characteristics of the military–industrial complex. The presence of few competitors reinforces the tendency toward agglomeration by encouraging firms to cluster.[36] Only with proximity can competitors watch one another's moves carefully, manage the market, and maintain market shares. Specialized services that enhance this oligopolistic structure cement the cluster, as do the requirements for frequent communication between monopolistic parts suppliers and their big final-assembly clients.

And because of the unique fact of government as monopsonistic buyer, clustering tends to encompass close proximity not only among competitors and suppliers, but also between buyer and sellers. With only one buyer, however complex, it pays to be nearby, with hired eyes and ears to the ground to detect future requirements, gather information, and market a continual supply of new military products. The aerospace industry thus becomes a "camp follower," setting up at least some of its operations in tandem with the military purchasing agents, planners, and funds appropriators in certain locales where this special client–seller relationship is present. This is especially true of certain types of operation, such as SETA, C^3I (command, control, communications, and intelligence), software, and systems engineers. The Pentagon and service agencies are located far from the major centers of commercial activity in the United States, raising the possibility that the preferences of the monopsonistic buyer powerfully helps determine which sites become new military production centers.

This geographically dispersed pattern of military–industrial production is reinforced by another feature of the Pentagon as buyer. Since cost is not a primary issue, the conventional pressure to minimize charges—for labor, transportation, and so on—is by and large absent. Instead, a premium is placed on being sited where the company can maximize its quality, reliability, and promptness in production—high cost or no.

Labor provides a good example. Highly skilled labor consumes a very large and ongoing share of the military procurement dollar, yet the location of such labor may not be at all crucial to the creation of a military–industrial center. This is because the government not only allows contractors to charge it for the costs of recruiting and moving skilled labor interregionally, but actually permits them to include these expenses in their cost base. Since contractors add their profit to this base, they have an actual incentive to move skilled labor around. One might even argue that the government has been running a massive for-profit population-resettlement program in the postwar period.

The new trend toward joint ventures also helps to anchor military-oriented producers in their new locations. The increasing sophistication of cold war weaponry has progressively emphasized the design stage and rendered it so complicated that no single firm is capable of turning out a new weapons system on its own. In the 1980s, just as the military services themselves were forced into greater cooperation and joint commands, the big aerospace contractors had to assemble teams to design, bid on, and eventually construct new weapons systems. This reinforces existing locations and favors proximity among cooperating firms. Often, since firms are based in disparate gunbelt sites, projects must be overseen by branch offices set up in selected central locations.

But the continual innovation inherent in cold war contracting has a contrary, destabilizing effect. The evolution of highly sophisticated computers with enormous computational capabilities may require ever larger contingents of private-sector contractors to write software and integrate systems located at the point where the military uses the equipment. And the new joint commands in the 1980s, made imperative by the incredible mobility and efficiency of modern weaponry, may accelerate the clustering of contractors that provide defense-planning services and C^3I around Washington, D.C., the central command-and-control headquarters of the nation's military effort.

In our tour through the gunbelt, then, we can suppose that military-production complexes develop in three stages. First, new centers emerge, a function of the peculiarities of the strategic mission of the cold war. Second, these centers have extraordinary agglomerative growth trajectories, because of the prolongation of innovation stages by the cold war and because of the unique feature of government-as-buyer. And third, as innovation alters the technology of warfare, new weapons and strategies themselves favor yet newer centers of activity, tailored to the requirements of the times. Older centers may compete, but existing business cultures often make this difficult. Together, these facets of the military–industrial complex heighten the tendency to cluster and draw the clusters toward locations favored by the military—locations likely to be found outside the traditional industrial heartland. And these features give a special role to the preferences and prejudices of individual actors: founders, managers, top military brass, promoters, boosters, and others.

Founders, Generals, Congressmen, and Boosters

Because of the unique market structure of military provisioning, both private- and public-sector actors can powerfully influence the selection of sites. On the supply side, the firm's behavior is well captured by the notion of profit-maximizing; but on the demand side, the picture is much more complex, encompassing bureaucratic "satisficing," strategic concerns, and electioneering goals. "Satisficing" means that Pentagon and military staff may prefer to maximize the size of their bureaus or the perks of their jobs, rather than modernize the defense services delivered to the nation.

Our story of the development of the military–industrial complex features two key groups of supply-side actors. First, there are the entrepreneurs or founding fathers (this story has no founding mothers) who set up the offices, plants, and facilities that ultimately grew to be major aerospace firms. Successful innovators require a nurturing environment, one that favors the fragile and risky initiative on which they embark.[37] Such an environment can be a hometown, the founder's actual birthplace or the seat of the university or firm for which he was working when he branched out on his own. It can also be a locale far from his home base, a place to which he flees because his local environment quashes his ambitions and refuses him the resources to succeed. Founders may be drawn to new locations by a number of factors: a lucrative defense contract, an irresistible offer from local boosters, or a sense that a new locale is the perfect place to live and work. Differential costs of production are generally unimportant in this first critical step, so personal preferences and/or serendipity may play an important role.

The second group of actors are the managers of established firms and branches. Their room for personal preference is much smaller. As technologies mature—in standard aircraft or electronics parts, for instance—defense managers feel the same pressure as their commercial counterparts: to lower costs by building plants in outlying locations or closer to end markets, profiting from proximity to the monopsonistic buyer. This is more likely to occur in lines of defense output where competition is intense; less so, where a firm has few rivals. In monopolistic situations, a manager may try to pass on the higher costs of a satisficing location in his contract. Or, if unable to, he may chose to trade off excess profits for the privilege of living and working in a favored place. Amenities, either cosmopolitan or environmental, may thus enter into the locational calculus. And in cases where a firm's status is judged by its letterhead, the mere "image" of being in Sunnyvale, Costa Mesa, or Chula Vista may shape a managerial location decision.

On the demand side of this military-equipment market lies the complicated institution of the state. Here, no single individual plays a dominant role, yet several sets of actors are alert to locational issues and employ their influence to shape the evolution of military-production geography. These actors include the generals and colonels responsible for military planning and strategy, the president (the military commander-in-chief) and his advisers who are responsible for foreign policy and budget formation, and the members of Congress who review and vote on military appropriations.

Military leaders are concerned primarily with strategic goals and therefore with the safety and efficiency of the "defense industrial base." Their notion of efficiency, however, may not be confined to issues of dollars and cents. For instance, Pentagon strategists may want defense facilities to be located in relatively remote interior areas where they will be less vulnerable to enemy attack. They may prefer to maintain duplicate and redundant facilities to ensure a source of supply. They may favor the siting of certain production and service activities close to their operational commands or procurement offices, to maximize interaction and cut down on delivery or installation time.[38] Such requirements may be written into contracts, even when firms are reluctant to comply. The costs of the consequent locational inefficiencies are absorbed by the service in question and covered in the contract.

The military may also use contracting power to create industrial communities that are more amenable to the defense presence. In the United States, unlike many other industrialized nations, the military top brass have never been accorded very high status in the cosmopolitan capitalist culture that emerged in the late nineteenth century.[39] Military leaders may thus favor the development of production facilities in communities that hold the military in relatively high regard. Forced to be very mobile throughout their professional lives, and scheduled for retirement at an early age, they may favor certain sites as potential retirement communities and may commit resources to these areas to enhance their attractiveness. San Diego, San Antonio, Los Angeles, and Colorado Springs, each with large concentrations of retired military, may have been favored in this way. Least attractive in this regard are large, established metropolitan centers dominated by a liberal social and business elite.

The location of private-sector defense activity may also be affected by military preferences. Remote places with residential communities of like-minded people may be favored over established industrial centers by military procurers, and by military personnel who have crossed over into private-sector management. The local politics and hardball labor practices that typify the industrial heartland—including collective bargaining, responsiveness to financial incentives, and job-hopping—are inimical to the military mode, with its rigid internal structure, narrowly restricted labor mobility, and emphasis on loyalty to the organization.[40] The search for commercial and community cultures congenial to military-industrial activity may draw contract dollars far from the Rustbelt.

Finally, rivalries among the service branches, and even within them, may emerge as powerful locational forces. During the 1950s, the struggle between the Air Force and the Army, with their very different visions of how strategic missiles ought to be made, was associated with a competition between Los Angeles and Huntsville for a major increment to the local defense economy. Many such controversies dot the history of strategic warfare. In some cases, the locational question is inconsequential in the larger conflict over weapons capabilities, service missions, and product management.[41] But in others, the fact that a certain military official is simply head of base x, y, or z, and that his personal prestige and chances of advancement will be greatly enhanced if he gets a certain new weapons system assigned to his territory, results in his lobbying hard for it, even if his location is not the strategically optimal one. National security policy-making is imperfect, so the literature tells us, allowing nonrational elements to come into play.

This most often happens at military middle-management level. Illogical factors may be embedded in the plans that colonels give their commanding officers for approval or in the requests that field commanders pass on to Washington. The top brass themselves may be indifferent to locational choices, although it is quite possible that generals will express preferences for certain key sites. Sometimes, the regional affinities of the topmost people will dictate the location of a military-related production complex. This has certainly been demonstrated in the case of the Houston Space Center, started when Lyndon B. Johnson was vice president.

Congress is a different matter. Indeed, much of the 1980s literature on the geography of defense outlays vilifies Congress as the agency most responsible for the skewed pattern.[42] The argument is that Congress treats the defense budget like a pork barrel, with every member scrambling for a chunk of contract dollars. Senators and representatives with the most clout—those chairing military-appropriations committees and those with the most seniority—can divert military dollars their constituents' way. Members of Congress have an incentive to maximize both votes and political campaign contributions, and thus can be expected to lobby hard for military contracts for their jurisdictions.

Overall, such a theory would suggest broad dispersion of defense contracts across the states, rather than concentration. Yet, while a few singular cases of the exercise of political muscle can be cited, empirical studies show a remarkable lack of general evidence.[43] A pork-barrelling model is difficult to defend, given the extraordinary concentration of prime contracts shown in Chapter 2. Congress can only approve or deny expenditures and is generally not involved in initiating a weapons system. The potential bidders are identified far ahead of time, and it is the preexisting location of defense factories and offices that explains the vast bulk of contemporary defense expenditures. Congress can be mobilized only very late in this process, making it more difficult to block an entire weapons system or to demand that a new plant be built in a virgin location. Although legislators from the industrial Northeast dominated Congress well into the 1970s, this region continually lost ground in defense production.

Congressional logrolling does reinforce the tendency of military production to cluster in centers that are not preoccupied with civilian production. Representatives of military-dependent districts may win support for bills favorable to defense firms by agreeing to vote in favor of other constituencies' priorities—agricultural states' farm bills, say, of the Midwest's auto and steel tariffs.[44] And since productive capacity tends to grow through expansions rather than new plants, existing centers would seem to have an edge over potential locations. Members of Congress may be more effective in responding to an existing constituency by blocking plant or base closings, than in selecting a new military-production site on the basis of the area's potential.

Congressional influence, then, is limited. Despite the fact that individual legislators loudly protest plant closings, complain about discrimination in funding, and demand that contracts be let locally, most of this is done principally to get the legislator's name into the local paper. Military managers have no incentive to maintain a high profile, nor would it be considered appropriate or ethical for them to do so, but in our view military managers figure much more prominently than legislators as creators of the gunbelt.

Local civic boosters constitute the last set of actors that engages in efforts to build military-production centers. This group may be motivated by a desire to expand the area's tax base, enhance real-estate values, and create jobs for local residents. Historically, the strenuous rival efforts of such groups often left their marks on the geography of military production. In the early decades of the twentieth century, San Diego, Los Angeles, and San Francisco competed fiercely to be the home of the Navy's principal West Coast naval base.[45] In the 1960s, Colorado Springs successfully competed for the title of space command center.

Local boosters—who include city officials, real-estate developers, locally tied business interests (newspapers, banks, sports teams), and even universities[46]—may offer defense firms and the military the same incentives that they offer other enterprises: land, infrastructure, financing for industrial plants and related housing construction, and tax breaks. But perhaps most important, they can offer military decision-makers the promise of enthusiastic acceptance by the local community and the city's elite, as well as the kind of business culture and environment that is so important to these groups.[47] As we shall see, such guarantees loomed large in the success of many gunbelt centers.

Military Places Rated

We now need to focus on the actual places on the American road map that compete for defense projects. Of course, "places" do not compete; their business elites do. Some fail; some succeed. To determine which characteristics seem to make for success, we will look at each area the way an economic developer would.[48] If you wanted to be a military–industrial town, how would you rate?[49]

Many factors—topography, climate, entrepreneurship, labor, government labs, universities, military bases, and local cultural and business climates—have been hypothesized to affect military–industrial location, especially the more glamorous, high-tech end. Many observers have stressed sun, clear skies, and flat terrain as ideal, simplifying construction of aircraft and missiles—important for small start-up companies[50]—and making it easier to test prototypes. Coastal sites provide access to international markets, very important in the pioneer days.[51] But, as mentioned above, for every case that seems to prove the rule, there are several that disprove it: Boeing did well in Seattle; Grumman, on Long Island; Honeywell, in Minneapolis. As we shall see in studying particular sites, climate was at best an eccentric and intermittent determinant.

Human Capital

Entrepreneurs cannot easily be treated as indigenous or fixed regional factors, since they are quintessentially mobile. Nevertheless, sometimes the location of a military-production plant may be explained by the simple fact that a founder started it in his hometown (Boeing in Seattle) or a place in which he settled and came to love (Douglas or Kindelberger in Los Angeles). Entrepreneurs, of course, can also be seen as products of their environments—and so it is helpful to know something of the cultural and industrial milieu where they spent their formative years.[52]

Skilled labor is quite another matter. Most of the literature on high-tech location stresses specialized pools of labor as a necessity.[53] But, as already argued, labor cannot be considered an exogenous, fixed locational factor, because so much of it has been highly mobile and so much of this mobility has been underwritten by government.[54] Since new military-production complexes have emerged far from traditional centers, it is evident that massive population resettlement occurred during the hot wars of the 1940s and 1950s, and continued throughout the cold war period.

Occasionally, already extant labor pools can be dipped into. Indeed, military bases themselves serve as sources of labor. Soldiers are recruited more or less ubiquitously from all over the United States, but the bases at which they live and work are concentrated in the Sunbelt. Mustered-out or retired military personnel composed the single largest group of interregional migrants in the years from 1969 to 1976.[55] They knew the labor market around their bases far better than that of their hometowns, a fact that encouraged many to stay in the vicinity. As we shall see, firms are attracted to these areas by the presence of people who have an institutional knowledge of weapons systems, the procurement process, and/or the services themselves, specialized training in operating certain weapons, and expertise in maintaining these weapons.

Universities may also be important regional suppliers of labor. Firms might locate near first-rate engineering schools, such as Caltech or MIT, to have "first dibs" on graduates. Employees seeking to advance professionally enroll in night classes and special "executive" programs for returning and working students; this, in turn, may make locating near a good university more attractive to employers.[56] Consulting by university professors for private firms, and the less frequent instance in which a professor sets up a contracting firm, are other ways in which universities may act as conduits of human capital for a nascent military–industrial complex. Universities, indeed, play a central role in the interregional redistribution of engineering and scientific talent. First, they admit students from all over the nation, with the better schools attracting high proportions of out-of-state entrants. Then, although many of these students are subsequently redisbursed nationally through their university's placement office, many choose to stay in the school's environs. This has been particularly true of the Boston area.

A great deal of the literature on high-tech industry has stressed the importance of amenities in the ability of firms to attract and hold professional and technical labor. The hypothesis suggests that professional and technical workers have a strong position in their labor markets, effectively pulling firms to the places where they want to live. But there is disagreement about just what those amenities might be. While some scientists may be infatuated with the opera, others may prefer the wide-open spaces, the seashore, or mountains to climb. Then, too, other studies dissent, noting that engineers and scientists have shown an extraordinary proclivity to follow the best job, wherever it is.

The availability of blue-collar labor was traditionally a major concern for aerospace companies. In the early decades, firms needed to be near a medium-size city; during the war years, government agencies and funds helped facilitate the recruitment of thousands of workers from labor-surplus areas to labor-deficit ones, even as they tried to decentralize manufacturing capacity toward areas of high unemployment. In certain places, the competition for blue-collar labor has been intense. Some authors suggest that there has been substantial labor-hoarding by aircraft-engine firms in New England and—to a lesser extent—by the airframe industry of the Southwest.[57]

But the "quality" of blue-collar labor matters, too: many defense contractors have shown an unusual antipathy toward unions and heavily unionized cities and regions, not principally because of wage demands, but for fear of work stoppages and resistance to changing work rules in an industry where timely delivery is critical and military models of labor relations prevail.[58] Like the military itself, these firms see themselves as having a mission to perform: they want their product to be "the best," and they need a dedicated, teamwork-oriented, pliant work force. Places without a well-developed industrial capitalist culture may thus fare better as potential military–industrial centers than Chicago, Detroit, Cleveland, or Philadelphia. Some may object that New England, a region with adversarial labor relations, disproves this theory, but New England suffered twenty years of deindustrialization before its military-based resurgence, decimating union ranks, and has benefited from its strong educational system. And Los Angeles, once a virulently anti-union town, had to accept unions as a part of the national wartime accords—organizing permitted but no strikes allowed.

Blue-collar labor, though, may not be the locational force it once was. With weaponry more and more dependent on innovation, the need increasingly is for very high-level engineering and technical expertise—the kind that comes from university Ph.D. programs rather than from trade schools. Today, a typical defense worker is more likely to be an engineer than a machinist, a software writer than a riveter, a skilled technician than an assembly-line worker, a physicist experimenting with gallium arsenide semiconductors rather than a metal bender. And, importantly, a member of a professional organization rather than a member of a union.

As with geophysical features, there are many examples where human capital has played a role, but also many where it has not. Many military bases have drawn no appreciable military–industrial activity, while some

successful defense cities, like Boston, have few bases from which to recruit. Some centers, such as Boston and San Jose, have benefited from the
presence of a major technical university, while other regions with first-rate
engineering schools continue to export most of their graduates. Many engineers swear by Seattle, Rockford, and even frigid Minneapolis; and win-
ters are long in New England, too. Remote cities like Colorado Springs
seem to have no trouble drawing highly educated workers, despite the absence of cosmopolitan cultural offerings. High rates of unionization do not
seem to have harmed the military–industrial cores of Boston and Los Angeles. In sum, no single element appears to be a necessary prerequisite to
the initiation of a military–industrial center. These labor features seem so
clearly crucial and yet so endogenous, evolving simultaneously with the
military production centers themselves.

Idea Mills: Government, University, and Corporate Labs

Another locational factor might be the presence of an "idea mill": a place
where military-oriented innovation is institutionalized as an ongoing activity.
Wellsprings such as government R&D labs, university labs, and corporate
labs might be expected both to generate new entrepreneurs and to attract
outside entrepreneurs, who would seek proximity to and contact with the
idea-makers.

The federal government runs and funds a number of major research laboratories around the country, including several elite national labs (Livermore,
Los Alamos) that do purely weapons-related work. They are much more
spatially decentralized than are either university or corporate labs.[59] We might
expect, then, that military idea centers would draw along in their wake new
forms of related for-profit activity. In fact, as we shall see, few have.

Universities might operate in the same fashion: their labs might generate
ideas that local entrepreneurs could pick up on. Certainly, this is the theory
behind the recently fashionable university research park.[60] And universities
may also be contractors themselves. As seen in Chapter 2, military RDT&E
contracts to educational institutions amounted to $850 million by the early
1980s. Several well-known concentrations of high-technology industry, with
strong defense components—Boston's Route 128, California's Silicon Valley,
and England's Cambridge Science Park—have been linked to major research
universities.[61]

Corporate laboratories, too, could devote some of their overhead to
military-oriented activities. In general, they are highly concentrated in the
traditional industrial heartland, near big corporate headquarters cities like
New York and Chicago, and key industrial enclaves for particular industries,
like Detroit. But this strategy would most likely depend on the prospects for
these firms in their existing markets. We might expect more experimentation
in regions with a structurally declining economic base, especially in eras of
major recession or depression.

Nonetheless, "idea mills" may prove very questionable locational factors.

Federal R&D centers tend to be heavily committed to secrecy and may offer their employees such favorable civil service perks that no local spin-off activity is generated. Well-paid and with job security for life, employees are less inclined to risk the rigors of the marketplace. Existing weapons labs show this clearly. Universities may generate the ideas essential to military innovation, but their host communities may not exploit the fact—as witness the top Midwest engineering schools. Conversely, many places without top-ranked research universities—including Colorado Springs, central Florida, Washington, D.C., and Huntsville, Alabama[62]—have been sites of high-tech military-oriented activities.

Defense Markets

Traditional location theory stressed the importance of overcoming the "friction of distance": industries would locate at sites that minimized the costs of assembling production inputs and reaching the market, all else being equal. But for modern defense industries, these assumptions do not work very well. In defense production, material supplies account for a small and shrinking share of total costs, and they are generally high in value relative to transport costs. Likewise, the cost of transporting the product to market does not matter much. Some assembled products, like ships, submarines, and aircraft, literally transport themselves to market, obviating transportation costs altogether.[63] Other products are designed for "mobilization," making the physical link to markets largely irrelevant. Military products that are stockpiled and stored for some future mobilization are placed in armories and receptacles—missile silos are a good example—whose locations are dispersed, classified, or frequently changed.

True, there are important exceptions. Overseas destinations may have mattered in the critical period of the 1930s, favoring coastal production sites. Military facilities might be needed for design and testing, or service and maintenance contracts may tie firms to a particular site. In one sense, the Department of Defense and Congress form the market, because they construct the budget and appropriate the money. If firms need timely or inside information, or if their client needs them close by to execute information-intensive C^3I contracts, we might expect them to set up shop around Washington, D.C. Conversely, contractors that want an inside track on the next innovative challenge may decide to establish storefronts or larger research-and-development branch offices close to leading-edge commands. Yet, all this said, city fathers of many towns have vigorously pursued military-related activity without success.

The important point here is that with the shift from large-volume, shooting-war production to small-volume, technology-intensive, prototypical design and testing, cost in the traditional sense no longer matters; what matters is getting or failing to get information. In this sense, defense industries are more like informational service industries than traditional manufacturing. The archetype is the SETA operations, which proliferated wildly during the 1980s and locate close to the contracting agencies, both at military bases and in central facilities in Los Angeles, Colorado Springs, and Washington, D.C.

It is going to be difficult to judge the relative effect of these conflicting factors—geophysical traits, human capital, idea mills, government presence—or to rank military-production enclaves according to them. We might try distinguishing between active factors—key elements that trigger the military-production-center building process—and passive factors that help maintain a center in place. The problem is that these elements may change over time as the technologies of warfare change and as the missions and fortunes of the services wax and wane. Thus we come full circle, back to the structural and behavioral forces that led to the construction of military-production complexes in places far from the old industrial heartland.[64]

How Military-Production Centers Are Built

How, exactly, do these new centers develop? Revolutionary breakthroughs in war technology, sudden shifts in foreign policy, and dramatic institutional changes within the military–industrial complex create ratchet effects that propel certain places to the fore. But something must be there to begin with: a critical element, like the grain of sand around which the oyster's pearl grows —a founding father who sets up a military-oriented plant, a preexisting industrial firm that decides to risk entering military-oriented production,[65] a local university or research lab with an interest in a particular military mission, or a strategic imperative that compels the government to start a new base or a new factory. In the twisted skein of cause-and-effect over time, distinguishing the initial cause may prove difficult, particularly if there are subsequent key events that might also explain a production center's success or failure.[66]

Once a site is selected for a military-oriented plant, agglomeration economies set in motion a dynamic process of local economy-building.[67] A specialized labor pool, a set of specialized business-service firms, and competitive spin-off firms begin to proliferate. New enterprises may be attracted by the resulting agglomeration of talent and ideas. "Progressive internalization" reinforces the process, as import-substituting activities supply specialized goods and services—as in Los Angeles in the 1930s and 1940s, where the airframe industry attracted machining, communications, electronics, software, and service industries, none of which had existed there before.[68] This tendency to agglomerate is very deep-set for defense-based industries: they will continue to cluster long beyond the point where economic rationality would suggest decentralization. Service procurement agencies may even be attracted by the resulting concentration of specialized firms. Thus, over time, entire metropolitan areas may come to depend substantially on military enterprise.

This is a multistage process, full of dynamic changes, discontinuities, and contingencies, unpredictable and sometimes random, and thus difficult to handle within the conventional static framework of neoclassical economics. It is analogous to a golf game, with the host cities as players of various sizes, strengths, smarts, and physical endowments. Each tees off with a certain strategy in mind; subsequent strokes are heavily shaped by the outcome of that first shot. Meanwhile, the weather may change, a crucial club may break, a competitor may make a brilliant move, their eye or their judgment may take a sudden turn. It is impossible to predict the final outcome or the best path to follow.

Five Models of the Military–Industrial City

We can distinguish at least five such paths to the development of a military–industrial city.

Model A: The Seedbed Transformed

An existing agglomeration of firms, services, and skilled labor pools may act as a "seedbed of innovation" for new defense-oriented activity.[69] Established centers with their corporate R&D labs, good universities, diversified business services, and extensive skilled-labor markets harness these resources to new tasks. An existing commercially oriented firm—in, say, instruments (Honeywell in Minneapolis) or radio (Raytheon in Massachusetts) or precision machining (Pratt & Whitney in Connecticut)—reorientates itself toward an emerging military mission and market. Successful entry on the ground floor leads to dependable, lucrative contracts for development as well as production. In turn, suppliers and/or competing rivals emerge around these key firms. This stimulates yet another round of skilled-labor-pool formation and local business services. A major obstacle to be overcome may be the hold that more established industries have on resources and, more subtly, on local attitudes.

Model B: The Upstart Military–Industrial City

A second, almost diametrically opposed model is one in which a single individual or small group starts up a military-oriented firm, sometimes with military support, at a site far from existing industrial centers. Founders, for reasons explored above, may prefer remote locations. Their Pentagon patrons, comfortable with frontier locations, may give them the initial contracts necessary for survival. The forces of agglomeration are thus set in motion, as in Los Angeles in the 1920s and 1930s.

Such a new center faces a formidable task. It must gather the multifarious resources that are readily available in existing seedbeds: a pool of engineers, scientists, and technicians; a technical-university system; and a crop of supportors in Congress. On the plus side, an upstart military developer has no encumbrances in the form of competing traditional industries and fixed business cultures.

Model C: The Booster-Incubated Military–Industrial Complex

A third model centers on the formation of an extraordinary local coalition, including members of Congress, to recruit military facilities and defense contractors. Since at key times the military–industrial complex shows a proclivity to relocate production plants or develop new bases, a town may be able to garner a share by vigorously promoting itself as an ideal site. Many such local efforts are mounted, but only a handful succeed. A favorable outcome usually hinges on an area's having something special: a local resource, a piece of land, surplus capital, or a unique environmental setting.

Once a locale attracts a military facility, it must develop agglomeration economies like those of established places. This may be difficult, since service bases and branch plants are often quite isolated, self-contained, and narrowly specialized. Thus the complex may have to be built in steps, through a grueling process of recruiting and wheedling in federal arenas. A military base, for instance, might provide the personnel to attract a few high-tech branch plants. Or it may draw around it special defense-service contractors. Or its military function may be upgraded. These, in turn, may further enhance the area's attractiveness as a defense research-and-production center, convincing other large firms to enter and encouraging local start-ups and spin-offs.

Model D: The Military–Educational Complex

Universities whose faculty and administrators face strong incentives to solicit outside research support may aggressively pursue military-funded research. Over time, some of these projects may evolve into off-campus research institutes or independent firms. Their military connections may allow, or even encourage, them to move from R&D into production. Agglomeration economies set in, and the area becomes a specialized military-production center, maintaining the university–industry link that affords it a steady supply of new ideas and talent. Stanford and Silicon Valley, MIT and Route 128, are the classic cases. Less well known is Caltech's role in engendering the Los Angeles aerospace complex, a tale we tell in Chapter 4.

Model E: The Installation-Based Military–Industrial Complex

Key military facilities—aircraft-testing grounds, defense nerve centers, deployment centers for missiles and spacecraft—may be positioned without local boosterism and may set off a growth dynamic, attracting production and/or service facilities. The military installation may generate a labor pool—short-term technicians and mechanics, intermediate-term engineers, and twenty-year retiring officers—who in turn may attract yet other firms. Such a center will most easily achieve the cultural characteristics that are favorable to an ongoing defense presence. In another version of this trajectory, the Pentagon may dictate the location of a defense plant for strategic reasons, and this may set off a process like that of the upstart-city model.

Model F: The Defense-Services Complex

A special variant of Model E is Model F, the defense-services city. The obvious example is Washington, D.C. The "installation" in this case is the core set of government institutions concerned with the military–industrial complex: the Pentagon, the White House, and the Congress. They constitute the command-and-control headquarters of the military–industrial complex, much in the same way that New York, London, and Tokyo operate as command-and-control headquarters for private financial and industrial capital in their respective countries. Just as for commercially oriented corporations, transportation and communication improvements have caused the major military-oriented firms to fragment their functions, with production far from the Washington center but large branch offices in nearby D.C. suburbs.[70] Such a defense-services city builds on these interconnections between government and private suppliers, developing a very specialized profile, with little or no manufacturing.

These models each posit a different initiating source and thus a different set of challenges and evolutionary steps. The end result for each defense-based city is a special kind of production complex, a function of its particular mission and of the period in which its greatest growth was engendered. Some cities may contain elements of more than one model.

Clearly, many aspiring cities fall by the wayside. Each model demands that a number of successive steps be taken. Simply attracting a plant or military base will not by itself ensure an agglomerative dynamic. Some military–industrial cities may remain one-plant towns. Others may fail altogether: San Antonio and Atlanta are examples.

Going Out on the Road

With the aid of this bulky atlas, we are now ready to tour the gunbelt. In the process, we will draw on a great variety of literature—some general, some applicable primarily to the places we are visiting—that can help throw light on the complex processes of building a military-production center. In addition, we will interview many actual decision-makers—military officers, university presidents, civic boosters, industrial executives—who have helped shape these stories.

We shall try to tell each story as an evolutionary, stage-by-stage process, in some kind of chronological sequence. First, the rise—and subsequent decline—of the pioneer defense industries in the American heartland, where they grew out of existing industrial traditions: the classic Model A. Second, the development of Los Angeles into the airframe and then aerospace capital of the world: an equally classic Model B. Third, the intriguing example of Seattle—the isolated Model B city, selected by a single founding father, that survived despite the odds against it. Fourth, New England as the Model A industrial region that successfully made the adaptation to high-tech industrial production—partly because its core, Greater Boston, was also a prototype of Model D: the military–educational city. Fifth, Colorado Springs, which combines features of both Model C, the booster-incubated complex, and Model E, the installation-based complex. And, finally, Washington D.C.: the special case of Model F, the defense-services complex.

4

The Third Coast: Aviation Pioneers Exit the Midwest

Whenever Dr. Morton Klein, vice president for business development at the Illinois Institute of Technology Research Institute (IITRI), visits the Pentagon, he sticks an aerial photograph in his briefcase. The photo shows the shoreline of Lake Michigan, with Meigs Field, a small commuter airport, in the foreground and the corporate offices of Chicago towering behind it. Klein is trying to generate more military-research dollars for his brain-powered organization, but finds his task difficult. "They often demur," says Klein, "since we are not 'on the coasts.' " Klein then whips out his photo and exclaims, "But here you have it, the third coast!"

Klein and others have discovered a hard contemporary truth: in the late 1980s, the third coast is well-nigh invisible on the defense-contracting map of America. As illustrated in Chapter 2, the industrial remapping of the United States has sucked defense manufacturing and research out of the industrial heartland and redistributed it along parts of the West, East,—and South—coasts. The Midwest is home to a mere handful of prime contractors, prompting representatives of these states to accuse the Pentagon and the armed services of purposely steering clear of the Great Lakes region.

At first sight, this bias is perplexing. The modern military–industrial complex was born in the midwestern industrial heartland, an area once said to contain the greatest concentration of engineering skills in the United States. Powered flight, the technological basis of the entire system, came out of the Midwest. The early history of the airplane, including its first military adaptation, is largely a history of the heartland, an "iron triangle" more than 500 miles wide but just over 200 miles deep, bounded by the third coast on the north and shaped by the great engineering cities of Chicago, Buffalo, and Dayton (Fig. 4.1). Detroit, midway between Chicago and Buffalo on the third coast, also played a fateful role in the early story.

The cities of this iron triangle form a virtual monument to the early history of aviation. Dayton, Ohio, was the home of the Wright brothers and the site of the Wright Company, formed in 1909 to sell the world's first military airplane to the United States government. Wright-Patterson Field in Dayton

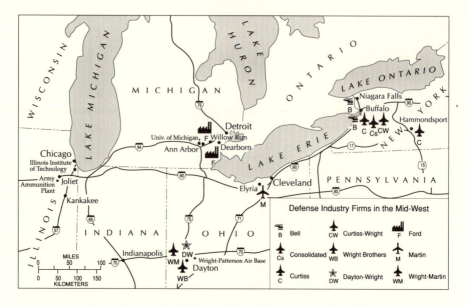

FIGURE 4.1. The Midwest: pioneer aircraft contractors.

became the Air Force's permanent headquarters for aircraft procurement. Buffalo, New York, was considered the first aircraft center in the nation. After early success with dirigibles, Glenn Curtiss started his Aerial Experiment Association in nearby Hammondsport, New York, in 1907. Assured of orders from Great Britain, Russia, and Italy, he expanded, renamed his operation the Curtiss Aeroplane Company, and moved to Buffalo. In 1918, the Glenn Martin Company set up shop in Cleveland, and the Martin Aeroplane Factory was opened in nearby Elyria, Ohio. The University of Michigan, in the early 1920s, offered one of only five aeronautical engineering programs in the nation. When the Detroit Aircraft Corporation was formed in 1929, its founders hoped that it would become the General Motors of the air. Chicago developed powerful electronics and optics industries that sold to the military early on. Up through World War II, and to a lesser extent during the Korean and Vietnam periods, the industrial heartland hummed with factories devoted to the production of tanks, airplanes, ordnance, and other war matériel.

The story of why the industrial heartland failed to keep this early lead in defense-based high technology is a stunning rebuttal to the "seedbeds of innovation" hypothesis, which predicts that centers of industrial leadership will continue to regenerate. Dayton, Detroit, Buffalo, and Chicago based their preeminence on heroic pioneering efforts by engineers-turned-airplane-entrepreneurs. Bicycle manufacture gave the Wrights in Dayton, and Curtiss in Hammondsport and Buffalo, the necessary expertise. Auto manufacture did the same for Henry Ford and for Packard's Henry Joy. Both the Wrights and Curtiss were midwestern founding fathers whose aircraft companies stayed in the Midwest.[1] Although each journeyed far afield to compete in air events, and both established Sunbelt training arenas, their pilot production plants were built within a few miles of home.[2] Henry Ford never left Detroit with his Tri-Motor, nor did he abandon his home base when the Ford Motor Company built Liberator bombers during World War II. The Packard company did have a branch plant in New York, but Detroit continued to be its aircraft home.

So the early lead in defense production was only logical, for these industrial cities were the nation's most innovative centers in metals, heavy machinery, autos, appliances, and consumer electronics. Why, with the largest concentration of the nation's corporate headquarters, private R&D labs, top engineering schools, and skilled managerial and blue-collar work force, should the iron triangle lose out so badly in the competition for new defense industries? For lose out it did. Decade by decade, especially after 1950, midwestern industrial cities lost ground to the emerging "gunbelt." Some firms picked up and moved, as did Glenn Martin to Baltimore. Others opened military-oriented branch plants elsewhere, as did Motorola in Scottsdale. Some lost business to competitors in the gunbelt and simply folded, or set their sights on commercial markets. Graduating engineers from the region's major research universities increasingly accepted outmigration as a way of life; by the 1980s, more than 50 percent of graduating classes left the region. New defense-oriented spin-offs, rather than clustering around the parent firm, migrated as well: of more than fifty that Klein's ITTRI generated, fewer than five remained in Chicago.

Companies born to and fostered in commercial cities were unable to survive the onset of the cold war and its unique demands. What happened to the early generation of inventor-entrepreneurs? Were the third coast and its bordering states ultimately inhospitable to military business? History makes clear the basic reason. Locked into consumer-oriented mass production and into the business culture it engendered, they found it impossible to adjust to the very different style of that peculiar, defense-dependent industry called aerospace.

To explain how this happened, we first tell the stories of four great urban production complexes of the iron triangle, and then interview the survivors in the biggest of them all, Chicago.

Dayton: Pioneers on the Prairie

Success four flights thursday morning all against twenty one mile wind started from Level with engine power alone average speed through air thirty one miles longest 57 seconds inform Press home Christmas Oreville Wright.[3]

Almost every American child would immediately see that the telegraph operator misspelled Orville Wright's name. Many could name the date and the place: Kitty Hawk, North Carolina, December 17, 1903. Fewer, perhaps, could identify "home." Home was Dayton, Ohio, where the Wright brothers had been building bicycles since 1892. Dayton, founded on the Great Miami

River in the middle of the southern Ohio prairie in the late eighteenth century, had a wide range of bicycle-manufacturing and other engineering shops by the 1890s. The safety bicycle, invented in England in 1884, was soon being mass-produced in the United States, bringing an industrial boom during the depression years of 1891 to 1898. A host of small but enterprising shops and subcontractors sprang up to meet the demand, many of them in the Midwest. In Dayton, Orville and Wilbur Wright started to repair and sell bicycles in 1892, and to make them about 1895. When, in 1900, the Wrights began their aeronautical experiments, their basic mechanical training, their workshop facilities, and their accumulated capital proved invaluable. Unsurprisingly, the resulting machine—although made of wood—looked remarkably like a flying bicycle.[4]

But there was a more fundamental tie: bicycles and airplanes shared a problem of balance, as the German aeronautical pioneer Otto Lilienthal noted in the late nineteenth century. Because of their background, the Wrights were able to see the airplane as an essentially unstable machine that had to be managed. Without benefit of much formal education, but with the necessary basic mathematics, they solved the problem of aircraft roll with a characteristic blend of theory, ground research, inspiration, and flying experience. They also found it easy to adapt the new gasoline engine to powered flight.[5]

But there was no certainty that the Wrights would make the world's first powered, sustained, and controlled airplane flight. Hundreds of people were in the race, and any of them might have won. Later, Wilbur said to his friend and collaborator Octave Chanute,

> If the wheels of time could be turned back six years, it is not at all probable that we would do again what we have done. The thing that impresses me as remarkable was the shortness of the time within which our work was done. It was due to peculiar combinations of circumstances which might never occur again.[6]

In fact, between 1898 and 1903, there were three major centers of early aviation experimentation, each with its lead inventors: Samuel Pierpont Langley worked in Washington, D.C.; Octave Chanute and Albert F. Zahm in Chicago; and Samuel Cabot and James Means in Boston. All appeared likelier candidates for success than the Wrights. Langley, secretary of the Smithsonian, produced plans for a full-scale flying machine in October 1897, and he used influential contacts—including Alexander Graham Bell—to obtain $73,000 in military funding. But because of basic structural and aerodynamic flaws stemming from an excessively theoretical approach, his "aerodrome" never flew in his lifetime, and made him a subject of national ridicule. (A Congressman derisively remarked: "You tell Langley for me . . . that the only thing he ever made fly was government money.") Twelve days after Langley's second flight trial ended ignominiously in the icy waters of the Potomac, the Wright brothers succeeded. The accumulated mechanical expertise of the Midwest bested the theoretical approach of the national capital.[7]

It continued to do so. In 1904, the Wrights built a new machine and arranged for a practice field on the farm of Terence Huffman, a Dayton bank president, eight miles from Dayton. In 1905, they solved their last control problem. Aware that they now had a marketable machine, they also knew exactly where the main market lay. Orville wrote in 1907 to the U.S. Department of War, "We believe that the principal use of a flyer at present is for military purposes; that the demand in commerce will not be great for some time." The war office, after going through the farce of competitive bids, finally contracted for a plane on February 8, 1908.[8]

Thus backed, in 1909 the brothers introduced outside capital to establish a new Wright Company; a new factory was completed by the end of 1910, and production immediately doubled. Two months later, work began on a new Dayton factory. Three years after Wilbur's death—in 1912, from typhoid—Orville sold the company to a group of eastern capitalists for a rumored $1.5 million. But just two years later, the Wright name again reappeared above a Dayton factory, thanks to another founding father.[9]

Edward Deeds and Dayton's Second Chance

Edward Deeds, a prominent Dayton businessman, was president first of the National Cash Register Company (NCR). In 1912, he had been sentenced to jail for "bribery and criminal methods in driving competitors out of the cash register business," but won his appeal. With Charles F. Kettering, he established Delco (Dayton Engineering Laboratories) in 1914. The next year these two, together with Harold E. Talbott, Sr., and Talbott's son and namesake formed Dayton Metal Products, a company that first made refrigeration equipment, and then produced fuses and war matériel. In April 1917, five days after the United States entered World War I, the same group set up the Dayton-Wright Airplane Company. The new company recruited some department heads of the old Wright company; Orville Wright, friendly with the directors, readily gave his name. The old Wright plant had already been sold, so the new company built a factory just outside Dayton, on land belonging to Deeds.[10]

Significantly, none of the founders had experience in airplane manufacture. Through Delco, their ties were with the automobile complex of Detroit, 200 miles to the north. The auto makers were looking to enter the aircraft industry, especially as war loomed. The Secretary of War appointed Deeds to the hastily assembled Aircraft Production Board chaired by Howard Coffin, president of Hudson Motor Car Company; all the civilian members of the committee had close ties with automobiles. In August 1917, Deeds was commissioned a colonel and put in charge of procurement. After divesting Dayton-Wright holdings, he was able to divert the lion's share of the Aircraft Production Board's funds to his Dayton friends.[11]

The result was a disaster. American mass-produced engines could not compete with the handcrafted European ones. To solve the problem, in July

1917 Deeds got top automobile engineers to design an engine in a hurry; the resultant Liberty engine eventually was produced at the rate of 150 a day and contributed significantly to the war effort. But no useful airframes were developed, and not one American attack plane or heavy bomber reached the field of battle. A Senate subcommittee on military affairs reported in August 1918 that a large part of the $840 million congressional appropriation had been simply wasted. The report was sharply critical of the decision to employ midwestern automobile manufacturers, unfamiliar with aeronautical problems, to mass-produce European designs. A presidential investigation, launched at the urging of the subcommittee, recommended that Deeds be court-martialed for awarding contracts to firms in which his friends had an interest and acting as confidential adviser to former business associates while in uniform.[12]

Deeds managed to wriggle off the hook, but the incident had profound consequences for the Midwest. For it built up a huge reservoir of resentment toward the auto makers on the part of the struggling airplane industry. Even worse, it shaped the basic attitudes of the young wartime officers who later rose to commanding positions in the Air Force—among whom the most significant was "Hap" Arnold, who never ceased to make clear his opinion that the auto makers were incompetent.[13] This contempt of young airmen toward Detroit proved to be the first nail in the coffin of the Midwest's hopes to be the nation's aircraft capital.

But the Midwest might still have succeeded as a center where the Air Corps would design and build its own planes. Had the arsenal system of "in-house" development won out over the practice of outsourcing to private companies, Dayton in particular would likely have become an aerospace capital. Shortly after Deeds's appointment to the Aircraft Production Board, the Army Signal Board, at Deeds's urging, selected Huffman Prairie, close to the Wright test field, as site for its Aviation School. As acting chief of the newly created Equipment Division of the Signal Corps, Deeds also was instrumental in the establishment of an adjacent site, which he owned, as the Signal Corps's central supply depot. Later, despite the scandal, the supply depot remained.

When, after war's end, the Air Corps proposed to relocate the Signal Corps's Engineering Division to Langley Field in Virginia, John H. Patterson, Deeds's successor at NCR, led a massive propaganda and subscription campaign to buy a site next to Wright Field. Four hundred thousand dollars was raised, and ground-breaking began in 1926. The Air Corps Act of 1926 authorized the Air Corps Matériel Division to establish permanent facilities for engineering (R&D), procurement, supply, and maintenance at Wright Field, the nucleus of the later Wright-Patterson Air Base. It grew from 20 buildings in 1927 to 40 in 1941 and to 300 in 1944, and from 2,434 employees in 1938 to 49,008 in 1945.[14]

The significance of Wright-Patterson was, of course, much greater than its direct role in the Dayton economy—although, with a payroll of between 23,000 and 31,000 since the mid–1950s, that was significant enough. Since 1933, it has been the source of procurement of Air Corps, later Air Force, equipment. Boeing, Douglas, and others came to Wright-Patterson in the 1930s to demonstrate their new designs. When a decision was made in 1950 to separate the new Air Research and Development Command from the existing Army Matériel Command, the new command's Air Development Center remained in Dayton, even when, in 1951, its headquarters was removed to Baltimore. So during the aerospace revolution, critical decisions about the creation of new weapons systems were made in Dayton[15]—but, significantly, this did not lead to local production.

At the outset, the Dayton facility was part of a grand scheme to replicate the arsenal system for the Air Corps. It would be, in the eyes of its military architects, a government production center, with aircraft designed by government-employed brain-trusters and produced by private manufacturers. This vision proved unworkable, primarily because the anti-arsenal inclination of the industry and the Air Force was already evolving, and the top engineers and designers preferred to work for the private sector. Despite the presence of the buyer, no new aircraft companies clustered around the procurement depot. Nor did Boeing, Douglas, or any other company that came to Dayton to demonstrate its designs set up production facilities in the area. And among the young Air Corps officers of the Army Industrial College, the notion of using aircraft companies for development as well as mass production took root—not least in the mind of Arnold, where it would have momentous consequences some fifteen years later.[16]

At this juncture, another key decision was made, altering Dayton's fortunes and demonstrating the powerful role of founding fathers and financiers in the rise and fall of military–industrial cities. In July 1925, Deeds abruptly withdrew his support from Dayton. He joined forces with George Mead and an Ohio businessman, Frederick Rentschler, to establish a business to build a new air-cooled aero engine that Mead, the engineering chief at Wright Aeronautical, had designed. Clarence Vought wanted to incorporate the engine in his plane, and the developers had visions of selling the plane to the Navy. Deeds, already chairman of the Niles Bement Pound tool company of East Hartford, Connecticut, convinced a Niles subsidiary, Pratt & Whitney, to supply half the funds needed for the project. Partly for this reason, partly because the Pratt & Whitney plant had plenty of spare space, perhaps partly because of a pool of skilled labor there, they located the operation at Hartford. The timing was strategic. Two months later, the Morrow Board report recommended a big increase in naval air procurement, and orders began to flow. Thus this is a case of a founding father who deserted his native city. Had Deeds not relocated, Dayton and not Hartford would have become the leading center of air-engine production in the United States.[17]

Curtiss, Martin, Fleet, and Bell: The Buffalo–Cleveland Connection

The Wrights' biggest competitor was yet another bicycle manufacturer. His location was less propitious. It was the tiny town of Hammondsport at the southern tip of Keuka Lake, one of the Finger Lakes in western New York

State, some seventy miles southeast of Buffalo. Strictly speaking, it was out-side the Midwest, but culturally it was very much part of the Great Lakes region. Glenn Curtiss, son of a Methodist clergyman, had like the Wrights only a rudimentary education. Notwithstanding, he pioneered the motorbike in 1901, a year after he took over a bicycle shop. In 1904, he began to provide engines for Thomas Scott Baldwin, the California aircraft pioneer, who re-located to Hammondsport after the 1906 San Francisco earthquake.[18]

Once involved in aviation, Curtiss found himself inevitably drawn into military work. The Aerial Experiment Association was founded in the fall of 1907, at the instigation of Alexander Graham Bell, to develop research for a military plane on a War Department contract. The work led to the formation of the American Aerodrome Association, with headquarters at Hammonds-port, in 1909. During the ensuing decade, Curtiss's company survived a num-ber of upheavals—not least, an epic patent battle with the Wright firm—to emerge at the end of World War I as the largest airplane company in the United States, so swamped with orders that it was reorganized as the Curtiss Aeroplane and Motor Corporation and moved to Buffalo.[19]

But this founding father was a less than able manager of his explosively growing firm. In order to build a third facility at Garden City, Long Island, to serve the war effort, Curtiss had to obtain financing from Willys Car Company. In turn, Willys imposed new management upon the firm, leaving Curtiss as president of the Engineering Division at Garden City and chairman of the board of the parent company. As the war drew to a close, Curtiss, claiming that he much preferred mechanical tinkering to administrative work, left the company and settled in Florida.[20]

Yet the Curtiss Corporation remained anchored in Buffalo. By the middle of the century's second decade, the company was the largest in American aviation, a distinction it held for thirty years. By the mid-1920s, its more than 2,000 employees produced over 150 planes a year. Curtiss aimed primarily at the military market. In the early 1930s, it was preeminent in fighter-plane design for both services. The Navy continued to be its major customer, award-ing many contracts for seaplanes and fighters. But the Army, too, was a steady buyer; Curtiss built fifty bombers for them in 1922 and 1923, at a cost of $24,000 each. In 1927, Buffalo built an airport to serve its fledgling aircraft industry, years before New York City and other large metropolises had air-fields of their own. The company merged with Wright Aeronautical in 1929, becoming Curtiss-Wright and doubling its clout.[21]

Yet—according to biographers Murray Rubenstein and Richard Gold-man—despite its early lead, Curtiss-Wright showed a remarkable and constant proclivity for disastrously poor designs. The company was not always to blame for this—often the military services, hoping to catch up with the Europeans, demanded that certain features be grafted to home-grown designs that could not support them. For example, in 1917 Curtiss attempted to introduce a European-designed fighter plane using the American-built Liberty engine to fill an Army order for 3,000. The war ended without a single fighter of American design seeing action.[22]

Among Curtiss's strategic mistakes was its partnership with the Navy in its long-standing advocacy of lighter-than-air dirigibles—"floating airships"—from which fighter planes would be launched, and the company's insistence on the superiority of the biplane. According to Rubenstein and Goldman, both a fighter-bomber and a dive bomber that Curtiss-Wright tried to sell to the Navy were plagued by technical problems. The latter was withdrawn from service in 1937, making it the last operational fighter Curtiss-Wright was ever to sell to the Navy. Over and over, Curtiss-Wright produced models that were slow, unwieldy, or ahead of their time. At first, the company, did well with its biplanes, ably switching, stretching, and shifting their designs. Curtiss-Wright stood by its visionary biplane design until 1934, when the biplane was outclassed by Boeing's much faster Army-backed monoplane. Curtiss-Wright then turned to monoplanes, belatedly, and targeted the Army Air Corps.[23]

World War II marked both the peak and the beginning of the end for Curtiss-Wright. The company went into the war as the preferred supplier of fighters for the Army Air Corps. Curtiss-Wright benefited from timing: the chief engineer of its Buffalo plant had developed a monoplane fighter, the famous Hawk, which ultimately became the P-40. Although—as Rubenstein and Goldman note—Curtiss-Wright's offering to the Army in 1939 was unquestionably inferior to the turbo-supercharged designs of Bell, Lockheed, and Seversky, the P-40 could be produced in quantity a full year ahead of any other aircraft.[24] Under pressure to supply planes immediately, the Army chose the Curtiss-Wright model.

Meanwhile, the engineering expertise of the heartland had attracted pioneer manufacturers from elsewhere—including California. Glenn Martin, who pioneered airplane production at Santa Ana, California, in 1905, merged in 1916 with the Wright enterprise to become the Wright-Martin Aircraft Corporation, based in Dayton, with a capitalization of $10 million. But in 1918, Martin left to start his own company in Cleveland. There he hired Larry Bell as manager and Donald Douglas as chief engineer; one year later, Bell hired J. H. Kindelberger.[25] Significantly, of these three Californians only the first would stay in the Midwest; the other two would become founding fathers of the Los Angeles industry. Martin himself moved to Baltimore in search of tidewater for seaplane construction and contracts with the Washington naval establishment. But, in compensation, Reuben Fleet's Consolidated Aircraft Company, founded in 1923 in Rhode Island, relocated in the following year to Buffalo, where Curtiss had already moved.

Bell was the stayer. He started his aviation career in California, joining Martin there in 1912, and then moving to Ohio to become manager of Martin's Cleveland operation. In 1928, a decade after directing production of the famous Martin bomber, he joined Fleet's Consolidated operation in Buffalo. When Fleet moved to San Diego in 1935, Bell stayed in Buffalo to start his own company, recruiting two top Consolidated men and soon establishing military contracts.[26] Times were hard at first for Bell: government orders were scarce, and the new firm survived by making wings on subcontract for Consolidated. The breakthrough came with the Airacuda fighter, commissioned

TABLE 4.1.   Company Fighter Plane Sales to Army Air Corps, 1940–1944

Year	Lockheed P-38	Bell P-39	Curtiss P-40	Republic P-47	North American P-51
1940	0	13	778	0	0
1941	205	926	226	1	136
1942	1,264	1,672	4,453	530	632
1943	2,213	4,965	4,529	4,135	1,711
1944	4,186	1,729	2,078	6,986	6,904
Total	7,868	9,305	12,064	11,652	9,383

Source: Rubenstein and Goldman, 1974: Appendix 2.

by the Air Corps in May 1936. That was just the start of the World War II buildup, which proved the basis of the company's fortunes. In its first five years, sales volume was just over $7 million; by V-E Day, it had reached $1 billion.[27]

World War II, then, sparked an employment boom in Buffalo. Both foreign and Army orders resulted in a 400 percent expansion of Curtiss-Wright's production facilities, swelling the company's employment roster to 45,000. Bell Aircraft also garnered military contracts and a new government-built plant at Niagara Falls. From 56 people on the books in 1936, Bell employment rose to 36,000 in the Buffalo area by 1943, with another 30,000 in Georgia a year later, and 2,700 in Vermont.[28] In addition, a Chevrolet plant was converted to manufacturing Pratt & Whitney engines, employing 11,500 at its peak. These three companies, accounting for most of the $3.9 billion in Buffalo aircraft-supply contracts, employed 87,000 workers in 1943. Buffalo did more war business with the federal government than all but four cities in the country, far more than its size would predict. With seven-tenths of 1 percent of the national population and labor force, it produced 2.5 percent of all war goods, which amounted to over $5,300 for every man, woman, and child. As one historian put it, "[Wartime contracts] resulted in the building of what amounted to a new airplane industry in the area."[29]

Curtiss-Wright was the largest defense contractor in the world during World War II. Wright engines powered B-17s, B-25s, B-29s, and tanks, and Curtiss propellers were incorporated in many competitors' aircraft. But as the war progressed, the company's flagship, the P-40 pursuit fighter, fell to competition from Lockheed, Republic, Bell, and North American (Table 4.1). The P-40 was an antiquated but tried-and-true design, despite late efforts to update it. In 1944, the 13,738th and last P-40 rolled off the assembly line.[30] Swamped by huge orders, preoccupied with mass production reminiscent of Ford, and comfortable in its position as number 1, the company simply did not achieve the technical gains that its coastal competitors managed. Meanwhile, jet engines under development elsewhere eroded the lead of the Wright engine operations, which had been committed to piston engines.

Both Curtiss-Wright and Bell had a hard time converting to peacetime production. Curtiss-Wright planned a postwar airliner version of its transport plane, but lost out to Douglas and Lockheed. An experimental torpedo bomber that Curtiss-Wright designed for the Navy lost out to Martin and Douglas. A final attempt at a Navy fighter ended in a crash in 1945. A Curtiss-Wright design for the Air Force's all-weather jet fighter turned out to be underpowered, allowing Northrop to win that contest in 1948 and prompting Curtiss-Wright to withdraw from military airplane competition.[31] Divisions were closed down, one by one. From 45,000 workers in 1942, Curtiss-Wright's Buffalo employment felt to 5,500 by September 1945. In early 1946, the company announced it was closing down almost all its Buffalo operations and consolidating them at its Columbus, Ohio, plant.[32] Bell, too, folded its fighter and bomber operations, barely hanging on in helicopters. With these cutbacks went an entire segment of the Buffalo economy.

The demise of Curtiss-Wright was more than simply a matter of management failure. The isolation of the company, far from more formidable competitors, and the local cultural orientation toward mass-production priorities also contributed. Buffalo was a workhorse city during the war, and design work took second place to output. Buffalo simply did not draw around it the unique infrastructure needed to support the adolescent aircraft industry; its fortunes relied almost entirely on its two stand-alone aircraft firms. When Curtiss-Wright failed the technological tests, alienating its Navy and Army patrons, the future of Buffalo as an aerospace center faded.[33]

Bell faced a similar challenge, but its location proved no handicap. As at Curtiss-Wright, business dropped catastrophically at war's end: from $317 million in 1944 to $11 million in 1946, and by 1947 only 1,800 employees remained at Niagara Falls Airport. Bell, who had a rare quality "which inspires dreamers to dream and hard-headed mechanics to convert those dreams into hardware," then made a brilliant decision: he backed production of a helicopter with electric controls, the design of which he had commissioned in 1941 from a young Pennsylvania inventor, Arthur M. Young. At a cost of almost $12 million in advance investment, the Bell helicopter was the first ever to be licensed, on March 8, 1946. Four years later, helicopters proved vital in Korea, evacuating almost 20,000 wounded soldiers. Almost simultaneously, Bell got into guided missiles and supersonic flight. On October 14, 1947, the Bell-X1 was the first airplane to break the sound barrier, making it the first of three Bell planes to beat all records. Bell stayed in the vanguard of technological progress, including automatic piloting in 1944 to 1945, automatic landing in 1955, and the first jet VTOL (vertical take-off and landing) in 1956.[34] But Bell alone could not ensure Buffalo's status as an aerospace city.

Buffalo was different from third-coast cities like Detroit, Dayton, and Chicago, in that its leading industries were predominantly port-related and increasingly run by large national firms not based locally. Bell apart, Buffalo was not a fertile seedbed. It had few of the corporate R&D labs that Chicago and Detroit could claim, and it had no one core propulsive industry that shaped its future. Although it had some motor-manufacturing history and wood- and metal-working skills, its leading industries—steel, grain, lumber, rubber—were primarily resource-based commodity processing.[35] Expertise in those fields offered little in the way of high-tech experience, at least of the product-design type so central to the nascent aerospace industry. In Buffalo, aerospace failure was in large part the product of an underdeveloped milieu.

Detroit: The Auto Makers Enter Aerospace

An intriguing question—and a critical one, for the Midwest story—is why the automotive industry did not successfully make the transition into aircraft production. Many aspects of automotive engineering, particularly the power plant, lend themselves to aircraft design and production. After all, it was Detroit's excellence in marine-engine making that propelled the city to prominence in early auto design. Eastern engine makers like General Electric and Pratt & Whitney managed to catapult themselves into the postwar military–industrial complex. Why did Detroit find it so difficult?

It was not for lack of trying. Several of the leading auto companies entered the industry during its early stages, well before the futures of West Coast firms like North American or Douglas were ensured. In wartime, up through the Korean conflict, auto firms in the Midwest produced both whole airplanes and engines in enormous quantities. Why this effort fizzled is perhaps best illustrated by the saga of Henry Ford's pioneer Tri-Motor in the 1920s and his company's World War II experience making Liberator bombers at Willow Run.

The Ford family had its share of air aficionados. Edsel Ford persuaded his father to help him build a small craft, powered by a Model T engine, in 1910; it rose six feet above the ground at the Detroit Country Club. As early as World War I, Henry Ford saw the possibilities for successfully moving his firm into aircraft. In 1917, he proposed to the government that the Ford Motor Company build 150,000 airplanes for the American and British services. He claimed that "aircraft could be manufactured as easily as motor cars," and wryly estimated that his product would cost 25 cents a pound.[36] Quantity and low cost, as ever, dominated Ford's vision: this would be the Model T of the air.

The proposal was never taken seriously. But Ford's expertise was soon urgently needed for the design and development of Packard's Liberty motor, also a Detroit product.[37] The Liberty was the only American product then considered superior to French and British aircraft designs. European allies ordered thousands, boosting employment at several Detroit firms. Ford engineers solved critical problems in cylinder and bearings design, winning a contract for 5,000 engines. Before the war ended, Ford employed 11,000 workers on the Liberty.

Preoccupied with lower production costs, Ford was proud that his partial assembly line achieved extraordinary production volumes. But the skills and equipment needed to build autos were not necessarily those needed for aero-engine manufacturing. Out of some 14,000 machine tools used on the Model

T, only 987 could be used on the Liberty. Fifty percent of Ford's plant and machinery had to be rearranged to produce the aircraft engine.[38]

Buoyed by his wartime success, in the 1920s Ford entered the aircraft industry competition in earnest. A local entrepreneur and engineering graduate of the University of Minnesota, William Stout, had designed a cargo aircraft that the government had rejected. In 1922, working in Detroit, he secured backing from local businessmen, including Ford, by appealing to local pride: Detroit led the nation in autos, why not in airplanes? To thank his backers, Stout coined a dreadful pun: his first craft became the "Maiden Detroit"; the second, built with heavy Ford support, the "Maiden Dearborn." In 1925, an impressed Ford bought out Stout and his firm.

Stout had tried to sell his revolutionary design—an all-metal, single-engined, mass-produced monoplane—to the Navy. But Ford was captivated with its commercial possibilities. Envisioning mass production for a mass market, he argued that once this was achieved, military production would be easy.[39]

> We are experimenting to see whether it is possible to produce an airplane which will require no more skill in its management than does a motor car, which can be manufactured and sold so cheaply as to be within the means of a large number of people, and which will be as safe from accident and as fool-proof as the motor car. . . . The step from the motor car to the airplane is not nearly as great as the step we have already taken from the horse carriage to the motor car.[40]

Ford underestimated both the performance demands of airplanes and the role the military would play in their development. But by 1924, the Maiden Detroit, then the best cargo plane in existence, won a coveted airmail contract. The government-subsidized airmail service in Washington was enthusiastic about Ford's plans for the famous Tri-Motor—a faster, larger-capacity craft that could run on two engines, or even one, safely and reliably. The Tri-Motor pioneered the transcontinental route over the Rockies; Ford's team developed radio guidance, setting up the first radio beacons.[41] The Tri-Motor's durability was beyond doubt; several are still flying in 1991.

Ford dreamed of serving a passenger-oriented industry. The individual consumer, after all, was his strong suit. But the market was not there. Like other fledgling companies, Ford inevitably turned to the military. The Tri-Motor was sold in modest quantities to the Army and the Navy—thirty-six in 1928; eighty-six in 1929. By the late 1920s, Ford was the dominant firm, selling more than 50 percent of all multiengine transports in the United States, to both airlines and the military. In 1929, with a goal of "a plane a day," the company expanded capacity by 165 percent in that single year.[42]

What happened to this fabulously successful aircraft firm? First, a dramatic slump in demand hit the industry. Poised on the brink of a depression he did not foresee, Ford by the end of the decade could fulfill in six months of normal manufacture the entire industry's need for the next four years. With airlines and airplane manufacturers being swallowed up by huge holding companies (Stout's own airline was taken over by the biggest such conglomerate, United Aircraft), Ford's commercial market dried up.[43]

There were supply-side problems, too. Boeing and Douglas planned faster two-engine, ten- to fourteen-seat, low-wing passenger transports. Ford tried outflanking its competitors by building a thirty-four-passenger liner; it was too heavy. A venture into small planes was abandoned when Henry Ford's personal pilot was killed in a crash. In the early 1930s, Ford began to decisively favor his auto over his aircraft business; in 1933, after selling 199 Tri-Motors, he shut down the program.[44]

He had good reasons. First, he was losing money: in 1932, the aircraft group's operating deficit was $5.6 million. And Ford, the consummate commercial capitalist, had always insisted that the airplane must be financially as well as mechanically successful. Second, with demand down and fierce competition from General Motors, he had enough problems in his auto business. Third, he was almost seventy years old, and his tyrannical style was beginning to hamper successful management of the firm. He claimed that his son, Edsel, was in charge of the airplane business:

> This work in the air, however, is not primarily my work. It was my son, Edsel, president of Ford Motor Company, who first became interested in aviation and it took a long time to convince me that it had a commercial feature. The direction of the work depends on my son. My generation brought out the automobile. It remains for the next generation to bring out the airplane.[45]

But he constantly meddled, never allowing Edsel to be the entrepreneur for aircraft that he himself had been for cars.

Perhaps the heart of the matter was Ford's personal passion: "He loved cars, not airplanes," reported a Ford historian.[46] He thought cars, and he was goaded by the competition of his Detroit neighbors, which thought the same way.[47] Other aircraft producers were far away, in places that had no alternative like the auto to vie for their attention. And underlying this was Ford's—indeed, Detroit's—fixation, a culture based on a ground-based transportation system for the masses. Ever since Ford triumphed with the Model T, he and his competitors had a vision of a world of assembly-line-produced, commercially oriented goods. He had difficulty applying this outlook to the aircraft industry, with its increasingly military clientele, high-tech product, and performance requirements that differed radically from auto making.

Nothing illustrates this clash in cultures better than Ford's response to the challenge of making the Liberator bomber in World War II. After Pearl Harbor, Ford offered his facilities, know-how, and manpower to the government.[48] He boasted that his company could swing quickly into production of 1,000 airplanes of standard design a day. He refused to produce only parts, insisting on making whole airplanes. At government-built plants, Ford's aircraft and aircraft engines were constructed using other firms' designs. In the

United States, during World War II, Ford manufactured 8,685 bombers, 58,000 aircraft engines, and hundreds of thousands of jeeps, military trucks, and armored cars.[49] True to the company's style, mass production was the guiding principle.

The showpiece was Ford's Willow Run plant, built to produce a Liberator bomber an hour. Top Ford management went to the San Diego plant of Consolidated, the originator of the design, and returned with contemptuous comments on Consolidated's primitive open-air production line, which aimed to make a bomber a day.[50] Although airplanes were infinitely more complex, the Detroit managers knew that Ford expertise could do better. Opened in early 1942, Willow Run was the largest single industrial structure in the world under one roof, the last designed by Alfred Kahn. Charles Lindbergh called it "a sort of Grand Canyon of a mechanized world." The *Christian Science Monitor* said, "It is, horizontally, what the Empire State Building is, vertically, to American industry. . . . It is a promise of American greatness."[51] The plant incorporated many of the ingenious ideas of Ford's assembly line. Ford's innovative temperature- and humidity-controlled interior prompted Consolidated to move its own assembly indoors in 1941. In engines, too, Ford proposed better materials, superior methods for machining, and higher precision inspection techniques, all of which were enthusiastically accepted by Pratt & Whitney.[52]

At first, Ford's bulk-production strategy ran into huge problems. Terrible tie-ups kept total bomber production down to only fifty-six by the end of 1942, less than three days' production at the vaunted plane-an-hour rate. Popular magazines asked, "Will it Run?"[53] A major obstacle, which captures the incompatibility between auto and aircraft philosophies, was that Ford depended on rigid, mechanically guided production lines, amenable to relatively unskilled labor. Ford wanted fixed specifications and unalterable hard-metal dies; Consolidated preferred rubber or soft-metal ones. Consolidated, like other West Coast aircraft companies, depended on a highly skilled work force to alter parts and make essential modifications. As Dutch Kindelberger, president of North American Aviation and consistent critic of the car companies, put it: "You cannot expect blacksmiths to learn how to make watches overnight."[54]

Ford's insistence on an elaborately tooled mass-production facility rankled Consolidated, where the Liberator was considered a makeshift craft. Consolidated was sure that the new breakthroughs would mean that this investment would be useless. In this struggle, Consolidated represented the culture of a company bred on continual, military-funded innovation, while Ford could not wean itself from the principles that had worked so well for it in the consumer market. This was true across the industrial heartland, as commercially oriented firms retooled for weaponry designed by coastal firms: GM had precisely the same battle with Grumman on the East Coast.[55]

Detroit's strategy finally worked: eventually, Liberators emerged from Willow Run at the rate of 428 per month. By 1944, Ford led all American engine manufacturers in horsepower shipments.[56] With $5.3 billion in military sales, Ford was America's third largest defense contractor during the war, after General Motors at $13.8 billion and Curtiss-Wright at $7.09 billion. Chrysler ranked eighth at $3.4 billion.[57] By ensuring output in the massive quantity required, Detroit almost certainly played a huge part in winning the war.

But at war's end, this achievement guaranteed no future for Detroit in the cold war–oriented aerospace industry of the future. Partly, this was because the war gave Ford and the other Detroit firms no major role in the design-and-experimentation phase of aircraft development. They had made huge process innovations, but product improvement was what competition in the aircraft industry was all about.[58]

But, fundamentally, Detroit's disengagement from aircraft was a result of its eagerness to rejoin the auto-production contest. As early as 1943, Alfred Sloan, president of General Motors, had delivered a speech called "The Challenge" to the National Association of Manufacturers, in which he prophesied an enormous pent-up demand for consumer goods after the war. Sloan and his competitors, like Ford and Chrysler, began to plan for conversion long before war's end. When it came, they were preoccupied with the enormous investments needed to retool; General Motors alone planned for a $500 million reorganization program.[59]

They were far too busy to think about flying. A major exception was Chrysler, which made persistent efforts to enter aerospace at the critical juncture: the mid-1950s. Then, as seen in Chapter 3, President Eisenhower accepted the Pentagon's recommendation that construction of the ICBM be given top priority, and the race between the Army and the Air Force was on. The Army had the advantage of a head start over the Air Force, because it alone had an established team entirely dedicated to missile design and production. The group, under Wernher von Braun, had been located since 1949 in the Army's Redstone Arsenal in Huntsville, Alabama. Successively titled the Ordnance Guided Missile Center, the Guided Missile Development Division of the Ordnance Missile Laboratories, and the Development Operations Division of the Army Ballistic Missiles Agency, the team achieved a series of missile "firsts," culminating in the launch of the Redstone—the "offspring" of von Braun's German V-2 rocket, a 500-mile-range surface-to-surface missile—at Cape Canaveral in 1953. While the Army was thus developing the Air Force's missile, the Air Force was ironically stuck with development of its Navajo cruise missile, which was really an Army weapon.[60]

The truly momentous resolution, to be told in Chapter 5, went in favor of an Air Force ICBM, the Atlas. Its design went to a new systems-engineering firm, Ramo Wooldridge, working directly with a new Air Force Western Development Division in Los Angeles. Its construction logically went to airframe and avionics firms, many of them in southern California. But as a consolation prize to the Army, development of a cruise missile, the Jupiter, went to von Braun's group in Huntsville. They promptly drew up the design in-house, and invited only the three big auto makers to bid. The production contract was awarded to Chrysler, as had been that for the earlier Redstone.

But Huntsville, too, had to depend on developments by airplane companies such as Convair for steering and North American for engines. These companies were now worried about potential competition from Huntsville, about the whole arsenal concept, about the challenge of the auto manufacturers, and, in particular, about the evident ability of Chrysler to invade their turf. Some Air Force officers shared their concern. They thought that the arsenal system meant lack of imagination, long delays, and inefficiencies. Some airframe manufacturers thought that the arsenal system was "socialistic."[61] They made a powerful coalition.

Chrysler by 1959 was in an advantageous position, with experience in missile production, a good reliability record, and a good working relationship with the Redstone Arsenal. But lacking the critical avionics capacity, it failed to secure the Polaris and Minuteman contracts and succeeded only with the Saturn I booster in 1961. Ford tendered for Saturn I and GM for Minuteman, but both failed. There were specific causes for these failures, but behind them was something more ominous: the fact that the Army by this point had lost control over long-range ballistic missile production. Not until the 1970s did Chrysler bounce back. Summarizing the Army–Air Force rivalry of the 1950s, one commentator concluded: "Each service tends to do business with firms it has grown accustomed to. Without this odd combination of events the automakers might today have a large role in the aerospace industry, for they tried to enter it at the innovation stage."[62]

There was a second exception to Detroit's retreat from the air. Henry Ford II, having decided to reexplore the aircraft business, bought several companies, including a key southern California firm, and merged them to create Ford Aerospace.[63] It was dramatically successful, especially during periods of cold war buildup. In the late 1980s, its over 13,000 employees worked almost entirely on defense and space operations. Ford built Mission Control at the Houston Space Center, and the company makes missile guidance and control units and space satellites, and engages in C^3I.

Yet none of this activity has ever taken place in Detroit. Principal operations are in Newport Beach, California, with others in Colorado, Texas, and Pennsylvania. Even the attempt to headquarter Ford Aerospace in Dearborn failed, because Ford's vice president for aerospace insisted that "we are in the kind of business where we should live over the shop."[64] Day-to-day discussions in this design-oriented business require the kind of proximity that worldwide auto manufacture and marketing do not. In 1988, after several years of tension, Ford Motor Company announced that it was setting up dual headquarters in Newport Beach, California—for "timely attention to operational issues and coordination among divisions"—and Washington, D.C., to enhance "Ford Aerospace's ability to anticipate and meet the nation's defense and space requirements."[65] For all practical purposes other than the multinational's bottom line, Ford Aerospace operates as a stand-alone business unit.

Detroit, then, had at least three chances at becoming an aircraft and aerospace center: first, through the city's early innovative lead in engines and transport planes; second, via its massive production of aircraft in World War II; and third, through its alliance with the Army's Huntsville team in pioneering American missile production. While the idiosyncracies of founding fathers like Henry Ford and entrenched interservice rivalries played important roles, what stands out in this story is the difficulty of a truly distinctive, revolutionary technology taking root in a region where another, entirely different one is still robust and commands resource markets and business culture. Detroit as an auto milieu failed utterly as a center for innovative aircraft activity.

The Strange Case of Chicago

Chicago has almost as great a claim as Dayton to be called the first city of American aviation. It was, for instance, the home base of Octave Chanute, the "grand old man of international aviation." Finishing a lucrative career in railroads, Chanute retired to the south end of Lake Michigan in 1889 to probe air-flight problems. Many of the earliest aerial flights were launched from his field in nearby Indiana, on the shores of the lake. Chanute was a critical figure in organizing and disseminating research results in the nascent aircraft community. In 1893, as part of the great Columbian Exposition, he helped Chicago host the first truly international conference on aerial navigation. At the turn of the century, Chicago was the nation's leading intellectual center for aspiring flyers. From here, Chanute encouraged the young Wright brothers to continue with their experiments. When the Wrights complained around 1905 that the winds at Dayton's Huffman Prairie were seldom strong enough, Chanute advised them to try the Kanakee Marshes, fifty miles from Chicago. Perhaps, if they had gone, the aircraft industry would have grown up in Chicago. But the marshes had not been drained, so the Wrights stayed in Dayton.[66]

Chicago attracted a large group of tinkerers, some of whom started early aircraft plants. Many of them joined the Aero Club of Chicago, formed in 1910. Finance was easily available, especially since Harold McCormick, heir to the reaper fortune and married to John D. Rockefeller's daughter, committed his family's money to getting the Chicago aviation community on a sound footing between 1910 and 1915. McCormick donated airport land, tried to start an airline, and designed an umbrella-shaped airplane that was a disastrous failure, resulting in his withdrawal from the industry and indifference thereafter. Perhaps this misadventure sounded the keynote for Chicago, for no major aircraft firm was to survive there beyond the 1930s.[67]

Among the top tier of American cities, Chicago's slippage as a major center of innovation is most striking. That it has historically served as a seedbed is undisputable. Out of the Greater Chicago area came major new industries like farm and construction machinery, industrial equipment, consumer appliances and electronics, and, most recently, pharmaceuticals. Originally, the area's dynamism came from the nineteenth-century symbiosis of a highly productive, relatively affluent, and labor-scarce agriculture creating unparalleled opportunities by offering both the capital and the markets for the nascent machinery industries. Skilled European labor was drawn in its wake. By the mid-twentieth century, Chicago claimed the nation's second largest concentration of corporate headquarters, with their center of gravity in the durable-goods industries.

Despite the early failure of local aircraft entrepreneurs, the resources that could have made Chicago a seedbed of defense technology remained well into the postwar period. The area still has a formidable share of the nation's corporate research-and-development labs. Its share of the nation's pool of engineers and scientists was, and is, quite high.[68] Yet its prominence as a center of high-tech activity is on the wane. Although the state of Illinois was the nation's number 2 high-tech employer as recently as the late 1970s in terms of total jobs, its position was eroding rapidly. With few exceptions, its high-tech industries—high-tech because they employ a disproportionate share of engineers and technicians—read like a roll call of America's industrial past. They are among the more mature segments of high-tech: for example, consumer electronics, construction machinery, telephone and telegraph equipment, photographic equipment, specialty dies, and switching gear. In recent years, Chicago's high-tech gains have lagged far behind those of many states and other cities.[69]

Chicago's slippage did not go unnoted at the time. In the early 1960s, Northwestern University's Albert Rubenstein, professor of industrial management and fresh from an assistant professorship at MIT, researched the poor showing of Chicago's electronics industry. He found, through interviews with sixty-one companies, that Chicago firms accounted for only 3 percent of the nation's electronic research, development, and engineering personnel, but for 18 percent of its electronics products. Chicago's electronics businesses were on the whole large and not noted for their leadership in R&D. The cause was not lack of local talent. The five major universities within a 150-mile radius of Chicago produced one-third of the nation's Ph.D.s in electrical engineering between 1954 and 1960. Of these, 200, almost half, went into private industry, but only 3 in the Chicago area.[70]

Yet Chicago's electronics firms were not suffering from their neglect of R&D. Even when size was taken into account, Chicago electronics firms grew faster on average than their non-Chicago counterparts in those crucial years in the 1950s when defense electronics was putting down roots elsewhere. Apparently, business was excellent, and as a result they were reluctant to undertake risky projects, especially for a military client. Rubenstein found relatively low levels of government sales. When asked, his interviewees stressed: "1) government business involves too much red tape and their company is not geared to such an activity, and 2) government business is typically less profitable and more volatile than alternative markets."[71] Rubenstein's own experience serving as a member of a mayoral task force devoted to examining why Chicago was not getting its share of federal dollars led him to believe that the banks were a major culprit. In general, bankers were

TABLE 4.2.   Percent Shares of Prime Contracts by Service Categories

	Army	Navy	Air Force	Defense Logistics Agency
Chicago	16	21	19	41
Illinois	32	13	26	23
California	18	31	44	5
United States	22	34	34	8

Note: Figures may not add up to 100 percent because of residual categories.

Source: U.S. Department of Defense, Prime Contract Awards, Fiscal Years 1983, 1984.

content with their robust big-business clients and indifferent, if not hostile, to small research-based enterprises that might be candidates for defense dollars.

Thus Chicago's eclipse as an electronics center was closely tied to the conspicuous absence of a defense-technology base.[72] Both the state of Illinois and the Chicago area were bypassed by the cold war defense buildup. Once a major center of matériel production, especially during wartime periods when large quantities of machinery and supplies were required, Illinois has seen its per capita prime-contract receipts decline steadily from 90 percent to 20 percent of the national average. A similar erosion has been experienced by all the surrounding Great Lakes states. Together, these states fall below 50 percent of the national average in per capita procurement and personnel receipts. In the important research-and-development category, the one that has been fastest growing in the 1980s, they have the lowest per capita defense receipts of any region. Thus the region has lost ground, particularly in the more innovative areas of the defense business.[73]

When Chicago does sell to the Pentagon, sales are apt to take the form of bulk commodities on standardized parts and equipment. Orders from the Defense Logistics Agency, primarily for food and other routine supplies, dominate Chicago's prime contracts, accounting for 41 percent compared with 8 percent nationally (Table 4.2). The state's orders are heavily skewed toward the Army, while both city and state fall far behind in filing orders for the Air Force, the service that has been most highly favored by the cold war buildup and is the most high-tech in its requirements. In contrast, California, one of the nation's major beneficiaries of the cold war buildup, has a far higher share of its orders originating from the Air Force.

The Chicago area possesses a comparative advantage in some types of military supply, particularly construction, photographic and matériels-handling equipment, petroleum, building supplies, and processed food. But in large and growing categories like airframes and related assemblies, aircraft parts, missile and space systems, combat vehicles, weapons, electronics, communications equipment, and defense services, the state ranks far below the leaders, the most prominent of which are California, Texas, Massachusetts, and Connecticut, followed by New York, Missouri, Florida, Virginia, and Maryland.[74]

The rather poor performance of Chicago is puzzling. Why, historically, did it not take advantage of enormous opportunities for growth in the defense

TABLE 4.3.   Northeastern Illinois Prime-Contract Awards over $10 Million, Fiscal
1983, by Firm, Plant, and Headquarters Location

Company	Northeastern Illinois Contract Location	Headquarters	1983 Primes (millions $)
Northrup	Rolling Meadows	Los Angeles	142.1
Sundstrand	Rockford	Rockford, Illinois	135.0
Amoco	Oak Brook	Chicago	72.6
Stewart Warner	Chicago	Chicago	22.2
Doesser Industries	Libertyville	Libertyville, Illinois	21.1
Sonicraft	Chicago	Chicago	18.0
Swift & Company	Chicago	Oak Brook, Illinois	17.3
Uniroyal	Joliet	Middlebury, Connecticut	16.9
Recon Optical	Barrington	Barrington, Illinois	15.8
Essex Electro Eng	Bensenville	Bensenville, Illinois	13.1
Honeywell	Joliet	Minneapolis	12.8
Teletype Corporation	Skokie	Skokie, Illinois	12.3
Kraft	Glenview	Glenview, Illinois	11.3

Source: U.S. Department of Defense, *Prime Contract Awards, Fiscal Year 1983.*

arena? The bulk of wartime provisioning activities, including sophisticated machinery like tanks and ordnance, had long been midwestern specialities. The area's expertise in machinery, engines and generators, electronics, and communications equipment—all building blocks for the new era of atmospheric warfare—was extraordinarily good. Electronics in particular was a Chicago specialty. In 1958, Illinois shipped 18 percent of the total value of all U.S. electronics products, 63 percent of which was electronic home entertainment and telecommunications equipment.[75] What explains Chicago's loss of momentum as the nation's premier center of sophisticated producers' goods? Why did a few firms manage to succeed where many others did not?

To answer these questions, we interviewed managers of twelve contemporary Chicago-area defense contractors.[76] Northeastern Illinois firms receiving over $10 million in prime-contract awards in fiscal 1983 are listed in Table 4.3. Eight of those interviewed were prime contractors, all of which were research facilities, engineering, optical, or electronics firms;[77] four were subcontractors.[78] Our sample included both large and small firms, the largest with $1.5 billion in sales, $516 million in defense sales. They ranged from giant operations with 15,000 to 16,000 employees, to a 3-person specialized product branch of a large national defense contractor. The majority of firms were single-plant operations headquartered in the region, although several had a number of satellite facilities. Product line varied greatly: one was a large construction firm; others made electronic products or electrical equipment; and three were research labs. Amazingly, despite their proximity, few links tied these firms together. None reported buying or selling to one another in substantial quantities.[79]

The majority of the firms started in the Greater Chicago area in nondefense-related fields. Six of the companies were successful producers in commercial markets prior to World War II. Like many midwestern industrial manufacturers, they aided in designing or manufacturing large quantities of defense materials during the war. All but one continued selling to the government once the war ended, although not all their plants remained in the Chicago area.

Most companies were in the Chicago area because their founding fathers were born or settled there. Subsequent chief executive officers have also come from this geographical area, thereby ensuring the companies' continued presence in the Midwest.[80] But the initial choice of Chicago by founding fathers does not explain why these particular firms survived in this location or why other companies founded there did not. Nor does the apparent absence of modern interlinkages deny that such links were important in the firms' earlier periods of growth, when they were more commercially oriented. The fact that these firms have managed to survive, in large part due to their position in national-market niches, does not foreclose the possibility that many others would have flourished had there been a core of interlinked activities or military facilities in the region.

Charting the location of spin-offs from these contractors is one way of following up these questions. We found that the majority of spin-offs were not located in the Chicago area or even in the Midwest. In fact, few of the contractors we interviewed reported engendering spin-offs. Some could remember none despite long histories. Spin-offs tended to come from the research labs or research-oriented companies. As noted earlier, the Illinois Institute of Technology Research Institute, Chicago's version of MIT, generated about fifty spin-offs since the 1930s, few of which took root locally. Most gravitated toward southern California, nearer to markets and competitors.

Chicago firms' branch offices tended to cluster around these same military-production enclaves. Several interviewees claimed that buyers and prime contractors on the West Coast would not cross a "Rocky Mountain barrier"—an imaginary line based on destinations within a two-hour flight from California. Therefore, midwestern companies had to open sales offices in the West in order to service them. Successful firms also transcended the absence of local interfirm linkages by resorting to air travel and shipment. IITRI's Morton Klein argued that distance to the major primes hurt Chicago-area contractors. "We could do better at marketing the Midwest," he argued. "Why not close down our Illinois Office of Marketing in Kuala Lumpur and open one up on the West Coast instead?"

The pull of military concentrations elsewhere appears to be more important than push factors like unionization in explaining contemporary branching decisions. While most firms told us that the presence of union workers did not handicap Chicago, the three companies with the most blue-collar workers reported that they had chosen to expand in geographic areas without unions. Yet Chicago's blue-collar work force was also defended by many contractors. Some stressed that the Midwest is especially attractive because the people are hardworking and highly motivated, less apt to "head for the beach." In a dissenting view, one vice president, mentioning Eastern Europeans and

Italians, asserted that ethnic backgrounds in the Chicago-area labor pool emphasize physical strength over intellectual strength, creating a work force ideal for large-scale, heavy manual labor but unattractive to the aerospace industry, with its small, light, and often hand-crafted components. Other firms and individuals vociferously contested this controversial viewpoint.

Although Chicago has been viewed by outsiders as poorly situated for recruitment of specialized labor such as engineers and scientists, we found no evidence for this. In individual cases, contractors reported that they had lost recruits to sunnier climes. Firms operating in more competitive labor markets noted that if potential employees were offered equivalent jobs elsewhere, factors like climate became important and made Chicago "a very difficult sell." But this too was controversial. One firm stated that Californians would not come to the Midwest, but another countered that "[Los Angeles] ain't what it used to be."

Yet despite difficulties in overcoming regional prejudices in cases of particular recruits, overall we found no lack of qualified professional and engineering personnel. This is reflected in prevailing salaries reported by the contractors interviewed. Most firms stated that their wages were competitive with those in other parts of the country. At least vis-à-vis Los Angeles, the lower cost of living aids firms in offering competitive or lower salaries, which in turn gives them an edge in bidding on contracts. Overall, the top research labs and companies in fields where the Midwest excelled had no problem recruiting top personnel. "Top people will come to the top lab," noted Allied-Signal's Patrick Stone. Most other companies targeted either the midwestern engineering schools or seasoned engineers of midwestern origin, and reported no difficulty in filling slots. Contrary to our expectations, most companies stated that the local universities were not utilized for research collaboration, but they did rely on such institutions for recruiting, for advanced training of personnel, and as a resource for engineers seeking MBAs.

We asked each company to speculate why the Chicago area has not fared better as a site for defense contracting. The answers were provocative. Several companies offered historical reasons for Chicago's failure to enter into defense-related work after World War II. They stated that the machine and manufacturing industries wanted to maximize their existing investments, which were in nondefense areas. The success of these companies in commercial markets allowed them to become complacent and not search for new products or markets.

Some executives advanced more creative explanations. One proposed a theory of differentiated ethnic mobility to account for the lack of high-tech and defense-oriented companies in the Midwest. According to him, immigrants from European countries such as Greece, Ireland, Poland, and Sweden came directly to the Midwest after arriving in the United States. Unlike Californians and other Westerners, the immigrants who settled in the Midwest did not move again. He personally felt that this complacency revealed a lack of pioneering spirit essential to the development of new industries, especially aerospace and high-tech. People who continued to move toward the West were ambitious and risk-taking, the fundamental qualities on which high-tech is based. Other contractors vigorously refuted this view, and one noted the extraordinary achievements of immigrants like Guglielmo Marconi, the physicist and inventor. Another startling charge was that "Boss" Richard J. Daley, mayor of Chicago from the mid-1950s to the late 1970s, opposed high-tech development in his city. According to a possibly apocryphal story, Daley believed that high-tech brought in engineers and scientists, and "those guys don't vote machine." The interviewer queried, "You mean he thought that they wouldn't vote Democratic?" "No—that they wouldn't vote machine!"

Other theories focused on some companies' belief that mass production and government production cannot coexist. Most successful midwestern manufacturers, such as the automobile-oriented suppliers, churned out a large number of mass-produced goods on assembly lines. This emphasis on quantity conflicts with government quality control and accounting practices, thus discouraging large manufacturers from seeking government money. Another respondent stated that the oligopolistic nature of Chicago's industries removed any incentive to look for new markets. A final informant stated that Chicago companies failed because they offended the Army, Navy, and Air Force by emphasizing commercial markets over the defense industry.

The Third Coast Explained

The Midwest in general, and Chicago in particular, thus refute the conventional wisdom that innovative industries are most likely to germinate in established industrial regions and cities. Such places, the theory runs, have a head start because they already have within their borders scores of entrepreneurs, sources of money capital, a skilled labor force, and a political structure amenable to change. Many innovations emanate from existing corporate R&D laboratories, which are heavily concentrated in a few major cities. Others are pioneered by smaller firms, headed by engineers or scientists who must rely on outside financing and support services like accounting, marketing, and legal help—all chiefly available in large, sophisticated urban centers. Regardless of their size, infant industries tend to cluster in areas where individual firms share in an environment of rapidly changing ideas, designs, labor pools, and specialized business services.

Cities that have this type of infrastructure are thought to function as "seedbeds of innovation." Even if they lose portions of industries they previously relied on, so runs the argument, new industries will spawn a reinvigorating supply of new jobs. The relative stability of the urban hierarchy, despite the dispersal of more mature industries, has been cited as evidence for this seedbed function.[81] Several recent studies have emphasized the skilled-labor requirement of high-tech and have suggested that the nation's major urban centers will continue to win the lion's share of high-tech jobs. The Joint Economic Committee study (1982) concluded that the Midwest, in particular, was poised to be a major gainer in high-tech, since it has all the necessary prerequisites.[82]

In fact, the seedbed hypothesis is actually an amalgam of several theories about the locational behavior of innovative firms. The reasoning runs more or less like this. Innovating firms demonstrate a high degree of dependence on specialized skilled labor (especially in the engineering, scientific, and technical fields), existing corporate R&D labs, good research universities, a diversified set of business services, and the presence of key competitors. Thus places that have a disproportionate share of these factors will be well positioned to attract and/or breed a relatively significant share of innovative activities. Also implicit is the assumption that these factors are more or less immobile and cannot easily be assembled at virgin locations.

In the 1980s, however, evidence proliferated that the seedbed theory is not supported by recent American experience. A number of empirical studies confirm that, since the 1970s, innovative activity has increasingly taken place in new centers.[83] Several explanations have been offered. First, new economic developments may be emanating not from corporate R&D labs, but from university and government labs.[84] Second, certain specialized research functions may be separable from the headquarters' operations; such technical branch plants, while they may not create spin-offs and new agglomeration, may constitute large high-tech complexes in and of themselves.[85] Third, accidents of history, particularly the preferences of firms' founding fathers for locating in their hometowns, may explain the birth of some new innovative centers.[86] Climate, too, has been suggested as an amenity factor that entrepreneurs and their prized technical staff may prefer. These explanations more or less focus on the forces of attraction that might characterize new innovative locations.

Another line of reasoning probes the forces of repulsion from established centers. Strong, if increasingly sluggish, traditional industries may dominate local resource markets in ways that deter new investors or entrepreneurs from setting up shop. Where some degree of oligopolistic power exists, large firms may enjoy an increment of profit that permits them to outbid other potential employers in the competition for labor, land, capital, and even political favors. Upstarts in new industries may find it impossible to assemble the resources they need. Or well-established companies may simply be so preoccupied with their existing markets that despite their ready cash and presumed managerial expertise, they are incapable of seeing new market potential and fail to be the instruments of diversification for their surrounding economies.[87]

A few empirical studies offer preliminary answers to the relative strength of locational factors in contemporary high-tech growth.[88] But what appears to have mattered five years ago or today may be different from what originally accounted for the decisions of entrepreneurs and firms to set up shop elsewhere. To probe the seedbed hypothesis, we need a historical body of evidence on the many sequential decisions of individual firms that together explain the relative success or failure of once-innovative cities to generate new industry.[89] Nowhere is that inquiry more compellingly called for than in the cities of the industrial heartland.

The Chicago area appears to have lost remarkable ground as a seedbed of innovation despite a very strong corporate, university, and professional/ technical culture. Given that military spending has been the single most important stimulant to postwar high-tech development, Chicago's slippage appears in large part to be a function of crowding out, on the one hand, and Pentagon boycotts, on the other. Those Chicago-area firms that did make it in cold war defense contracting have relatively long histories and successfully moved into defense contracting from an earlier specialty in commercial markets. Many still have substantial commercial-product lines, and some reported that they had been driven into more defense work simply because of the rapid deterioration in the 1980s in their nondefense markets. Most had developed state-of-the-art products and had few or no competitors. Yet the striking fact is that there are so few of them.[90]

Traditional locational factors do not appear to explain Chicago's fall—or, by extension, that of the Midwest generally. Almost all the firms reported that remoteness from military purchasing offices, military users, other contractors, or suppliers was not a major impediment to their success in selling from Chicago. They were on the whole adamant that the quality of labor, universities, and business services was quite high there. Nor did they report difficulties in attracting personnel to the area. None reported having to pay higher than national salaries, and some reported slightly lower rates. Why have so few companies won defense contracts? And why are there virtually no new plants in the area, and so few start-ups oriented toward defense high-tech?

The absence of branch plants can be explained rather easily. In our interviews, Los Angeles–based defense contractors, many of which are trying to disperse production from congested, high-cost southern California, never mentioned the Midwest as a possible site. In addition to the two-hour-flight limit—the aforementioned "Rocky Mountain barrier"—many would not consider areas with relatively high degrees of unionization. There appear to be rules of thumb about which places are attractive—Colorado Springs and Huntsville rank high—and almost a herd instinct about where to go next. Most branch-plant decisions are driven either by the need to be near a particular military facility or concentration of contractors, or by routine functions that are dependent on blue-collar or technical laborers who favor states with a good labor reputation. Indeed, almost all the Chicago-based companies we interviewed that had located branch plants elsewhere had chosen Sunbelt, relatively rural, or overseas locations. The Los Angeles prejudice against the Midwest extends to the siting of technical branch plants as well, those requiring well-educated staff. Given our Chicago-area respondents vouching for the high quality of the local engineering and professional work force, it remains more of a mystery why more California-based firms do not open branch plants in the cosmopolitan Midwest.

Partly, the answer is that the creative agents of the military–industrial complex spurned the Midwest. Historically, there have been very strong factors drawing the airframe industry and earlier shipbuilding toward the coasts and away from the heartland. The combination of strategic concerns, the siting of key military facilities (early Air Force bases, missile research facilities, the Kennedy Space Center, and so forth), boosterism, the preferences of certain founding fathers—including military men—for places like Los Angeles, and logrolling politics all help to explain the development of a "defense perimeter" outside traditional centers along the third coast.

But in addition, we detect a strong push factor in this evolution. Until the late 1970s, the major midwestern companies, heavily invested in producer goods and highly successful in consumer-durables markets, saw no reason to pursue defense outlets. It was difficult to serve two masters; many companies felt compelled to choose either one type of market or the other. Government regulations and performance requirements are more cumbersome and rigorous, orders much more sporadic, than commercial demands. Despite the high levels of defense production in wartime, including the Korean and Vietnam eras, midwestern companies have been eager to return their plants to commercial production with peacetime.

Bell and Howell is a good example of this. Following forty years of leadership in the movie-camera business, it became a dedicated producer of military optical equipment in World War II, making gun cameras for the Air Corps and other equipment for the Army, Navy, and NSA. After the war, management was eager to convert back to making cameras for a society with a booming birthrate. In addition, said former CEO Donald Frey, the company had become fed up with military contracting. The procurement process is not a "free market," he noted, and firms had to put an enormous investment into figuring out how to get contracts. Doing "defense" did not fit into Bell and Howell's culture; the firm was not a big Washington player, like its larger optics rival, Kodak, which continued its association with the Pentagon.

Nervousness about patent protection proved another barrier to midwestern interests. Many midwestern fortunes had been achieved with legal monopolies, creating an extraordinarily conservative and secretive strategy by which patents were not even applied for until markets had already been penetrated. For instance, Goodyear in Akron, Ohio, had an aerospace division that primarily made brakes for aircraft. Interested engineers could not convince top management to pursue government technology-intensive products. The administrators feared that designs would be replicated before their return on investment had been realized.[91]

It was not that the Midwest failed to innovate; just that innovation is carried out so differently in commercial and in defense markets. Particularly in consumer goods, the product has to be very simple—"user friendly" in today's parlance. In Frey's view, making a product that simple is actually much more difficult than making sophisticated cameras for Hollywood. It requires considerable technological know-how.[92] From Henry Ford to Bell and Howell, the Midwest had devoted its energies for more than fifty years to making everything from automobiles to televisions and cameras in large numbers relatively inexpensively, so the middle and working class could buy them. Midwestern firms had become masters at mass production, no mean feat. This produced a management style inimical to that favored in defense procurement, where tailor-made esoteric equipment is fashioned with little concern for cost and no presumption of long-term mass production.

But if the great midwestern corporations had once been entrepreneurial in product and process design, they became less so in the postwar period. Their markets remained strong and deep until the late 1970s. After earlier decades of mergers and cutthroat competition, a handful of firms came to dominate these markets, reaping persistent oligopolistic profits. They developed their own peculiar internal practices, marked by preoccupation with market-share maintenance, adversarial labor–management relations, and conservative investment and product-development decisions.[93] Even in the high-tech durable-goods industries, like optomechanical and electromagnetic equipment and consumer radio and television, most midwestern firms never made the transition into the electronics age. Corporate culture in the Midwest, then, increasingly diverged from that favored in the heavily government-dependent, performance-conscious defense high-tech corporations clustered in new centers, such as Los Angeles. The midwestern corporate culture appears to have created a political environment in its own image: highly adversarial party politics, a preoccupation with the interests of commercially oriented business and labor, and an indifference at best to the possibilities for defense pork-barreling. Despite members of Congress (e.g., Everett Dirksen, Daniel Rostenkowski) with impressive longevity, Illinois and surrounding states seem never to have competed vigorously for the key military facilities that were to draw many contractors in their wake. Several of our interviewees complained bitterly of the lethargy of the Illinois congressional delegation in reversing the dwindling share of the defense dollar that comes back into the state. But in large part, this apathy is a function of the small size of this constituency among many larger and well-organized ones.

Another cultural factor may have handicapped the heartland. A disproportionate number of scientists who fled from Nazi-occupied Europe were resettled in the American West, where they worked on military research and pioneered the unique government–science partnership that was to endure into the cold war era. Fewer émigrés joined universities or private-sector labs in the industrial heartland, where ample numbers of scientists were already ensconced. Among those who did were Leo Szilard and Enrico Fermi, who worked at the University of Chicago on the crucial chain reactions for the Manhattan Project. But soon after Hiroshima, Szilard became a public critic of the use of atomic weapons, and pioneered, with other Chicago colleagues, the *Bulletin of the Atomic Scientists*. Scientific opposition to the cold war remained headquartered in Chicago. It is difficult to determine whether this further added to Pentagon repugnance for the industrial heartland.[94]

In the end, then, the third coast and the iron triangle lost out because of a complex set of causes and events. In the crucial decade of the 1930s, it lost aircraft production to Los Angeles and because entrepreneurs like Ford were too busy competing in the relatively depression-resistant auto industry. In the 1940s, its leadership in mass-producing fighters, bombers, and engines resulted in only short-lived prosperity. Once the war was over, the design-conscious West Coast firms pulled ahead, while Ford, Packard, Bell and Howell, and similar companies focused almost entirely on serving pent-up consumer demand. Over the decades, would-be aircraft entrepreneurs tended to migrate to the perimeter, where local promoters were eagerly handing out land and tax breaks, and where military facilities offered testing fields and markets.

In the postwar period, the military–industrial complex has risen in tandem with the cold war, but it barely touched the Midwest. East and West Coast electronics firms got their start on Pentagon research and procurement dollars. Politicians beholden to new defense-oriented constituencies in states like Massachusetts, California, and Texas came to dominate the presidency and relevant congressional committees. Although the occasional midwestern congressperson pointed out the vulnerability of coastal aircraft plants and insisted that defense-research facilities be located in the Midwest, such demands fell on deaf ears.[95] By the end of the 1950s, the industrial heartland sat back on its haunches, proud of its great industrial boom, to find that it had lost out on the newest wave of infant industries. It was hard to swallow, but the truth was, as Donald Frey put it, "that the Midwest had no Fred Terman and no Tip O'Neill." By the 1980s, this absence had become a major issue.

Can the Third Coast Rise Again?

Is there hope from the Pentagon for the heartland and its depressed industrial cities like Chicago, Detroit, and Buffalo? Can defense-related, high-tech activity be increased there? The answer is probably not. While the Reagan buildup exacerbated the midwestern handicap, it was really events decades earlier that sealed the region's fate.[96] Forty years of a national effort to construct the nation's cold war defense-production base has resulted in new agglomerations built elsewhere to perform the bulk of this work. The defense build-down now in progress further limits the growth potential from Pentagon sources.

The problem does not appear to be a lack of appropriate talent. The presence of outstanding engineering schools, large concentrations of corporate R&D labs, and an ample professional/technical work force has simply not been sufficient to generate a defense-technology base. On the contrary, impressive numbers of Midwest-educated engineers are immediately recruited to the defense perimeter every year. And given the relatively negative assessment of universities as sources of development ideas, it is unlikely that an emphasis on upgrading universities, education, and/or technology-transfer mechanisms will reverse this situation. Indeed, it may only exacerbate the problem: the Midwest is supplying, at regional taxpayers' expense, a well-educated stream of outmigrants whose exit is of no benefit to their home states.

Among the more striking responses to our questions were the confirmations of defense-oriented firms in the Midwest that they had little or no connection or interdependence with similar firms in the area. The Midwest as a whole does not command a large enough share of any key defense product to bring about a new agglomeration. Nor do any of its cities. In a bold move to rectify this inadequacy, the recently organized Illinois Defense Technology Association (IDTA) launched the Arsenal-21 Project, which proposes to develop a portion of the present government-owned Joliet Army Ammunition Plant as a defense R&D center.[97] The project is modeled on the success of the Redstone Arsenal in Huntsville, Alabama, which now employs about 31,500 people and has attracted many private contractors to the area since 1950.

Convincing the Army and, in turn, the Department of Defense and Congress that such a facility is needed will be difficult. The military budget is not a bottomless pit, despite the beliefs of some critics, and strategic and performance characteristics loom large in the Pentagon's annual allocations. While research continues to consume a growing portion of defense dollars, very little of this money has been directed to Illinois. For example, Illinois companies and universities received only $154,000 of the $1.1 billion set aside for SDI research in fiscal year 1985, compared with California's $365 million and Massachusetts' $202 million. When Illinois' tax contribution to SDI is considered, it ranks worst in the nation.[98]

It is hard to avoid the conclusion that the midwestern economy's strengths, including its high-tech prospects, lie in its established commercial sectors rather than in defense technology. The Chicago area has a critical mass of high-tech expertise in areas like pharmaceuticals, medical technology, machine tools, chemicals, and metallurgy, as well as in central management functions and business and financial services. Its technical specialities in manufacturing are heavily skewed toward chemical, mechanical, and metallurgical engineering, in contrast to the electrical and aeronautical engineering favored by the defense-oriented industries of the perimeter.[99] Those defense-oriented firms that have survived are really vestigial arms of a previous body of civilian producer goods industry, by now detached from a coherent core.

Illinois and the Midwest in general would be better advised to invest in efforts to redirect national priorities and resources away from the current reliance on military-led innovation and toward commercially oriented industries. In fact, most new public-sector initiatives in the Midwest are aimed at nondefense arenas.[100] Although several of the contractors we talked to volunteered that their efforts to develop the Illinois Defense Technology Association were predicated on a pessimistic view of the prospects for commercial markets and on the belief that military-based R&D was going to be the only game in town for the forseeable future, with the dollar's fall and caps on defense spending likely, this view may be out of date. One stated unequivocally that there would not have been an IDTA without the Reagan military buildup. When asked what would happen if national budget priorities were changed, IITRI's Morton Klein replied, "Heck, we don't have to be the Illinois Defense Technology Association—we could be the Illinois Waste Management Association!" suggesting that the biological and chemical expertise on his staff could easily be redirected toward solving the nation's waste-management problems.

Leadership for such a change in national priorities is most likely to come from the Midwest, since it is the region that has benefited least, along with most other interior states, from the defense buildup and the increasing militarization of research and development in the United States. As one contractor put it, "If we could get the Department of Commerce organized to do what the Department of Defense does on the research front, we wouldn't need another new agency to do this. But no one is really coordinating a policy for competitiveness at present." Of course, the rationale for a nonmilitary innovation policy is based on expected benefits encompassing much more than balanced regional growth. But for the third coast generally, our research suggests that putting energy into redirecting the nation's goals would achieve much greater payoffs for the Midwest than any effort to win a "fair share" of defense dollars.

5

Aerospace Capital of the World: Los Angeles Takes Off

The approach to Los Angeles International Airport offers one of the world's most spectacular urban panoramas. And the best place from which to enjoy it, for the dedicated student of cities, is by the airplane's left window. As the plane swoops down over the ocean, the Santa Monica Mountains in the foreground, there appear the movie stars' homes of Beverly Hills, an apparently endless march of offices and penthouses down Wilshire Boulevard, the famous "Hollywood" sign on the hillside, and the unmistakable juke-box-record stack of the Capitol Records tower. This is the L.A. everyone knows: the capital of movies and television, glitz and glamour, kitsch and schmaltz. Then, as the plane dips toward the right into a giant U-turn, the traveler sees a second L.A.: downtown, marked by the memorable outline of city hall and the huge skyscrapers of Bunker Hill. This is a less recognizable, but older and equally significant city, the city of financial power, political and media clout, boosterism and ballyhoo, and political games played for huge stakes.

The plane completes its turn and levels out for the final approach, heading toward the ocean. Below, partly obscured by the smog, emerges yet a third Los Angeles: one far less familiar than the other two, yet in many ways the most significant of all. It is marked by the cluster of huge, squat structures around the airport perimeter, and by other buildings strung between the palm trees along the huge arc of the San Diego Freeway, I-405, as it curves southeast from West Los Angeles, through Inglewood, Torrance, and Long Beach into Orange County. This is "Aerospace Alley": the greatest concentration of ultra-high-tech weapon-making capacity in the world (Fig. 5.1).

Here are some of the greatest names in the Fortune 500, although their products are seldom advertised on television and never offered on super-market shelves: Rockwell (formerly North American Aviation), Northrop, TRW, Hughes, McDonnell-Douglas, Lockheed, Litton. Far more than oil or movies or banking or tourism or any of the other more celebrated props of this southern California metropolis, they have represented the real motor that has driven the dynamic economic growth of city and region for the past half-century and more. Nearly one-quarter of all prime aerospace contracts,

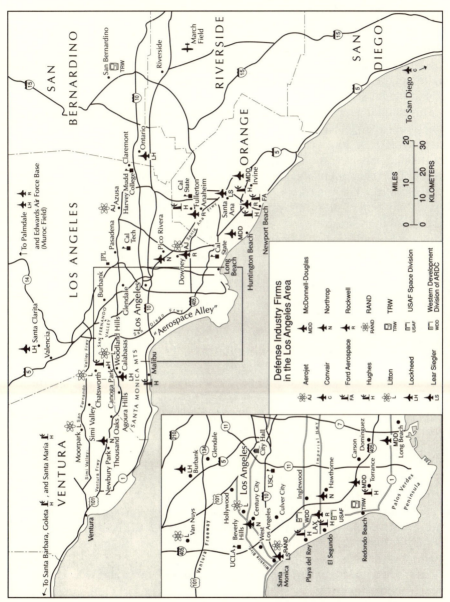

FIGURE 5.1. Los Angeles: defense-industry firms.

83

in any typical year, go to California; and of these, well over one-half come
to the Los Angeles Basin.[1] True, aerospace still accounts for only 7.7 percent
of the region's employment;[2] Los Angeles aerospace, avionics, and systems
companies are but one strand in the complex weave of this metropolitan
economy. But they generate relatively high wages and, in turn, many jobs
(multiplier effects), which give them a far greater economic impact than simple
statistics might suggest.

This chapter addresses three basic questions about Los Angeles aerospace.
First, about the past: How and why did Los Angeles become the number 1
center of defense contracting in the United States, particularly in the areas
of airplanes, missiles, and defense electronics? Second, about the present: Is
Los Angeles maintaining its dominant position in the industry? Do the economies of inertia, labor markets, scale, and agglomeration continue to provide
a crucial attraction, or are they being outweighed by the growing congestion
and costs of doing business in Los Angeles? How far are aerospace companies
taking the big plunge and relocating outside the region? And third, about the
future: Will the balance of forces—centrifugal versus centripetal—remain the
same? Will some critical breakpoint arrive, exploding the industry outside
the Los Angeles Basin? How do current aerospace managers see the prospects
of relocation in the years to come? Out of the area—or within it?

History 1: Founding Fathers, 1905–1935

L.A. aerospace is a story that goes back a long way—almost to the Wrights'
first flight. At the beginning, no one would have bet on its chances. Many
other places seemed poised to do better: Dayton, Detroit, Buffalo, and New
York, home of several pioneer companies. Within California, the San Francisco Bay Area clearly surpassed Los Angeles in industrial capacity and population, and held early promise as an aviation center. Its Hall-Scott Motor
Car Company made the airplane engine most prized by early experimenters
(including Martin and Boeing). Its Pacific Aero Club was heavily supported
by the banker William Crocker.[3] Los Angeles was the upstart city in the far
southwestern corner of the continent that took on both the heartland and the
older California metropolis for leadership of the new defense-based high-tech
industries—and won.

How could that happen? Los Angeles achieved this extraordinary feat
through actions taken by key local figures at critical historical junctures, each
corresponding to a different period in the evolution of American strategic
policy and companion development of the military–industrial complex. First,
early in the era of interwar isolationism, several founding fathers of pioneer
aircraft firms relocated to southern California, often enticed by civic boosters.
Second, building on that foundation, a military–scientific–industrial complex
emerged from the mid–1930s onward. In a third critical period, the pioneer
manufacturers into mass producers during World War II. Fourth, after a
transitional period during the late 1940s, there was the race into aerospace

during the cold war era of the mid–1950s, which marked the real birth of the military–industrial complex. Each era presented a new challenge with a new set of opportunities. Each time, Los Angeles responded innovatively—hence, successfully—to the challenge.

Like Dayton and Hammondsport, Los Angeles had its founding fathers. It was a pioneer center of flying experimentation and flying sport: the first major air show in America was held there in 1910—significantly, in Dominguez Hills north of Long Beach, in what became the heart of Aerospace Alley. Pioneer airplane production in southern California had already begun, simultaneously with the Wrights' efforts in Dayton, and by the mid-1920s a number of immigrants from other regions as well as native Californians had set up shop.

Glenn Martin

As seen in Chapter 4, Martin pioneered airplane production at Santa Ana in 1905. He built his first plane in 1909. Three years later he was working in an abandoned church in Los Angeles, listed in the phone book under "Amusements".[4] He merged with Wright and moved to Dayton, then left and opened a new factory in Cleveland in 1918.

Donald Douglas

Douglas roved widely before settling in Los Angeles. Drawn to the air in preference to the sea, he left the U.S. Naval Academy as a midshipman to become one of MIT's first graduates in aeronautical engineering in 1914. A year later, he was hired by Martin in his new Los Angeles plant. After a World War I stint with the Army Signal Corps, he rejoined Martin in Cleveland in 1917. But he wanted to strike out on his own. While working in public relations for Martin, he met Bill Henry of the *Los Angeles Times,* who lobbied him hard and introduced him to the Los Angeles business community. Henry's efforts paid off.

In 1920, supported by $15,000 raised by Harry Chandler, publisher of the *Los Angeles Times,* Douglas established his own company in southern California because of the area's climatic advantage, cheap buildings, good labor conditions, and general economy—the second case, following Curtiss, of a deliberate locational decision. He was also influenced by his wife's view that Los Angeles was a better city than Cleveland in which to raise children. He wrote to his former colleague George Stompl—whom, with others, he convinced to join his company—in June 1920:

> LA is much the same as ever and I certainly would hate to think of going back East now that I am here again. It would not be far [*sic*] to me to recite the many advantages of this old burg, for that might bias your judgment, so I will say no more about it now.[5]

Using his contacts in Washington and the eastern military establishment, Douglas developed a thriving defense business in the 1920s, producing out of an abandoned movie studio on Wilshire Boulevard in Santa Monica. He prospered in the 1930s after he lured designer Jack Northrop from Lockheed and set him up in a separate division located in El Segundo. Northrop's celebrated Douglas Commercial designs—above all, the DC-3—gave the company a near-monopoly of commercial aviation before it went on to make some 10,000 military versions in World War II.[6]

The Lockheed Brothers

Allan and Malcolm Loughead, born in the late 1880s in Niles, California, were migrants from northern to southern California. Early flight hobbyists, they started a seaplane company in San Francisco in 1912 but moved in 1916 to Santa Barbara, where they built two Navy flying boats. After failing, they restarted in 1926 as the Lockheed Aircraft Company, located in a Hollywood garage. Here their designer, Jack Northrop, produced the revolutionary monocoque design, the Vega. In 1927, short of space, they moved to Burbank. After a buy-out by the Detroit Aircraft Corporation and that firm's failure in the Great Depression, they were taken over in 1932 by brothers Robert and Courtlandt Gross. By 1936, they had substantial military orders. Two years later, they received an order from the British RAF for 250 reconnaissance bombers, the biggest order ever placed with an aircraft company. Thus, on the eve of World War II, they were firmly placed as both military producers and suppliers of civilian aircraft. During the war, they went on to produce over 19,000 planes and to expand from 2,500 workers in late 1938 to 60,000 by early 1945. By this time, Lockheed was the biggest aircraft company in the United States.[7]

North American

North American Aviation, a holding company that included the Buffalo-based Curtiss Aeroplane and Motor Corporation, was created by Clement M. Keys in the aircraft boom of 1928 and 1929. During the Depression, control passed to General Motors. In 1934 the management put the aircraft production division under the control of "Dutch" Kindelberger, who had been hired away from Douglas. Obtaining an Army order for a training aircraft, Kindelberger seized the opportunity to move North American's base from Baltimore, where it was located for a short time, to Inglewood, next to the Los Angeles Municipal Airport, in 1935.

Lee Atwood, hired at the age of twenty-nine as chief engineer and later chief executive, recalled that this move was due primarily to personal preferences, availability of suitable buildings, and the fact that Los Angeles was an established aircraft center. The general intellectual quality was better on the East Coast, but "people felt they could build a better airplane here," with a feeling of greater independence. The city and county "did not knock themselves out" to attract North American, Atwood said, although they gave the firm "practically a bean field" next to the municipal airport at a low-rent lease. But Kindelberger himself believed that boosterism had been a major factor, as we shall see.

Military-based expansion followed. Between January 1939 and September 1945, North American produced over 42,000 planes, 10 percent more than its nearest rival, Convair, and 14 percent of American World War II production. By war's end, it had 100,000 employees in Los Angeles and in two wartime branch plants at Kansas City and Grand Prairie, Texas. But Kindelberger, pessimistic about the future—perhaps due to poor health—likened the industry and the city to "a Donald Duck inflatable figure, about to deflate" and deliberately reduced the size of the company.[8]

Jack Northrop

In the 1920s, Jack Northrop thrice set up airplane companies in the Los Angeles area. After seven years in partnership with Douglas, specializing in the production of military planes at his El Segundo plant and expanding rapidly in the military buildup of the late 1930s, in 1938 he broke away to start his own company—his fourth, and the third with his name. After a search for alternative locations, he chose to remain in the Los Angeles area on the basis of climate, lower plant costs, and skilled labor. Accordingly, he set up shop in 1939 in Hawthorne, where he developed a whole series of military aircraft during and after World War II.[9]

Howard Hughes

Howard Hughes, born in Houston in 1905, reaped a fortune when he inherited his father's oil-drill manufacturing company. He moved to Los Angeles in 1925, more or less on a whim, to start a movie-making business. At first regarded as a playboy, he had a number of successes, culminating in *Hell's Angels* (1930), an aviation drama that sparked his interest in flying as a sport, spurring him to start a company to build sports planes. As design chief he hired a Caltech graduate, Richard W. Palmer, who brought in a group of his fellow graduates. Starting in a leased corner of a hangar at Grand Central Airport in Glendale in 1934, the company's airplanes were successful in racing events in the 1930s. But its overambitious plans during World War II—when it expanded (in 1941) into new premises west of Culver City, close to the Los Angeles Airport—proved a disaster. Its experimental projects—the wooden D-2 bomber and its successor the XF-11, the S-43 plywood Hercules cargo flying boat—never made a successful flight. Emerging unscathed from a congressional inquiry in 1947, Hughes largely ignored the aircraft company to pursue his motion-picture interests. Under the skilled management of two former Air Force officers and a former executive of Ford Motors, the company began to wax successful by developing top-secret military electronics. Simon Ramo and Dean Wooldridge, who were principally responsible for this success, resigned from the company in 1953 to protest Hughes's erratic management style and to set up on their own.[10]

One crucial factor in their resignation was Hughes's unsuccessful attempt in 1950 to relocate the research laboratory to the desert outside Las Vegas, a move prompted by his obsessive desire to avoid California income tax and by a complex deal involving the exchange of federal land. Ramo, Wooldridge, and others opposed the move because "they doubted that first-rate scientists would settle in the neon, honky-tonk world of Las Vegas."[11] Hughes eventually backed down and approved a major extension of the facilities at Culver City. But the incident, so typical of his maverick management style, was one of many that eventually led to Ramo and Wooldridge's defection.

The Los Angeles Boosters

Whether founded by native Angelenos or by in-migrants, these infant firms were located in places that had plenty of cheap land, often beyond the built-up limits. Lockheed went north to the San Fernando Valley, which happened to be the favored area for airport location in the 1920s and 1930s. Douglas, Northrop, Hughes, and North American went west toward the ocean, locating close to what would become the Los Angeles International Airport (LAX). But this was not entirely a matter of chance: civic boosterism helped propel them there.

Lee Atwood, in our interview, asserted that the city had made no effort to attract North American in the 1930s; but his own chief, Dutch Kindelberger, said in 1935 that the Chamber of Commerce "for a number of years, has worked assiduously on this company and its predecessor, the old General Aviation Corporation." Kindelberger also praised "the forward-looking policy of the city in modernizing its wonderful Municipal Airport."[12] In fact, Los Angeles throughout the late 1920s and 1930s was a classic example of civic boosterism. And the aircraft industry was a key target.

Here, again, a founding father plays a role. Harry Chandler was the publisher of the *Los Angeles Times* for over forty years, during a critical period of the city's and paper's growth. With an early reputation for "getting things done in a hurry," he played an incalculable role in the establishment of an independent port at San Pedro, the Owens River aqueduct, the development of the San Fernando Valley, the downtown redevelopment of the Civic Center, and the restoration of Olvera Street. He helped start Western Air Lines, the All-Year Club to publicize southern California, and innumerable other promotion ventures. His land syndicates speculated on an enormous scale, at one time controlling 1.5 million acres. He was the director of thirty-seven important organizations. A later editor of the *Los Angeles Times* said that Chandler had thought of the paper more as a tool for building southern California than as a newspaper per se.[13]

Immediately after World War I, Chandler and his business associates systematically began to seek out major eastern industrial enterprises that they could attract to the city. They also urged the Chamber of Commerce to promote the city's climate as an advantage to plane makers. In 1919, Chandler gave his sports columnist, Bill Henry, a year's leave to work in Glenn Martin's aircraft factory in Cleveland, where Henry met Donald Douglas. The following year, he was mainly responsible for the $15,000 financial backing that allowed Douglas to fill a $120,000 Navy contract for three torpedo planes from a base on Wilshire Boulevard in Santa Monica, on land leased by a Chandler syndicate.[14]

Chandler also played a leading role in promoting airport facilities in the Los Angeles area. A 1929 editorial cartoon portrayed the city as the aviation hub of America. A Chandler syndicate first financed the Western Air Express company and later—on Chandler's prompting—merged with an eastern firm to become Transcontinental and Western Air (TWA) in 1929. Here, as in the matter of the port and water-supply facilities, as well as in power generation, the city pursued an active policy of municipal socialism. Pressured by the Chamber of Commerce to develop a municipal airport after passage of the Air Commerce Act of 1926, it commissioned a survey that identified Mines Field, an open barley field near the ocean in what was then the undeveloped Inglewood area. A local citizens' group, including real-estate developer Harry Culver, the founder of Culver City, and Frank D. Parent, chairman of the Inglewood Chamber of Commerce, obtained an option on the Inglewood site and began to campaign for a "super airport" that would include both airfield and manufacturing facilities. It is not clear whether Chandler was a member of the group, although, given the extent of his interests, it seems extremely likely. The city finally leased the site in June 1928, opening the facility in 1930. Failing to develop as expected because of competition from the established Grand Central Airport at Glendale and the United Air Terminal at Burbank, the airport was used by flying schools, airplane agencies, and private planes during the 1930s.[15]

Particularly, the city attracted manufacturers to the site of the future LAX. Jack Northrop established his second plant there in association with Douglas in 1932, and North American leased twenty acres at the southwestern quarter in 1935, moving into a permanent facility in January 1936. No argument favoring Los Angeles as a factory site was neglected by the Chamber of Commerce.[16] Only after the city bought the site and the government funded development in 1937 to 1939, did firm plans develop to centralize major airline operations there. Ironically, these plans were delayed by war, during which the federal government took over and developed the site as the main delivery base for the thousands of aircraft produced in the adjacent Douglas (former Northrop) and North American facilities.[17] Thus when the new Los Angeles Airport opened for business in 1946, it was already the core of the greatest concentration of aircraft manufacture in the United States.

The activities of Chandler, Culver, and others illustrate a key point about Los Angeles in the 1920s and 1930s: the tradition of civic boosterism allied to land speculation and development on an epic scale, in which private profit joined with public spirit to promote growth.[18] It is clear that Los Angeles was only the most spectacular example of this tradition, which also characterizes San Francisco and San Diego. And active promotion by key booster-developers, as well as by chambers of commerce, played a key role in setting up Douglas in his first business, in attracting North American to Los Angeles and Consolidated to San Diego, and in establishing Northrop after his break with Douglas.

History 2: The Rocket Scientists and the Generals, 1925–1946

Pioneer entrepreneurial wit, coupled with aggressive boosterism, may have been enough to launch the infant aircraft industry of the 1920s and 1930s. But they would not be enough to engineer the critical next step: the translation of aircraft into aerospace. The crucial foundations were laid in the late 1920s and the 1930s, when a remarkable alliance developed between visionary scientists and a top Air Corps officer.

Millikan, von Kármán, and Caltech

Harry Chandler played a critical role in persuading Robert A. Millikan to head the physics laboratory and the executive committee at the California Institute of Technology in 1921. In 1925, Donald Douglas pointed out to Millikan that laboratory facilities in southern California were lacking. Early the following year, Millikan approached the Guggenheim Foundation for help. Ten days later came a $2.5 million grant to finance major programs at Caltech, Stanford, the University of Washington, the University of Michigan, New York University, and the Georgia Institute of Technology.[19]

That was not enough for Millikan. In 1927, he wrote to Harry Guggenheim of "the urgency and, indeed, the inevitableness [sic] of the airplane development in Southern California, and the desirability of having it directed along sound lines, especially in view of the fact that this has already become an airplane production center of the first importance."[20] This brought Guggenheim funds to establish the Guggenheim Aeronautical Laboratory of the California Institute of Technology (GALCIT). Already, at the end of 1926, Millikan had invited Theodore von Kármán to Caltech in order to try to lure him from his chair in Aachen, Germany. At the two men's first interview, Millikan repeated his view that "I am convinced the aircraft industry will be attracted to Southern California. So, with your help and the Guggenheim Foundation, I think we can make Cal Tech the nation's center of aeronautics."[21] In 1929, von Kármán accepted the job, and at Caltech—from 1936 onward—began the work on rockets that eventually, in 1943 with Army support, was institutionalized as the Jet Propulsion Laboratory (JPL).[22]

Thus Caltech stole a considerable march on Dr. Robert H. Goddard, the pioneer of rocket technology, who could—and indeed did—claim to be a prophet without honor in his own country. Goddard patented a multistage rocket in 1914, wrote his classic paper on the principles of rocket propulsion in 1919, and achieved the first practical launch of a liquid-fuel rocket in 1926.

Ignored by the American armed forces, but supported by Guggenheim funds, he had developed, by 1941, virtually every concept of rocket propulsion used since. But he refused to share his work with others, and there is no direct line from his work to what happened later.[23]

"Hap" Arnold

The line of development proved to lie with others elsewhere: at Caltech. Here was added yet another critical link in the chain of individuals and institutions that built Los Angeles aerospace. Henry H. "Hap" Arnold of the U.S. Air Corps served as commander at March Field near San Bernardino from 1931 to 1936. Arnold had easy contact with leading Los Angeles personalities. He invited movie stars to open days for public-relations purposes. More germanely, he resumed close links with Donald Douglas, a friendship begun in 1924. During their quail-shooting outings, Douglas told Arnold about technological developments. "Douglas, more than any other manufacturer, gave him an opportunity to study the aircraft industry from inside, to learn about its needs, its limitations, and its potential output."[24]

In the spring of 1933, Arnold was approached by Millikan, whom he had known in World War I, for help in experiments with cosmic rays. "The scientist became a frequent visitor, and he and his assistant, Johnnie Mattson, spent considerable time at the Arnold kitchen table, talking half the night away."[25] Through Millikan, Arnold met von Kármán, whom he convinced to serve as consultant to the Army Board of Ordnance on the aerodynamic characteristics of projectiles at supersonic speeds. Two years later, the Army commissioned the Caltech Jet Propulsion Laboratory to work on long-range jet-propelled missiles and provided $3 million in new facilities.[26]

Significant here is an incident related by von Kármán. Arnold in 1938 organized a committee, under the sponsorship of the National Academy of Sciences, to sponsor two projects: one on visibility from bombers, the other on rocket-assisted takeoff. Jerome Hunsaker, head of the Guggenheim Aeronautics Department at MIT, said, "Well, we'll take the problem of visibility. Kármán can take the Buck Rogers job." MIT, von Kármán heard, refused to take any money from Guggenheim for rocket work. MIT's Vannevar Bush said to Millikan and von Kármán, "I don't understand how a serious scientist can play around with rockets."[27] Not everyone in the young Los Angeles aircraft industry shared von Kármán's vision. Top members of the research team—von Kármán, Frank J. Malina, Martin Summerfield, John W. Parsons, and Ed Forman—had ignored discouraging opinions from Northrop and other aviation experts. They had launched Aerojet to develop the new technology commercially. But skepticism persisted. As late as 1947, a perceptive Dutch Kindelberger opposed the idea of a new center to study supersonic flight and ballistic missiles, because—according to von Kármán—people like him "understood products like an airplane, but they were not yet attuned to the coming research revolution."[28] But rocketry prevailed. In just over twenty years, Aerojet grew from a 6-person company with capital of $1,200 to become the "GM of rocketry," employing 34,000 people and doing $700 million worth of business a year.[29]

Arnold reluctantly left California in 1936 to become, successively, assistant chief of the Air Corps, chief of the Air Corps, and chief of Army Air Forces. But his California experience influenced him profoundly. In 1944, he embarked on his last major mission:

> As Chief of the Army Air Forces, I had yet another job. That was to project myself into the future; to get the best brains available, have them use as a background the latest scientific developments and the air arms of the Germans and the Japanese, the R.A.F. and determine what steps the United States should take to have the best Air Force in the world twenty years hence. There was no doubt in my mind but that a different pattern must be followed in so far as radar, atomics, sonics, electronics, jet planes and rockets were concerned. . . . To get the best thought on the subject, I went to my friend Dr. Robert Millikan at California Tech.[30]

After long discussions, Arnold brought in von Kármán to chair his committee. He told them to look ahead about twenty years and to use "their boldest predictions." "I see a manless Air Force. . . . For twenty years the Air Force was built around pilots, pilots, and more pilots. . . . The next Air Force is going to be built around scientists—around mechanically-minded fellows."[31] The committee's first report, dated December 1945, "Toward New Horizons," was not declassified until 1960. It described low-range ICBMs and multistage earth-orbiting satellites.[32] It was the brief for the aerospace revolution.

At about the same time, Arnold asked another long-time Los Angeles friend, Donald Douglas, to set up an independent civilian research center at his Santa Monica plant. Known as RAND, for Research and Development, it was to be based in the Los Angeles area partly because Douglas happened to be there, and partly because Arnold wanted it to be as far away from Washington as possible. Its first report, issued in 1946, correctly predicted the development of an earth-orbiting satellite. Originally part of the Douglas organization, RAND soon hived off as an independent nonprofit corporation, moving to its own headquarters close to the Santa Monica beach.[33]

History 3: Aircraft on the Assembly Line, 1941–1945

The 1930s thus saw a shift in the geographical pattern of the aircraft industry. Due to the relocation of North American and Consolidated, by 1938 five major airframe builders clustered in southern California—four of them in the Los Angeles area, and two of those four newly arrived in the mid-1930s. And by 1939, 44 percent of floor space and 33 percent of all employment in the aircraft industry was in California, representing a major shift of the airframe industry in the 1930s.[34]

World War II saw a huge expansion of the entire aircraft industry. Firms

TABLE 5.1.   Major Aircraft Manufacturers: World War II Production,
July 1, 1940–August 31, 1945

North American	41,188
Consolidated-Vultee	30,903
Douglas	30,696
Curtiss	26,154
Lockheed	18,926
Boeing	18,381
Grumman	17,428
Republic	15,603
Bell	13,575
Martin	8,810
Chance Vought	7,890

Source: Goldberg, 1957: 91.

that had produced a few hundred planes, or even fewer, were turned almost overnight into huge mass producers, becoming in the process some of the largest companies in the United States. Of the top five producers (Table 5.1), four were based in southern California, three in Los Angeles. But the war also brought a marked decentralization as new federally funded plants were opened or expanded in the interior of the country. Yet at war's end, an equally sharp contraction produced a reconcentration in the industry's traditional production centers. The geographical pattern of 1950 was close to that of 1940, although there had been some shuffling of the rank order of states and metropolitan areas. Los Angeles remained the chief center, the New York City area the second, although the shares of both were somewhat smaller; St. Louis and Dallas–Fort Worth (where Chance Vought had relocated) had emerged as major centers.[35]

Reflecting on this pattern in 1951, the geographer William Cunningham concluded that traditional locational factors such as raw materials or market access were of little significance; even the location of military activity seems to have explained very little. Skilled labor was more important, and—given the size of some plants—it had to be present in large quantities. Cunningham, however, overlooked the fact that in World War II, labor had been moved around at the taxpayers' expense in response to the needs of the industry. There were two special topographical factors: a mild, sunny climate, not merely for flying but for open-air construction, and flat terrain.[36] But these were not overwhelmingly important. Curtiss-Wright remained anchored in Buffalo, Grumman on Long Island, and Boeing in Seattle. Nor did all early California pioneers stay there. Martin, bucking the trend, moved back to the Rustbelt.

History 4: From Aircraft to Aerospace, 1946–1960

The immediate postwar period represented a kind of intermission for the defense industries. The Air Force in 1946 gave Convair of San Diego a contract to develop what would become the Atlas ICBM, but canceled it a year later. Convair and its successor, the Convair division of General Dynamics, kept the engineering team together, hoping for reinstatement. Behind the scenes, aircraft companies again lobbied hard for government support, as they had in the 1920s. As the cold war intensified, flaring into a hot war in Korea, the Los Angeles aircraft complex floated a number of ideas to win desperately needed federal dollars.

The next key juncture came with the decision to build the intercontinental ballistic missile. This was the outcome of a long struggle between Air Force chiefs of the World War II vintage, headed by Curtis LeMay, and a new generation of officers committed to missilery, among whom Bernard Schriever came to take a lead. Indeed, Schriever played as important a role in this fourth chapter of Los Angeles aerospace history as Arnold had played in the second.[37]

Schriever was a new type of officer: not a scientist or technologist, but "basically . . . a military manager, with a fund of technical knowledge and a quality for dramatizing the need for technological progress."[38] Significantly, he was a product of ROTC, not West Point, and had returned to civilian life after his initial flight training. By 1953, in charge of space and missile programs, he was battling LeMay for what many saw as a "Buck Rogers" idea. He formed an alliance with Trevor Gardner, the equally abrasive civilian newly appointed as special assistant on defense. It was Schriever who approached John von Neumann and Edward Teller, asking them if the H-bomb could fit into the nose cone of an ICBM. All became members of the Strategic Missiles Evaluation Committee—the famous "Teapot Committee," chaired by von Neumann. Significantly, it had two Caltech representatives, plus a third Caltech alumnus who had joined Hughes. In February 1954, it reported that an ICBM with an H-bomb warhead was indeed possible, and recommended a six-year crash R&D program. The Air Force, and shortly thereafter the foreign policy elite, fell in line.[39]

Then, in an amazing saga of interservice rivalry, the Army and Air Force behaved like competitive capitalist corporations. The Air Force had been freed from Army control as late as 1947. The agreements of that time restricted the Army to a subsidiary role in missile development, which ill-accorded with the ambitions of von Braun and his team at Huntsville.[40] Meanwhile, the Air Force—the most logical agency—was suffering from its "own enduring love for airplanes."[41] The Teapot Committee broke this impasse: a small "political coalition, spearheaded by Gardner and von Neumann, gained momentum" and countered both Army and Air Force views; finally, it overcame even "Eisenhower's commitment to frugality."[42]

So the Air Force, somewhat against its will, was chosen to implement the costliest crash program in defense history. The question now was how to do it. Several key people, in both industry and the military, envisioned a West Coast–based effort. At the time, Air Force contracting was divided between the Air Research and Development Command (ARDC), based in Baltimore, and the Air Matériel Command (AMC), at Wright-Patterson in Dayton. In

July 1954, just after Atlas had received top Air Force priority, Trevor Gardner created the Western Development Division (WDD) of ARDC, based in Inglewood, California, and headed by Schriever. In August, just after Schriever took command of ARDC, AMC established the Special Aircraft Project Office, responsible for Atlas procurement, at Inglewood.[43] The Air Force had moved to Los Angeles.

Schriever later recalled: "When I went out to the West Coast, to take over this job, the betting was fairly high that I wouldn't last more than six months."[44] He stayed for five years, until he returned to Wright-Patterson to head ARDC. His move west had the crucial effect of taking key decisions from Dayton and putting them into the heart of the Los Angeles air-production complex in Inglewood.

Southern California continued to dominate early missile development. In the summer and fall of 1954, a successor to the Teapot Committee, the Atlas Scientific Advisory Committee, considered how to organize the huge task of research, development, and production. It had technical help from two systems engineers who had defected from Hughes: Simon Ramo—a long-time acquaintance of Gardner—and Dean Wooldridge. WDD itself lacked the capacity. The only possible production contractor, Convair, had the aborted 1946 contract and had continued to do research on an ICBM with its own funds. But the scale and complexity of the program meant that one company could not carry the huge double load of systems engineering and production. Other possibilities for overall systems engineering—a major university like Caltech or MIT, or an independent research organization like RAND—proved impractical. Significantly, the notion of using von Braun's Redstone group apparently was never seriously considered. The committee recommended that overall development should go to an independent civilian organization working in close contact with WDD, to be headed by Ramo and Wooldridge.[45]

Ramo and Wooldridge, in the technocrats' view, were the best people, and they were on the spot. Simon Ramo had came to Los Angeles as director of research for the radio division of Hughes Aircraft in 1946. A Caltech graduate from the Jet Propulsion Laboratory, he later recalled that "we had a strong case of California-itis" after ten years of working for General Electric.[46] Together with Dean Wooldridge, a former classmate at Caltech who had earlier worked at Bell Labs, Ramo had built up at Hughes the second largest scientific and engineering organization after Bell Labs itself, staffed by over 400 Ph.D.s concerned with scientific problems of air defense and manufacturing complete aircraft-control systems.

The Ramo–Wooldridge team pioneered military electronics, a field that established contractors were ignoring because there was no money in it. But in 1952, Ramo, Wooldridge, and two other Hughes vice presidents broke with Hughes's autocratic deputy, Noah Dietrich, and in August 1953 Ramo and Wooldridge resigned, precipitating a major showdown between Hughes and Secretary of Defense Harold E. Talbott. In September 1953, with the backing of Thompson Products Inc., a Cleveland aircraft-engine firm seeking to diversify, the engineers set up their own firm "to apply creative science and technology both to military and nonmilitary applications." Ramo later recalled that the firm consisted of himself, Wooldridge, a secretary, and an assistant. By 1957, it was overseeing 220 prime contractors and thousands of subcontractors. By 1960, Ramo-Wooldridge—which in 1958 merged with the Cleveland-based Thompson Company to become TRW—had no fewer than 5,182 employees.[47]

The ironic result, one observer pointed out, was an organization that uncannily resembled the Army's arsenal system of procurement, which the Air Force professed to reject. So there were now two rival arsenals, one in Los Angeles working on the Atlas ICBM, the other in Huntsville working on the IRBM cruise missile, through different contractors. The extent of the rivalry between the two can be gauged by the fact that when an Air Force group visited Huntsville in 1958, Simon Ramo was excluded by the military director, General John B. Medaris, who could not bear the idea of his organization being evaluated by a rival. The two "arsenals" differed dramatically in location and style. Huntsville was far from any existing center of aircraft production. It emphasized the Army's preference for in-house weapons fabrication in its own arsenals, which accorded well with von Braun's history with the German Army Board of Ordnance. When it had to contract, it went to Chrysler, an automobile manufacturer, intensifying the fears of the airframe producers that they were being cut out. But it too had to depend on developments by airplane companies such as Convair for steering and North American for engines.[48]

The Air Force's philosophy, in sharp contrast, was—as Schriever put it— "going to industry and having industry develop and produce for us."[49] All its top defense contractors—Boeing, North American, General Dynamics, and United Aircraft—were airframe manufacturers. They already understood that unlike airplanes, missiles would be produced in limited numbers, would need relatively little airframe work, and would be expensive to develop; therefore, it was crucial to their survival that they move into the aerospace field. They were worried about the competition from the "socialistic" arsenal system at Huntsville—and from Detroit. By eschewing any in-house capacity, the Air Force developed a big, well-heeled constituency of scientists, organized labor, and industry, while its impeccable free-enterprise credentials removed most of the stigma from the surge in public spending that this recruitment entailed. WDD placed its prime contract, as expected, with Convair in San Diego; huge subcontracts went to other airframe and electronics firms.[50]

When Gardner promoted Schriever to head the ICBM program, he immediately established WDD in Los Angeles because most of the industrial facilities—as well as top systems engineers like Ramo and Wooldridge—were there. Air Force logic virtually demanded the step. Once the critical decision was made, it gave another turn to the screw. By locking the development process into Los Angeles, it gave the local airframe firms a means to remain innovative. They had some advantages: their existing contacts with the Air Force and their huge engineering staffs. But they also had heavy odds stacked

TABLE 5.2.   Leading Firms' Share of the Missile Market, 1956 and 1961

Company	Date	Missiles as Percent of Military Sales	Missiles as Percent of Market Share	Military Sales ($000)
Boeing	1956	—	—	79.3
	1961	36.8	11.1	1,173.3
Convair	1956	20.6	9.1	515.8
	1961	46.1	15.5	1,309.5
Douglas	1956	1.4	1.0	797.5
	1961	39.3	3.5	343.4
Lockheed	1956	—	—	574.0
	1961	69.4	17.3	973.2
Martin	1956	9.7	2.3	271.9
	1961	87.5	13.6	606.6
McDonnell	1956	2.8	0.4	162.0
	1961	18.9	1.4	296.5
North American	1956	—	—	743.2
	1961	40.3	10.8	1,046.5
Northrop	1956	33.7	7.3	253.0
	1961	35.5	1.2	134.6

Source: Simonson, 1968a: 234–36.

against them. They had to move into a new and relatively unfamiliar field, with different production requirements involving huge programs of reinvestment plant renovation and expansion. Their main competition came not from Detroit but from the electronics manufacturers, chiefly in New England, which the airframe firms met by investing heavily in avionics. Even by 1954, they employed 6,200 electrical and electronic engineers, 45 percent of whom worked on guided-missile R&D. By 1959, despite Air Force threats of retaliation against their moving into avionics, they were employing 27,000.[51]

In making the new product, then, neither the old auto nor the airframe manufacturers could monopolize the field. The electronics manufacturers, developing and manufacturing the crucial guidance and control systems, could readily enter, even at a small initial scale, as subcontractors; some could graduate to become main contractors on smaller space vehicles.[52] Thus in 1959, of the top sixteen missile contractors, eight were originally in aircraft, six in electrics and electronics, one in automobiles, and one was a subsidiary of a rubber manufacturer. Of eighteen top NASA contractors in 1961, only eight were in aircraft.

So not all airframe makers did equally well. Only eight of the fourteen major ones managed to make the transition into missiles. Of these, Boeing, Convair, Lockheed, Martin, and North American were conspicuously successful, achieving more than two-thirds of the total value of missile sales in 1961. Douglas and Northrop were much less successful (Table 5.2). Firms that failed to get into significant missile production included Curtiss-Wright, Grumman, Fairchild, and Republic—all, significantly, East Coast operations.

Nevertheless, the remarkable fact is that the airframe makers managed to increase their share of total missile sales from a mere 23.5 percent in 1956 to an impressive 74.5 percent in 1961. And the "big five" scored notable successes with individual missiles: Convair with Atlas, Martin and Titan, Boeing with Minuteman, Lockheed with Polaris, and North American with Hounddog.[53]

The chairman of one of the successful firms, Dutch Kindelberger of North American, had earlier been skeptical of the new technologies; but he made a decision in 1947 or 1948, about the time of the Berlin airlift, to employ scientists to develop the new products. He hired a scientist from MIT's Radiation Lab.[54] In 1955, Lee Atwood told us, North American had anticipated missile work and restructured the company into new divisions—Rocketdyne (engines), Aeromatics (guidance systems), Missile Systems (systems engineering), and Atoms International (warheads)—putting them in business with contracts for guidance systems, rocket propulsion, and the Minuteman, Thor, and Condor missiles. They moved deliberately into these new areas, with a heavy scientific input.

Was it true, then, that West Coast firms demonstrated greater entrepreneurial capacity to adapt and occupy the new market niches? Lee Atwood doubted this. East Coast and midwestern labs had been fully involved in early scientific work. Grumman and other Long Island companies had done early missile work, but made a major mistake in staying with propeller planes for the Navy. Atwood found it difficult to say why midwestern firms had faded away. Was it, then, that the West Coast companies gained an advantage from proximity to the military-procurement people? It was true that the heart of the effort was in Los Angeles under Schriever, and that Edwards Air Force Base had attractions for test flying. But Schriever had gone to Los Angeles because the main players were there and because work on Atlas and Thor was already under way. Maybe, too, Lockheed was helped in its early missile work by its proximity to the Ames Test Center, the Stanford Linear Accelerator, and Lawrence Livermore Labs. There may have been synergy among West Coast firms, but Atwood could not say: as he put it, "Where do fashion designers go?"

History 5: Summing Up

Thus in the history of Los Angeles aerospace, two capacities were equally important: the capacity to found a firm, and the capacity to lead it in new directions. But time, chance, and aging could and often did intervene at both stages, particularly between them. Success in the first stage was no guarantee of success in the second.

Almost without exception, the founding fathers were young engineer-entrepreneurs during the 1920s—technical enthusiasts rather than top managers. Often highly mobile across the nation, they shared a love of flying and of airplanes. They faced many vicissitudes during the Great Depression, sometimes going out of business and reconstituting. Their firms remained small and struggling until the growth of commercial aviation in the mid–1930s, some until the defense buildup of the late 1930s. Somehow, almost all of them met the extraordinary managerial challenge of converting to mass production during World War II. Those that flourished under the profits and government-financed increases in capacity during World War II were thus much stronger at the war's end. But, in retrospect, this growth was small in comparison with the challenge of the postwar period, when businesses had to convert from airplanes to aerospace. That meant an entirely new attitude to R&D, a capacity to think about the future in futuristic terms, and a need to create areas of expertise in the marriage of aviation and electronics. And by that time, the founders themselves were in late middle age, mostly still in charge of the firms they had started. Some did supremely well in this new environment; some less well; and some failed completely.[55]

What did geography have to do with all this? A great deal—but not in the conventional sense. True, in the early days of aviation, climate was indeed a significant factor. Year-round flying, first demonstrated in a grand style during the aviation meet in Dominguez Hills in January 1910, demanded good visibility and freedom from the vagaries of hurricanes, blizzards, and weeks of drizzle; in these respects, the Los Angeles area was ideal. In addition, temperate climate allowed for the assembly of airplanes either outside or in open-air hangars. Mild weather appealed not only to manufacturers, but also to military managers, who needed year-round testing of airplanes and operation of air bases.[56] Desert and ocean provided aviators with the space, isolation, and often secrecy to build expansive facilities, test their planes, and hide their inventions from curious eyes—a vital factor in the postwar age of high-performance aircraft and rocketry.

All this was true, but, for manufacturing, not crucial. Aerospace manufacture could successfully take place under the gray skies of the Northeast and Midwest, and indeed did. The real reason for L.A.'s success was not physical climate but mental or cultural climate. In the founding period of the industry, between 1910 and 1930, entrepreneurial talent flourished in a number of centers where key participants showed an early interest in aviation. Outstanding among them were older industrial centers—such as New York City, Buffalo, the Dayton–Cleveland axis, and St. Louis—and two new ones—Los Angeles and Seattle. Yet in the second period of adaptation, between 1950 and 1960, Los Angeles emerged as overwhelmingly the most successful center. Key individuals and institutions, notably scientists and Air Force officers, contributed to this. Millikan and von Kármán at Caltech supported work on rocket propulsion in the 1930s, when other scientists scoffed at this "Buck Rogers" idea. Arnold encouraged them and later, through the von Kármán committee and the creation of Project RAND, played a key role in steering the Air Force toward long-term technological planning. Key California entrepreneurs like Kindelberger at North American, and later Ramo and Wooldridge, contributed to the state's technological culture, developing a highly innovative, speculative attitude toward R&D.

We conclude that Los Angeles in the 1940s, as in the 1920s, had become—in the language of Philipe Aydalot—an innovative milieu. This was no accident. Key individuals helped build institutions, in both the private and public sectors, that were dedicated to undertaking high-risk research and to selling to the government. In turn, they reacted on one another synergistically to create a technical climate based on the suspension of disbelief, that the impossible could be made possible. There was an atmosphere of optimism, of invention, free of the old industrial and business traditions left behind in the East. No dominant manufacturing corporations, with their conservative banker friends, hoarded the political, financial, and human assets of the city. In the early stages of an industry, such a climate encompasses much more than the mere cost differentials of materials, labor, shipment, or weather. The aviation pioneers and their military patrons liked being far away from what they felt to be the cramping, archaic business climate of America's traditional industrial centers.[57]

It is perhaps no accident that Los Angeles, the City of Dreams, should have provided the unique atmosphere for this process. As Carey McWilliams perceptively put it, in 1946:

A nearly perfect physical environment, Southern California is a great laboratory of experimentation. Here, under ideal testing conditions, one can discover what will work, in houses, clothes, furniture, etc. It is a great tribal burial ground for antique customs and incongruous styles. The fancy eclectic importations soon cancel each other out and something new is then substituted.[58]

It is surely no accident that two of the new technologies that have captured America's imagination in the twentieth century, flying and cinema, were brought to maturation in Los Angeles. As with film-making, aerospace is not simply another standardized industry that relies on cost-cutting and efficiency for success. Rather, it thrives on innovation, risk, and cleverness—indeed, on imagination. Los Angeles was a place where people came to leave behind their old ideas about cities, industries, and culture. The unique culture of the early twentieth century gave Los Angeles a special momentum, which it has exploited to this day.

The nature of military–industrial city building is difficult, perhaps impossible, to capture. It depended, in this case, on the presence of a critical mass of creative, aggressive, and well-placed individuals, organized into appropriately supportive institutions. This may happen at one time and not another. It happened, for instance, in the late nineteenth century in Berlin and in the Boston–New York axis, but both centers later lost their momentum, the first completely, the second in part.[59] Policy may aid it or hinder it; but to a considerable degree, serendipity enters in.

Present 1: Agglomeration Versus Congestion

From the mid-1950s onward, Los Angeles aerospace rapidly came to develop a unique set of what economists call agglomeration economies. At the most basic level, firms could share suppliers, infrastructure, facilities, and skilled labor, thus reducing fixed costs. But beyond that, they could engage in joint projects with neighboring contractors, not merely for production but also for design—an increasing necessity, given the huge scope of the new missile projects. There are big advantages in keeping engineering, design, and production close together. "It's good to grow within the area . . . to keep a tight network," a Hughes manager told us. But the resulting synergism goes even further: it means that firms are tied into a shared system of specialized knowledge, in which one idea begets another, and one firm begets another.

The polycentric, low-density, urban–suburban latticework of Los Angeles lends itself to the need for synergy. The industrial suburb, a new type of land use, was spawned in part by the aircraft industry, which is centrifugal at the regional scale but centripetal at the local scale. From very early on, it was unusually suburbanized.[60] But within these suburbs, firms tend to build new facilities close to their old ones. The perpetual struggle to stay innovative encourages firms to put their workers, at least their key people, together. Assembly of big items, too, may require a stand-alone, self-sufficient division capable of taking on a $100 to $200 million project employing 2,000 people.

This vast labor pool of engineers, scientists, technicians, and managers provides Los Angeles with its greatest resource for aerospace production. For this is a business driven by innovation, not cost-cutting, and labor matters in a way no other factor does. Because it is so big, the L.A. labor market is highly flexible, and this benefits both the firms and their workers. In Seattle, when Boeing is on the downturn, there are no other big aerospace employers to turn to; the same is true for Grumman on Long Island and McDonnell-Douglas in St. Louis. Yet in Los Angeles, when TRW is down, Hughes may be hiring; Northrop may be expanding just as Rockwell is completing a project. Firms lay off thousands, and then take on thousands a few months later; workers swap jobs on a scale and at a speed that would seem irresponsible and threatening in traditional heartland industries. As one observer noted, "Job-hopping is not only acceptable in Los Angeles aerospace circles, it is essential."[61] This structure—based on entrepreneurs and consultants—is characteristic not only of aerospace but of the city's other project-oriented industries: electronics, motion pictures and television, construction, and real estate.

The nature of the labor market means that much labor recruitment takes place among firms as each goes through the fluctuations of expansion and contraction. A spokesperson at Litton stated that over two-thirds of the company's new engineering hires come with experience rather than directly from college, and that most of these engineers are already working in the Los

Angeles area. Over time, industry pressures have helped build the area's universities into another important source of new employees. Such nearby schools as the University of California, Caltech, USC, the Claremont colleges (particularly Harvey Mudd College), and the Fullerton and Long Beach campuses of the state university system are obvious sources.

Historically, of course, the professional and technical labor pool in Los Angeles was composed of a large number of migrants from other regions. But in the 1980s, the area's aerospace companies have had a difficult time recruiting from elsewhere in the nation. California candidates understand the southern California landscape, climate, and culture, and are often hooked on the distinctive Los Angeles life-style and acclimated to the area's congestion, pollution, and, above all, high housing prices. Young graduates from engineering schools in the Midwest, East, and South are not. "We can't get MIT, Cornell, Duke—those kinds of engineers to move to Southern California," a TRW official told us. "Our biggest university source is Cal State–Long Beach. . . . Unless you have lived in Southern California, you don't know what it is like to live here, and you don't want to pay the tariff to move here." Companies like TRW have experienced significant recruiting difficulties in the 1980s aerospace boom. Young, entry-level, family-oriented engineers often balk when they learn about the region's high housing costs. Companies such as Hughes have found that even local graduates leave in search of cheaper housing after about five to seven years. Recruiting middle-level management is also hard.

The specter of a daily bumper-to-bumper commute under smoggy skies scares many away. Congestion clogs access between an aerospace company's facilities in different locations in the L.A. Basin. Despite a complex network of freeways and access roads, Los Angeles still ranks seventeenth among U.S. cities in miles of freeways per million population—a statistic that undermines the city's popular image as the freeway capital of the nation. Predictions suggest that congestion, already serious, will worsen.[62] Gridlock is the constant specter on the horizon, and mass transit is not a viable option in such a decentralized area. Additionally, the growing perception that Los Angeles has become an overcrowded, sometimes violent urban agglomeration filled with strange people—a West Coast version of New York—has tainted the romantic image that once tempted the pioneers. Companies have countered these negative impressions by offering higher salaries, help with finding a house, payment of relocation costs, and mortgage subsidies, often with the help of the taxpayer. Of course, the relatively uncompetitive structure of the industry helps, too.

Nevertheless, many aerospace companies complain about the time and money costs of development in the Los Angeles area, as well as about unionization of the blue-collar labor force. Related to these is a more general concern about an ostensible "antibusiness climate" in southern California, a concern that encompasses higher taxes, higher payments for state worker's compensation, Coastal Commission efforts, and other environmental restrictions, such as the regulation of paint solvents—a major problem with aircraft manufacturers. When, in the 1970s, Governor Jerry Brown wanted to impose a 6 percent tax on business inventory, Douglas decided to build a fully mechanized, $100 million spare-parts facility in Las Vegas, right over the Nevada state line, dubbed by some the "Jerry Brown Memorial Warehouse." In the 1980s, Hughes, after threatening to put all expansion out of state, actually did relocate low-cost assembly operations. But the firm also built millions of square feet in California. Bolting to non-California locations is in fact rare, and most threats to do so seem to be in response to factors that irritate aerospace firms, but will not force them to move elsewhere.

Moves from one part of California to another, however, are not uncommon. Douglas left Santa Monica in 1975 after over fifty years, claiming that the city had "invited us out of Santa Monica" by restricting expansion; the firm went to Long Beach. Cities such as Palmdale, and others on the periphery of the Los Angeles metropolitan area, are seen as more receptive to aerospace firms. El Segundo, the small community just south of LAX, has been a traditional center of aerospace; very cooperative with developers and flexible with zoning, it acquired Rockwell, Hughes, and TRW in the 1970s. But more recently, a local head tax on employees, plus greater public pressures to limit urban growth, have encouraged commercial tenants to look elsewhere.

There are other considerations: the political and business liabilities of excessive concentration in one area, of "putting all one's eggs in one basket"; strategic considerations, which loomed large in the 1950s but seem irrelevant in the age of the ICBM; and the case for dispersion across the nation to strengthen political support for controversial projects. Rockwell's successful lobbying campaign to revive the B-1B project, which emphasized that parts for the bomber were to be built in almost every state of the nation, was widely regarded within the industry as a masterly public-relations coup. But as one commentator put it: "Yes, it is a factor, [but] . . . not big enough." Although California's congressional delegation does not have a strong reputation in defense matters, lacking the clout of southern representatives such as Georgia's Sam Nunn, political factors are unlikely in themselves to cause dispersion.

Present 2: Moving Around the Basin

Given all these concerns about housing costs, recruitment, congestion, and lack of space for expansion, and complaints about antibusiness attitudes, one might expect a great deal of aerospace relocation out of southern California. Of the original attractions for aviation pioneers—cheap and expansive land, environmental appeal, country atmosphere among orange groves—only the climate remains, and that tainted by smog. Yet there have been surprisingly few expansions of Los Angeles–based aerospace operations outside the state, and even fewer relocations. Instead, overwhelmingly, firms have chosen to relocate *within* the Los Angeles Basin and immediately outside it, to the north and west. One aerospace spokesman put the calculus succinctly: "Orange

County is still in the area. From Santa Barbara south is all southern California. I wouldn't distinguish within the area. The thing to watch for is moving out of the state."

In the early days, L.A. aviation was concentrated in Santa Monica, Burbank, and other locations adjacent to the city of Los Angeles. But the current aerospace complex covers a vast expanse of southern California terrain. As already noted, the industry helped spur the area's characteristic urban sprawl, as it spread east through the San Fernando Valley and up the coast toward Santa Barbara, north to Palmdale and Antelope Valley, east out toward San Bernardino and Riverside, and south to Orange County and beyond. By the mid-1940s, the aircraft industry was already more highly suburbanized than other heavy industry.

The most common direction is southeastward into Orange County. This movement does not represent a jump out of one area into another. Rather, it is a continuous sprawl over the nearly imperceptible border between Los Angeles and Orange counties. No topographic barriers block the path; on the contrary, two freeways—the San Diego and Santa Ana, which flow from L.A. into Orange County before joining at Irvine—have assisted it. And despite some antigrowth sentiments in Orange County, there have been no political obstacles.

Although Orange County has a long history of aviation,[63] starting in 1909 with Glenn Martin's first airplane in Santa Ana, the area's phenomenal growth is a postwar phenomenon, associated with the big move of the airframe manufacturers into missiles, satellites, and above all electronics. Essentially, the area is the avionics capital of America and one of the nation's greatest high-tech manufacturing centers. Unlike Greater Boston or Silicon Valley, the Orange County complex did not grow through spin-offs from university research; it grew through in-house development of electronic components in pioneering firms like Hughes and North American. Because by the 1950s space was lacking in the aerospace core around the Los Angeles International Airport, these firms developed branch plants at the urban periphery to the southeast. Then, in the 1960s, Orange County developed through spin-offs and subcontracting into an industrial complex of small firms, characterized by dependence on a common labor pool and infrastructural services.[64]

The attraction has been simple: plenty of land, close enough for easy communication with existing operations in Los Angeles County. When Rockwell expanded into Anaheim many years ago, the area was still just building up and land was cheap. The city was cooperative, for Anaheim's city fathers needed the industrial base. Housing was available, and there were more than enough home builders interested in keeping up with demand—and workers ready to move to Anaheim or to make the then-easy commute along the new freeways. Older developed areas were not even considered. They were too congested, and they lacked adequate parking. As one aerospace real-estate manager joked: "Show me your parking lot; I'm sure I'll like your building." And they did not have the right atmosphere: to quote a Rockwell veteran, it was "not the kind of place you would want to be."

Over time, the area built up a huge labor pool and extended the agglomeration economies to the whole of the L.A. Basin. Long Beach, just north of the county line, has been colonized by companies like TRW and Hughes. The firms' rapidly expanding labor pool allows them to rotate employees between facilities in both counties. Likewise, Hughes operations in Irvine and Newport Beach allow executives and engineers to permute work sites without changing residence. Ironically, Orange County has become the victim of its own success. In the 1980s boom, it was often hard for companies to get enough labor, and housing costs increased dramatically, as in Los Angeles.[65]

The aviation complex has also expanded northward, to places such as Palmdale, fifty miles north-northeast of the Los Angeles International Airport, and Edwards Air Force Base, ten miles farther north. Edwards has been the test location for nearly every military plane built since World War II and for some commercial planes as well. Its history effectively started in 1910, when the Corum family established a small town in the desert. They named it Muroc, their name spelled backward. In 1933, soldiers arrived from March Field, outside Riverside, to lay out and maintain a bombing and gunnery range. After Pearl Harbor, two major air groups/squadrons were set up there, and flyers were trained in B-25s, P-38s, and B-24 Liberators.[66]

But the area's unique potential awaited the coming of the jet age. The planes developed immediately after World War II were much larger, heavier, and more powerful than any before. They needed long, smooth, massively constructed runways. The dry lake bed—naturally smooth and hard, capable of supporting several tons per square foot—proved an excellent, almost infinite "natural" runway. The remote, unpopulated location was ideal for security, and emergencies would not threaten populated areas.

These qualities, plus almost no rainfall and perpetually good flying weather, made the area an ideal military airfield. The first American jet aircraft was tested at Muroc AFB on October 1, 1942. By 1946, Muroc was a center of engineering and flight testing of new aircraft. The base was the site of two historic "firsts": Chuck Yeager's flight when he broke the sound barrier, and the maiden flight of Northrop's unique "Flying Wing."[67] Captain Glen W. Edwards died on this plane in June 1948, and the base was officially given his name on January 27, 1950. A year later, the USAF Experimental Flight Test Pilot School was moved to Edwards AFB, mainly because of poor weather conditions at the existing site in Dayton.

Edwards symbolized the new generation of jets and their pilots—a world aptly captured in Tom Wolfe's *The Right Stuff,* distinctly western and epitomizing the close links of military aviation and space operations. Rocket test stands set up there were used by North American's Rocketdyne, NASA, and other pioneers. The impressive hangars of the major manufacturers stood along nearby "contractors' row." Edwards—isolated, secretive, barren, expansive, far away from traditional midwestern and East Coast military industries, a veritable tabula rasa of sand on which new designs and new institutions were laid down—visually epitomized the rise of the western military–industrial complex.

Ten miles south lies Palmdale, which emerged as an important assembly location for large aerospace projects. There Rockwell, in its government-owned, corporate-operated (GOCO) facility, began building its B-1B bombers in the 1980s. The site was ideal: close to Edwards and to the company offices in El Segundo at the Los Angeles International Airport, with an air-taxi service between the two—a convenience that would not have been possible with an out-of-state operation. During the 1970s, Rockwell had considered setting up in Palmdale as an alternative to El Segundo, since the latter was getting too expensive to operate. Yet this idea was eventually dropped, in part because of a classic Catch-22 dilemma facing boom–bust industries. When a company has plenty of contracts, there is no time to think about future plans; when there are few, there is no money for anything. And Rockwell engineers were very reluctant to make the move north into the desert. Palmdale therefore still has the disadvantage of remoteness; when Lockheed chose it in the 1970s for assembly and testing of its technologically admired but commercially disastrous L-1011 Tristar, it found the labor pool too small. The company had to recruit from Burbank and encourage people to move, or move them daily in company buses.

Eighty miles due west of Palmdale, on the Pacific Coast, lies Santa Barbara, the location of Hughes Aircraft's large research center. Just as the remote dry desert lake symbolizes the heroic side of the jet–space age, so the consciously idyllic, campuslike seaside setting of aerospace research centers like this (and similarly in Malibu and Newport Beach) symbolizes the cerebral side. Interestingly, when Hughes wanted to expand into manufacturing, the city resisted. In 1980, Hughes found a site farther up the coast at Santa Maria, just east of Vandenberg Air Force Base. It now has several thousand employees. Housing is relatively cheap by L.A. standards, and there is room to expand. This location represents a significant new northern coastal perimeter of Los Angeles aerospace.

In the traditional center of the industry, the San Fernando Valley has also seen great expansion of aerospace firms. Separated from the rest of Los Angeles by the Santa Monica Mountains, the valley is nevertheless part of the city—an odd legacy of early days, when the city annexed it to gain access to its water rights. Lockheed has been there since the 1920s. North American Aviation's Rocketdyne division also has a relatively long history there. After the war, the company began work on rockets in its Downey facility and tested them in Simi Valley, a then sparsely developed area west of the San Fernando Valley. It needed a remote place because rockets were noisy and potentially dangerous. The company also went westward in the San Fernando Valley to Warner Ranch, now Canoga Park, and bought property there for its operations.

But probably the most interesting move into the San Fernando Valley was that of Litton Industries, which is headquartered in Beverly Hills. In 1960, expanding into guidance and control systems, the company transferred some operations to Woodland Hills, on land from the Warner Ranch. Since then, it has incrementally moved farther west along both the Ventura Freeway and the Simi Valley–San Fernando Valley Freeway, about eight miles farther north, building facilities in Canoga Park, Calabasas, Agoura Hills, and Moorpark. At that time, there was cheap available land and a work force nearby.

These locations offered not only cheaper land and less congestion, but also an edge in attracting aerospace workers already living in the San Fernando Valley and points farther west. "Well, at Litton, our move will be toward Moorpark, of course, Ventura and that area, rather than toward Palmdale, Valencia, etc., because everything goes out that way, and that's where our current employees are," noted a Litton executive in Beverly Hills. "They're all in the west San Fernando Valley or further out." Litton has found that the possibility of a shorter commute, as an alternative to the long drive to El Segundo and other aerospace workplaces farther south, has a big appeal:

> One of the reasons that we located to Agoura . . . is that you have a nice building with a big sign on it: "LITTON." We're finding out that lots of engineers live further out in Thousand Oaks and elsewhere in Ventura County, and they drive by that every day to McDonnell-Douglas, or Lockheed, or someplace, and they have another half-hour to go. When we put an ad in the paper, we were able to get a few engineers that way, just by location. . . .

Since Litton produces electronic systems and components rather than large airframes, it understandably lacks interest in a move to Palmdale.

To sum up: a clear first motivation for the outward push has been the search for space. Firms have sought large chunks of land that is cheaper or more plentiful than it is in the Los Angeles area. There is a certain attraction— sometimes economic, sometimes psychological—in a greenfield site offering complete design control over a new consolidated office complex. Second, there is the draw of a government facility, such as Edwards for Rockwell, or the Air Force's ballistic missile office in San Bernardino for TRW. Third, and of growing importance, there is the pull of labor in the new residential areas at the region's perimeter.

Here, a major distinction has to be drawn. Blue-collar workers for Douglas often came from Carson, Dominguez, Huntington Beach, and Downey; those at Northrop often lived in Hawthorne or Torrance. Executives and senior engineers tend to live in the most desirable areas that are reasonably close to the facility: Hughes and TRW in the Palos Verdes Peninsula; Northrop in Bel Air, Beverly Hills, and Century City (the company's headquarters); Lockheed in the San Fernando Valley.

But, conversely, a significant factor in location of the facility may be the CEO's residential preference. Hughes corporate offices were recently moved several miles northwest from El Segundo to Westchester, just north of LAX; the chairman lives not far away, near Culver City. When asked why Northrop had its corporate offices in Century City, our respondent explained that the chairman lived in Bel Air and wanted corporate offices in nearby Century

City. Litton's Beverly Hills location provides another example. There are "probably fifty or sixty rules that you have to follow for location studies, but the fifty-first is the most important—where the CEO lives," noted one aerospace veteran.

Present 3: Moving Out

Despite the expense and congestion of latter-day Los Angeles living and working, aerospace companies have generally preferred to move around than move out. But some have bucked this trend and established new operations in the Southwest, in and around Colorado Springs, throughout the South from Texas into Georgia and Florida, and in the vicinity of the nation's capital. Most of these are small assembly facilities, or testing and maintenance operations at military installations. The work is fairly straightforward, with little engineering (outside of production engineering) done on-site. The standardized nature of the tasks at hand means that communication with the main office in Los Angeles is easily satisfied through periodic visits to the site by management and engineering staff. But a few represent larger and potentially important moves toward establishing new aerospace complexes in these predominantly southern-tier states.

A small-scale operation, originally called Colorado Electronics, was set up by TRW in Colorado Springs in the early 1960s. The company was attracted by the area's lower labor costs, combined with pleasant climate, the right mix of white-collar and blue-collar labor, and good transportation for its relatively high-volume manufacturing operation. The small staff of engineers performed mostly product engineering; in fact, this "build-to-drawing" operation probably came closer to volume production than any other TRW defense-related activity. Unlike more recent TRW operations in Colorado Springs, such as work on the Consolidated Shuttle Operations or the Space Defense Operations Center, closeness to the customer was not a factor. This move came before the establishment of USAF Space Command in the town.[68]

Hughes has also experimented with setting up smaller branch-plant operations in other parts of the country, including five locations in the South (in Georgia, South Carolina, Mississippi, and two in Alabama) during the early 1980s. These five, which served Hughes operations in either California or Tucson, were considered "slave manufacturing plants," because they needed relatively unskilled labor. Hughes balked at the idea of relocating other types of work out of Los Angeles, such as its satellite operations, which it felt were too large and complex to be moved.

The appeal of these Sunbelt locations was their lower labor costs and lack of unionization, proximity to technical schools and an airport, lower cost of living (including lower housing costs), an attractive environment (important for the families of engineers), and good schools. States made vocational training available, which could be used to retrain the local textile workers.

Tax breaks and Industrial Revenue Bonds (IRBs) were also offered to "sweeten the deal." Nearby universities, such as Georgia Tech and Clemson, and their advanced engineering programs mattered in the cases of the Georgia and South Carolina facilities. An additional appeal of the area was that ephemeral beast, the business climate. One Hughes manager called it "the American dream revisited down there. . . . States have reputations," and these Sunbelt states have positive ones: receptive economic-development organizations, favorable work ethic, and so on. Another Hughes official stated: "What one really wants is a general pro-business climate. Plant closure legislation is death for aerospace."

When McDonnell-Douglas bought Hughes Helicopter in 1984 for $470 million, it moved most of its southern California operations to Mesa, Arizona, a town of 150,000 just southeast of Phoenix.[69] McDonnell-Douglas found the area's good weather, open space, available cheap land, and labor supply attractive for its operations, which include testing and flying. A Douglas official lauded the advantages of being near a national forest—it means a dearth of residents to complain about noise, especially for testing. An additional appeal of the Mesa location was the significantly lower labor costs of the area. Hughes found that it had to pay engineers 22 percent more in California than in Mesa.

Austin has also emerged as a chosen center of California aerospace expansion. Perhaps the most dramatic move was that of some of Lockheed's operations to the Texas college town. Although Lockheed is based in Burbank, this particular relocation involved the company's operations in the heart of Silicon Valley at Sunnyvale. Lockheed was attracted by the heavily endowed University of Texas and the city's labor force, as well as the responsiveness of Texas to the potential move. "You want to be liked," noted a Lockheed spokesman. "Texas won out over other places, they wooed us. More than the Duke [Governor Deukmejian] would do."

Many in the industry see Lockheed's move to Austin as "one of the great success stories." The company did a good job of selling the location to its reluctant employees, including bringing in Austin housewives to "sell" the city, providing salary increases, and offering to move any employees back to California after two years if they were unsatisfied. In the end, few returned to California. "Austin is a real long-term bet," stated a Lockheed spokesman. "We moved there on a big leap of faith that you provide the business for them to continue to grow." The bet seems to have paid off. In fact, Austin has grown so quickly that some in the industry are wary of moving any more operations there. The city is seen as "saturated," with MCC, Lockheed, Motorola, and the new Sematech project. One aerospace executive expressed his doubts: "Austin has nothing that Colorado Springs doesn't have," and went on to say that it is more difficult to convince people to move to Austin than to a place like Colorado Springs. Hughes also seems somewhat hesitant about an Austin location, for it, too, finds the city crowded. Although a firm often does not want to be the only one in town, too many companies in a small city can cool other companies' interest. This is a particular concern when—as in the early 1980s—a city like Austin is growing fast in boomtown fashion, since the local labor market and infrastructure often cannot keep up.

In general, Los Angeles aerospace companies look to the South and the Mountain states for possible expansion sites, rather than to the traditional industrial Midwest or Northeast. A Northrop official stated that there was "no reason to go to the other coast," since there was nothing there that was unavailable in the West. States such as Utah, New Mexico, and Colorado, with sites only one to two hours away by plane, were preferred. But, compared with other L.A. firms, Northrop seems to display a greater tendency to stay concentrated and not venture too far from southern California.

Other L.A. aerospace companies placed importance not on closeness per se, but on accessibility. In other words, being far across the country was not as much a problem as being far from a hub airport. Therefore, places such as Orlando or cities in North Carolina, lacking direct flights to Los Angeles, were not considered workable. Litton reiterated the need to be near a major airport. "We have to get people in and out of there quickly, otherwise we don't do it." All the firms we interviewed echoed this sentiment, stressing that the airport is needed for testing and shipping or, more commonly, because the company has to move its top personnel quickly from facility to facility. And in the case of large airframe makers, such as Douglas, a direct taxiway to the airport was considered essential.

Just as labor is the major factor within the Los Angeles area, so is labor often the biggest issue affecting out-of-state expansions. Often assembly-type, less geared toward R&D and management, these facilities have lower skill requirements than operations in the Los Angeles area. Several firms stated that they found a high female labor-force participation rate to be a locational attraction. Yet some top engineering skills are needed, making universities a valuable amenity. Areas with a plentiful supply of low-cost labor may lack skilled workers and educational amenities. Conversely, an area with a skilled labor force may house other high-tech firms, meaning competition and high-skill labor shortages.[70]

Some critics have noted that aerospace firms pointedly avoid unionized areas of the country. Certainly, the L.A. companies have steered clear of traditional industrial areas in the Northeast and Midwest, although these areas have other liabilities as well. But unions do make aerospace firms wary, especially in cost-sensitive or strike-sensitive plants. A spokesman for Litton, a firm explicitly charged with union-busting, claimed, "Unions as such don't determine whether we go to a place or not—certainly the labor costs do.... If you are a big employer, the unions are going to follow you anyway. We don't avoid unions, but we don't particularly want to go to a place that's highly unionized." Other sources suggested that it is not the potential cost-push of unions that matters so much as the threat to meeting delivery dates. In other cases, the Pentagon appears to have directly encouraged union-avoidance or bargained for concessions from organized labor.

These expansions, such as the five "slave manufacturing plants" established by Hughes in the South, must be distinguished from those that directly serve government facilities. Whereas the former are driven primarily by labor considerations, the latter are driven by their need to be close to military bases and other military installations, such as early warning or missile bases, where testing and maintenance take place. For example, TRW has several hundred people working in Huntsville, Alabama, with a software-maintenance contract at NASA-Marshall, plus work there with the Army Missile Command and its subsidiary, the Missile Intelligence Agency. In addition, TRW has facilities at other military installations, including Warner Robins AFB (just south of Macon, Georgia) and Wright-Patterson AFB in Dayton, Ohio. Firms see some potential competitive advantage in being close to government customers. Although these operations give a company such as TRW a defense-electronics presence in many parts of the country, they are quite small relative to the TRW complex in Los Angeles. They are designed to serve the government customer at the site, and generally are not encouraged to develop new business on their own.

There is a final reason why Los Angeles contractors may be tempted to disperse outside California: the political advantages of broad geographic representation and, more specifically, to gain congressional support by putting a facility in a key representative's district. One L.A. aerospace official in charge of finding potential expansion sites was quite blunt:

> We were going after a big program, and I had to have options in Virginia and Texas, because those were the two prime guys sitting on the decision-makers.... We were locating it strictly on the basis of "we are going to employ a whole bunch of people in your state . . . to encourage the vote."

Nevertheless, he stressed that such a strategy is not binding, because one does not need to commit the company to a specific site before the contract is awarded: "We just put that in our plan . . . but it would have to work also . . . and it was the type of thing that you could have located anywhere: an electronic assembly operation." A congressional staffer concurred that such "on-paper" dispersion was often just window dressing. "How many of those B-1 bomber parts were actually ordered from the plants targeted in the propaganda?" she asked. "Not that many."

It becomes clear that L.A. aerospace firms have a "mental map" of the defense-business landscape. Its high points are places with good labor, schools, amenities, transportation access (particularly by air, but also by highway), and a "positive" business climate—although this is often hard to define. The ideal city size varies according to the scale and skill requirements of the operation, but it must be large enough, with existing businesses and infrastructure, for the firm to be not too much of a pioneer or the center of a one-company town. Yet it must not be too large: major Sunbelt cities like Dallas, New Orleans, and Miami are rarely mentioned, let alone northern cities such as New York, Chicago, and Detroit. The picture is of a town with from 50,000 to perhaps 1 million people, open to new businesses, and not dominated by an established, unionized employer; a place with amenities, a supportive government, a balanced labor force, and the right infrastructure. Examples include Colorado Springs, Boulder, Phoenix, Oklahoma City, Salt Lake City, Austin (despite concerns about "saturation"), Albuquerque (notwithstanding a perceived lack of good schools), Huntsville, northern Virginia, and the Greater Atlanta area.

This map clearly has a western and southern bias. It rejects most mid-western and northeastern locations. The grounds are the usual ones: snow, grime, antiquated infrastructure, high labor costs, inadequate space, unions. Behind this is an assumption that these places offer nothing that the West lacks, and that it would be foolish to locate the industry of tomorrow in the cities of yesterday. More oddly, the Pacific Northwest, a young and growing region, is missing—perhaps due to indifference, perhaps to the perception that the region's largest city, Seattle, is dominated by Boeing and therefore "off-limits."

The highest-rated cities are all Sunbelt locations, mainly in the Southwest. They represent growth, vitality, youthfulness, and a break with the industrial traditions of the past—the qualities that appeal to West Coast defense firms, match their high-tech image, and make them feel at home. These are also, curiously, the same places that military retirees find agreeable. The leading edge of the military–industrial complex rooted in the quadrant, surrounded by communities constructed with its dollars, in its image.

Future: The Calculus of Relocation

The Sunbelt cities favored in this latest round of expansion are what aerospace firms would like L.A. to be, and what it perhaps was long ago. Yet, as seen, firms will move only their most marginal operations. The aerospace core remains locked into the basin. And indeed, there are good reasons why this is—and will remain—so.

First, given the scale of investment there, relocation is enormously expensive. And the need for close integration of different operations precludes simply breaking off a chunk of the operation and moving it to Denver or Georgia. An extreme example is the satellite business. When TRW began to outgrow "Space Park," its "campuslike" complex several miles south of LAX in Redondo Beach, company officials—after considering a move—ultimately conceded that the satellite complex—with its expensive test chambers and environmental facilities, major investment in "high bay" areas, and so on—had to stay. "There is just no way that they diversify something like that geographically," noted a TRW official. North American also considered a major relocation after it outgrew its Los Angeles facilities. Possible sites included Salt Lake City, Denver, Kansas City, and some midwestern locations. But the company decided to stay, not wanting to disturb its employee base, pay enormous relocation costs, or risk its performance on key contracts and bids.

There is thus a powerful inertia in all this, especially for large companies involved in massive contracts, stressing the best products made by the best people. "[Y]ou'll locate where you are already located," a Rockwell official in El Segundo told us. "And so we are here, and we just can't pick up and move. . . . If we get another 100 B–1 bombers, we know where we are going to locate the additional [production] . . . because it is there, right?" At Northrop, our respondent answered: "If one was building one's first plant, one wouldn't put it in L.A. . . . Los Angeles would not even be in the top ten. [But] there is a terrible cost to move." At Rockwell, the response was: "Well, I think it is obvious we don't like it, but we're here." This "yes, but" mentality was repeated at Hughes: "Everybody says 'we need to move, but not me.' " An official at TRW answered: "[Y]ou're right. The cost of living here is high, the traffic situation is terrible, and we'd move if I had anything to say about it. But we'll probably stay here." The answer at Lockheed was similar: "If you were starting over, you wouldn't come to California. But aerospace grew up here."

So there is a crucial difference between what firms will do, given their present location in L.A., and what they would do if they were to start all over. This underlines the powerful and lasting role of early locational decisions made by aviation pioneers, and the subsequent the compulsion to stay. It is this anomaly that helps keep the industry concentrated in Los Angeles long after the original locational attributes have vanished or become irrelevant. Of course, most industries follow a life cycle of concentration, and then dispersion.[71] But in aerospace, the process is continually truncated by the predominance of innovative, developmental activity, on the one hand, and the absence of long production runs amenable to the assembly line, on the other.

Yet these considerations do not work with equal force for all companies. Some firms have begun to explore dispersion strategies in the nation's southwestern states, while others seem mired in southern California, no matter what the cost. Some have expanded north and west into the San Fernando Valley, Palmdale, and beyond; some have headed south into Orange County. Some seem sensitive to politics or business climate; others do not. The fact is that L.A. aerospace is not monolithic. One critical difference is in product. Producers of large airplanes (such as Lockheed, Rockwell's North American Aviation, McDonnell-Douglas, and Northrop) need correspondingly large hangars and other massive installations. Thus although Northrop is traditionally not one of the largest contractors in the state, at least before the Stealth bomber contract, it is one of the largest users of space, commanding roughly 20 million square feet of space in California by 1985. Access to an airport is essential due to the nature of the product. These companies also handle large airplane parts (such as wings and fuselage sections), often shipped in by suppliers, which necessitate access not only by air, but often also by ship, barge, or rail. In contrast, the electronics and systems houses—TRW, Litton, and Hughes Aircraft—usually produce either much smaller projects or "products" in the nonmaterial form of electronic information (e.g., software). They have greater need for office space and favor more compact assembly and testing facilities. The airframe and electronics producers also have differing labor requirements. For example, Douglas Aircraft in Long Beach still employs a significant number of blue-collar workers for large-scale production work, which contrasts with a company like Hughes.

Parallel to the distinction between airframes and electronics is a difference between "big-ticket" and multiproduct contractors. A fighter-plane or bomber prime contract is by its very nature exceedingly large, and it often makes up the lion's share of a company's revenues. Such dependence creates enormous volatility in employment and facility requirements as the monolithic project passes through the production cycle. At the other end of the spectrum are the producers of communications systems, software, and other electronic equipment that is designed and manufactured on a smaller scale. At Hughes, one official noted, "We don't build platforms; we build the electronics for it." In this regard, Hughes identifies more with Hewlett-Packard and Raytheon than with Northrop and other plane makers. Hughes, a company with about 1,500 contracts at any one time, claims that if it were to lose its 10 largest contracts, it would lose only about 40 percent of its business. TRW, similarly, has steered away from simply building the platforms (otherwise known as the "bus" or the "truck"), and instead has concentrated on the payload. In an era in which the emphasis, cost, and indeed the competitive edge in winning contracts are shifting from producing the best hardware to designing the best software (i.e., the payload), TRW is well situated for being competitive for future contracts. A firm like Lockheed would fit somewhere between the extremes of Hughes and Rockwell's North American Aviation, since it has many different contracts, yet still makes "big-ticket" items.

The nature of the product can also shape the relationship to the military customer. If a company produces a fairly standardized, self-contained item such as a McDonnell-Douglas KC-10 tanker, then there is little need for close daily contact with the Air Force. A more experimental aircraft, such as Rockwell's B-1B bomber, requires extensive testing and modification, which, in turn, makes access to military testing grounds (Edwards AFB, north of Palmdale) crucial. On the electronics side, there is an equal, if not greater, variation in the need to be close to the customer. For example, when Litton produces standard parts that will be built into airplanes, there is little need for this subcontractor to be near the military customer. Yet when a firm like TRW is involved in a project such as missile support or installation of a radar tracking system, the project may require constant attention at the actual military facility. For example, TRW has placed itself near its primary customer, the government, by setting up operations in many locations outside California: Fairfax County, Virginia (the Pentagon), Colorado Springs (USAF Space Command), Warner Robins, Georgia (Robins AFB), Dayton (Wright-Patterson AFB), and Huntsville (NASA-Marshall). The key determining factor with regard to government-customer access thus seems to be not just the end use of the product, but also the degree of tailor-made product versus standardization, and corresponding needs for design, testing, and modification in close cooperation with the customer.

One final factor is the relationship between commercial and military products. Among the area's four major military-airplane makers, only two have also traditionally made civilian aircraft—and of these, McDonnell-Douglas is the only survivor, since Lockheed dropped out after its L-1011 brought the company to the verge of bankruptcy. In contrast, North American (Rockwell) and Northrop never entered the postwar civilian-airplane market.

But product alone does not explain all the differences between L.A. aerospace contractors. Corporate history is also important: some firms—for example, Hughes—have grown through internal expansion; others—for example, Litton and TRW—through aggressive outside acquisition. The latter may find their facilities dispersed around the country, while companies that expand internally are more likely to remain where they are. Although one firm located in a high-quality residential area because its CEO prefers to live there, and has many facilities throughout the San Fernando Valley, perhaps only one-quarter of its operations are in the Los Angeles Basin. Its other operations are spread throughout the country. But several leading L.A. aerospace firms have local headquarters and other facilities that give them a greater sense of California identity. Lockheed is headquartered in Calabasas in the San Fernando Valley, northwest of the company's complex in Burbank, and two of its four operating groups—Aeronautical Systems and Information Systems—are still based in Burbank. Jack Northrop was also a local product, which may help explain why the company he founded has, in the words of one official, "a conscious commitment to California." Northrop has tended to grow in tight concentric circles, with its current Century City headquarters just down the road from its previous Beverly Hills location. Hughes also has its roots in the Los Angeles area; of the firm's six divisions, three are in El Segundo and one each in Fullerton, Torrance, and Canoga Park.

In contrast, TRW and McDonnell-Douglas have their corporate headquarters elsewhere. Yet their California components have long traditions of autonomy. When Thompson Products purchased Ramo-Wooldridge in 1958, it retained its Cleveland headquarters despite the California division's domination of aerospace. Likewise, when McDonnell bought the much larger Douglas in 1967, it kept its St. Louis corporate offices. The same year, Rockwell merged with North American Aviation. At first, it retained the Rockwell name and Pittsburgh headquarters, even though Los Angeles had assumed increasing corporate responsibilities within the hierarchy. Recently, it bowed to the primacy of its aerospace business and moved its headquarters to El Segundo. In each case, a traditional midwestern industrial company acquired a larger or prominent high-tech aerospace company in California. So certain decisions affecting facilities, budgets, and geographic strategies will be made at the out-of-state corporate headquarters. Yet there is no evidence of a diminished commitment to southern California.

To sum up: although the large prime contractors in the Los Angeles Basin exhibit many common approaches to location, two companies will often react differently to the same situation. The main reasons lie in the nature of the product and in accompanying differences in labor, facilities, product mix, and the relationship with the customer. In addition, the institutional structure of a company—shaped by its history, geographic origins, founding fathers, and present headquarters—also helps explain these different approaches. And certain locational anomalies can only be ascribed to chance and circumstance.

Past, Present, Future: Los Angeles in Review

In the end, there is the basic question: To what extent will Los Angeles remain the center of defense aerospace? Clearly, there are pressures for the industry to disperse from the crowded, expensive L.A. Basin. There are many communities throughout the South and West that are attractive to aerospace. Yet the industry remains concentrated in its southern California birthplace. The area's almost century-long history of involvement in aviation still exerts a huge inertial pull. The regional complex of major contractors, suppliers, consultants, universities, research centers, and government installations is both impressive and self-reinforcing. Above all, the vast high-tech labor market plays a crucial role in the L.A. Basin's dominance, counterbalancing the growing diseconomies of traffic congestion, housing costs, and lack of space for expansion. As long as producing for the Pentagon remains an innovation-prompted activity, this anchoring of the industry in Los Angeles will not be challenged.

True, out-of-state expansion has occurred and will continue. Yet in every sense it is marginal. It is quantitatively small, and it is concentrated in the lower-skilled, assembly-oriented, cost-sensitive parts of the industry. It does not threaten the core of the industry, which is driven by the need to find and recruit engineers, scientists, technicians, and other highly skilled workers. The historic shift—from guns and ships to high-tech aircraft and missiles packed with electronics—proved decisive in establishing California's competitive advantage in the 1950s, and there is no sign of a reversal. Nor is there any evidence that the region has lost the innovative capacity that was the basis of its meteoric industrial rise.

But what impact will the end of the cold war have on Los Angeles? The ease in tensions between East and West, combined with the American budgetary squeeze, has already led to a decline in defense contracts, which, in turn, has lowered revenues and employment at various Los Angeles defense contractors. These cutbacks will have a ripple effect in the rest of the Los Angeles economy: declines in the number of suppliers and subcontractors to the large defense companies, as well as all the businesses that serve their employees. Large contractors such as Rockwell and Hughes have already had to lay off employees, and there may be some hard times ahead, with some of the unemployed leaving town.

However, the city of Los Angeles should not be dragged down too far with the decline of the cold war. There are four reasons for the city's resilience.

First, relative to the enormous reduction in the threat of war with the Soviet Union, the initial cuts in defense spending have been surprisingly small—certainly not the "peace dividend" that so many have hoped for. (And the war in the Persian Gulf may delay them indefinitely.) Second, much of the proposed defense cuts come from closing military bases, not from canceling contracts. So Los Angeles should fare better than those towns with only Army, Navy, or Air Force bases; many of these smaller cities are heavily dependent on the bases and will suffer much the same woes as a mining- or steel-company town does after the mine or plant shuts down. Third, although Los Angeles may dominant American defense industries, defense does not wholly dominate Los Angeles. The city's other thriving sectors, including finance, trade, real estate, tourism, entertainment, and producer services, will help buffer the loss of defense dollars. Finally, the diversity, professional expertise, and technical sophistication of the Los Angeles defense-contracting sector should make it easier for its employees to find work in the civilian sector—a flexibility not found in older American industrial regions that produce warships, tanks, or ammunition.

In the end, the cold war has pumped thousands of skilled workers and engineers, invaluable technical expertise, and billions of dollars into the Los Angeles economy over the past forty-five years. One can essentially regard this as a massive high-technology economic-development program for southern California. Even if the 1990 thaw in Eastern Europe finally spreads to the American military budget, Los Angeles may have irreversibly become the high-tech center of North America.

6

The Winning Transition Team: Props, Jets, and Avionics in New England

Everyone knows that New England is really Old New England[1]—the quintessential traditional industrial region that made a successful transition to high-technology manufacturing and services. Highly urbanized, the first region of the United States to experience the Industrial Revolution, it successfully reversed a long-run industrialization trend: from 1968 to 1975, it lost 252,000 manufacturing jobs; from 1975 to 1980, it created 225,000 new ones. This remarkable rate of job creation—far more rapid than in the United States as a whole—was dominated by high-technology sectors.[2]

Two facts about New England are not widely appreciated. First, the industrial recovery of the late 1970s and early 1980s, as well as an earlier one in the 1950s, has been overwhelmingly defense-based. Massachusetts and Connecticut have been among the leading recipients of prime military contracts over the entire postwar period. And this reflects the fact that Massachusetts, in particular, was one of the key places where, during World War II, the military–scientific complex was born.[3] Avionics in Massachusetts, helicopters and aero engines in Connecticut, airplanes and missiles and control equipment on Long Island—this last outside the region in a strict sense, very much part of it in a wider functional sense[4]—have become New England's basic industries.

Second, New England is not a continuous industrial area. In a week's tour of high-tech defense-based firms in New England, the typical business tourist may start at the foot of Boston's Beacon Hill, looking across the Charles River at the Massachusetts Institute of Technology, and end in a yuppified fishing port on the shore of Long Island. In the intervening days, traveling from one part of this intensely industrialized and urbanized region to another, this visitor will tour for hours through forests, farms, and charming New England towns, each replete with white-boarded churches and schoolhouses. The urban–industrial parts of the region are still, despite vast suburban growth, essentially islands that stand out against a background of rural America: no megalopolis here, at least not in any physical sense.

This physical separateness further emphasizes the distinct urban–industrial character of each area. The key to understanding this region is that, quite unlike Los Angeles, there is no one dominant industrial tradition that has progressively swallowed the others. Essentially, there are at least three New England economies, each with quite separate origins, industrial traditions, and growth trajectories. True, as the entire complex has grown during the post–World War II period, these three industrial complexes have become more functionally interrelated, but they remain physically and economically distinct (Fig. 6.1).

Greater Boston, the first, is now so extensive that its northern suburbs wash right into neighboring New Hampshire. States in New England are more like counties elsewhere, so the state line is only a fifty-minute drive from Boston City Hall. Greater Boston encompasses scores of small New England towns, including some revered places of American history. Lexington and Concord are now prestigious suburbs close to the Beltway. Gleaming commuter trains roar past Thoreau's Walden Pond.

Boston's economy, perhaps earlier than any other in the United States, was based on the commodification of knowledge. In large part, this was due to massive plant closings and outmigration when traditional industries like shoes and textiles faltered. Unlike the Midwest, Boston viewed these setbacks as an opportunity to gear up for a new type of activity. Greater Boston today is home to a vast proliferation of information-technology industries, dependent on electronics, that trace their origins to scientific research in the region's cluster of universities, especially the Massachusetts Institute of Technology.[5] In that sense, the region should truthfully be called Greater Cambridge, with the real powerhouse of the economy on the north side of the Charles River.

One hundred miles to the southwest is the region's second nerve center: the Connecticut Valley. Its origins were quite different from those of Greater Boston. First settled a few years after the Massachusetts core, this fifty-five-mile line of industrial cities—Springfield, Hartford, Meriden–Middletown, New Haven—rose into prominence in the mid-nineteenth century with the second American Industrial Revolution. The first Industrial Revolution had created the mill towns of Lawrence, Lowell, Providence, Fall River, and New Bedford. This second revolution was more distinctively American and consisted in the mass production of precision-engineered products like guns, sewing machines, typewriters, and small machines, as well as the first large-scale information-technology industries. At Pratt & Whitney, airplane-engine manufacture was a natural outgrowth of this precision-engineering tradition. And though quite physically separate, Pratt & Whitney's major rival engine manufacturer, General Electric at Lynn, twelve miles north of Boston, comes out of a similar engineering tradition.

Some sixty to eighty miles south of Hartford, in the "bedroom communities" on both sides of Long Island Sound, is a third set of places with a distinctive tradition of early aircraft and component manufacture. Here started pioneers like Sikorsky, Chance Vought, Republic, Grumman, and Sperry. Some had begun operations in New York City but moved out in

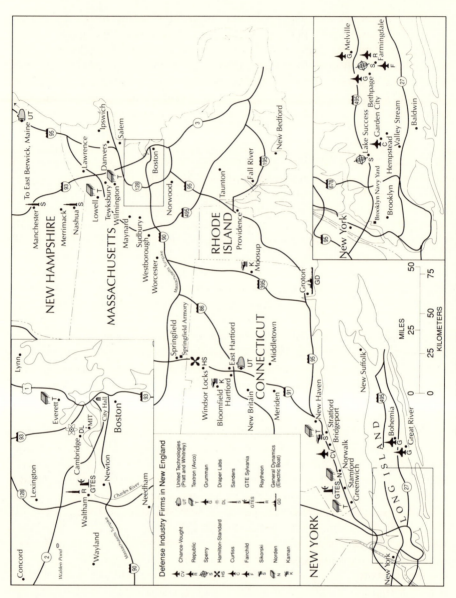

FIGURE 6.1. New England: defense-industry firms.

120

search of space and, where seaplane manufacture was involved, access to water. Three—Sikorsky, Chance Vought, and Standard—were swallowed by the giant United Aircraft Corporation in the merger mania at the end of the 1920s and were moved out into Connecticut: the first two to Bridgeport, the third to Hartford. On the Connecticut side of the Sound, therefore, this complex merges with the Hartford complex, which has absorbed it. On Long Island itself, there are three major survivors: Republic and Sperry, in Farmingdale, and Grumman, in neighboring Bethpage, twenty-five miles east of Manhattan. And separate both geographically and historically, but emerging from the same fertile New York seedbed, is the submarine-making complex of General Dynamics, formerly Electric Boat, at Groton-on-Thames at the far end of Connecticut.

Because today's northeastern defense-based enclaves have such different industrial histories, they warrant separate treatment. And, because historical chronology follows the reverse order of the route from Boston south, we will start in the New York suburbs.

The New York Aircraft Complex: An East Coast Los Angeles

Nassau County, in suburban Long Island, is unquestionably the major East Coast aerospace center. Its rise, first in the form of start-up companies in the 1930s, then in their translation into aerospace in the 1950s, uncannily parallels that of Los Angeles. Here, close together in a number of plants, are some of the major names in high-performance aircraft, missiles, and spacecraft—Republic, Grumman, Sperry, Arma, Fairchild—all heavily engaged in defense work. Sperry, with twelve separate divisions in Nassau County, is world leader in electronics, radar, guidance, systems, and specialist computers. Arma and Fairchild build jet engines, missile components, and satellite ground stations. And around them is a huge network of thousands of specialist subcontractors, which already employed more than 75,000 people by the early 1960s.[6]

The history effectively starts, as it did for Los Angeles aerospace, around 1910. And the beginnings were virtually identical. Aviation enthusiasts formed the Aeronautical Society of New York in 1908, soon renamed the Aero Club of America. Glenn Curtiss, among others, made exhibition flights at Morris Park in the Bronx. In 1909, exhibitions fled the congestion for the Garden City Aviation Field at Hempstead Plains on Long Island, where the flat topography was ideal; other fields were soon established nearby. During World War I, the area became a center for military flying, and Mitchell Field was retained as a permanent base between the wars, surviving until 1949.[7]

The first firms were born in New York City. The LWF Corporation and Chance Vought had been started in Queens, expanding greatly during World War I. In 1917 Grover Loening, an aeronautical engineer who had worked for Orville Wright, founded Loening Aircraft Engineering, building Navy fighters in a mid-Manhattan loft and then in a three-story plant on the East River. He developed innovative flying boats and amphibians, keeping the

150-employee works viable during a difficult time after World War I. The Curtiss Airplane factory opened on Hempstead Plains, Long Island, in the fall of 1917 and soon employed 3,000. It continued to make airplanes until 1931, when operations were centralized in Buffalo.[8]

Sperry and Other Newcomers

Not all early pioneers were initially aircraft builders. Some were inventors of gear and equipment essential to safe and effective guidance under conditions of battle. Edgar Sperry developed the gyrocompass, designed to overcome distorted compass readings on iron ships, a serious problem for accurate gunnery on warships and submarines. The Navy showed great interest, partly because the Germans were installing a rival compass, and in the pre–World War I naval-armaments race, ample funds were forthcoming. With backing from a New York financier, Sperry formed a manufacturing company in 1910, and three years later set up a small plant in Brooklyn, close to the Brooklyn Navy Yard.[9]

With an astute appreciation for the next expanding field, Sperry now moved into aviation. He became the world's foremost pioneer in airplane stabilization. During World War I, with his son and a few engineers, he developed patent applications on aircraft instruments, including the gyrocompass. At war's end, the Navy canceled the contract. Undeterred, he developed an "aerial torpedo," a type of flying bomb, on a Curtiss flying boat. In this and other efforts, he was encouraged by the Navy's head of aviation, Captain Washington Irving Chambers. At the end of the war, Sperry said that the Navy and War departments had used his firm as "nothing short of a 'brain mill' and experimental laboratory . . . for developing . . . intricate and even abstruse instruments of high precision." The Sperry name now became synonymous with sensitivity and precision in the control of ships, airplanes, and other technology.[10]

Centrifugal movement out of New York City and onto Long Island was well under way by 1920. Sperry's son founded the Lawrence Sperry Aircraft Company, based on the aviation department of Sperry Gyroscope, with a large workshop and hangar at Farmingdale, Long Island, and capital assets of $50,000.[11] It was this company that provided the base for the subsequent development of the Sperry empire on Long Island. A number of other small companies made airplanes on Long Island in the 1920s, including Sikorsky. But none developed full-scale production, due to the industry-wide depression. Some, like LWF, failed.[12]

Then, in the euphoria of the late 1920s, came significant firm formations, solidified during World War II. In 1925, Sherman Fairchild incorporated the Fairchild Airplane Manufacturing Company, and three years later moved to Farmingdale, producing 138 planes with a value of $1.9 million that year. Fairchild continued to make engines there through World War II. Alexander de Seversky founded his Seversky Aircraft Corporation in Manhattan in 1931 with the aim of building high-performance military airplanes, and established a plant near Farmingdale in 1934; in 1939 de Seversky was forced into retirement, and the firm was reorganized as Republic Aviation Corporation. The new firm immediately won a $3 million Army contract for the P-47 Thunderbolt. Major orders followed, and during World War II Republic produced 9,000 Thunderbolts at Farmingdale. At peak, it employed over 25,000 on its 560-acre site. Sperry likewise grew massively, building a huge plant at Lake Success for advanced instruments and employing over 32,000 at the new plant, in Garden City, and elsewhere, by 1943. And, of course, there was Grumman.[13]

These early New York firms enjoyed extraordinarily good shopworkers. Aircraft building at that time was a one-of-a-kind or few-of-a-kind business. Wood, fabric, wire, and simple metal fittings were assembled by skilled woodworking and metalworkers, the great majority first- or second-generation immigrants. Italians, Germans, Poles, and other Middle Europeans, who had learned their skills in the apprentice systems of their homelands, were attracted by the challenges the new industry offered. New York, as a major gateway city, provided a pool of these skilled mechanics. They moved from shop to shop.

The Grumman Story

Grumman, which ultimately became dominant firm in this area, started in January 1930 with a staff of twenty-one. Nearly all were former employees of Loening, which was moving to Bristol, Pennsylvania. Roy Grumman—son of a Norwalk, Connecticut, carriage maker; Cornell- and MIT-educated; an ex-Navy test pilot—had been manager at Loening since 1920.[14] Making a bold decision to concentrate on military aircraft, Grumman developed a fighter for the Navy with a new Wright engine. Reflecting Grumman's personal preference, the firm stressed informal small-scale, "familial" style, high quality, and great engineering innovation: in quick succession came stressed-skin construction, retractable landing gear, unorthodox fighter design, and the utility amphibian. The approach paid off. In 1932, Grumman was still the newcomer among half a dozen competitors for Navy work; by 1937, it was leader of only three. Sales rose from $109,700 in 1930 to $276,100 in 1932 and $1,719,000 in 1936.[15]

Grumman's history shows how contractors often metamorphosed several times in early stages. The firm kept outgrowing its premises at extraordinary speed. The first plant, at Baldwin, about twenty miles east of Manhattan on the south shore of Long Island, gave way in 1931 to a bigger plant at Valley Stream, about eight miles east, and a year later to yet bigger premises at Farmingdale, sixteen miles farther east. Grumman finally moved into even larger and better-equipped premises at Bethpage, a few miles north of Farmingdale, in 1936, expanding there in 1938.[16] Thus as in Los Angeles, the move was always toward the urban periphery. On Long Island, Grumman was a major agent of suburbanization.

During World War II, the firm grew into a huge operation, producing more military planes than most other aircraft companies, and adding 19,000 to a prewar payroll of 6,500. Afterward, Grumman made a precocious decision not to get into vertical flight. Instead, it systematically pursued high-tech military and space work. Although the company had acquired its first electrical engineer only in mid-1939, it later went heavily into avionics. Its culminating triumph, the lunar module for the historic 1969 moon landing, had more than 1 million components and required massive subcontracting. MIT Instrumentation Laboratories got the guidance systems for the command and lunar modules; the descent engine for the lunar module came from TRW; and the ascent engine was built by Bell and the Rocketdyne division of North American Rockwell.[17]

The basic nature of the Grumman operation remained unaffected by its scale. During World War II, General Motors agreed to produce Grumman airplanes in spare plants. Grumman's historian tells the tale:

> What followed was the clash of two worlds. GM started out with the idea that it would show the aeronautical industry in general and Grumman in particular how to mass-produce airplanes. Grumman started out with the idea that GM would be lucky if it managed to produce one airplane. GM, or Eastern, was more wrong than right; Grumman more right than wrong. ... The essential difference, of course, was that the automobile-maker and the aircraft-builder produced two vehicles with vastly different requirements and by different production methods.[18]

The essential difference lay not in scale but in the fact that aircraft tolerances were much tighter, coupled with the fact that in aircraft the aluminum skin has to carry the load, and parts have to be constantly modified on the job. Interestingly, the same rules proved true on perhaps the most sophisticated construction job in world history, the lunar module. Tom Kelly, the Grumman engineer in charge, had this exchange with writer Richard Thruelsen:

> *Kelly:* There is no real production involved in spacecraft. They are handmade. It's almost like the old cottage industry where an individual craftsman painstakingly molds or files or does something with great skill.
>
> *Thruelsen:* It is closer to the old XFF-1, the first Grumman plane, for instance. Where, at Baldwin and Valley Stream, they had an order for, originally, I think, two planes, and they built them by hand.
>
> *Kelly:* That's right. Much more like that, except that this involved very high technology. Very sophisticated, very demanding equipment.[19]

In 1986, 22,000 workers checked in each morning at the huge Grumman complex at Bethpage, originally established far out in rural Long Island but since swallowed up by the suburban sprawl of the 1950s and 1960s. This is quintessential suburbia. The original Levittown is a few miles away. But as Grumman has grown on Long Island and the suburbs have grown around it, it has changed character. It has become more and more an electronics and data-processing firm involved in high-tech prototypical work. "An aircraft," our Grumman respondent told us, "has become a thing to carry electronics." And in this process, the firm has increasingly found itself in complex contractual relationships that have important impacts on its location. Customer requirements, whether from the military or from major contractors like IBM, and political pressures may leave the company little freedom of action.

In any case, we heard, "Long Island is now a very expensive place to do business." Although nearly two-thirds of Grumman's 36,000 employees worldwide remain at the Bethpage plant, which is also the site of administration and much of R&D, since about 1980 the tendency is for aerospace manufacturing to be propelled to other locations by both push and pull factors to other locations. Officials claim that the area, dominated by environmentally sensitive suburban communities, is not favorable to business. Traffic congestion and long commute times—seventy-five minutes "if lucky" for a thirty-two-mile drive—are getting steadily worse.

And besides, costs are becoming more and more crucial for the operating divisions, both in civilian and in defense business. Basic manufacturing will stay on Long Island, but "separable" new operations—each under its own vice president—will be floated off elsewhere. Construction cost differentials, especially for very expensive operations like super-secret rooms, might be significant. Grumman's new facility at Melbourne, Florida, costs 30 percent less to run than an equivalent in Bethpage, and this is typical. In extreme cases, costs might even be two-thirds lower in the South. Not only are direct costs like utility charges much lower—less than half—but living costs are also much less. Unskilled labor is also much easier to attract elsewhere, and even skilled engineering talent is becoming scarce in the Northeast because of competition from small high-tech firms. The old tradition, then, that if you worked in electronics on Long Island you came here, is weakening. One advantage is the second income earned by spouses working in New York City, but this apparently does not outweigh the handicaps. Senior managers might be difficult to persuade to move, but those who have moved found that they liked the change. And although previously Grumman had no need to consider land costs, it now has only one remaining piece of land within its perimeter. When this is full, the company faces costs of $500,000 to 700,000 an acre against $5,000 to 15,000 an acre elsewhere. But relocation presents a number of problems, including the difficulties of trucking materials and flying senior management back and forth. A new plant would have to be built in the corridor between North Carolina and Florida. And access to a good airport is essential.[20] For its surveillance-equipment project in Melbourne, for example, Grumman had to locate an airport that could accommodate 727 aircraft without much commercial traffic. Beyond that, Grumman would not want to compete with other major corporations in the same area, which would inevitably drive up costs. In addition, Grumman could not easily move far from its customers: "Defense is a tough business," we were told, "your customer lives with you." For example, a maintenance contract with IBM at Fishkill, New York, required Grumman to locate within ten miles of the IBM plant (later extended to twenty to thirty miles). Air Force contracts would be limited to a radius of 100 miles around Washington. As a result of all these constraints, Grumman remains surprisingly centralized on Long Island.

As a Navy supplier—the Navy still accounted for two-thirds of Grumman's $3.3 billion in revenues in 1988—Grumman is now reeling under the shocks of defense-budget cutbacks. Grumman lost its chance to build the Navy's next attack aircraft, and its A-6 Intruder bomber, F-14 fighter, and electronic jammer craft are also in deep trouble. Grumman eliminated 1,500 jobs in 1987, 2,600 jobs in 1988, and 3,100 in 1989, most of them on Long Island.[21] The losses fell predominantly on blue-collar manufacturing workers.

In conjunction with a nearby Fairchild closing that idled 5,000 workers in 1987, the Grumman cutbacks have had a powerfully negative effect on the Long Island economy. While never as fully elaborated as the Los Angeles economy, Long Island has developed over the decades a system of hundreds of subcontractors and suppliers in the immediate environs. The A-6 attack bomber, for instance, engaged 2,500 workers at Grumman, but supports another 5,900 in the region.[22] As Grumman projects are canceled and new bids lost, suppliers heavily dependent on Grumman are having a difficult time shifting their sights elsewhere.

Meanwhile, one rather spectacular recent relocation decision illustrates how Grumman's activities have been forced to change with the rise of Star Wars and space defense. In 1988, Grumman let it be known that its space systems group was looking for a new home. The top competitors read like a roster of the gunbelt: Atlanta, the Carolinas, northern Virginia, Denver and Colorado Springs, Huntsville, Dallas–Fort Worth, Houston, and San Diego. Ultimately, Houston ended up the winner.

Wooed enthusiastically by an economic-development council formed in 1984 to combat the city's oil slump, Grumman apparently responded favorably to several Houston attributes. First, Houston has NASA's Johnson Space Center. Second, it offered extraordinarily low costs. Compared with the head-quarters area around Bethpage, it cost half as much to build in Houston; housing costs were one-third as much; and property taxes 60 percent lower. Third, Houston offered Grumman land at an old Army Air Corps base, a perfect and inexpensive proposition. Last but not least, Houston seemed to have "the right stuff." "The political leaders in the state really wanted us to come," said a Grumman executive quoted in a New York newpaper. "They are not liberals who don't have leverage. These guys are militarists, like us."[23]

As the cold war frontier shifts toward space, Grumman finds itself forced to focus on its defense electronics and space operations, currently less than 20 percent of its sales. In turn, this shrinks its work force and shifts its occupational mix away from production workers and toward white-collar engineers and technicians. Space-oriented work draws it away from its traditional home on Long Island. The Houston facility will employ 1,500 people, of whom few will be relocated from Long Island, and the Texas payroll is anticipated to grow to 4,000 if the firm wins key space and aircraft parts-building contracts. In another recent decentralizing shift, Grumman operates a $1 billion management oversight contract for space station work in Reston, Virginia, drawn there by forces we will document in Chapter 9. So even Grumman, the nation's most successful military airframe builder outside of the South and West, is slowly shuffling toward the locus of its major competitors.

The Connecticut Shore

On the other side of Long Island Sound, in Stamford and Norwalk, is another cluster of firms, which moved from New York City in the 1920s to become part of the United Aircraft complex. Among the aerospace survivors, the most important is Sikorsky, founded by a Russian émigré in the 1920s. The Sikorsky helicopter company moved from its original New York City site to Bridgeport in the late 1920s when it was taken over by United Technologies. Although Sikorsky experimented with helicopters at that time, he was diverted into work on Pan Am's famous Clipper flying boats. It was not until 1938, at the start of the defense buildup, that the United Aircraft management decided to back further work. The first helicopter flight, a mere ten seconds in duration, took place on September 14, 1939. Progress was rapid, and military deliveries started in April 1942; eventually, 580 were delivered. Facing difficult problems of adjustment after World War II, the firm concentrated on military helicopters after the start of the Korean War.[24]

Another, indirectly related industrial tradition deserves a chapter to itself. Aerospace and avionics are the central theme of the New England renaissance, but—as already seen—many of the firms around Long Island Sound have had long associations with the Navy, especially the Brooklyn Navy Yard. And some twenty miles east of the estuary of the Connecticut River, at Groton near the mouth of the smaller Thames, stands the electric boat division of General Dynamics, one of the main producers of submarines for the United States Navy. Its origins are curiously similar to those of the nearby aerospace companies. John Holland, an Irish immigrant to the United States, taught school for a living—first in Boston, then in Paterson, New Jersey—and dabbled in submarine design at night. He built his first model at Paterson in 1878; he then lived in Newark and worked in New York, eventually incorporating his own company in 1893. His contacts with Lieutenant William Kimball in the Brooklyn Navy Yard proved useful, but were insufficient to overcome the prejudices of the Navy's conservative top brass. Although Holland rarely exhibited impatience, he once asked, "What will the Navy require next, that my boat should climb a tree?"[25]

By the late 1890s, prospects for the submarine had been transformed by two unrelated developments: safe and efficient electric storage batteries, replacing petroleum engines, and the outbreak of war with Spain. At this point, Isaac Leopold Rice, a brilliant lawyer, professor, and financier, arrived on the scene. He had founded the Electric Storage Battery Company of Philadelphia to make batteries and had soon acquired almost every competitor.

The prospect that the submarine might use battery power naturally attracted him. In the summer of 1898, he began to finance Holland and then formed the Electric Boat Company, which acquired the assets of the Holland Torpedo Boat Company. That same year, the company rented the Goldsmith and Tuthill Yard in New Suffolk, a summer resort in Cutchogue Harbor, at the far eastern end of Long Island. In 1899, it won a Navy contract for six submarines.[26]

From the start, Holland found the atmosphere at Electric Boat inhospitable. The brilliant inventor-pioneer was pushed aside by more "practical-minded" managers, and he finally left the company in 1904, aged sixty-three. Earlier, Rice forged a series of foreign agreements, including one with Vickers of England that lasted from 1900 to 1939. Without these, Electric Boat could not have survived. "That is what we live on principally," he told Congress in 1908. Soon after the first Navy sale, he began to develop a plan to make Electric Boat into a major provider of international arms, by arranging a licensing deal with Vickers (the Royal Navy had a huge budget compared with the U.S. Navy).[27]

The oddity was that—apart from the tiny New Suffolk station—the Electric Boat Company was a shell, with most of the work done by subcontractors. In the early years, Electric Boat never had a shipyard of its own. The headquarters were in New York; hulls were built by Bethlehem at its plants in Quincy and San Francisco, and in a Seattle yard; the engines came from Bayonne and elsewhere. Determined to have their own yard, despite the fact that the New York directors refused to provide funds, the technical staff, led by Frank Cable, raised their own capital. They opened a subsidiary, the New London Ship and Engine Company (Nelesco) at Groton-on-Thames in Cable's home state of Connecticut. There they completed the company's first twelve diesel submarines, begun at Quincy.[28]

After World War I, Electric Boat fell on hard times. From 1918 to 1931, the company did not build a single submarine. It limped by, building commercial ferries and tugboats, repairing ships, and, doing assorted foundry work and odd jobs, was shrunk back on to the Groton yard. Yet when orders started again, Electric Boat was the only submarine manufacturer to have survived the Depression. War brought enormous expansion at Groton. In 1936, at the start of growth, the company could build perhaps three boats a year. By 1944, with $20 million of Navy investment, it could turn out three a month and had 14,000 workers, including many women. Groton built seventy-four submarines during World War II, more than the combined output of the five other shipyards.[29]

Electric Boat was the cornerstone of General Dynamics. John Jay Hopkins, Electric Boat's president, created General Dynamics in 1952. "A regal adventurer, Hopkins was quick to respond" to the challenge of new technology.[30] "Grow or die" were the words he used. He was anxious to acquire new territory, catering to Admiral Hyman Rickover's enthusiasm for the nuclear submarine. He acquired Convair from Floyd Odlum, a master of "special situations" who wanted to be divested of it. The deal meshed perfectly with Hopkins's high-risk strategy to build what he himself called a "General Motors of defense." The result was a mega-organization with 106,000 employees and nine divisions, each with its own jealously guarded traditions, each essentially a corporation in its own right.[31]

The Connecticut Valley Complex: From Six-Shooters to Jets

The Connecticut Valley, from New Haven through Hartford up to Springfield in Massachusetts, is the industrial heart of New England. Yet it is a very different New England from, say, Greater Boston. This is a major center of traditional engineering industries. Despite its role as insurer to America, Hartford is an old-style blue-collar town, in a way that New York and Boston no longer are. And that particularly applies to East Hartford. The visitor, leaving downtown and crossing the railroad tracks and the Connecticut River, immediately senses that this is the factory side of town. For East Hartford is home to Pratt & Whitney, one of the core businesses of the sprawling United Technologies Corporation (UTC) complex, which seems to occupy most of the manufacturing space in the valley floor.

It is not UTC's only home. The multinational giant's 185,000 workers are found in many other subsidiaries: Otis Elevator in Farmington; Hamilton Standard, the propeller manufacturer, in Windsor Locks; Sikorsky in Stratford; Norden in Norwalk; Carrier in Syracuse, New York; other divisions in Indiana and Colorado and California. No fewer than two in five of its workers are overseas. Even Pratt & Whitney has outgrown East Hartford, its original home, and has established offshoots in Columbus, Georgia; North Berwick, Maine; and West Palm Beach, Florida. Most of these operations are where they started, before UTC acquired them.[32] But UTC's corporate headquarters are in Hartford. Pratt & Whitney started its shop in 1860 in East Hartford, and is that city's dominant employer. Indeed, UTC is probably the largest private employer in Connecticut. The Pratt & Whitney division employs 30,000 in the state; the entire company, 45,000.

Pratt & Whitney is another "founding fathers" story, except that this time, the name is really that of the founding grandfathers. In the mid-nineteenth century, the Connecticut Valley, between Springfield, Massachusetts, and New Haven, Connecticut, had become the world's greatest center of mass-produced precision-engineering goods. This was a result of the methods of gun manufacture first employed at the U.S. government's Springfield armory from 1814, and then emulated by former employees who went into commercial manufacturing, such as Colt and Smith & Wesson. After the Civil War, with the catastrophic decline in the demand for guns, these armorers began to apply the same production methods to a great variety of both capital and consumer goods. Both Francis A. Pratt and Amos Whitney worked for the Colt gun works between 1850 and 1852. They went into partnership in 1854 and opened their own gun and machinery works in 1860. By the end of the century, reorganized as part of the Niles-Bement-Pond Company, the firm was producing machine tools, gun-making machinery, typewriters, bicycles, and many kinds of industrial machinery.[33] But neither Pratt nor Whitney ever conceived of making aircraft engines.

The true founding father was Frederick B. Rentschler. In 1925 Rentschler, a former board member of Wright Aeronautical Company, and Dr. George W. Meade effectively took over Pratt & Whitney in order to develop air-cooled radial engines. Obtaining most of their venture capital from the Niles Tool Company of Connecticut, which owned the well-established machine-tool concern in Hartford, they decided to lease idle space and draw on the firm's general mechanical reputation and pool of skilled labor.[34]

Rentschler was then thirty-seven. A 1909 liberal-arts graduate of Princeton, he had become interested in aircraft-engine manufacture as a World War I serviceman. From 1919 to 1924, he had managed the Wright plant at Paterson, New Jersey, with an able team including Donald Brown, George Mead (an MIT-trained engineer), and Andrew Van Dean Willgoos. But he found himself at loggerheads with the directors on commitment to R&D funding. A passionate advocate of the minority view that the future of the airplane lay in bigger craft, higher speed, and greater ranges involving more powerful engines, Rentschler proposed to Pratt & Whitney that it move into the production of air-cooled radial engines—a step sought by the Navy's Rear Admiral W. A. Moffett. As described in chapter 4, Clarence Vought hoped to incorporate the engine in his plane, and there were high hopes that the Navy would buy it. Pratt & Whitney, Rentschler found, had surplus cash and surplus space. The locality had plenty of skilled labor and small engineering shops that could act as subcontractors.[35]

The Hartford management accepted and contributed $250,000, half the cost. They agreed to form a new Pratt & Whitney Aircraft Company, independent of the parent company but with two common directors: Colonel Edward A. Deeds and Sanford G. Etherington. Deeds, as we have seen, had helped build up Dayton as a major aeronautical center. Now he switched allegiance. Already chairman of Niles-Bement-Pond, he was instrumental in negotiating the project and getting Pratt & Whitney to finance it. This, then, is a clear case of two founding fathers who deserted their native city. Had this decision not been made, Dayton and not Hartford would surely have become the leading center of American air-engine production.[36]

In August 1925, Rentschler moved from Dayton to Hartford with his team of six top Wright people—Mead, Willgoos, and Ryder, all gifted engineers, and Brown, Marks, and Borrup, each with extensive machine-shop experience in the engine-design field. The parent company's shop was so well equipped that virtually everything could be fabricated in-house. Between June and December 1925, the team developed the engine that became the Wasp. It took to the air in May 1926, in a Navy test flight in Washington.[37]

The timing was strategic. Two months later, the Morrow Board report recommended a big increase in naval air procurement, and orders flowed. The Wasp was an immediate success, arriving at exactly the right moment to go into a new generation of high-performance aircraft that quite suddenly lifted the American aircraft industry into a top world position. By 1930, together with its more powerful sister, the Hornet, the Wasp represented more than 60 percent of total shipments of the largest twenty-five firms. Wasps and Hornets powered virtually all Navy and a large share of Army Air Corps planes as well as 90 percent of commercial aircraft. They powered such notable planes as the AAC's long-range high-altitude bomber and the Navy's fast carrier task force. The first strategic bomber, the XB-17 Flying Fortress of 1935 built for the AAC, had Hornet engines at its trials. It incidentally sparked a Wright–Rentschler rivalry that lasted throughout World War II.[38]

This was a classic new firm. One observer recalled:

> They were not only an able people in those early years, but they literally worked like hell. . . . They all knew that there was a hell of a lot to be done. You see, they were a little outfit that had blossomed, early in life, into a big one, and they did not have the ponderousness that goes with size.[39]

A veteran later remembered:

> It never occurred to any of us in that era that the hosiery industry outranked us in annual sales dollar volume. It never struck us that if you had put our entire industry into one unit, it would have numbered less than the employees of a single General Motors automotive division.[40]

It was the era of late trust-building, and the air industry was not immune. During 1928, Rentschler took the lead in forming United Aircraft, embracing Pratt & Whitney Aircraft, Hamilton Standard (propeller manufacturer), Sikorsky Aircraft, and Chance Vought, together with five airlines that became United Air Lines. The company moved all three newly incorporated companies into Connecticut—Chance Vought to the company's Hartford base—necessitating a move from the original building on Capitol Avenue, Hartford, across the river to new premises at East Hartford. By 1940, United was the second largest aircraft manufacturer, and Connecticut was one of the industry's leading centers, with 13.5 percent of national employment.[41]

During the war, Pratt & Whitney Aircraft and its licensees produced 50 percent of all the horsepower required by the American armed forces. This, curiously, put them at a disadvantage. For the federal government determined that existing engine manufacturers, notably Pratt & Whitney, should continue to produce propeller engines after the war. It would finance two electrical companies with knowledge of turbine manufacture, General Electric and Westinghouse, to develop jet engines. Pratt & Whitney nonetheless financed development of jet engines without government assistance—a decision that enabled it in the 1950s, to focus on the civilian-jet market while GE remained heavily defense-based.[42]

Pratt & Whitney, we began to realize, had an entirely different locational calculus from the airframe companies we had interviewed in Los Angeles and on Long Island. Both the firm's traditions and its relatively self-contained

East Hartford location were not at all the same as in Los Angeles. This emerged as soon as we began to talk recruitment. Pratt & Whitney recruits its top scientists and engineers both locally and from all over the country. With one or two exceptions, it has no special relationship with Connecticut universities. Back in the 1950s, UTC realized that higher scientific education in the locality was inadequate. It therefore persuaded the Rensselaer Polytechnic Institute, based in Troy, New York, to establish the Hartford Graduate Center. Much later, UTC gave money to the University of Hartford and the University of Connecticut to establish scientific centers. Today, UTC funds these centers to the extent of $8 to $9 million a year, mainly to help provide continuing educational opportunities for its younger research workers and to train manufacturing engineers who do not readily migrate from one place to another.

Hartford, our respondent argued, is quite a strong locality for national recruitment. It is close to New York; there is local skiing and sailing; and the general standard of living and local environment are good. The company has encountered no difficulties in keeping all UTC's R&D work at the Hartford headquarters site. About one-third of the facility's work is corporate, one-third for the firm's divisions, and one-third directly contracted from government. Under the previous president, the firm had relocated its headquarters to downtown Hartford, for reasons of image-building, but the new president intended to take it out to the suburbs.

The blue-collar labor market is of course, quite different. Pratt & Whitney needs large numbers of skilled workers. It recruits locally, drawing on a good pool of skilled machinists that has effectively grown up with the company. There is a great deal of fluctuation in demand, although UTC's multiple contracts gave the workers a greater degree of stability than did other aircraft companies. Perhaps because it is so heavily dependent on blue-collar labor and hence cost-sensitive, perhaps because UTC is a multidivisional company with such diverse origins, the firm's manufacturing operations, in sharp contrast to its R&D, are widely decentralized. The firm has located major facilities at North Berwick, Maine, and Columbus, Georgia. Its object is to find places with loyal, low-cost, nonunionized, unskilled, but trainable labor. Incentives had also played a role, our respondent surmised. Both the North Berwick and Columbus facilities make parts that are assembled in East Hartford, since the necessary specialized labor and facilities are there.[43]

United Technologies Corporation's contemporary locational choices differ from those attractive to Los Angeles firms, even though the factors cited are quite similar. Critical in such decisions, our respondents stressed, are the needs of each operating division. From the military viewpoint, some groups must be sited near bases, especially for maintenance. For instance, UTC maintains a Sikorsky plant close to the Army base at Fort Rucker, and an Air Force facility at San Antonio. Beyond this type of link, the important criteria are labor costs, nonunionization, and labor availability. UTC reported that it seeks the cheapest labor for a particular job at a particular time, and it considers only right-to-work states. Next in importance comes access to the interstate highway system. A site must be within a twelve- to fourteen-hour truck ride from Hartford, which rules out a site in Alabama and narrows the choice to a belt from Virginia to Georgia. Then follows the availability of the right kind of plant. Political factors enter into the final corporate decision only if the other factors are nicely balanced. The company has never considered a site in the Mountain or Pacific states, and has never located a defense facility in the Midwest or parts of the Mid-Atlantic region. Cleveland and New Jersey, we were told, were absolutely out of the question on labor grounds. It would consider almost anywhere else that met its criteria, but some sites—Birmingham and Huntsville, Alabama, and San Antonio, Texas—are thought expensive, the last two precisely because they are military bases. Company officials fear that the right quality of labor would not be available at the right price.

But recently, the tendency has been to contract back to the Hartford base.[44] Within two years, twenty-three strategic business units have been cut to three, but the company might expand elsewhere again if the right opportunity came. According to our respondents: "With this company it's hard to know"; Pratt & Whitney is "tied into the bedrock" here; Sikorsky would be difficult to move because it is like Pratt & Whitney; Hamilton Standard and Norden could fairly easily be relocated out of Connecticut, although operating management would fight the move.

For all its size and internationalism, UTC has not formed the core of a larger aerospace agglomeration. The company is not at all closely tied to the ups and downs of the Connecticut economy because it operates and sells worldwide. There has been a limited number of local spin-offs, all defense-oriented. The new firms generally perform the same tasks they did before they broke away, all of them with fewer than fifty employees. But together, they had generated fewer than 1,000 jobs since 1970, our respondent estimated.

The Connecticut Valley contains a number of other small defense firms that have developed there because of the general industrial traditions of the area. One, Kaman, in Bloomfield, Connecticut, seven miles north of Hartford, had just passed its fortieth anniversary when we visited it in 1986. Founded in Bloomfield in 1945 as a helicopter company, it diversified into military–scientific work in the 1950s, first at Albuquerque, then in Colorado Springs. Since then, the company has grown to more than twenty-four subsidiaries working in a broad range of technologies and industries from high-tech defense to industrial-parts distribution and musical instruments. Two thousand of its 6,500 employees are here, primarily still making helicopters for the Navy. Because of past crises and strategic planning, Kaman keeps diversified, with over 2,000 contracts, mainly in specialized defense work, and subcontracts extensively to other aircraft companies like Boeing and Lockheed.

On the defense side, Kaman officials estimate that one-third of the staff is professional and technical, one-third administrative, and one-third blue-collar. They do not often recruit new graduates, but prefer to hire experienced professionals from all over the country, especially from leading aircraft-production centers like Los Angeles and Dallas. So they do not have an active campus recruiting program. Links with local universities are not critical. The nature of Kaman's work takes its management and technical people all over the country: on marketing to potential customers; on proposal writing; on design reviews, engineering changes, and logistics support; and to solve day-to-day problems. This travel is mainly to other suppliers like Boeing (in Seattle or Wichita) or Lockheed (in California or Georgia), to specialist suppliers, and to defense contractors. "The aerospace industry," we were told, "is a relatively small circle of businesses. Everyone knows each other. While competing for some contracts, contractors may team up and work together or do subcontract work for each other." Much of this travel is out of the local Hartford airport, which the company finds quite adequate for most purposes; occasionally, travelers go via New York.

Skilled blue-collar labor, we heard, was becoming scarce in the area, with unemployment down to 4 percent; it could take two weeks to find a materials handler. Housing costs and congestion, our respondents recognized, could pose problems in the future, and they registered the usual complaints about the business climate. But, as was very evident on our visit, Kaman has plenty of land for expansion. In general, the problems that loomed large for firms in Los Angeles or on Long Island did not seem very important here. And that, we surmised, is equally true for UTC, Kaman's neighbor down the road.

Kaman's greatest worry is the prospect of reduced military spending. It sees much more competition for contracts and few of them awarded. Cuts in defense and associated program slips or delays will significantly change the way defense contractors now do business. Particularly, the shifting of increased financial burden of investment to the industry is driving some contractors out of the business. They are pushing for more industry–government cooperation and less adversarial counterproductivity.

With all this military activity, from Sikorsky to General Dynamics to UTC, the state of Connecticut is per capita the most defense-dependent state in the nation, three times the national average. More than 25 percent of its manufacturing shipments go to defense. In addition to those mentioned, sizable Connecticut firms such as the Singer Corporation, Colt Firearms, and Avco make military products ranging from machine guns to satellite surveillance devices. During periods of defense buildup, as when our interviews took place, Connecticut is flush with cash and jobs. In the mid-1980s, the state had one of the strongest economies in the nation. It was the richest beneficiary of the Reagan buildup. In 1983, the Pentagon spent over $5 billion in the small state, or $1,625 for each resident, far exceeding the per capita spending for military equipment in any other state.[45]

During "normal" times, Connecticut's unemployment rate mirrors that of the nation. But during the Reagan buildup, it plummeted to a low of 4.3 percent compared with 7.1 percent nationally. Pentagon dollars also feed into the state's income stream. By 1984, Connecticut ranked second in the nation in per capita income. In contrast, during the post–Vietnam defense contraction of the early 1970s, the state's unemployment rate escalated to more than 12 percent. In the 1990s, defense cuts could mean anywhere from 5 to 65 percent of the defense-dependent work force.[46]

Greater Boston: Aircraft Engines and Avionics

Boston's two-stage industrial renaissance—the first in the 1950s, the second in the late 1970s and 1980s—has won Massachusetts its reputation as perhaps the world's most outstandingly adaptive old industrial region. It has been based principally on the electronics industries that stem from research in Cambridge laboratories. These postwar success stories cluster around the interchanges of Highway 128, the city's original beltway. All this is part of Sunday-magazine legend. What is less known is that much of this activity depends for its existence on defense contracts, in which for the past twenty years Massachusetts has stood second only to California.

Few could have predicted that development in the years down to Pearl Harbor. Massachusetts' early electronics manufacturers grew out of a very old tradition of electrical manufacture in the region, which goes back to Edison's great inventions of the 1870s. One of the early results was the establishment in Lynn, once an independent factory town, now one of Boston's northern suburbs, of Pratt & Whitney's chief competitor in the aircraft engine business: General Electric.

General Electric's survival in Massachusetts was the result of mergers and conscious business strategy after considerable migration around the East Coast. In 1878, Professors Thomson and Houston of Philadelphia developed an effective electrical generator, and two years later founded the Thomson-Houston Company in New Britain, Connecticut, to manufacture it. Meanwhile, in Lynn, an early center of shoemaking, a former shoe salesman named Charles A. Coffin was building his empire. Eventually Coffin's group absorbed the little generator company and merged in 1892 to form General Electric. It was decided that the Lynn plant should concentrate on lighter products, the Edison works at Schenectady on heavier products, and the Edison works at Harrison, New Jersey, on lamps.[47]

The Lynn works was a precision-engineering operation early on. One of General Electric's fastest-growing areas of business was in turbo-alternator manufacture, an activity with strict standards of analytical engineering to achieve high revolution speeds. The turbine blades for this work were engineered and manufactured at Lynn. Its major competitor was the Pittsburgh-based Westinghouse concern.[48] GE and Westinghouse received a great boost during World War II, when the federal government financed their development of jet engines, notably through GE's locations in Lynn and in Evendale, outside Cincinnati. Lynn's fate was sealed when the government constructed a new plant for GE at nearby Everett in 1941.[49]

The electrical engineering traditions of the Boston area also begat electronics. And this was to prove the really decisive development. For Massachusetts' distinctive contribution to the military–industrial complex was in avionics, and this contribution came directly out of research at the Massachusetts Institute of Technology. What Caltech did for rocket propulsion in Greater Los Angeles, MIT did for electronics in Greater Boston. In both places, the creation of dedicated, large-scale scientific research laboratories working for national defense began almost simultaneously, at the start of World War II.

In Boston, this military high-tech dividend was dominated by a few key individuals and institutions. In the 1920s and 1930s, Dugald Jackson built up MIT's electrical engineering department, founded as early as 1882, to a position of towering preeminence in electrical and electronics research. In 1920, Vannevar Bush, an associate professor at MIT, made an adventurous decision to team up with his old Tufts classmate Laurence Marshall and, with self-taught machinist John A. Spencer, to form the company that became Raytheon. At first, Raytheon manufactured thermostatic controls for electric irons. It then moved into vacuum tubes for radios, which involved a long and grueling patent fight with the AT&T–RCA pool. Resolving this by a cross-licensing agreement in 1928, Raytheon barely survived the Depression, remaining a small and experimentally oriented firm and moving from its original Cambridge base into old mills, first next door to Newton, then to Waltham.[50]

During World War II, Raytheon stood to benefit enormously from demands for radar. In 1940, as director of the federal National Research and Defense Committee, Bush played an indirect role in bringing the British radar team to work with Professor Edward Linley Bowles of MIT on radar devices, thus forming the nucleus of the (deliberately misnamed) Radiation Laboratory at MIT. MIT's James Killian arranged lab and hangar space in a few hours, beating out the competition from Bolling Field in Washington, D.C. The "Rad Lab" worked on three key items: a flying radar, a gun-laying system, and a long-range navigation system. Bowles, who worked with Raytheon, persuaded his British colleagues to let the firm, still a small one with a mere 1,400 employees, compete with Bell Laboratories on manufacturing the necessary magnetron equipment. By early 1945, Raytheon had increased production forty times, and was producing 80 percent of all magnetrons. Faced with bankruptcy at war's end and forced to reorganize, Raytheon prospered in 1950 with a test rocket that, building on its wartime work, intercepted and destroyed low-flying aircraft. By 1950, boosted again by the Korean War, the company was a vast undertaking, with five large and twenty smaller buildings, many bought from the Navy on terms that gave the government priority use.[51]

Each of these Massachusetts initiatives was timed with beautiful precision. The birth of electrical engineering at MIT came at the right time to feed basic research in the American electrical industry. The creation of Raytheon came at just the right moment to supply the burgeoning commercial radio industry of the 1920s. MIT's entry into radar came in the critical two-year period before Pearl Harbor, when America was girding itself for war but had not yet made the commitment. Bush's move to Washington virtually guaranteed MIT a leading role in wartime electronics research. Raytheon, which had gone through bad times as a vacuum-tube manufacturer in the 1920s, became heavily involved in military contracts through its wartime connections with MIT's Radiation Lab, and achieved a breakthrough with a commercially viable magnetron, which set it on a rising trajectory.[52]

MIT itself became a defense contractor unlike any other American university. MIT's willingness to take military contracts during the 1950s gave it a head start in high-tech defense electronics. The Radiation Lab became the Electronics Research Laboratory, and it was joined by the Lincoln Laboratory (founded shortly after the war to do research for the Air Force in radar, computer technology, and space applications) and by the older established Instrumentation Laboratory, now the independent Draper Labs. Around MIT, a whole electronics complex began to grow from the mid-1950s on. It was never paralleled elsewhere on the East Coast.[53]

Military patronage was key to the formation of this agglomeration of electronics firms, large and small. In a late-1950s study of the Boston area electronics complex, Al Rubenstein found that its roots lay deep in World War II, when a large pool of engineering expertise assembled in and around the wartime labs.[54] The Radiation Lab and the Harvard Countermeasures Lab alone spawned several dozen research-based enterprises, and many others evolved out of other area labs. Rubenstein found extraordinary degrees of defense dependence in the crucial infant-industry decade of the 1950s:

A very large percentage of New England's New Research-Based Enterprises (NRBEs) are in the electronics business, and a very high proportion of the electronics business comes from government contracts. Most of the region's NRBEs, therefore, are highly (in many cases completely) dependent on the level and composition of defense-electronics contracts and subcontracts. (pp. 21–22)

Rubenstein argued that many of these firms would not have existed without government support:

The major advantage in many cases has been the gift of corporate existence itself. Without the initial study contracts on which their companies were founded, many technical-entrepreneurs in the field would still be working for someone else. Further, once some of these firms secured one or more contracts they had some assurance of continued existence for a period of months or years during which time they could begin to develop an economic role for the longer pull. For example, many of these firms were started on the basis of a contract to study a particular weapons system or a component or military operations problem. The income from the contract enabled them to employ competent specialists, purchase equipment, and build a support organization with capabilities beyond the requirements of the immediate contract on which they were working. (p. 22)

Rubenstein's report suggests that defense business was quite profitable and shows how, as a consequence, the Boston banks were more than willing to lend funds to electronics contractors:

> There has been a lot of security derived from having one large customer with what at times seems like an inexhaustible thirst for the technical talent provided by the NRBE and who, in most cases, pays its bills regularly and whose credit is such that banks will honor its contractual commitments almost up to the complete amount of anticipated progress payments. Indeed, this very security has attracted some investors into NRBEs with a heavy government-contract commitment because of the certain, and sometimes lucrative return on investment, where initial investment was quite small. (p. 21)

Rubenstein was writing in the late 1950s, when doubts about the military–industrial complex had been expressed by none other than Dwight D. Eisenhower, and a severe recession threatened to cripple the already ailing New England economy. His research was a response, in part, to a storm of recent criticism within the region directed at the overdependence on government contracts of New England's electronics sector. Furthermore, he found that the Pentagon did not always favor the smaller and more innovative firms, making them particularly vulnerable in a downturn. Increasingly, too, with the rise of the integrated weapons systems, the smaller firms had difficulties making original contributions to a major project.[55] Yet overall, Rubenstein found that military contracts were the crucial factor in engendering the nascent electronics complex, built on the professional and technical labor emanating from wartime labs and area universities.

Yet Boston was only one of a number of East Coast centers that were actively pursuing early electronics research. At Harvard, Howard Aiken did pioneer work on the development of the computer during the 1930s, supported by IBM. At the University of Pennsylvania, John Mauchly and John Eckart produced the ENIAC, generally regarded as the first true digital computer, in late 1945. At Princeton, mathematical genius John von Neumann acted as consultant to the University of Pennsylvania's pioneer ENIAC and then began work on more advanced computers, narrowly rejecting an offer to join the MIT team.[56]

But the starkest contrast is found in Bell Labs, a preeminent pioneer in electronics, which never did spawn a military-electronics cluster around it. Bell Labs, relocated in 1941 to laboratories in Murray Hill, New Jersey, was the birthplace of the transistor, in December 1947. Bell, which, like Western Electric and Douglas, had its share of defense contracts, was a prime contractor for the Army's Nike ground-to-air radar-guided missile. From 1954 on, in a research facility built during World War II and expanded in 1955 at Whippany, New Jersey, Bell developed the radio-inertial guidance system used for the Thor and Titan ICBMs.[57]

The question is: Why Massachusetts and not New Jersey? One answer is Bell's legal commitment to make the technology freely available to licensees.

Although several new firms—including Transistron, Texas Instruments, and Shockley Semiconductor—were founded by former Bell Labs employees, they were not locked into proximity to Murray Hill or Whippany. Bell, perhaps because it eschewed secrecy or proprietary patent battles, did not generate any agglomeration effect. Once the integrated circuit was patented, semiconductor manufacturing abruptly changed character, from assembly to component fabrication, and the locus of the industry shifted from Massachusetts to Silicon Valley. Firms like Raytheon and Transistron dropped out of transistor manufacture. The East Coast had almost nothing to do with the subsequent development of the semiconductor. The early promise of areas like northern New Jersey or Philadelphia withered on the vine.[58]

In contrast, Greater Boston overcame the challenge, as new firms shifted into more and more sophisticated military- and then civilian-electronics assembly, the region's main strength. The new Greater Boston complex—in contradistinction to its well-known rival, Silicon Valley—was from the start involved in electronics assembly rather than in basic semiconductor production. Its success lay in the combination of two factors, unique to the Boston area.

The first was university-based research. This is odd in a way, for MIT apparently played relatively little conscious role in the whole commercialization process; Harvard none at all.[59] It was based on new, innovative firms, especially in the field of minicomputers. MIT research was vital, though, in an indirect sense. Its laboratories provided both the basic links to military-oriented research and the founding fathers of the new firms.

Key, however, was MIT's unusual willingness to pursue military contracts. Witness Draper Lab, which was established back in 1930 and concentrated after the war on work for the Navy, and, later, the Lincoln Laboratory. This tradition continued: MIT contracts are the main reason why Massachusetts has an unusually high proportion of its defense contracts in the research and development, test, and evaluation (RDT&E) sector, and why an unusually high proportion of the state's awards go to the nonbusiness sector.[60] In particular, MIT's role in radar research was crucial.

Arising from a 1949 MIT initiative, Project Charles at MIT was carried out in 1950 in the teeth of opposition from those in Washington, led by Edward Teller, who wanted to give priority to the H-bomb. It led to a recommendation for a computer-controlled defense system and a strengthened early-warning radar surveillance along the U.S.–Canadian border, plus a permanent laboratory to continue to develop air defense technology. Accepted by Truman, it resulted in the establishment in September 1951 of the Lincoln Laboratory, the so-called Manhattan Project of air defense, at MIT. Ironically, the project was soon overtaken by the ICBM. But the laboratory survived, and MIT's primacy in computer and radar-based air defense systems was assured.[61]

From there, the Boston laboratories soon developed a tradition of industrial spin-off. Perhaps the first such firm, Wang, was started by a Harvard graduate in 1951. But this was a false dawn, since MIT, not Harvard, proved to be the true source of start-ups. Perhaps the most notable was the Digital

Equipment Company (DEC), founded in 1957 by Ken Olsen, a former manager of MIT's Lincoln Laboratory, in an old woolen mill at Maynard, Massachusetts. DEC developed what proved to be a completely new product, the minicomputer. Then, a process of breakaway and swarming occurred. By the early 1960s, 175 start-up firms had been founded by former full-time employees of MIT or associated institutions. Another 45 started after 1965.[62]

The second Boston factor was the way in which a few old firms successfully adapted. This was not true in the industrial heartland as a whole. Raytheon expanded again during the Korean War, but in a very structured way under Charles Adams, the new chief. For Raytheon, 1952 and 1953 were record years, the best since 1944. In 1953, sales were $179 million, profits $3.8 million, the bulk coming from government contracts. Staff totaled around 18,000. Much of the work consisted of research and development in avionics to go into the new missiles.[63]

The whole process was underpinned by the region's huge supply of qualified workers drawn in through the universities' nationwide recruiting, availability of venture capital, and the development of agglomeration economies. The Greater Boston area, colloquially Highway 128, thus became the first great electronics complex in the United States, predating Silicon Valley by several years. Highway 128, the original orbital highway around the city of Boston, started in the 1930s but completed only in 1951, links no fewer than twenty towns in the Greater Boston area, many of them with old established manufacturing and service functions.[64] Most of the firms siding Highway 128 had moved there from sites close to the city center: 59 percent had been located within a 2¼-mile radius of the center of Boston, 79 percent within a 4½-mile ring. This dispersion continued into the 1960s and 1970s, although new firms were now more apt to be oriented toward a commercial market, making Boston, with Los Angeles and Chicago, one of the three greatest concentrations of high technology in the United States in sheer number of jobs.

Today, after nearly forty years of evolution, this is a mature industrial area. But unlike its heartland counterparts, this city's new core industries are not inclined to bow out or relocate elsewhere. As our interviews along Route 128 showed, these firms feel themselves tied to the Boston area because of its unique concentration of research activity, much of it still financed by the military. That fact keeps them there, even though most other considerations—congestion, housing costs—would drive them out. The same calculus that locks aerospace firms into Los Angeles or Long Island, locks these avionics firms into locations within forty miles of the Charles River bridges. The most they can do is to move outward *within* the region. And even then, there are extraordinarily tight limits.

Let us look more closely at the military–industrial success stories in their contemporary guise. Sylvania Electrical Products merged with General Telephone in 1959 to form GTE. Raytheon and Sylvania are the two great survivors of the Massachusetts electronics industry. Founded before World War

II to manufacture lamps and vacuum tubes, Sylvania moved into defense-related electronics work in association with MIT laboratories during the war and remained there afterward. GTE-Sylvania has 8,500 employees in Greater Boston, in a variety of locations strung out along the 128 (now I-95) beltway: Danvers, Salem, Ipswich, Waltham, and Westboro. About 5,000 work in defense production, chiefly in guidance and C^3I systems, at GTE Government Systems located at Needham. Raytheon has 20,000 employees in Massachusetts, including 10,000 at its Lowell missile-manufacturing plant. Both firms have been heavily involved in microwave electronics from the birth of the science.

The third beltway company we visited, Avco Systems, today a division of the Textron company, is in contrast a 1950s start-up. It is the brainchild of a Cornell physicist, Arthur Cantarowich, who invented a missile-reentry system and who interested the president of an older engineering company, Avco. Avco already had a more or less independent research division at Everett, a northern suburb of Boston; the new division logically belonged under its wing. Locating first in an old mill in Lowell, the new division built a prototype in eighteen months. Expanding as an Air Force contractor in this early missile era—it was and is the only reentry specialist apart from GE—it moved into the complex of buildings at Wilmington, close to Lowell, in 1958. Wilmington, we were told, had an optimal location close to Route 128, Boston proper, and Logan Airport. Today, this operation is five times the size of the Everett laboratory, with 2,500 employees.

All three companies—Raytheon, GTE, and Avco—depend heavily on recruitment of new engineering graduates, including substantial numbers of Ph.D.s. You cannot buy microwave engineers, we were told; you have to grow them. Both GTE and Raytheon recruit widely. GTE takes 10 percent or less of its scientific work force from Massachusetts, although a number have done degree work or had other contacts there. Raytheon recruits from Illinois, Cornell, Pennsylvania, and Penn State, but not from the West Coast. There is also a heavy recruitment of overseas engineers, aided by immigration procedures that are easier than on the West Coast. At Avco, 60 percent of the work force is white-collar, down from 75 percent in previous development stages; the white-collar share may fall to 40 percent as the company switches into production. Avco recruits extensively from local universities. Scientific and professional graduates from local colleges are attracted by the idea of working on a state-of-the-art Department of Defense product. But Avco maintains contact with universities nationwide.

All firms, however, agree that the local concentration of universities is crucial in another way. New graduates are attracted above all by the quality of the work and of the city, particularly the potential to interact with university scientists and the prospect of earning a Ph.D. or another advanced degree work. Avionics employees are reportedly in and out of MIT constantly, although general graduate programs are not offered to outsiders and special release courses are expensive. Boston's "European" cultural attributes are a powerful attraction, as are the recreational opportunities nearby. Greater Boston, we were told, was a big metropolitan area, but still felt very comfortable.

In comparison, conventional transportation factors are unimportant. Movement of people is considered more significant than movement of goods. For a minority of top people—10 or 15 percent—there is intensive two-way traffic with the military contractors. Travel is mainly by air to more distant locations like Washington, D.C., Huntsville, Florida, New Mexico, and Silicon Valley, but by car to closer locations like the Navy establishments at Portsmouth, New London, and Groton; United Technologies Corporation at Hartford; and General Electric at Pittsfield. Since the work also involves much use of complex optical and semiconductor equipment, top people also have to travel to vendors in both the local area and Silicon Valley. "You have to see the equipment work," one contractor said. There is also a great deal of seminar and conference travel—"their life blood." "If this activity were on the moors," we were told, "we'd have to go." Because such meetings involve large numbers of East and West Coast people, some rotate between the two locations. Another firm maintains field operations in four locations and field marketing in three. But the great advantage lies in keeping everything together. Respondents from this firm told us that though their main contractor had always been the Air Force, California firms had no particular advantages of access over them.

The main deterrent to location here is the high cost of housing compared with the typical places from which the recruits come. To overcome this, all three firms offer attractive relocation packages. It now takes a two-hour commute into New Hampshire to find a real break in housing costs, we were told, but New Hampshire residents working in Greater Boston still pay Massachusetts income tax. All three firms report a high wastage rate for their top personnel, with a large number taking university appointments. Avco told us that it loses 12 to 14 percent of its labor force each year in the division we were visiting, but does not find poaching to be a major problem.

Yet despite these complaints, all three firms remain rooted in Massachusetts. One respondent was not sure why, but felt that the reason was the "Boston factor," especially proximity to MIT. It was difficult to imagine an alternative location for the kind of work done here. Similarly, another interviewee told us, labor and the general engineering environment were overwhelmingly the most important locational factors, locking the industry into a relatively restricted radius around Boston and Cambridge. So they would stay, despite the costs of recruitment and higher overheads.

Relocation, our Raytheon and GTE respondents told us, would thus be difficult. It would have to be to an area with similar qualities, such as Research Triangle. According to Avco officials, however, volume production, as of routine munitions, into which the firm is now moving, could be carried out elsewhere. Indeed, it has planned such a facility, and location consultants have investigated sites in the Sunbelt and Maine.[65] The firm also hopes to produce what it invents, not hand it over, as it has done in the past. That kind of work requires proximity to government testing grounds, the right skills, and availability of materials. Unionization was not a factor for Avco, since the work force here was nonunion, although other parts of Avco were unionized. The other two firms, in contrast, told us that their manufacturing work force was quite extensively unionized, although not uniformly, and one firm reported two "hairy" strikes. But this appeared to be a relatively minor consideration in comparison with the general advantages of the area.

Local movement is altogether different. Plenty of it is happening, but to only a few places. Currently, the big growth of firms—GTE, DEC, Prime— is in the western sector between Route 128 and the newer beltway, Interstate 495, twenty miles farther west, and even as far as Worcester. Lowell, to the north, was also a popular location. The general tendency is for high-tech industry to move out toward Interstate 495, where Wang, Digital, and Apollo are already established.[66] Developers have provided plenty of new buildings, many still lying empty. But there is a limit to this deconcentration: the point where "Boston is no longer Boston." Southeastern Massachusetts, the area on Interstate 95 south of Mansfield, is regarded as outside the pale. Some top engineering design people are reluctant to relocate to places like Wayland or Sudbury. This dovetails with other recent findings that suggest that the benefits of Massachusetts high technology are closely confined to the immediate Boston area, and have actually led to a worsening in the state's regional income distribution.[67]

Spin-offs, we found, are far less common than in the past. Years ago, spin-off support shops took the form of precision engineering as well as electronics firms, but nowadays that kind of work is unnecessary. Start-ups are usually in the form of one or two individuals working as consultants and then diversifying into hardware. The established companies offer such attractive employee benefits that people are reluctant to take the plunge. One firm did report spin-offs in energy, medical, and laser applications, where research programs had not coincided with the company's corporate objectives. SDI and related Defense Advanced Research Projects Agency (DARPA) projects have underwritten the formation of a few firms in artificial intelligence or neural networks spun off from the universities. In any case, there is a great deal of interaction among well-established firms and the MIT labs because they are all working at the scientific–technological frontier. For this reason, the individual units remained locked into the area.

Typical beltway firms, therefore, will not move far; nor do they produce many start-ups. But one or two firms have located farther afield, especially on the preferred western and northern corridors. One such is Sanders. Royden C. Sanders came to Raytheon during World War II from RCA with two other scientists because they found the large firm too structured. At their Lab 16, they developed continuous-wave subsonic radar from the end of the war, winning against formidable competition in the development of the early Lark missile for the Navy. In 1951, unhappy because he no longer enjoyed the close camaraderie he had known earlier with top management, Sanders left with twelve of his scientists to start his own organization, Sanders Associates.[68]

They established themselves in Nashua, five miles north of the New Hampshire line on Highway 93, finding very cheap space in an old textile mill that had just shut down. They also found a well-educated work force by the standards of those days, with a good work ethic. Over the years, the company's fortunes have mirrored the general state of defense contracting—down in the 1970s, up in the 1980s. Sanders stayed in New Hampshire during periods of expansion, finding this a good location from the viewpoint of land, infrastructure, labor, community factors like housing and schools, and "business climate." It developed facilities in Maine, Virginia, Massachusetts, and New York, but sold them when the going got tough. Sanders Associates is the largest private employer in New Hampshire. Its Manchester plant was greatly expanded in the mid-1960s, and the company also maintains its flagship plant at Nashua and another facility in Merrimack.

Southern New Hampshire, according to a Sanders spokesman, "just exploded" in the mid-1980s. The resulting problems do not compare with those of Greater Boston or of Orange County, and the business climate—no local income tax or sales tax—still represents a powerful advantage, particularly in recruiting labor. But housing is tight, since this is now a major bedroom community for Boston. You would have to go thirty miles north, we were told, to find low-cost blue-collar housing. Nevertheless, Sanders has little problem in recruiting blue-collar workers—25 percent of its labor force—because it offers high-wage jobs, despite being nonunionized.

Sanders recruits its professional staff mainly from the local universities such as MIT, Northeastern, the University of Lowell, and the University of New Hampshire. These universities offer no direct benefits in terms of research, but their presence makes recruitment easier. Most new Sanders employees come from a fifty-mile radius. Salaries are on a par with those in Boston, although the income tax bite is softer.

Sanders contracts to all three services almost equally, generally as a prime contractor on smaller contracts, although it acts as a subcontractor too. Were it ever to have a facilities problem, its first approach would be to try to operate in existing plants, then to lease nearby or expand an existing facility, and finally to construct nearby. The firm retains small maintenance and repair facilities at Wright-Patterson Air Base, and at Huntsville, Fort Dix, Fort Hood, and Fort Major. It stressed that one factor keeping it in New Hampshire was the synergy between central corporate management and the operating divisions, each of which had a product line geared either to Army, Navy, or Air Force requirements. Like the beltway "bandits," the firm's work involves a good deal of travel—especially to Washington, but also to military bases and other contractors, particularly in California—making access to a major hub airport important. Boston's Logan is within one hour's drive.

Overall, Sanders feels it occupies a particularly advantageous location. Some twenty miles beyond Highway 128, it is near enough to Boston to enjoy virtually all the region's agglomeration economies, yet far enough away to avoid some of its disadvantages—and on the right side of a rather significant state line.

Yet the diseconomies of continued regional growth were beginning to make themselves felt. But as in Connecticut, the greater worry is the prospective defense build-down. When we visited them in 1986, these firms, like the rest of the area, were still on the crest of a boom. The problems were all those of an overheated economy. But this is a very cyclical and volatile business; a 1970s-like depression could mean losing as much as 70 percent of the professional work force. Engineering design in particular works on a very short cycle, as little as eighteen months. The MX missile had already been phased out at the time of our visit. A new Department of Defense policy for dual sourcing for each product also threatened home-based jobs.

Conclusion: Military–Industrial Diversity

The northeastern military–industrial complex, then, grew out of the ashes of an older industrial tradition. In contrast to the Midwest, the seedbed here was fertile, perhaps because industrial decline was so deep and irreversible. The chief agents of high-technology buildup in the Boston nexus were a set of scientists and engineers at MIT, whose work in electrical engineering and eagerness for military funds led to a long line of laboratories and spin-offs in the environs. The precision-engineering tradition, spread more broadly down through Connecticut and Long Island, enabled a number of firms to move into high-tech aerospace and naval projects. Helpful, too, were the policymakers at city and state levels, who charted strategies to revitalize the depressed northeastern economy and organized permanent lobbies to secure funds from Washington.[69] To Washington went politicians like Tip O'Neill, who looked after his hometown's ongoing needs for taxpayer infusions. No other industries competed for center stage, as they did in the more youthful, mechanically oriented Midwest.

Yet the northeastern military–industrial complex is also more diversified than any of the others around the nation. It has a share of government proceeds in almost every major weapons category, and is more evenly patronized by the three major services than are other regions. Within it are smaller concentrations with varying degrees of maturity, some still primarily research-intensive, others much more heavily engaged in engineering and production. This makes a difference in their future prospects. Areas like Boston will continue to flourish as long as American foreign policy strategists place a heavy priority on a technological lead in weaponry. Contractors in areas like the Connecticut Valley and Long Island face tougher pressures to decentralize their operations to lower cost sites.

In southern New England, a typical contractor is large, corporately managed, and prone to decentralize decision-making to its operating divisions. It is under pressure to cut costs and is open to political influence. It has been headquartered in its present location for a half-century or more, but is very likely experiencing constraints on its operations especially so if it is close to New York City. Therefore, although it might prefer to continue operating in its traditional locale, it increasingly tends to float off operations to places in the Southeast, leaving only certain functions—headquarters, R&D, key assembly operations—at the original site.

The typical company in this region does not feel tied to its traditional location by agglomeration economies. At most, it depends on the skills of its blue-collar craft-engineering workers, but it may worry about losing them. It does not draw on a pool of scientific and technical labor out of local universities, but recruits all over the nation. It thinks that its present location has some attractions for such scarce technical talent, but also perhaps some disadvantages. It is basically here because it has always been here, and because there is not yet a pressing reason to pull up stakes, especially since the company has a huge investment sunk in land and buildings. But it does not see any unique advantage in the location. If it is Pratt & Whitney, it stays where it is because in East Hartford the constraints are not severe. If it is Grumman, it actively looks for locations where it can float off some activities.

The Massachusetts and New Hampshire electronics firms—many of them still small, others grown large—occupy a completely different mental world. Big or small, for them Boston and Cambridge represent the center of an intellectual universe on which their lives depend. Again and again, they sing the same refrain: the nearness of MIT; the ability to drop in, to use facilities, to attend seminars; the sense that here and only here one could keep abreast of the state of the art; the cultural ambience; the crucial importance of all this in recruiting new graduates; the sense that even southern Massachusetts is somewhere off the edge of the world.

Thus despite the disadvantages of which they were all so well aware—escalating costs of housing, congealing traffic on the expressways—they would never leave. Although all these firms were middle-aged and some were reasonably large, they retained the attitudes of small start-up companies. They sought agglomeration economies in a single specialized industrial quarter, in the same way that similar companies do in southern Los Angeles and neighboring Orange County.

These differences clearly go right back to the origins of the companies. The southern New England group arose from early entrepreneurial craft traditions, surviving cycles of depression and takeover, massively expanding and bureaucratizing during World War II, and increasingly organizing their own in-house R&D. The Massachusetts and New Hampshire electronics firms, on the contrary, are steeped in basic university research traditions. Despite the convergence of aircraft manufacture and electronics, the two industries organize their business in different ways and have quite different mental pictures of their own locational needs.

The cliché, as so often, is profoundly true: New England is old, and its remarkable industrial renaissance has sprung from the entrepreneurial agility that has allowed old industries to find new roles, thanks to the emergence of the cold war. As so often in this story, this agility has manifested itself at critical historical turning points: the beginning of World War II, the military buildup of the 1950s. Individuals, whether university researchers or garage manufacturers, caught critical waves and floated on them to positions of great economic power. Without those waves—the timing and size of which were determined by America's changing strategic role—the New England economy would have fared very differently. Above all, this was true of the 1980s. New England's economic turnaround in that decade was specifically triggered by a national military buildup that focused on technology rather than personnel and on the multiplier effects thus created.[70] But what one wave can lift, another can cast down on the beach. As Lynne Browne and Sarah Gavian found of the 1970s, the defense industry's impact on the regional economy is greater than size alone would suggest simply because it is so volatile.[71] They showed that during the Vietnam War, jobs in the aircraft industry rose from 80,000 in 1963 to 99,000 by 1967, falling back to 70,000 by 1971. Substantial multiplier effects magnified the way that these ups and down ricocheted through the regional economy—in service, trade, and construction.[72]

In 1989, one press report followed another on the travails of New England and Long Island defense contracting, and the resulting contraction of the region's economy. Between 1985 and 1988, fiscal spending on prime military contracts in New York State fell from \$5.5 billion to \$4.9 billion.[73] By mid-1989, the state of Massachusetts was in serious financial trouble, with the governor's top financial aide quoted as saying, "If the state were a business, we'd be insolvent. We'd be eligible for Chapter 11."[74] A defense-dependent economy can feel wonderful, even to a Democratic presidential candidate, while Pentagon hawks rule the roost. But it can be exceedingly uncomfortable when they lose their perch.

As the region enters the last decade of the century, its communities, firms, labor unions, and policymakers have become preoccupied with looming defense cutbacks. In 1989, analysts estimated that about 11,000 defense jobs would be lost in New England in 1990 alone, with greater cuts on the horizon. By 1989, New England, with 5 percent of the nation's population, received 12 percent of the nation's defense outlays. Four of the region's biggest employers—United Technologies, Raytheon, General Dynamics, and General Electric—depend primarily on defense contracts. About one in fifteen employees in Connecticut and Massachusetts works in defense-related business. The research-intensive nature of many contracts will help shield the region from cutbacks, but that will do little for the blue-collar workers whose jobs are more immediately threatened.[75]

7

Seattle: Aerospace Company City

Seattle seems like the last place in America to build planes, or even to think about building them. It is separated by a continent from the nation's capital, by hundreds of miles from any procurement center or any other major aerospace production site. The Pacific storm tracks bring huge gray rain clouds that scud across Puget Sound, dousing the B-747s, B-767s, and Air Force jets that sit in Boeing Field waiting for their test flights. Behind airfield and city lie the Cascades, and beyond them, deserts and more mountains.

A Seattle tour guide might point out the Space Needle on the old World's Fair site, the controversial new downtown high-rises, and on clear days, snowcapped Mount Rainier. Yet the alert tourist immediately notices something far more pervasive: the hundreds of hangars, warehouses, factories, and offices that dot city and suburbs, all carrying that unmistakable BOEING sign (Fig. 7.1). Indeed, almost the first Seattle sight, on Interstate 5 from the airport to downtown, is the Boeing company's sprawling Plant Two site, next to Boeing Field.

Seattle is thus unique: not a "company town," like an old-fashioned steel or coal town, but a "company city," the only major American city so clearly dependent on one contractor. Boeing dominates Seattle's economy. It not only is the only major defense contractor and by far the largest manufacturing employer, military or civilian, in the entire region, but also is the largest employer, public or private.

The price has been a boom-and-bust pattern. During the Reagan defense buildup, Boeing jobs in the area soared from 60,000 in the mid-1980s to over 100,000 by the end of the decade: more than twice the World War II peak. Similarly, the cold war, the golden age of jet travel, and the Apollo program sparked employment booms. But always, booms have been followed by busts that have hit the city hard. During the famous "Boeing Bust" of 1968 to 1971, when Boeing's employment plunged from over 100,000 to less than 40,000, a billboard placed near the freeway exhorted: "Would the last person to leave Seattle please turn off the lights?" And in the current era of defense-budget cutbacks, the Washington economy is expected, by one estimate, to lose more than 13,000 jobs a year during the early 1990s.[1]

Boeing's dominance of the Seattle economy has other effects. As the

148

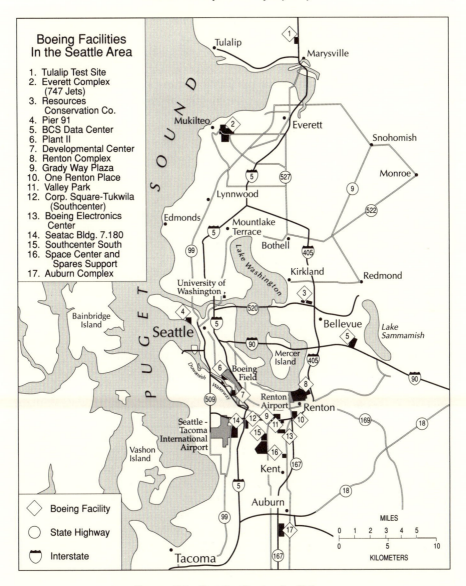

FIGURE 7.1. Seattle: Boeing facilities.

largest employer in the area, it shapes the local labor market as no single defense contractor in New England or southern California ever could. The Seattle high-tech labor pool of engineers, computer programmers, software specialists, and the like, is essentially the Boeing labor pool. Most other high-tech companies must operate in Boeing's shadow.

In a broader sense, Boeing's dominance means that Seattle differs dramatically from Los Angeles or Boston in complexity of supplier networks, industrial linkages, and service support. Seattle does not benefit much from agglomeration economies like those that stem from contracting activities in these other cities. In addition, Seattle has not been a traditional center of industrial innovation. The isolated timber and shipping town would have once seemed an improbable location to run a massive high-tech operation. How, then, could the nation's—indeed, the world's—most successful airplane manufacturer develop here, overcoming the massive disadvantage of isolation and lack of local business networks?

These are not the only unique aspects of Boeing's situation. Boeing is also the only military-airplane maker that has had equal or greater success in the commercial market than in military sales in recent years. McDonnell-Douglas, despite some successes, has struggled with its commercial jets ever since problems with its DC-10. Lockheed dropped out of the market after its ill-fated L-1011 program, and Convair never successfully made it into the commercial-jet age.

But, conversely, Boeing also represents a rather unusual case of a contractor that has had consistently bad luck in gaining "big-ticket" and "follow-on" defense contracts. Since the 1960s, its failed bids include the TFX, C-5A, B-1, KC-10, MX, C-17, and C-5B. Partly as a result, Boeing was not one of the leading defense contractors for the Vietnam War, and indeed saw the defense proportion of its company revenues decline during the 1960s. All these elements make the history and development of the Boeing Company significantly different from those of other major contractors.

The story of why Boeing is in Seattle involves no complex corporate and geographic histories such as TRW or Litton Industries, nor does it need any elaborate theory of industrial location. What is interesting is why William Boeing stayed in Seattle after he produced his first seaplane there in 1916, rather than moving south or east, why he had such success, and whether Boeing's location in Seattle played a role. Did, for instance, Seattle steer the company into certain types of products and production methods, as well as an association with one military service rather than another?

Another set of questions concerns the future prospects of Boeing's operations outside the Puget Sound area. The two largest such operations are in Wichita, Kansas, and in Philadelphia, each arising from acquisition of preexisting facilities rather than greenfield expansions. Yet there are many other, smaller Boeing facilities around the country, many of them recent expansions in the Southeast. They reflect both push and pull factors. They also symbolize a larger concern of this book: the changing regional distribution of defense manufacturing and its role in the economic remapping of the United States.

A Short History of Boeing

Early Years

Boeing, of course, was the creation of its founder, William Edward Boeing, who was born in 1881 in Detroit. Boeing's German-born father and Viennese mother had large holdings of timber and iron ore in Minnesota's Mesabi Range. Young Boeing studied engineering at Yale's Sheffield Scientific School, but left in 1903, a year before graduation, and moved west. In Seattle he acquired timber on his own, and was also involved in yacht-building and outfitting Alaska-bound expeditions.

Seattle was then a small town, growing rapidly bigger. A turn-of-the-century boom had taken it from a mere village of 3,500 people in 1880 to 81,000 by 1900 and 237,000 ten years later.[2] Yet by the 1910s, growth had slowed, and new industries were not being developed to sustain growth and development. Seattle badly needed a Boeing.

Boeing became increasingly fascinated with the young sport of flying, an interest honed after he attended the Los Angeles Aviation Meet in January 1910. With Conrad Westervelt, an engineer in the Naval Construction Corps at the Puget Sound Navy Yard, he experimented with both boat and airplane construction. Boeing's inherited wealth afforded him a level of independence to pursue aircraft design in the industrially obscure city of Seattle and freed him from the pressures of turning an immediate profit. It also allowed him to take flying lessons from Glenn Martin's operation in Los Angeles and to purchase a $10,000 Martin seaplane in 1915. By June 1916, the first of two Boeing & Westervelt seaplanes was completed and flown. Built in Boeing's converted Heath shipyard on the Duwamish River in Seattle, it used a Hall-Scott engine from San Francisco and much aeronautical information from Jerome Hunsaker at MIT. The next month, Boeing formally established his company as the Pacific Aero Products Company; a year later, it was renamed the Boeing Airplane Company (Table 7.1).[3]

The company received early boosts from military orders during the latter part of World War I, but suffered with the rest of the airframe manufacturers after the armistice. The market was glutted with surplus wartime planes. Barnstormers were reluctant to purchase new, expensive planes destined for frequent crashes. So Boeing turned to the construction of furniture and sea-sled boats: a shift not as odd as it may seem, since early airplanes were made not of metal, but of wood, and Boeing employed many skilled ex-cabinetmakers and shipwrights.

Seattle, like Boeing, was vulnerable. The fact was masked by wartime shipbuilding and lumber booms, but peace brought an immediate end to the new jobs. Massive shipyard layoffs provoked a strike in February 1919, leading to a general strike that brought no gains to labor. The city seemed to be retreating to its earlier role as a processor and shipper of raw materials: lumber, fish, and wheat. National recessions during the 1920s, and still more during the Great Depression, were felt particularly hard. By 1939, Seattle manufacturing employment was half that of 1919, and although the value of materials handled was roughly the same, manufacturing value-added had dropped by almost 50 percent. Seattle was becoming more of a way station for raw materials than a valuable processor of these materials.[4]

Boeing's star rose faster than Seattle's, although it too showed ups and downs. The postwar slump in aviation began to abate in the early 1920s as the economy improved and the military showed increasing interest in Boeing's

TABLE 7.1. The History of Boeing by Era

Year	Period	Selected New Products
1916–1918	Start-up and early World War I contracts	B&W seaplanes
1918–early 1920s	Postwar downturn	B-1
Early 1920s–1926	Early defense buildup	MB3-A, P-9
1927–1929	Commercial boost through airmail contracts	Model 40, Model 80
1929–1934	United Aircraft and Transport Corporation era	Model 247, Monomail, P-26
1934–1939	Depression woes and the rise of the big plane	B-17, Stratoliner
1939–1945	World War II	314 Clipper, B-29
1945–1947	Postwar downturn	YC-97, B-50, Stratocruiser
1948–1957	Cold war and the jet-bomber era	B-47, B-52, B-707, KC-135
1957–1961	Downturn	B-720
1961–1968	Space buildup and big growth in civilian-jet aviation	B-727, B-737, Minuteman
1968–1971	Recession and the "Boeing Bust"	B-747
1972–late 1970s	Diversification and recovery	AWAC, LRV
late 1970s–1990	Defense buildup and boom in commercial aircraft	B-757, B-767

products. By 1922, Boeing's timber was selling again. The company completed an order for 200 MB3-A pursuit planes for the U.S. Army Service in 1923, and by 1926 was one of the largest U.S. producers of military aircraft. Boeing's first major step into commercial aviation took place in 1927, when it won the bid to operate the Chicago–San Francisco airmail service, using its new Model 40 transport plane. The remote location of the firm was clearly no deterrent to buyers in either military or commercial markets.

United Aircraft and the Depression

The Boeing of today, like so much of the airplane industry, was powerfully shaped by corporate mergers on the eve of the Great Depression. The late 1920s were a time of heavy speculation on Wall Street, with airplane manufacturers a popular target of investment and acquisition. Charles Lindbergh had flown the Atlantic in 1927, increasing popular interest in aviation. In this heady, pre-Depression climate of 1928 and 1929, Curtiss and Wright were merged, bringing together two of the oldest and biggest operations in aviation. Fearing this giant, Fred Rentschler (of Pratt & Whitney fame), Clarence Vought, Bill Boeing, and others decided to consolidate the best companies in airplanes (Boeing, Chance Vought, Hamilton Metalplane Co.), engines (Pratt & Whitney), propellers (Hamilton Aero and Standard Steel Propeller), and transport systems (Boeing Air Transport, Pacific Air Transport, etc.) in a textbook example of vertical integration.

Although their original strategy was to include only military and transport companies, Wall Street investors—convinced of the viability of the new aviation industry—pushed for inclusion of private commercial manufacturers. So Rentschler purchased both Stearman (in Wichita, Kansas) and Sikorsky (in Bridgeport, Connecticut), two companies that were soon in trouble after the stock market crashed and the demand for private airplanes plummeted.[5] The resulting conglomerate, which included many other operations, was named the United Aircraft and Transport Corporation (UATC) and was based in Hartford, Connecticut. All the companies retained their own operating names.

One could see the effects of the merger in Boeing's Model 247, a twin-engine monoplane, first flown in 1933. Its motors were made by Pratt & Whitney. Its variable pitch propeller came from the recently consolidated Hamilton-Standard, which now had a virtual monopoly over propellers. Phil Johnson of Boeing also convinced Rentschler to replace the entire United fleet with the 247. Yet this vertical integration may have also hurt Boeing's commercial-aviation chances. TWA also wanted to purchase the 247, but as a competitor to United, UATC refused to sell to TWA until United's order for sixty planes was completed. TWA, along with other competitors, turned to Douglas and its new DC-1. Douglas began to dominate the 1930s commercial market at the expense of Boeing.[6]

Allegations of unfair airmail-contract allocations led to the Air Mail Act of 1934, which mandated the separation of all companies' aviation-manufacturing divisions from air transport (airmail) subsidiaries. United Airlines was split off to operate the transport companies. The transport link thus severed, UATC decided to divide the manufacturing concerns into two groups, with Boeing to operate the western units of the disbanded conglomerate: Boeing's Seattle operation, Boeing Aircraft of Canada Ltd. in Vancouver, and Stearman Aircraft in Wichita. Hence the roots of Boeing's presence in Wichita lie in the breakup. The resulting Boeing group was the weakest of the three in capital and in backlog of business. Bill Boeing, who had already withdrawn from active participation with UATC and had begun selling stock, now bitterly severed all aviation connections.[7]

Military Buildup and Wartime Production

The 1930s proved a critical era for both Boeing and its rivals. The Depression, plus undependable commercial markets and stiff competition, made this a do-or-die era for fledgling aircraft companies. By the time the decade ended, Boeing had become a massive industrial operation, buoyed by the growing military interest in strategic bombing. Yet at the mid-point of this crucial decade, there were few signs of future success. The year 1934 was particularly difficult: P-26A pursuit planes were sold at a loss; production on the 247 commercial line ended; and the Douglas DC-2/3 series dominated the market.

Undaunted, Boeing took steps that would shape the company's future direction and pay huge dividends in the coming years. It shifted from smaller planes and pursuits to larger, four-engine planes that would serve as both bombers and transports. It started to develop a new four-engine plane that eventually became the Stratoliner, and the Flying Fortress bomber that became the B-17, and a larger, long-range bomber—the XB-15 (X for experimental, B for bomber)—that boasted engineering that fed into the transoceanic commercial clipper. These projects, deliberately spanning military and civilian markets, were particularly significant because they gave Boeing early experience with large planes, positioning the firm to benefit from tremendous military demand by the end of the 1930s and civilian demand after the war.

The looming world war fueled Boeing's assembly lines from 1936 on. Some 173,000 new shares of stock were sold, and despite the fact that engineering hours and costs of R&D for big airplanes were rapidly increasing, ambitious expansion plans were made for Boeing Field, to be called Plant Two.[8] By 1939, Boeing had a large backlog of orders for B-17s, Stratoliners, and Clippers; but it also was registering major losses, and bank credit had dried up. The scale of production was qualitatively different, requiring a shift in thinking about airplane production, development costs, and funding.[9]

The Boeing Company continued to invest in new and better military designs. In 1939, it unveiled a new superbomber, the B-29 Superfortress, to meet the military's need for a 4,000- to 5,000-mile-range bomber with better armament. Congress was reluctant to provide support, since the United States was officially neutral, and such bombers were seen as "aggressive." But the invasion of Poland in September, and the Air Board's report showing how air power could threaten the Western Hemisphere, eroded resistance and the funds were released.

Boeing was well placed to flourish from the American involvement in hostilities. When, just after the fall of France, President Roosevelt announced a massive program to produce 50,000 military airplanes, orders came in for hundreds of B-17s, as well as two prototype versions of the new B-29 Superfortress. By 1941, Boeing had undertaken large-scale expansion programs in Seattle, Vancouver, and Wichita, plus a new plant in Renton, just south of Seattle. The Superfortress came on-stream in 1943; by the end of the war, it constituted the bulk of Boeing's production. At the time, the B-29 program was the "greatest single industrial undertaking ever underwritten by the War Department" and, given the complex network of suppliers and assembly plants, "the most organizational airplane ever built."[10] No less than 46 percent of all total bomb tonnage dropped in Europe was from B-17s, and 96 percent of all tonnage in Japan was from B-29s. The atomic bomb that destroyed Hiroshima was dropped from the *Enola Gay*, a B-29. Thus while the B-17 spanned the distances of the Atlantic to fight the war in Europe, it was the Pacific based, longer-range B-29 that changed the character of military aviation.[11]

Boeing represented perhaps the only significant opportunity for Seattle to create a new economic base. The company was the principal agent for the city's second major boom period from World War II through the 1960s. It employed only 4,000 people in 1939, rising to 30,000 by the end of 1941 and peaking at 50,000 in 1944.[12] Yet, just as in World War I, Boeing military-aircraft production failed to diversify the Seattle economy or even set off an agglomeration process. Most of the needed raw materials and parts continued to be imported into the region, which failed to develop the complex supplier networks seen in cities like Los Angeles. As noted by Roger Sale,

> Boeing was like a gigantic baby dropped into Seattle's lap. Wartime procurement can always wreak havoc on a local economy, especially one as frail as Seattle's has been.... The very simplicity of the operation, for all the huge complications involved in altering designs, procuring material, and keeping employees in a tight labor market, gave Boeing little flexibility in its operations. It was not its own boss, and it could do little to help Seattle's economy except provide its huge payroll.[13]

Postwar: From Boeing Boom to Boeing Bust

War's end brought the abrupt termination of production and massive layoffs. Boeing's Seattle employment dropped from a wartime peak of 45,000 to 15,000 by November 1945.[14] Production of B-29s in Wichita was terminated, and the entire government-owned Plant Two was closed down. But soon, the rapidly escalating cold war and the pent-up demand for commercial planes provided new markets. And technological breakthroughs in jet engines, "pilotless" aircraft, and missiles offered new possibilities for R&D contracts.

Boeing, unlike Curtiss-Wright or the auto companies to the east, eagerly and successfully tackled both market segments. Key to its strategy was its early advantage in the jet-bomber market.[15] In turn, military-jet technology gave Boeing a crucial headstart on civilian-jet transportation.[16] No other U.S. company had as much jet experience in engineering and wind-tunnel testing. Time after time, military demand filled a commercial gap. For instance, the need for midair refueling of the huge B-52s led to a jet tanker, which turned into the commercial 707. Its 707 thus giving it a head start over Douglas's rival DC-8, Boeing had taken the first step toward becoming the Western world's most successful producer of commercial jetliners.[17]

But the result was dangerous dependence for the Seattle economy. Whereas only about one in five King County manufacturing employees was at Boeing in 1947, this figure rose to one in two by 1954. The only other growth sectors were real estate and home building, both dependent on the Boeing boom. And, of course, they were quite vulnerable to sudden changes. Boeing employment plunged in the late 1950s and early 1960s when military contracts were completed. It picked up again with the Apollo program, the boom in commercial jetliners, and early work on a supersonic transport. Overall, the years from 1954 to 1967—when employment peaked at 148,000—were some of the best that Boeing, and Seattle, ever had. Seattle during the

1950s and 1960s was a kind of colony, importing many of its basic needs and exporting aircraft to the government and the airlines.[18]

From the late 1960s through the mid-1970s, major layoffs and unemployment wracked the company. The "Boeing Bust" stemmed not only from cutbacks in Vietnam spending, but from a drop in demand for commercial jets and failure in military design competitions. The huge expense of developing the 747, coupled with lower-than-predicted sales at first, heavily strained the company and brought further employment cuts. Another 7,000 jobs evaporated when the Senate canceled the Supersonic Transport (SST) in 1971, a project that Boeing had actively pursued since the late 1960s. The SST, once the proud emblem on local bumper stickers ("SST Seattle Stands Tall"), now became symbolic of the Seattle recession.[19] And no "big-ticket" military-airplane contracts came to replace the old B-47s, B-52s, and KC-135s as their production tailed off. Boeing temporarily diversified into unfamiliar territory, such as making light rail vehicles.

At first, the necessary cuts were achieved through attrition, since huge turnovers were common in the aircraft industry. Boeing employment in Washington fell from 100,000 to roughly 80,000 between 1968 and 1969. Then came direct layoffs, slashing employment to a mere 38,000 by 1971; 28,400 people were dismissed in 1970 alone. The hardest-hit were not the middle-class engineers, who took significant cuts in income but were usually able to find new employment, but those lower down the economic ladder. Workers with the least experience and education were the first to go.[20]

Surprisingly, the local economy had a certain resilience. Few people left the city, per capita incomes fell by a quarter but remained just above the national average, and consumer spending did not drop as much as expected. High pre-recession incomes had generated cushions in the form of savings accounts. Unemployment insurance and other payments helped, and those who still had jobs enjoyed rising incomes.[21]

The determination of most ex-Boeing workers to stay in Seattle was a long-term blessing for the city.[22] Although it meant an unemployment level of 12 percent, twice the national average, it did prevent the kind of "brain drain" of highly skilled employees that has decimated the economies of cities struck by similar massive layoffs. Many workers eventually returned to Boeing; others used their skills and education to create spin-off enterprises. The commercial market soon recovered, and Boeing's risky investment in the 747 began to pay off. In the 1980s, the new 757 and 767 models, plus the highly successful 747 and 737, again boosted sales and jobs. As the decade came to a close, the newspapers repeatedly announced record-breaking sales of new Boeing commercial liners. And a further fillip came from the defense buildup.

Boeing Today: The "Two-Engine" Strategy

Boeing is the largest aircraft manufacturer in the Western world, the second U.S. exporter, and, according to a *Fortune* magazine survey, America's third most admired corporation.[23] It is a company whose fortunes have gone through dramatic periods of feast and famine, yet it remains one of the enduring success stories in the industry. Unlike its two traditional domestic commercial-aircraft competitors, McDonnell-Douglas and Lockheed, Boeing has been able to maintain both a healthy portion of defense contracts and the lion's share of commercial business. As *The Economist* put it, "Boeing's trick in its 70-year history has been to give the market what it wants, not what its engineers think it wants—a commendable achievement in a company where engineering commands the greatest prestige."[24]

Boeing remains one of the nation's leading defense contractors, with sales of over $6 billion in 1986. Ironically, the public knows it best for its commercial products. In part, this is because Boeing lacks a recent, readily identifiable military product, like Rockwell's B-1B or Northrop's Stealth bomber. Indeed, the most famous Boeing military planes date from the 1940s and 1950s: the B-17 Flying Fortress, the B-29 Superfortress, and the B-52. In the 1960s and early 1970s, as the 707 and 727 made Boeing the leader in commercial aviation, some analysts expressed concern about Boeing's apparent past neglect of defense: "[Boeing] may be paramount in civil aircraft, but in the military and space arena there is a clutch of equally impressive rivals—e.g., Rockwell, General Dynamics, McDonnell-Douglas, Lockheed, United Technologies, General Electric."[25]

But not all observers agree that in the past Boeing simply "neglected" the defense side of its business and thereby lost big-ticket contracts. It is hard to explain Boeing's failures in the source-selection for the TFX (1962), C-5A (1965), B-1 (1969), KC-10 (1975), MX (1979), C-17 (1981), and C-5B (1982) in terms of technological inferiority. Time after time, Boeing failed to achieve the traditional pattern of follow-on defense contracts to the same company: the follow-on contract to its Minuteman went to Martin-Marietta (the MX), the KC-135 successor to McDonnell-Douglas (the KC-10), and the B-52 follow-on to Rockwell (the B-1).

One possible reason for this is that Boeing's commercial success perversely proved its undoing in defense contracting. Boeing has tended to lose contracts to competitors that were suffering financial crises. The TFX went to General Dynamics in 1962 after its failure in commercial jets, despite four successive unanimous recommendations for Boeing's design. The C-5B contract went to Lockheed in 1982 after that company's huge losses on the L-1011; the KC-10 went to McDonnell-Douglas in 1976, after poor sales of the civilian version (the DC-10). Boeing, ironically thwarted by its own commercial success, was left scrambling for subcontracts or systems like the MX and B-1. James R. Kurth and others have charged that large, visible, and politically manipulable contracts have acted as a Pentagon industrial-subsidy policy to bail out troubled companies and thus keep everyone in business.[26]

In the 1980s, Boeing reoriented its business toward defense, becoming the fastest growing major contractor. By 1984, military sales provided Boeing with more than 70 percent of its profits and nearly 50 percent of sales.[27]

Because the company must pay for commercial development but the Department of Defense is likely to absorb the costs of military weaponry, military work gains higher returns.

This lucrative defense work is concentrated in three Boeing divisions: Boeing Aerospace and Electronics, Boeing Military Airplane Company (BMAC), and Boeing Helicopter Company. Estimates in 1985 put the military share of total Boeing employment at 35 percent in the Puget Sound area, more than two-thirds in Wichita, and 90 percent at Boeing Helicopter (in Philadelphia).[28] Military work relies on a low-profile strategy, based on the production of helicopters, command aircraft, tankers, and space systems, and on major subcontracting of bombers and missiles, without any distinctive product like the 747 or 767. But the low-profile segments add up to a whopping $6 billion.

The two-engine strategy of pursuing both civilian and military contracts has benefited Boeing. The company can hedge against boom and bust in these two highly cyclical markets—unless, of course, the two occur simultaneously. It can develop products for both markets, thus lowering overall development costs: the strategy embodied in the XB-15 experimental bomber and Pan Am Clipper of the 1930s, the B-17 and Stratoliner of the 1940s, the B-29 Superfortress and Stratocruiser of the late 1940s, and the KC-135 and 707 of the 1950s. And although no commercial planes directly arose from the B-47 and B-52 bombers, they did give the company invaluable and transferable experience with jet technology, including swept-back wings and engine placement. A clear exception is the 747, which Boeing developed despite the loss of the parallel C5-A transport contract to Lockheed in 1965, and which it again failed to sell to the military as the C-X (C-5B) in the early 1980s.[29] By sharing information, plant space, equipment, and personnel between the commercial and military divisions, Boeing also achieves considerable economies of scale and scope. This sharing between Boeing's commercial and military operations extends to recruitment; however, problems with security classification, as well as differing programs for affirmative action and hiring foreigners, sometimes require separate military and civilian hiring programs.

Boeing survival depends on its ability to solicit both production and R&D work from the Pentagon. With the Pentagon more closely scrutinizing contractor costs, Boeing is counting on its unrivaled experience with automation and large-scale production of commercial aircraft, particularly on its 737 and 747 lines, to give it a competitive edge for future defense contracts. As Thomas V. Jones, chairman of Northrop, noted, "The existence of Boeing's commercial business definitely helps the military side."[30] Boeing recently began pursuing one huge Pentagon plum—the Advanced Tactical Fighter (ATF), a joint project with Lockheed and General Dynamics—although it has not made a fighter in over forty years. Another strategy Boeing has used to increase its share of defense business is aggressive solicitation of R&D contracts, often seen as the key to future prime contracts. Boeing was the largest winner of such contracts during the 1980s, and is also a leader in SDI contracting. Boeing is also gaining market share as a military-electronics contractor.[31]

Boeing's dramatic growth as a defense contractor during the 1980s, coupled with recent record contracts for its commercial jets, suggests that the
company has benefited dramatically from its two-sector strategy. But this may
not be so successful in the future. The growing gap between the requirements
of commercial and military aircraft makes it harder to develop these two types
of aircraft in parallel. Furthermore, the upturns and downturns in the two
sectors may not permit smooth switching from one to the other, although the
current international demand for commercial planes does appear to be soft-
ening the blows from defense cuts.

Boeing and the Seattle Economy

Just what does this volatile giant's presence mean for its host region? Seattle's
economy rests on three foundations: banking and finance, overseas trade,
and high technology. Seattle is the undisputed center of banking for the Pacific
Northwest. By exploiting containerization and fast sailing time to Asia, the
ports of Seattle and Tacoma have grown dramatically to become the second
largest cargo-handling region on the Pacific Coast, behind Los Angeles/Long
Beach, but ahead of San Francisco/Oakland.[32] Seattle has also become home
base for a smattering of high-tech firms in electronics, computers, and medical
equipment, including the headquarters of Microsoft software and branch facilities of Hewlett-Packard.

But Boeing dominates. Even the legendary Microsoft employed only 500
people in 1985.[33] Other high-tech firms generally either depend on Boeing
subcontracts or are relatively small operations. Boeing receives the vast majority of all the region's defense contracts: $2.6 billion in 1983, or 72 percent
of the contracts in the Puget Sound area. The Seattle economy remains heavily
vulnerable to the company's ups and downs. The "Boeing Bust" of 1968 to
1971, with its ripple effects on the region's real-estate and consumer markets
and its long-term damage to the city's psyche, was just the most dramatic
reminder that the city has tied much of its fortunes to those of the aerospace
giant.

Since those bleak years, Seattle has not seen such wild fluctuations. Yet
the city continues to be subjected to Boeing's unpredictable cycles. The 1982
downturn hit harder and longer in Seattle than elsewhere: "We are in
a recession that is somewhat deeper and will be somewhat longer lasting
than that of the general national economy," said Cleveland Anschell, associate economist at Rainier National Bank.[34] The reason was that Boeing
was suffering from declining commercial demand and had just lost a big
MX missile contract. The company laid off many engineers and machinists,
recruited only one year before, fueling previous accusations that it overhires
during booms.[35]

Such layoffs hit Seattle particularly hard, since Boeing is the only major
aerospace employer in town. Although by 1982 only 10 percent of all Seattle
employment was at Boeing, down from 19 percent in the big bust of 1968,

this is still an extraordinary rate of dependence for a major city.[36] "It isn't like Los Angeles, where if Lockheed lays off you can walk across the street to Northrop," notes a union official. Leaving Seattle to find aerospace work elsewhere is unusually difficult for Boeing workers, who are reputed to be strongly attached to their city's superb natural environment, slower pace of life, clean air, and relatively low costs of living.

Boeing claims that it has successfully dampened its employment swings by subcontracting out more work. Yet this logic is suspect. If the subcontractors are local, then they too are affected by downturns. If not, then this practice has essentially lowered employment permanently in boom times. The subcontracting strategy is essentially a tactical means to deal with the symptoms of Boeing's cyclical business, rather than a strategy to deal with the structural causes of these ups and downs. This course of action is doubtless consistent with Boeing's low-profile, hands-off style, based on its self-image as a conventional, engineering-based private company.

Of course, Seattle's tradition of dependence on a single industry did not start with Boeing. The city relied first on lumber, then on shipbuilding, before Boeing came on the scene. When it did, Seattle simply continued its pattern of enjoying the booms while neglecting to cushion itself against the inevitable busts. Thus when Roger Sale asks why Seattle "continued for so long to be so nakedly dependent on its one magnificently successful company," the answer is precisely *because* it was so magnificently successful.[37]

Diversifying the Seattle Economy

Seattle's roller-coaster history reflects its dependence on the size of the defense budget and the demand for commercial aircraft, both of which are controlled by sources far from the Washington State capital. It is surely no accident that the "export-base" model of economic growth was born at the University of Washington during the 1950s, a time when Boeing was booming.[38]

So Seattle badly needs to spread its economic base. One way this could happen is for Boeing to diversify internally. Or more Boeing subcontractors could locate within the Puget Sound area. Spin-offs from Boeing could form new high-technology companies. New, non-Boeing-related sectors could develop. Each of these strategies deserves discussion. Boeing has tried internal diversification over the years, starting with its short-lived excursion into furniture and sea-sleds after World War I. More ambitiously, after the "Boeing Bust," the company turned to streetcars, hydrofoils, land reclamation, water desalinization, and real estate. Yet these efforts met with mixed success. Perhaps the reason was lack of corporate experience in these fields, coupled with necessarily long development lead times. But perhaps also it was Boeing's unwillingness to invest substantial resources, since the company expected to get back into airplanes as soon as it weathered the storm. Once again, a short-term tactical adaptation prevailed over long-term strategy.

Relatively few of Boeing's subcontractors have ever been located nearby. Even during World War II, Puget Sound businesses never provided more than 5 percent of Boeing's subcontracting services.[39] Boeing, as we have seen, actively encourages a widespread network of suppliers, ostensibly to reduce the local economic impacts of downturns. Whatever the merits of this policy, it may have inhibited the development of ancillary services to help counteract military-induced fluctuations.

Boeing spin-offs are conspicuous for their absence. In contrast, expatriates from Hughes, the largest aerospace employer in California, built two of the largest defense contractors in the region: TRW and Litton. Although these spin-offs are in the same business, they broaden the economic base for the region, and they help develop the complex network of suppliers, labor markets, and scale economies that distinguish southern California aerospace. Why have Boeing employees not done the same? Even in the bust of 1968 to 1971, which provided both maximum incentive and available human capital for spin-offs, financial resources and market opportunities were limited. A few new medical technology firms were the only visible result. Whatever the reason for this failure—differences in place, technology, company structure, or mere chance—it is one of the most disturbing features of the Seattle defense economy.

Diversification might happen through new, non-Boeing-related sectors. The Seattle–King County Economic Development Council was established in 1973 for this explicit purpose.[40] Yet the city has traditionally not been very effective in diversification, and seems to resort to it only in times of crisis. Some have blamed existing organizations and interests: Dave Beck and the Teamsters, it was alleged, inhibited new businesses through their attempts to "subsidize" existing ones.[41] The local banking community has been assailed for its reluctance to provide venture capital for new and risky businesses. City officials, and the community generally, have tended to see development in terms of a glossy image of ballparks and downtown buildings, ignoring the manufacturing base. No one has given much though to import substitution in order to develop a broader economic base and to improve the city's trade balance. All in all, Seattle remains a classic example of an ossified single-sector economy, where one or a few firms dominate local resource markets.[42]

Boeing and the Seattle Labor Market

As the largest employer, as well as the only major aerospace employer, in Seattle Boeing has a huge impact on the regional labor market. The Puget Sound high-tech labor pool is essentially the Boeing labor pool. To be sure, Boeing is not the only defense contractor in the region: the Puget Sound Naval Shipyard employs more than 11,000; the new Trident submarine base, up to 7,000. But neither is in aerospace.[43] In economic jargon, Boeing is a monopsonist, a dominating buyer, in this local labor market. This gives it major advantages. It has a largely captive skilled labor pool, which has a lower strike potential because of the lack of alternative work. For the same reason, Boeing can afford to invest more heavily in building its employees' skills.

Yet there is a downside too, even for Boeing. In booms, when labor is tight, it cannot "raid" other local aerospace corporations, as Los Angeles firms do. It can hire only from outside, entailing major relocation expenses. These factors, plus the risk to the worker of moving to a one-firm city, may drive up Boeing wages. The company thus lacks the short-term flexibility and surge capacity that characterize its Los Angeles competitors.

But if monopsony is problematic for Boeing, it creates much bigger travails for the region's other firms. During the aerospace boom of the late 1980s, Boeing was willing and able to pay electricians about $4 more per hour than local shipbuilders. This has exacerbated problems for the latter: Lockheed Shipping, Todd Shipyards, and Marine Power and Equipment Company have suffered major financial difficulties.[44] If (or when) the boom ends, Boeing wages will doubtless sink again to those of the shipbuilders, as they did during the great bust. But some shipbuilders may not be around to benefit.

Geographic Concentration and Political Power

Unlike many of its competitors, Boeing concentrates its operations in one sparsely populated state. It is one of the few major aerospace companies with no major facilities in either California or the Boston–New York corridor. This affects its strength in the political battle for defense dollars. Boeing is only too well aware of its concentration in a state with relatively little political clout. It is doubly aware of this since the loss of senators Warren Magnuson and Henry "Scoop" Jackson, two powerful voices in the nation's capital. Like other major contractors, Boeing tries to build "geographic constituencies" to solicit broader political support. As one Boeing official put it, "It's wise to be nationwide."

Two key questions thus arise about Boeing in politics. How has the political dimension of location in Washington State influenced the company's operations? And how influential have powerful voices in the United States Senate been for Boeing? Some key defense-contracting decisions provide interesting evidence.

The TFX Controversy: Place, Product, or Industrial Policy?

Earlier, we cited the TFX/F-111 decision of 1962 as a case of defense-contractor bailout. Yet the Pentagon's choice of the General Dynamics/Grumman design for a new, variable-sweep-wing tactical fighter, over the apparently superior Boeing design, had a political dimension too. General Dynamics planned to produce the plane at its Fort Worth facility, and some suggested that these new jobs in Vice President Lyndon Johnson's home state were a component in the Kennedy reelection strategy. Others pointed to personal ties between the Department of Defense and New York, the location of subcontractor Grumman.[45] During the resulting Senate investigation, called

by Senator Jackson of Washington State, Defense Secretary Robert Mc-
Namara rejected allegations that the TFX decision was influenced by political-
geographic bias, and none was proved.

Yet a third explanation comes in an excellent account by Robert Art.[46]
Art highlights the rivalry between McNamara and the armed services.
Boeing's proposed TFX was a risky yet powerful design, the "best plane at
any cost" favored by the armed services. General Dynamics/Grumman offered an ostensibly safer, more cost-effective design that appealed to the
efficiency-minded McNamara. The decision represented a victory for Mc-
Namara's value-for-money style over the top Air Force brass. Whatever the
true explanation—and maybe all three played a part—the company lost its
first chance in years to produce a new military airplane to follow its B-47 and
B-52. Instead, Boeing expanded into commercial jets, a market much less
affected by geopolitics.

The "Senator from Boeing"

Even though Washington was a relatively sparsely populated state far from
the nation's capital, for several decades it had a loud, powerful voice in
Congress. Henry "Scoop" Jackson, a Puget Sound native, elected first to the
House in 1940, then to the Senate in 1952, was dubbed "the Senator from
Boeing" during his 1958 reelection campaign. Ironically, the most controversial issue at the time was a right-to-work proposal that pitted Jackson, on
the side of the unions, against Boeing president William Allen. Allen reportedly referred to the freshman senator as "that goddamned socialist,"
although the two eventually became friends.

A deeper irony was that the Jackson era was primarily notable for the
contracts that Boeing either failed to obtain (the TFX, the C-5A) or saw
canceled (the SST, the Dyna-Soar).[47] It was not for want of trying on Jackson's
part, however. It was at his instigation that a Senate subcommittee convened
for ten months to review Boeing's loss of the TFX award to General Dynamics/
Grumman. A decade later, Jackson and his colleague, Senator Magnuson,
fought a long, hard battle to retain government funding for the SST. But the
economic and ecologic arguments were just too strong, and the SST went
down to defeat. These cases underscore the implausibility of explaining
military-spending patterns solely as a function of strenuous efforts by senior
members of Congress.

Perhaps Jackson's most spectacular pro-Boeing efforts came in the early
1980s. The Air Force was seeking a replacement for the aging and troubled
Lockheed C-5A transport plane, needed to move troops quickly to trouble
zones worldwide, to be called the C-X (Cargo EXperimental). In January
1981, three contractors submitted bids: Lockheed, McDonnell-Douglas, and
Boeing. They were the three survivors in the commercial-jet market, and
envisioned rich commercial spin-offs from the contract.

The battle narrowed to a choice between a new design, the C-17, from
McDonnell-Douglas, and an updating of forty-four existing Lockheed C-5s

in that company's Georgia and California facilities. The Lockheed bid promised a cheaper, faster plane. Besides, the company was in major financial trouble following the failure of its L-1011 widebody commercial jet, and its Georgia plant lacked work. In January 1982, against strong service opposition, the Department of Defense announced that Lockheed had won. As a consolation prize for McDonnell-Douglas, there were extra orders for that company's KC-10 tanker/cargo plane and F-15 fighter jet. Only Boeing was left empty-handed.[48]

Boeing officials were furious. The decision hit the firm particularly hard, for its commercial-jet business was in a mini-recession. Belatedly, Boeing offered to convert forty-eight used 747 commercial jetliners to military transport planes; it maintained that if cost and speed of delivery were crucial, then this would be the best solution. But the 747 was too small to carry large military equipment such as M-1 and M-60 tanks or many helicopters, it lacked easy loading capabilities, and it needed better runways than the Lockheed planes, making it less useful on war-torn battlefields.

Senator Jackson, along with his home-state colleagues Senator Slade Gordon and Representative Norman Dicks, lobbied mightily for the Boeing 747 over the Lockheed C-5B. Senator Robert Dole of Kansas, where the 747 modification work would be performed, supported the Boeing proposal. Senator Sam Nunn of Georgia, the location of Lockheed's Marietta plant, opposed it and reminded his colleagues that they would not buy International Harvester combines over M-1 tanks just because Harvester was in trouble. Senator Jackson, who was skillful at rounding up votes, was helped on the day of the Senate vote when Braniff Airlines went bankrupt. The Senate voted 60 to 39 for the 747s over the C-5B. But Jackson's, and Boeing's, victory was short-lived. Pentagon officials and Lockheed met in secret conclave, the C-5B group, to lobby the House. One tactic was to threaten cancellation of several Boeing military contracts. Two months later, on July 21, 1982, the House voted 289 to 127 for the Lockheed C-5B.[49]

Boeing depends on federal support even for its commercial endeavors. In 1982, when the Reagan administration announced plans to eliminate the Export-Import Bank, Boeing swung into action. The company is a huge exporter, and its commercial sales had benefited greatly from the bank's credit activities. It fought hard to save the bank, rallying nearly 5,000 of its suppliers in every state of the country into geographically broad-based lobby. This time, Boeing succeeded; the Export/Import Bank stayed.

Seattle is a city of contrasts. Some critics have charged that the city's reliance on Boeing induces its leaders and residents to support indiscriminate cold war spending. Only in such an extraordinarily defense-sensitive economy could a local newspaper wonder in its headlines, "Would a Lasting Peace Be Devastating to Area?" Yet Seattle is also the home base of the Sane/Freeze organization, which has actively lobbied for disarmament and economic diversification.[50]

Boeing and Seattle: The Balance Sheet

If all the aerospace companies in the Los Angeles Basin are located at the metaphorical "center of the tree," then Boeing in Seattle is at the end of the branch. Seattle is far from a traditional center of industry; its economy is more noted for port, shipbuilding, and natural-resource industries. It is an odd site for a major airplane producer needing a complex and sophisticated network of suppliers and subcontractors. Indeed, perhaps only William Boeing's independent wealth and Navy connections allowed him to pursue airplane production in such a distant corner of the country. As Gerald Nelson noted, "In 1916, only a madman or a rich visionary would have incorporated an airplane factory in Seattle."[51]

Boeing officials are wryly amused by what they see as the sun-and-surf snobbery of their Los Angeles competitors. As one put it to us: "We're not out in the woods." The company's vast size and diverse facilities throughout the Puget Sound area give it a particular advantage. Although there is some dispersion of Boeing operations within the region, to cities like Bellevue, Kent, Auburn, and Everett, all these locations are comfortably within the Greater Seattle housing and labor market. This fact gives Boeing unique internal agglomeration economies, such as flexibility in using plant capacity and labor mobility—particularly helpful features in an industry that suffers cyclical fluctuations.

Boeing has exploited this economic advantage through a systematic company-wide, employee-initiated internal mobility policy, unique to the aerospace business. For example, production of the 707, 727, and 737 was consolidated under one roof during the "Boeing Bust." Occasionally, such transfers are more complex and costly. The 747 buildup in 1966 and 1967, for instance, involved a massive transfer of production workers from the Wichita plant to Seattle and Everett.[52] But generally, Boeing's concentration in the Puget Sound area means that redeployment is relatively painless.

University Ties

A number of institutional and cultural features helped to anchor Boeing in Seattle and enabled it to thrive. The most prominent of these features is the University of Washington. Once more of a local educational center, the university has evolved—especially during the 1960s—into a solid research institution with significant federal grants. Boeing has close ties with the university, encompassing sizable grants, recruitment, and continuing education of Boeing employees. Boeing takes advantage of the advanced-degree programs at Seattle University, the University of Puget Sound, and Pacific Lutheran, too, and the company also sends its employees to schools outside the region, such as Stanford, for classes and seminars.

The University of Washington's involvement in aeronautics dates back to Boeing's earliest days. In 1916, William Boeing, a young mining and timber heir, recruited a number of engineering students from the nearby campus, including Claire Egtvedt and Phil Johnson, both of whom would play significant roles in the company for decades. In 1917, the year that a chair for the teaching of aeronautics was established,[53] Boeing donated a wind tunnel, patterned after the first such tunnel at MIT. When the armistice diminished interest in aviation, the chair was abandoned and the aeronautics courses were removed from the engineering curriculum. But four years later, F. K. Kirsten, a professor of electrical engineering, revived the courses and put the wind tunnel back into service. Kirsten was appointed to a permanent chair in aeronautics in 1926.

It was probably this ten-year history of aeronautical education that attracted the attention of the Daniel Guggenheim Fund for the Promotion of Aeronautics. Guggenheim money had already supported aeronautics programs at New York University, Caltech, Stanford, the University of Michigan, and MIT. A belated concern about geographic distribution led in 1928 to a grant of $290,000 for the University of Washington's program; the Washington State legislature added $50,000 for equipment.

At the suggestion of William Boeing, Professor E. O. Eastwood, head of the mechanical engineering department, was appointed director of aeronautics. The Daniel Guggenheim Hall of Aeronautics was opened in 1930, and eight years later the school completed a third, larger wind tunnel with funds from Boeing, the Washington legislature, and the federal Works Progress Administration. Boeing and the school used the facility jointly; no other Guggenheim school appeared to have nearly as close a relationship to a single aviation company.[54]

The first six bachelor's degree students were graduated in 1930. After a slow start during the Depression, average class size climbed to roughly sixteen by the late 1930s. Some graduates went to work for the government at Wright Field or Langley Field; others to aviation firms around the country. Many joined Boeing. By the end of that decade, the majority of the company's engineers had been trained at the University of Washington.

Boeing's engineering teams are no longer dominated by University of Washington alumni, and although Boeing continues to use the university's tunnel for low-speed test work, the company has long since built its own facilities. The university never generated ground-breaking new research on a par with legendary figures like MIT's Jerome Hunsaker and Charles Stark Draper or Caltech's Theodore von Kármán and Clark Millikan. Yet it made important contributions to the development of multi-engine bombers and transport planes, and it helped establish the Pacific Northwest as a center of aviation and aeronautical-engineering talent.

Recruitment and Retention

Turnover in the aerospace industry is high, and Boeing hires about 1,000 new employees a year in the professional and technical fields. Although recruits come from a cross section of the United States, the company finds it easier to hire people from the Midwest and the West, rather than from the East.[55] Within California, recruiters sometimes refer to the SLO (San Luis Obispo) line, named for the modest-size town halfway between Los Angeles and San Francisco. Professionals and technicians from north of the SLO line are more willing to go to Seattle than those living south.

Boeing salary offers are usually $1,000 to $2,000 less per year than those of Los Angeles aerospace companies, but Seattle's relatively low cost of living and high quality of life make it an attractive place to live and work. In general, housing costs are lower and traffic is less congested than in Los Angeles, Boston, and other urbanized regions. The appeal of Seattle is one of the main reasons that Boeing also has a strong hold on its workers, as could be seen in the surprisingly low out-migration during the bust years of 1968 to 1971.

Labor Relations

Unlike other defense-contracting firms, Boeing has a long tradition of unionism. The company's employees are served by both the International Association of Machinists and Aerospace Workers (IAM), the largest Boeing union, and the United Auto Workers. In 1986, the IAM counted 28,000 members in Seattle, 9,000 in Wichita, and 1,100 in Portland.[56]

Some Boeing officials told us that labor relations have improved over time, but that might be because management has won major wage concessions, starting with a two-tier wage scale adopted during the 1983 recession. This agreement lowered starting salaries and specified that annual lump-sum payments would be awarded in lieu of general wage increases. Security analysts estimated that these measures saved Boeing $100 million in the three years following the contract. Surprisingly, despite a boom in business and a $317 million profit in 1986, management was able to win union agreement to maintain this wage structure.[57]

Management has also won greater flexibility and cost savings through union acceptance of increased plant automation in exchange for retraining. In addition, the contracting-out of traditional in-house work—a policy Boeing began during the 1970s downturn—has cut the company's payroll. This loss of jobs, coupled with the fact that contracted-out work often goes to nonunion shops, has spurred IAM officials to step up their organizing efforts.[58]

Boeing and Taxes

Tax rates are seldom seen as one of the important factors shaping the location decisions of defense contractors. Rather, firms are believed to be attracted by labor-market quality, proximity to universities and government facilities, high-tech agglomeration, and amenities. Nonetheless, like any other large business, defense contractors face significant taxation, and they are often adept at lowering the burden. Citizens for Tax Justice ranked Boeing number 3 among the nation's leading corporate tax freeloaders. At the state level, nonfinancial businesses like Boeing have been exempted from business and occupation taxes on their interest income. In 1987, Governor Booth Gardner tried to close this loophole, but he was thwarted by Boeing lobbyists. Boeing officials have threatened to move some operations out of the state if the tax burden is not lowered. Such tactics have led some legislative staffers to refer to Boeing as the proverbial "800-pound gorilla."[59]

In general, despite protests about tax rates, Boeing management seems to have no fundamental dissatisfaction with its Seattle location. Isolated suggestions that the corporate headquarters be moved to Washington, D.C., or New York have been dismissed out-of-hand. For the question of whether Seattle is an "ideal" location appears out of place; Boeing is a Seattle company, both by inertia and by long tradition.

Yet Boeing does find its heavy cyclical impact on the Seattle economy to be a problem; it would actually prefer not to be so dominant in the area, if only for public-relations reasons during downturns. And the lack of congressional clout, compounded by the absence of a powerful voice to replace Senator Jackson's, provides a further incentive for Boeing to disperse its operations.

Boeing's Second Homes: Wichita, Philadelphia, and the Southeast

Although its headquarters and most of its employees are in Seattle, Boeing has large facilities in other parts of the country. The most important are the huge Boeing Military Airplane Company in Wichita, Kansas, and the Boeing Helicopter Company in Philadelphia, the latter a somewhat autonomous organization. Both became part of Boeing through acquisitions: the Wichita facility in 1934; the Philadelphia division with the purchase of the Vertol Aircraft Corporation in 1960. Smaller facilities, which are mostly in the South and Southeast, are interesting for what they reveal of the firm's recent dispersion strategy, including decisions on product lines and plant expansions.

Wichita

Boeing's operation in Kansas resulted from the short-lived United Aircraft and Transport Corporation (UATC), when the Stearman Aircraft Company of Wichita was first added to the huge conglomerate in 1929 and then attached to Boeing after UATC's dissolution in 1934. Lloyd Stearman was a native of Wichita, but his company originated in Venice, California. In 1927, ten Wichita businessmen raised $60,000 to move it to the Wichita flying field, where production of sport planes and mail planes began.[60] But despite its commercial origin, the Wichita plant owed its survival to the rise of atmospheric warfare. The private airplane market was hit hard by the Depression, forcing Stearman to turn to production of military trainers to keep solvent. Business picked up considerably, and in September 1939 Stearman received a new contract to produce 255 more trainers, to be known as Kaydets. By 1943, the company had produced more than 7,000 trainers.[61]

The mass-production experience that the Kayder trainers provided for the Boeing work force proved invaluable when Boeing's Wichita plant became the country's main producer of B-29s. An initial order for 250 of Boeing's new B-29 Superfortress in 1941 led to massive wartime expansion after the military decided that the production plant for these bombers should be away from the danger of coastal attack. Employment jumped from 2,500 to over 27,000. By war's end, Wichita had produced a staggering 1,644 B-29s. In comparison, 1,050 were produced at Boeing's Renton plant (just southeast of Seattle), 668 by Bell Aircraft in Marietta, Georgia, and 536 by Martin in Omaha.[62]

In the days after the war, the government-owned Plant Two closed, and the greatly reduced staff withdrew to the original Plant One. B-29 production ended at Wichita, while modest production continued in Renton. But when the Berlin airlift began in 1948, the Air Force decided to modernize World War II B-29s, and, following the recommendations of the Finletter Report for further aircraft-plant dispersion, Boeing was asked to reopen Plant Two for the work. And the B-47 Stratojet, designed in Seattle and first flown in late 1947, represented a major new Boeing production line.

Boeing wanted to produce the B-47 in Seattle, in its own plant and with its existing organization and engineers. But the Air Force's General Kenneth Wolfe, at Wright Field, insisted on Wichita. Boeing president Bill Allen, maintaining that his home plant was being bypassed because of its supposedly vulnerable Pacific location, appealed to Stuart Symington, the new Secretary of the Air Force:

> We are not as close to the coast as many plants. We have to do this job with people. Certain kinds of people. And people have their own ideas of where they want to live. We'd lose a lot of our ability if we tried to move them all inland. If our country has an Achilles heel, won't the enemy strike at that heel wherever it is? Isn't dispersal of industry the answer, rather than just geographical location?[63]

The Seattle community also responded to the threat of "decoastalization" of the B-47 and the upcoming B-52 program.[64] E. L. Skeel, a former head of the city's Chamber of Commerce, founded a group called: "Save Boeing—Defend Seattle." Skeel argued that given the many important national security facilities in the area, including Hanford, the Bremerton Naval Shipyard, and the hydroelectric dams on the Columbia, a more prudent strategy would be to improve the defenses of the Pacific Northwest. According to Skeel, Los Angeles, with its high density of defense contractors, was more vulnerable than Seattle.[65] When Boeing even tried to solicit the southern California industry's help, Oliver P. Echols, a retired officer who was chairman of Northrop, responded: "That's strictly a Boeing problem." Lee Atwood, president of North American, was philosophical: "I can't see how the industry can help Boeing if the Air Force is pressuring the firm to concentrate its military production at Wichita."[66] Nonetheless, the Los Angeles firms were concerned that they would be forced to move to surplus war plants in Tulsa, Oklahoma City, Omaha, and Fort Worth.

Some in Seattle even saw a plot: "Nationalization Seen as Motive in Moving Plants," read one newspaper headline. A *Seattle Times* columnist conjectured that the attempt to move Boeing and other airplane manufacturers to surplus, federally owned plants in the Midwest and elsewhere was part of a larger scheme to gain complete government control of the industry.[67] Secretary Symington ultimately concluded that it was in the government's interest to have the B-47 produced in Wichita, but that the production of B-50s and C-97 transports (both propeller planes) and the mock-up of the B-52 would stay in Seattle. Because the B-47 was then a cornerstone of air-defense strategy, the project had top priority, forcing Boeing to shift executive from Seattle to Wichita and to massively expand its Wichita operation. Wichita received a further boost in October 1952 when the Air Force selected it as a second site for the B-52.[68]

The decision to concentrate military production in Kansas fundamentally affected corporate strategy in Seattle, spurring management to push for commercial projects for the Seattle facilities and labor force. Certainly, that side of Boeing business has remained firmly on Puget Sound, with no hint of a transfer to Wichita. Yet eventually, as we shall see, the attractions of decentralization would jeopardize this commitment.

Wichita Today

The Wichita facilities are currently the headquarters of the Boeing Military Airplane Company (BMAC), one of seven Boeing operating companies. By the late 1980s, they employed over 20,000 people, including about 1,000 workers at Boeing Computer Services. Although this is a far cry from the 35,000 who worked there in 1957 at the peak of the B-52 program, it is still a dramatic increase over the 14,500 employees of late 1982 and the mere 5,000 of 1971. Boeing's Wichita operation is not well known outside the area, but it has been the largest employer in Kansas for much of the 1980s. Its approximately 16,000 employees in 1981 comfortably exceeded the 13,000 at Cessna, 10,000 at Beechcraft, and 3,000 at Gates Learjet.[69] Boeing's premium pay scale allows it to compete with these three other aviation firms for Wichita labor.

Attempting to transform the company's image in Kansas from a "prairie sheet metal shop" to a modern facility, Boeing has undertaken a major modernization at Wichita. It also purchased the old government-owned plant in 1979 for $44.7 million—the biggest property sale in the General Services Administration's history, involving 573 acres and 69 buildings, and requiring congressional approval.[70] The Wichita operation was also restructured through the formation of BMAC—a partial response to a string of military-contract losses. Expansion at Wichita has involved participation in the Air Force Aeronautical Systems Division's technology modernization program, with new automation and flexible machining equipment to produce components for the Common Strategic Rotary Launcher, a cruise missile launcher, and for the A-6 re-wing program.[71]

Yet it is doubtful that Boeing–Wichita will ever transcend its subordinate role to Boeing–Seattle. Despite expansion, it will remain a facility for producing parts, not new aircraft, directly dependent on Seattle for its future. As a Boeing spokesman in Seattle recently commented on the company's bidding for the Advanced Tactical Fighter (ATF):

> Assignment of actual production work to Wichita isn't likely to have a major effect on Boeing employment or business here [in Seattle] but it will help assure the business future for that business. . . . It's always been our policy that the up-front technology work in the BMAC is done here and Wichita does the production work.[72]

Boeing in the Southeast

Boeing also has operations in scattered cities throughout the nation, with a distinctive cluster in the southeastern United States. These include KC-135 tanker maintenance in Lake Charles, Louisiana; aircraft refurbishing and repair in Greenville, Mississippi; aerospace operations at Cocoa Beach, Florida, and Houston, Texas; computer services in Huntsville, Alabama; aircraft and missile-system components fabrication and assembly in Oak Ridge, Tennessee; and electronics facilities near Dallas, Texas, and in Corinth, Texas. Although significantly smaller in size and employment than the operations in Seattle, Wichita, and Philadelphia, they reflect a broader, more recent trend in the company and the industry toward the Southeast.

Oak Ridge is an interesting although somewhat unusual example. Boeing originally contracted with the federal government to build and operate a uranium-enrichment facility there. The contract was canceled in 1984, since the Boeing plant was designed to manufacture centrifuge equipment, and the Department of Energy was shifting to a laser process. Boeing decided to convert the facility, where it had assembled a good labor force, to manufacture aircraft and missile parts.

There have been other motivations for the expansion in the Southeast. Lower labor rates are one, particularly in places like Louisiana and Mississippi. States and localities have been very helpful, sometimes because of civic boosterism, which tends to be strong. When in the mid-1980s Boeing was considering an expansion of its work force in Huntsville, Alabama, from 750 to 2,000, a local realty company sponsored relocation seminars for prospective employees.[73] Proximity to military facilities, as well as the political advantage of having a broad geographic base, have also played a role, as has lack of space at Wichita. Boeing also says that some moves were prompted by the opportunity to tap new labor pools, particularly at Huntsville and Oak Ridge. And the political advantage of having operations spread around the country needs no underlining.

In some cases, problems have arisen with the dispersion policy. Although the Oak Ridge expansion was apparently smooth, other southeastern localities have not had the requisite skill level. A great deal of unanticipated training has been needed, and Boeing has had to bring in its own people to help. There did not seem to be much resistance to this: as one Boeing official commented, the people on the Seattle staff are "good soldiers."

Sometimes, too, these branch operations are not able to maintain sufficient work. The Greenville, Mississippi, facility was originally established to install new wings on the Navy's A-6 attack aircraft. The state contributed $10 million, the city and county offered $5 million in bonds, and the federal government added another $5 million in grants to construct a new building and refurbish hangers at the city's old military airport. Yet the A-6 project never came about, nor did the anticipated 1,000 workers. In late 1988, when temporary work on the Navy's C-9 military transport began to wane and no new work was scheduled, Boeing announced that the plant would shut, affecting about 250 workers.[74]

A new Boeing facility was planned for a remote site in north central Oregon, just west of a large Navy bombing range. The planned 6,000-acre space-research center would conduct research and development on space chambers, lasers, missiles, and a proposed transatmospheric space plane. The site was selected from fifty-one others in the Pacific Northwest, apparently because of its remoteness from radio and television transmission and heavy-vehicle traffic. Boeing originally leased 93,000 acres in 1964 to develop a space-age industrial park, but the project never jelled. The huge tract was acquired from ranchers, sometimes through condemnation, following a special Oregon legislative session, and with $1.9 million in Oregon Department of Veterans Affairs money to purchase land. Governor Mark Hatfield referred to Boeing's plans as "a major bid to thrust Oregon into the space age."[75]

Another rather special Boeing location is the recently acquired $275 million ARGOSystems in Sunnyvale, California, part of an attempt to gain a stronger foothold in defense electronics. ARGOSystems produces such military electronics as communications reconnaissance equipment, electronic warfare equipment, and systems engineering in signal processing. It employed 1,200 people at the time of acquisition. It operates as an independent subsidiary, reporting directly to corporate headquarters in Seattle, rather than to Wichita.[76]

Boeing's Future: Seattle Versus the Rest

One central question emerges from this discussion: To what extent will Boeing continue to decentralize? It seems that top management increasingly questions the wisdom of such heavy concentration in Seattle. There is concern about the stresses on local infrastructure and services during bursts of growth and, equally, about the effect of massive layoffs on the city's economy during periods of slump.

It is important to distinguish between organizational and geographic decentralization. When asked about decentralization, most defense contractors tend to think of internal corporate structure, rather than geography. Within Boeing, there even appears to be a slight move back to organizational centralization, to give the CEO a better handle on the company. Yet there is also a conscious desire to decentralize geographically. Telecommunications and air travel make it less vital to have all operations close to one another. And other locations, particularly in the Southeast, appear increasingly attractive.

Yet these southeastern locations remain relatively small. In the mid-1980s, there were only 600 employees at Oak Ridge, and 800 at Boeing Electronics outside Dallas, compared with about 100,000 in the Seattle area. Although further centrifugal growth may occur, it will not challenge Seattle's clear dominance in the Boeing hierarchy. Southeasterly expansion has greater significance for the smaller communities like Oak Ridge, or Corinth, Texas, than for Seattle. Seattle remains unconcerned, for these operations are expansions, not transfers of existing operations. The major corporate elements of Boeing seem firmly entrenched in Seattle, with even less talk of major relocation than we heard from Los Angeles aerospace firms, due in part to the absence of high housing costs, congestion, and pollution.

Thus despite its isolation, Boeing has demonstrated astonishing longevity and inertia. Its size, experience, and ability to straddle commercial and military markets have given it rare flexibility, internal agglomeration economies, and an ability to "go it alone" in the northwest corner of the nation. It is the gigantic solitary survivor. And Seattle, "Boeing Country" for more than seventy years, will remain so for many more to come.

8

Space Mountain: Generals and Boosters Build Colorado Springs

Colorado Springs is an unusual site for an aerospace complex. Poised on the abrupt junction of the High Plains and the Front range of the Rockies, flecked in winter by snow on the mesas and backed by the stark flank of Pikes Peak, it is totally unlike typical high-tech sites such as New England, Los Angeles, and Seattle. Yet something remarkable has been happening there. The natural landscape, dramatic as it is, has been overwhelmed by the man-made. Ubiquitous housing subdivisions march across the undulating plains, bringing to mind a vast military encampment—an appropriate image in light of the surprising fact that Colorado Springs, in post–World War II America, has become an archetype of the new military–industrial city.

Ironically, though, the key military underpinnings of this community are not nearly so visible. The nation's strategic defense nerve center, mimicked in the film *War Games,* is buried deep inside Cheyenne Mountain. The new National Test Bed for the Strategic Defense Initiative is being installed ten miles east of Colorado Springs, at Falcon Air Force Station. The newly unified United States Space Command operates out of adjacent Peterson Air Force Base; the Army's Fort Carson lies two mesas away to the southeast. And to the northwest, the most celebrated symbol of the military presence, the lovely Cadet Chapel at the Air Force Academy, pushes 150 feet skyward, its seventeen spires tucked up against the foothills (Fig. 8.1).

Because Colorado Springs is still relatively small and simple, it is like a fishbowl for researchers. Its people—including top military officials, private contractors, and past and present leaders of the city's business-development efforts—are easily identified and were more than willing to be interviewed. Time and again, these people mentioned the interplay between private companies, military leaders, and city boosters, revealing a way of thinking and business culture that has been central to the rise of both the gunbelt, and the cities of the Sunbelt.

Compared with the places previously explored in this book—New England, Seattle, even Los Angeles—Colorado Springs is a relatively new center of defense production. Its rise to prominence began only in the

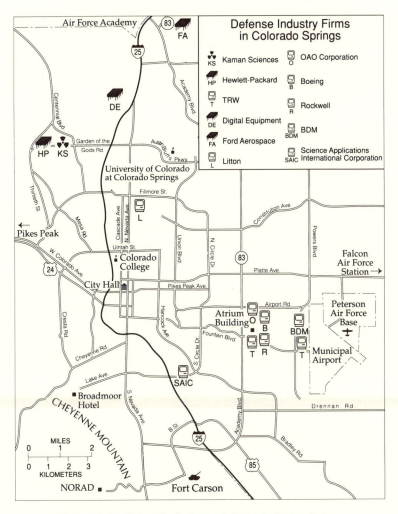

FIGURE 8.1. Colorado Springs: defense-industry firms.

1950s. It boasts no roster of industrial founding fathers: pioneer engineer-entrepreneurs who staked their talents, ambitions, and modest fortunes on their preferred locale. Instead, it owes its fortune, and even its existence, to another kind of founder: one with no particular scientific or manufacturing expertise, but possessed of intense civic pride and an urge to develop and promote the city, often for high returns and personal profit. Colorado Springs is a creation of its boosters: an odd amalgam of local officials, business and real-estate leaders, and military elite, most seeking financial gain, prestige, or both, who conspired over the decades to establish the Springs as the "Space Capital of the Free World."

They were amazingly successful. Even in relation to the other stories in this book, the Colorado Springs saga is extraordinary. At the start, the city had none of the traits considered essential for a high-tech future: no high-

TABLE 8.1.   Colorado Springs Military-Related Personnel, 1985

Installation	Military	Civilian	Total
Peterson Air Force Base	5,213	1,869	7,082
Fort Carson	20,166	3,284	23,450
Air Force Academy*	7,068	2,137	9,205
Other[†]	2,234	63	2,297
Retirees	15,819	3,584	19,403
Total	50,500	10,937	61,437

*Includes 4,459 cadets.

[†]Includes reserves and National Guard.

Source: Air Force Space Command, Directorate of Cost, "Department of Defense FY 85 Economic Impact on Colorado, Colorado Springs: Peterson Air Force Base," May 1, 1986.

tech labor force, no local companies of any note, no research university, no hub airport. It still could not claim the last three as late as the mid-1960s. Yet from a tiny Depression-ridden resort town of fewer than 35,000 residents at the end of the 1930s, by 1985 it had grown almost tenfold to 306,000, with 27 percent of its output in manufacturing and some 15,200 high-tech employees in more than 20 facilities. How did this apparent miracle happen?

The most obvious answer is direct military investment. By 1985, Colorado Springs housed 35,000 military personnel,[1] its total population 50 years earlier, plus 7,300 civilian federal employees. Three independent military complexes—Peterson Air Force Base, with its associated NORAD (North American Air Defense Command) and Space Command; the Army's Fort Carson; and the Air Force Academy—each accounted for a minimum of 5,000 personnel (Table 8.1). Together they had generated a local population of nearly 20,000 retirees. The town captured almost one-half of the state's total military payroll—$507 million a year—and its military complexes were responsible for more than 60,000 livelihoods.

Yet this is not the story of one Congressman landing a coveted military base for his hometown. Rather, it encompasses a complex sequence of activities and decisions, involving key military installations and private company plants and labs, that occurred over several decades. The phenomenal development of Colorado Springs powerfully illustrates the value of a dynamic location theory that incorporates historical change and within which the dependent variables of one era become the independent forces of another.

Four eras in the Colorado Springs story are distinguishable. First, in the late 1930s, the tourism-depressed local business community saw its chances in the incipient war and lobbied relentlessly for a share of the nation's new military facilities. They won both a large troop-training base, Camp Carson, and an Air Force base to train pilots, Peterson Air Field. Second, desperately struggling to stave off postwar recession, in 1951 the community secured one of the new cold war plums—the Air Defense Command, later to become NORAD. In the same era, the community landed the prized United States Air Force Academy, the chief educational institution for the newly ascendant Air Force.

Third, in the mid-1960s, the town garnered yet another military facility: the "hot war" Fort Carson, which made a large and ongoing contribution to the local blue-collar work force through dependents and mustered-out soldiers. Simultaneously, and continuing over the next decade, a number of commercially oriented high-tech plants located in the area, to take advantage of amenities for their professional work force and the relatively low cost of local nonunionized labor.

Finally, in the 1980s, Colorado Springs emerged as what local enthusiasts call the "Space Capital of the Free World," or more truly the military space capital, with the capture of the military's Consolidated Space Operations Center and certain key Star Wars facilities. A number of large military-dependent research and development labs, plus several dozen smaller, service-oriented branch plants, have gravitated toward this space defense complex to serve the nation's military space mission.

What were the chief locational factors in each of these eras? How do the attributes built into the community's resource base and culture in one era contribute to the next round of sitings? To understand, we start with the city's earliest history.

Importing Wealth and Income

Colorado Springs was born in the post–Civil War era of western mining and railroad booms, a town not appreciably different from thousands of other tiny communities in the West, with a handful of promoters trying to induce thousands of people to join its few hundred residents. A half-century later, the town stood markedly apart, due chiefly to adroit land-speculation efforts of a small group of exceptionally rich and lucky men. Through influential contacts and powerful if overstated marketing, they succeeded in importing to their tiny colony several dozen medium-size fortunes, especially second sons of the English gentry and tubercular eastern society types. In the latter half of the nineteenth century, the Springs' cabal alternatively styled itself "Little London" and "Newport of the Rockies."[2]

A few townsmen prospered by monopolizing transportation and gold-mining services and by successfully reinvesting profits in speculative mining ventures. The highly uneven distribution of income and wealth generated pleasure palaces, large landholdings, and other public attractions that became permanent assets for community building, while the promotional effort remained tightly controlled in the hands of a few. Spencer Penrose and Charles Tutt cornered the market on Cripple Creek gold processing. With the profits, Penrose built the outlandishly elegant Broadmoor Hotel, which was to play a key role in military boosterism.

Colorado Springs, then, benefited from a curious type of founding father. Here, we find no indigenous high-tech entrepreneurs, pilots, researchers, or educators. Instead, we discover a determined clique of civic boosters, continually exploring new gimmicks with only sporadic success. For all of its pre–

World War II history, this community had grown only when wealth or profits could be raked in from elsewhere. As we shall see, this tradition continued through World War II and the cold war era.

Wartime Recruits: Camp Carson and the Army Base

In the late 1930s, Colorado Springs was in deep trouble. With a population of a little over 30,000, 1,500 housing units, almost 20 percent of the housing stock, lay empty. The Depression had suffocated tourism, and people fled in droves. When war in Europe and rumors of American involvement in the hostilities began stimulating the American aircraft industry, residents with skills began to emigrate to southern California. One old-time promoter, Joe Reich, reported, "Well, when it was clear there was going to be a war, some of us decided to try to get something out of it." They decided to seek a small military installation, with a price tag of a modest million.[3]

Pearl Harbor and FDR's decision to build up the Army Air Corps created the need for instant overnight air bases, principally for training pilots. These "one design"—easily built and quickly constructed—bases were best located where the land was cheap and the weather sunny, since large tracks of land were needed and pilots had to be trained as quickly as possible. Colorado Springs scored on both points. Because it had been hit by the Great Plains drought, Colorado Springs in the late 1930s seemed to have more annual average sunshine than usual. Furthermore, pre–World War II eastern Colorado was riddled with abandoned farms that could fulfill the need for inexpensive land.

The Springs' promoters—who included the Tutt family, the executors of Penrose's Broadmoor trust, and a banker, a dentist, a hardware man, a restaurateur, and a man with a plumbing business—raised $28,000 from private businessmen to plug Colorado Springs as a base site. These boosters prevailed over dissenters such as ranchers, farmers, and traditionalists like the Territorial Daughters of Colorado. "The Army was not just throwing bases around," reported Reich. "The town had to want it and support it, with energy, water, and so on."

The boosters, under the auspices of the Military Affairs Committee of the Chamber of Commerce, developed a case for the Springs as a base location and sent their strongest suitors—the bankers, the Chamber of Commerce types, and the Broadmoor people—to Washington to lobby. Their major opponent was President Roosevelt's coordinator of war, William S. Knudsen, who asserted that Colorado Springs was snowbound from October to June. The group countered every objection, and held out as an inducement a 35,000-acre parcel of free land. In January 1942 the effort paid off, and Colorado Springs won not one, but two facilities—Camp Carson and the small Peterson Army Air Base. Together they would provide a payroll of $5 million per month. To build Camp Carson, the U.S. government spent $30 million and hastily threw up 1,650 buildings to train a total of 30,000 troops.[4]

But the Springs had even more going for it. The Broadmoor and its downtown sister, the Antlers Hotel, became war facilities of sorts. Tutt and his friends wined and dined the top brass of the services at a new club they set up. They called it "Rest and Aspiration." This "time-out" for war-weary generals, including Dwight Eisenhower, permitted the military men to "get tight and tell their woes," according to Reich, one of the key promoters. The generals began to think of the Springs as both a pleasure ground and a place where the military was respected. The personal ties forged between the Colorado Springs and the service elites in this manner proved highly valuable in later local efforts to preserve and extend military capacity.

At the war's end, the government closed Colorado Springs' training facilities, as they did across much of the sparsely settled interior of the nation. Peterson Field, which had served as an air base, reverted to the city of Colorado Springs as a municipal airport. Political competition over base closings was intense in Congress, and Colorado Springs had no special congressional clout. Following the war, the Chamber of Commerce regrouped to tackle the problem of inevitable postwar loss of military funds. City officials elected to continue to seek outside sources of income and jobs for the community—a strategy that had so often succeeded in the past. As the cold war stepped up, Colorado Springs moved quickly to lure some of the new military facilities coming on line.

Cold War Trophy: The Air Defense Command

The rise of cold war in the late 1940s forced the military establishment to reexamine its priorities. "Defense" took precedence over offense, as new threats came from strategic bombers, with their devastating nuclear deliveries, and the possibility of submarine-launched missiles. The newly independent Air Force picked up many of these responsibilities. The technologies central to the Air Force's mission were radar, communications systems, and the new jet-fighter interceptors, like North American's F-86 Sabrejet and Lockheed's F-94, "all-weather" interceptor.[5] One source put it this way:

> Air defense . . . occupies a major position in the thinking of the U.S. Air Force. During the days of World War II, the Air Force's primary object was carrying the fight to the enemy. But there is a new line of thought today . . . and for the first time in United States aviation history, a separate major command has been established to handle that feature of the operation.[6]

The Air Force grew rapidly during this era, and it created new commands to meet the challenge. In 1950, it decided to establish the Air Defense Command (ADC) to act as the nerve center for the nation. By centralizing and streamlining operations, the ADC would oversee a large and growing number of dispersed fighter bases.[7] The question was where to locate the new command. ADC's precursor organization, headquartered at Mitchell Field on Long Island, was now considered undesirable, since coastal locations would be vulnerable to attack if submarine-launched missiles were developed. The

Air Force already maintained eastern and western operational wings for fighter forces in Newburgh, New York, and in northern California, and sought a safer interior location. Furthermore, the new ADC could not be too close to the Strategic Air Command's headquarters in Omaha.

The ADC siting was not a political football; the decision was made entirely within the military hierarchy. How did Colorado Springs manage to land this plum, which would eventually grow into the elite North American Aerospace Defense Command and United States Space Command, when dozens of other interior communities were equally as likely sites?

Once again, the Colorado boosters, with their extraordinarily good military connections and gusto for recruitment, provide the answers. In 1950 one local paper speculated that "in view of the wide popularity Colorado Springs has enjoyed in the past in Air Force circles, it appears likely that some installation probably will be established here."[8] The long years of grooming the Broadmoor as a top-brass vacation center gave Colorado Springs inside information and a head start. As K. G. Freyschlag, who headed the Chamber of Commerce in the late 1980s, put it, "winning the ADC was an outgrowth of positive relations with the second Air Force." The Broadmoor's Thayer Tutt, chairman of the Chamber of Commerce's Military Affairs Committee, personally invited General Ennis Whitehead, the ADC's new chief, for an informal visit weeks before his committee toured other prospective sites. Joe Reich, a fellow committee member, recounted, "He looked it over and said he thought it an ideal location for the headquarters." Here is a striking counterpart to the "founding father" thesis of defense-plant location—a military VIP who had a strong preference and made it stick.[9]

Colorado Springs attracted the general not just because of the hospitality of the Broadmoor clique. The town's promotional effort was by this time slick, innovative, and unabashedly pro-military. To demonstrate the community's eagerness, the Chamber of Commerce offered the idled and available Peterson Air Field on attractive terms and pledged to build 1,000 units of housing, much of it rental, to shelter the incoming work force. Simultaneously, it aggressively sought designation as a "defense area" under the new $3 billion Defense Housing Act, which provided up to 90 percent of the cost of such new units through an extension of the Federal Housing Authority. To ensure a congressional voice for their strategy, the chamber helped bankroll the successful House campaign of J. Edgar Chenoweth, a pro-military Republican who defeated the Democratic incumbent. The chamber's lead role continued after the base was won: through 1951, it operated a Military Housing Office out of its own quarters, from which it both allocated existing space and worked assiduously with developers to create more.[10]

All these efforts were successful and were the initial experiments in what was to become a formula for the local boosters: an all-out effort on every conceivable front to win increments of a new kind of external income-generating capacity—U.S. military activities. A key and explicit argument was that Colorado Springs was a military-friendly place. As the chamber's Freyschlag described it: "It was eyeball to eyeball. . . . We have one of the most outstanding military-civilian relationships in the nation. We do not like to call ourselves 'civilians' and them 'military,' we just call everybody 'citizens.' "

In U.S. society, where the status of military leaders among other national elites is relatively low, this type of welcome was unusual and rewarded.[11]

Winning the Air Force Academy: The "Postmark of Colorado Springs"

As specialized and durable as the air defense function was, it could not by itself boost Colorado Springs into clear stature as a military enclave. Air defense could be shifted to other locales relatively easily, as much would be in the late 1970s. The gem that permanently gave Colorado Springs its respectability as an elite and singular military town was the Air Force Academy.

Interservice rivalries, and the birth of an independent Air Force, played a key role in this increment to the Springs' defense complex. In 1948, General Hoyt Vandenberg, the Air Force chief, announced tentative plans for a separate Air Force Academy. He argued that it would be too costly to expand either West Point, where Air Force cadets were currently trained, or Annapolis. Of course, the status of the emerging service would also be considerably enhanced by building and operating its own educational institution. Joe Reich, a Colorado Springs restaurateur and chair of the Chamber of Commerce's Finance Committee, read the notice in the local newspaper while having his hair cut: "Newly Formed Department of the Air Force to Seek Academy." Reich, who became known as "Mr. Air Force Academy," went across the street to the president of the chamber—and within weeks, the chamber had set up an Air Academy Committee and solicited $10,000 for its lobbying effort. It assigned the task of site selection and promotion to Tutt.

The siting of the academy turned out to be a six-year ordeal. Colorado Springs made the final list during the first review in 1950. But the Korean War derailed the process, and the quest was not resumed until after the election of General Eisenhower, who had been on the original committee recommending a separate academy. This time, Congress and the Secretary of the Air Force, Harold Talbott, considered over 528 sites in 45 states. Air Force General Carl Spaatz again headed the committee, which included four others: General Hubert Harmon, who was slated to become the first superintendent of the academy; Dr. Virgil Hancher, president of the University of Iowa; General Merrill Meigs, vice president of the Hearst Corporation; and Charles A. Lindbergh. If they could agree on a site, Secretary Talbott had to accept it. If not, they were to recommend three, and Talbott would then choose. Reich believed that the committee was predisposed to Colorado Springs.

The members of the Springs Air Academy Committee aggressively used their connections with the military's top brass. According to Freyschlag, "Mr. Tutt was personally acquainted with General Eisenhower and Secretary Talbott, and everyone knew General Harmon." The committee sent two retired generals to West Point to pick up inside information on site requirements. And Father Paul Potter, a Catholic priest who was a friend of the secretary of the selection committee, "used to leak words of advice" on the Springs' suit, our interviewees told us. Colorado Springs boosters found out that the selection committee sought "15,000 acres in a naturally beautiful area with a four-seasonal climate without extremes of hot and cold." The committee was also concerned with proximity to a major city, water supply, transportation, an airport, and cost.

Tutt and his cohorts saw their big drawing card in the land category. Tutt had originally offered 4,000 acres next to the Broadmoor, but on finding that this was insufficient, the committee chose instead a huge parcel on the north side of town. Prompted by the Air Academy Committee, the Colorado state legislature quietly appropriated $1 million to buy the land. The committee hoped that the natural beauty of this site and the extraordinarily low cost of the land would give Colorado Springs a comparative advantage in the competition.

The Springs' effort faced formidable obstacles, including high altitude, distance from centers of higher learning, fear of rheumatic fever, and water shortage. The committee members assiduously worked to overcome these stumbling blocks. They secured a City Council commitment to furnish the academy at least 2 million gallons of water a day. They offered to donate Peterson Air Field. They found experts to testify that the altitude was not a problem.

Month after month, they sent envoys to Washington to present their case. Their group, renamed the Air Force Academy Foundation (AFAF), raised more lobbying money, and put together a dazzling book with a fighter jet streaking across its cover to further Colorado Springs' case. They wooed each man on the siting committee personally. They invited Lindbergh out to "fly and see for himself," which he did to his satisfaction. They catered to General Harmon's desire for a front entrance only, and to General Meigs's wish for a lake. They promised to continue AFAF activities once the academy arrived, and, indeed, they went on to raise private funding for the academy's stadium and Eisenhower golf course.

A final underrated factor, reflects K. G. Freyschlag, was the attitude of local people. "The committee did a lot of homework. They came out and talked to elevator operators, gas-station attendants, shoe clerks, and bankers" about their feelings toward the military. They were impressed—the towns-people did indeed seem to be eager to have the cadets and their educators in Colorado Springs.

In the end, the members of the selection committee could not make a unanimous choice. So they presented Secretary Talbott with three sites: Colorado Springs; Alton, Illinois; and Lake Geneva, Wisconsin. Talbott reportedly asked President Eisenhower if he would like to make the final choice, and he replied, "Not on your life!" In the end, the advantages that Colorado Springs presented—a fantastic land deal and a comfortable spot for Air Force top brass—paid off. On June 24, 1954, Secretary Talbott announced that the Springs had won the competition.

The win paid off handsomely. The Air Force bought $3.75 million of land, in addition to the state's contribution of $1 million. Over $250 million went into the physical construction of the academy over the ensuing years. More than any other facility, the academy represented a permanent commitment of operating revenues and employment to the community. Unlike other bases, its chances of being shuttered were almost zero. But more importantly, the academy became a surrogate for a university, albeit one without graduate programs, giving Colorado Springs the type of prestige that a place of learning entails. The Air Force Academy is, in Freyschlag's words, the "postmark of Colorado Springs."

Revitalizing Fort Carson

Neither the ADC nor the Air Force Academy was a particularly large installation. Each was relatively self-contained, with few linkages to the larger economy beyond demand for land, housing, and services. Few personnel from either entered the local labor force, except for the growing numbers who retired. But a third facility, Fort Carson, played a major role in Colorado Springs' labor-force expansion. A basic army training facility to prepare troops for combat in Korea, Vietnam, and, today, the Persian Gulf, it dwarfed the other installations in sheer manpower and population-generating potential.

Camp Carson, as it still was called in the early 1950s, was in trouble. It had been on standby since World War II, nearly closing after the Korean conflict. The Military Affairs Committee worked hard on its behalf, and in 1954 secured a change in status that elevated the camp to Fort Carson. Again, $13 million of congressionally approved housing funds were secured for building 1,000 units of family quarters, a first for an otherwise "temporary" base that had already exceeded its life expectancy. Each incremental change was a part of what Freyschlag calls the "permanizing strategy."

"Permanizing" was also going on at the Air Defense Command. In 1954, it was expanded to a joint command when the Army antiaircraft and the Navy radar system were integrated into its C^3I (command, control, communications, and intelligence) network. In 1957, the binational agreement with Canada led to its expansion into NORAD. At that time, the decision was made to build a heavily guarded and survivable "hole in the mountain" from which to run the nerve center, a decision that guaranteed Colorado Springs a long-term strategic role.

But permanizing was more like trench warfare than a blitz. By the late 1950s, Fort Carson again faced trouble. Similar bases were being closed across the West, and efficiency experts argued that Carson was too far from main transportation arteries and population centers. Houses were hard to sell, and people leaving the base were forced to sell their homes for closing costs. Again, the town fathers responded by forming an organization of civilian well-wishers and boosters to lobby for Fort Carson. They signed on 5,000 people, and sent the roster to the Secretary of the Army, Brucker. "For four years," remembered Freyschlag, "we had the biggest Army Association of any community in the world!"

In the early 1960s, the Cuban missile crisis and the Berlin wall justified the reactivation of two Air Force divisions. The site-evaluation board went to Colorado Springs, and as the official history puts it: "Major General Heintges . . . looked over the reservation and was impressed. The next morning, unable to sleep, he rose early at the Broadmoor Hotel and took a walk. In the beauty of the Colorado morning, he decided that Carson should remain open."[12]

Fort Carson received one of the new divisions, finally solidifying the military sector of the Colorado Springs economy. Each success, remarked Freyschlag, helped to strengthen and permanize the existing installations. While none among this modest agglomeration of military facilities had extensive links with the others, they all were products of and contributors to what was fast becoming the hallmark of Colorado Springs—its military-friendly culture.

Creating Silicon Mountain

The military-induced growth that powered the Colorado Springs economy through the late 1960s also created greater vulnerability, especially as the United States pulled out of Vietnam. The local business community once again went hunting for additions to the city's economic base. After much study, the business leaders concluded that their best bet was high-tech manufacturing—not homegrown firms, but branch plants of outside companies.

Two contextual factors elevated their chances of succeeding. First, the dramatic military-based growth of the local economy had enabled them to climb well beyond a minimum threshold size. The community could offer substantial private and public infrastructure, a respectable business-services sector, and a willing and diverse labor force to prospective employers. Second, the congestion and escalating costs in the booming high-tech centers of southern California, Silicon Valley, and the Greater Boston area had created a general interest among large corporations in dispersed branch plants.[13] Many other communities could have benefited from these features. That Colorado Springs did so well is due to both its strenuous boosterism in the 1970s and its promotion of the unique opportunities associated with its success as a diversified military center.

The Pioneers: Kaman Sciences and Hewlett-Packard

The first phase of branch-plant recruiting began in the 1950s, when the Chamber of Commerce borrowed money from local banks and invested in a large tract of land near the picturesque, red-walled Garden of the Gods to entice outsiders. Few took the bait, however, with two noteworthy exceptions: Kaman Sciences arrived in 1957 and Hewlett-Packard in 1962. Although distinctly different—the former a defense-oriented research operation, the latter a technical branch plant of a major commercially oriented firm—these two facilities pioneered the relocation of important scientists and engineers to a remote location.[14] Together, they provided the inspiration for the high-tech strategy that emerged in Colorado Springs in the 1970s.

Kaman Sciences

Although the National R&D Labs have not generated many for-profit spin-offs, Ken Erickson of Sandia Labs was an exception. In 1957, he and a group of scientists gained the backing of the newly successful Kaman Corporation of Connecticut to set up Kaman Sciences in Albuquerque, doing high-level, classified work in nuclear physics for the Pentagon. Two years later, they found themselves boxed in, having exhausted all the available space in their lodgings behind a five-and-dime store and a beauty parlor. They first looked to expand on the outskirts of Albuquerque and found a one-acre plot near the airport. Company president Charles Kaman nixed the proposal; burned by expansion difficulties himself, he counseled them to find a much bigger parcel. But the larger local options were too expensive. Kaman felt rebuffed by the city of Albuquerque, which appeared indifferent to the firm's dilemma.

Kaman Sciences had worked almost exclusively on military prime contracts, mainly with the Air Force. Its work did not mandate geographical linkages to any other contractor or supplier, nor was it sensitive to the location of military users. Industrial recruiters caught wind of Kaman's plight and moved in. "Word got out," reported Albert Bridges, current president of Kaman Sciences, "and the Colorado Springs people came down." So did suitors from Oregon, Florida, and other places in New Mexico.[15]

For management, only two things mattered: inexpensive and abundant land, plus an attractive living environment for their employees. Colorado Springs was aggressive on the former; it offered the land cheaply and even gave Kaman an option to name the road. Colorado had attractive housing costs, too, and recreational opportunities galore—mountains, skiing, fishing. Bridges reported that during a previous West Coast stint, he had tried to buy a house in Santa Barbara. "People insulted you if you were going to pay with an FHA loan and not full price," he said. Colorado Springs, in contrast, welcomed every type of housing loan available. "People here have really opened up their arms," Bridges concluded.

In 1959, Kaman Sciences moved to the Garden of the Gods site in Colorado Springs, along with the entire Albuquerque science and engineering staff. Despite sometimes difficult communications with headquarters, Kaman never failed to recruit good scientists to the Springs. Kaman was a pioneer among "footloose," highly specialized, defense-dependent technical branch plants. Assured of continued contracts regardless of location, the company gave first priority to its site needs and preferences of its technical staff, mostly Ph.D.s in physics.

Hewlett-Packard

Colorado Springs' Industrial Foundation, another offshoot of the Chamber of Commerce, used Kaman Sciences as its "guinea pig," reported Bridges. Every time a new entrant got as far as visiting the relatively remote community, it would be taken around to Kaman, where the management would enthusiastically detail the virtues of the Springs. In the early 1960s, Hewlett-Packard was one such visitor.

At that time, Hewlett-Packard employed about 1,500 people in Palo Alto, California. The company was growing rapidly, and both Hewlett and Packard believed that one of the firm's great advantages lay in its small size, with people knowing one another on a first-name basis. The best way to preserve that, the firm believed, was to divisionalize. In 1959, it took one of its four products lines and set up a plant in Loveland, Colorado, close to Colorado State University, which offered a good electrical engineering program.[16]

By 1961, Hewlett-Packard was considering another divisional relocation. Then a fortuitous event occurred, one that comes closest in this story to an instance of a "founding father." David Packard, who had grown up in Pueblo and whose parents had attended Colorado College in the Springs, was driving back to Denver airport after a visit home. He stopped in the Springs to see a friend and, while there, decided that this would be a nice place for the new division. At the time, Hewlett-Packard had four criteria for an acceptable site: within one hour from a major airport; within two hours' flying time from California; near a good university with engineering programs; and the presence of enough local entry-level employees, with a proper work ethic and desire to learn. While Colorado Springs was deficient on at least two of these criteria, the Loveland success sold Hewlett-Packard on Colorado, and it eagerly sought another site in the state.

Hewlett-Packard's new Colorado plant would be very labor-intensive, building oscilloscopes for the company product line, and labor availability was critical. The work required a fair mix of engineering and design, as well as assembly. Although blue-collar labor was available in the Springs, Hewlett-Packard had to relocate management and engineers from California in 1964. Even though many of the 150 who moved had reservations, only a half-dozen cashed in on the guaranteed return ticket to California.

For technicians and machinists, Hewlett-Packard again looked far afield. "We found that machinists are a tight-knit group," recalled John Riggen, a former plant manager. "We hired a few from the Midwest, and they called their friends, most of whom moved on their own." The same experience held for technicians, who came from all over, but paid their own way to Colorado Springs. Most of the production workers Hewlett-Packard hired were local women, the majority of them wives of Fort Carson military personnel. In addition, a number of draftees and enlisted men stayed around after their stints, which helped Hewlett-Packard improve its minority recruitment.

The absence of a university posed a major problem, though. Packard tackled this directly, according to Riggen:

> He stopped in to see Governor Steven McNichols in Denver and pointed out that there was not a university here, and that . . . Hewlett-Packard required . . . a major university in the community. McNichols said that he would be willing to put a branch of the University of Colorado there, if it was that important. Packard said it was. And that's what started Hewlett-Packard in Colorado Springs and also started UCCS at the same time.

Unlike with Kaman, local chamber recruitment played a relatively minor role in Hewlett-Packard's decision to start up a Colorado Springs plant. Hewlett-Packard's decision was initiated as part of an innovative dispersion strategy by the firm's management and shaped by the personal preferences of one of the firm's founders, David Packard, and his remarkable access to the governor.

At first glance, neither Kaman nor Hewlett-Packard appears to have chosen Colorado Springs because it was a diversified military complex. Neither claimed to be attracted directly by the presence of the military as customer or by the availability of a military-related labor force. Yet without the military installations, it is unlikely that either would have come to the Springs. The three installations created the size community that each found necessary for a support staff, business services, and an adequate community social life.[17] Additionally, the Air Force Academy gave the place a touch of class, a landmark, and an active elite that set Colorado Springs apart from a dozen other western communities competing for such branch plants.

The Quality Economic Development Initiative

Despite the welcome entry of Kaman and Hewlett-Packard, Colorado Springs remained a heavily military-dependent town in the early 1970s. By one estimate, the military and enterprises relating to it composed over 50 percent of the Springs' total payroll.[18] Fort Carson boomed during the Vietnam war, swelling the community with housing-construction activity and related services to support a combat-ready military contingent. Direct military employment increased from 15,000 to 37,000, and direct civilian support by about 3,000. Meanwhile, the town's Industrial Foundation effort had attracted only four new commercial plants with 2,000 jobs.[19] As opposition to the Vietnam War mounted, the community became concerned about its future.

In 1969, a group of developers—"concerned visionaries," as one of the originators, Steve Schuck, referred to himself and his colleagues—concluded that the overheated local economy could not be sustained without some new economic base. "We had to diversify, to wean ourselves from the public teat." Led by three developers, colloquially known as the "Three Ss" because their

names were Sunderland, Schuck, and Shepard, the group took over from the
Chamber of Commerce's Industrial Foundation and proposed an aggressive
Quality Economic Development (QED) program. Taking their cue from pub-
lic and private economic-development efforts of five larger cities (Austin,
Houston, Albuquerque, Atlanta, and Denver), they produced a manifesto,
titled "A Program for Quality Economic Development."[20]

The committee highlighted the Springs' problems. Although it ranked
132nd in the nation in population, the city ranked 229th in average income
per household, 10 percent below the national average. Welfare costs were
high, amounting to 35 percent of the county property tax levy. The lackluster
growth of civilian jobs of all types—fewer than 2,600 per year while school
districts produced 4,000 graduates each year—made the situation especially
difficult for the young. The manifesto summed up the situation: "In short,
our major source of economic growth for the last decade will probably offer
little future support to economic expansion."[21]

The conclusion was obvious: "In the final analysis, economic progress
requires import of money into the economy"—the same conclusion another
group of ambitious men reached a half-century earlier. The QED backers
focused on new primary export activities, especially those that would generate
good-paying jobs. Specifically, they aimed to double the number of manufacturing jobs from 7,000 in 1971 to 14,000 in 1980, boosting the manufacturing
share of civilian jobs from 9.6 percent to 13.3 percent. To do so, they mapped
out a set of tactics prosaic by today's standards but quite novel at the time,
particularly for a city of Colorado Springs' size. These included a study of
comparative prospects by a professional firm; the targeting and active wooing
of specific firms; land banking and site preparation, including financial assistance for the construction of "spec" buildings; and an aggressive public-
relations effort to change the town's image from "a small, isolated wintry,
cowboy-and-Indian tourist town" to a high-technology center.[22]

The QED program managed to raise about $80,000 per year for its activ-
ities. It targeted branch plants and overlooked no opportunity. It personally
called on all prospective firms. "Ambassadors" visited the big cities—New
York, San Francisco, Chicago—and when companies came to recruit at the
University of Colorado's Business School in Boulder every year, Colorado
Springs attempted to turn the tables and recruit the companies. Believing the
city's unity to be their trump card, the ambassadors talked of "comraderie
and brotherhood," characteristics they assiduously nurtured by coaching every
conceivable participant. They even taught taxi drivers what to say to visitors
on their way in from the airport. They stressed the high productivity of the
labor force, arguing that military-related personnel in particular made good
workers: "less sick leave, and more showing up at work on time," reported
the chamber's Freyschlag. The "military spouse market," as Economic Development Council director Jim Devine dubbed it, was also a selling point,
especially for firms that ran three shifts, wanted low-cost labor, and did not
mind the turnover.

But the going was not easy. In 1973, the local counterpart of Colorado's statewide environmental movement swept into the city council.[23] These "no-growthers" were backed by Colorado's soon-to-be governor and unabashed environmentalist Richard Lamm, who headed a movement called Citizen's Lobby for Sensible Growth. They aimed to slow down in dramatic fashion the activity that they felt was diminishing their quality of life. As opposition leader Schuck recalled, "Their goals were laudable—who wouldn't want a better quality of life, cleaner air, less congestion and more park? But all of us who live in the real world appreciate trade-offs." On June 28, the Springs' no-growthers placed a moratorium on natural-gas permits, "a day of infamy" in the history of Colorado Springs, recalled developer Schuck.

The reaction was swift. New housing starts plummeted from an annual average of 10,000 to zero, and construction jobs evaporated. Employment in the Springs fell from 70,000 to 50,000. Tax-base growth halted, and real-estate values dropped. "The Chamber of Commerce and the developers were left holding the bag," reflected Hewlett-Packard's Riggen, "with empty houses and lots of unbuilt land."

For six months, the no-growthers ran city hall, pursuing their antigrowth policies without consulting the business community and traumatizing those leading the QED effort. Of course, the post-Vietnam builddown would have probably brought to a halt the frenzied spurt of housing starts that had erupted in tandem with the no-growth movement. Schuck acknowledged this: "Clearly we were in for a major adjustment, but I'd rather see the marketplace dictate the changes, rather than an emotionally-driven political decision." Ironically, the brief no-growth era apparently solidified boosterist support behind the nascent QED program and permanized its location outside city hall. Within a year, hard lobbying and campaigning by many groups with a stake in the growth agenda began to chip away at the no-growth initiative.

"Little California"

If in the 1870s, Colorado Springs had styled itself as "Little London," a century later it turned westward and tried "Little California," directing its recruitment efforts at California firms. The strategy attracted new firms from Silicon Valley or the Greater Los Angeles area, and a few even came from Boston and Minneapolis. The QED campaign produced an agglomeration of sorts, a new satellite concentration of electronics branch plants.

QED's first "catch" were predominantly nondefense-oriented electronics branch plants. Honeywell, NCR, United Technologies, Mostek, Inmos, and Ford Microelectronics began fabricating the bulk of their integrated circuits (ICs) in Colorado Springs. Litton started a communications equipment branch, and Digital arrived to make disk drives and controllers. The major new entrants are listed in Table 8.2, along with their employment levels in 1986.[24] Although the immediate market for their output was the parent firm, much of what they produced ultimately ended up in military products.[25]

Each firm was looking for a site at which to assemble several types of

TABLE 8.2.   Colorado Springs Private-Sector High-Tech Employment

Company	Date of Entry	Jobs in 1986
Kaman Sciences	1957	500
Hewlett-Packard	1962	2,700
TRW EPI	1968	1,000
TRW Colorado Systems	1969	400
Honeywell	1975	1,026
NCR	1975	300
Litton Data Systems	1976	350
Ampex	1977	1,200*
Digital Equipment	1977	2,600
SAIC	1976	95
Ford Aerospace	1979	1,200
Texas Instruments	1979	550
Mostek/Inmos	1979	1,850*
Rolm	1980	300
United Technologies Corporation	1980	300
Data General	1981	500
Ford Microelectronics	1981	300
OAO	1982	56
Computer Sciences Corporation	1982	200
TRW Defense Systems	1983	210
Litton Mellonics	1984	100
Cray Supercomputer	1988	300

*By 1989, both Ampex and Inmos had closed and left.

Source: Economic Development Council, "Companies Locating Initially or Expanding in Colorado Springs, 1975–86," 1986, and interview data.

labor: engineers, technicians, and low-skilled assembly workers. All sought to decentralize operations away from congested headquarters or divisional home-base locations, where wages and housing costs were rising. All did manufacturing that required some engineering support, and all had important testing operations, while some performed design and development functions as well. Both Kaman and Hewlett-Packard were powerful exhibits, regularly included on the circuit for prospective clients. They showed that high-salaried engineers and scientists could be recruited to a relatively isolated place, and that good blue-collar workers could be found here as well.

Litton's profile of its employees is noteworthy. Lacking the space to expand and facing rising blue-collar labor costs, Litton decided to spin off an equipment-manufacturing operation from its Data Systems group in Van Nuys, California, in 1976. It considered ten sites; Colorado Springs eventually won out.

The group moved only fifteen to twenty people from Van Nuys, mostly management and systems testers, and their relocation was indirectly charged to the Department of Defense through Data Systems' final product. Like Hewlett-Packard, Litton hires most of its assembly workers locally, many just out of school or the military. And like Hewlett-Packard, women make up 70 percent of this blue-collar labor force, and Hispanics compose 23 percent. Fort Carson supplies most of the technician labor—some 50 to 70 percent come from the Army base—with other technicians migrating on their own from the Midwest. New management is sometimes drawn from the military ranks because the cost of recruitment is relatively low.[26] Like Litton, other firms found that the Springs offered an attractive labor mix. The QED's emphasis on the qualities of military-trained labor seems to have won them points. Many employers preferred locations with a nonunion work force and a good work culture, and found both in the Springs, particularly in the Fort Carson area.

Both Fort Carson personnel and company managers volunteered that the Fort's pivotal role as a supplier of labor is vastly underrated in the community. In sheer numbers, by 1986 the Fort's 20,000 military personnel supported 27,000 other family members and accounted for almost 30,000 retirees and related family members in the area. This means the Springs has an abundance of temporary workers and people who are available for various work shifts. Also, the Army heavily subsidizes military personnel after they leave the service, through VA hospitals, post social activities, and the PX, which encourages them to stay near a military base and enables them to live adequately with lower wages. In addition, military-related workers are young, mobile, and politically apathetic and show a low propensity to vote. Thus despite the considerable number of blue-collar workers in the labor force, the citizenry of Colorado Springs votes overwhelmingly Republican (around 70 percent), ensuring the continued pro-military stance of both local and nationally elected politicians.

Unlike blue-collar labor, however, engineers must be recruited from outside Colorado Springs, often uprooted from their homes in amenable places like California or Boston. Even so, most of the firms reported that engineers were not hard to recruit to Colorado Springs. Irving Burg, facilities manager at Digital, related his own experience in this regard:

> When you drove on this property, you could feel it. I looked out . . . and I could see Pike's Peak, and not a single other man-made object—nothing between here and that peak. Engineers . . . just oohed and aahed, especially if you came out of the Northeast Corridor. An engineer, if he just takes a look at this and that's his thing, he's gonna end up saying, "you got me."

And finally, the Air Force Academy, Kaman, and Hewlett-Packard had already established an engineering community in town, creating the potential for professional and social networks for newcomers. When asked if there were any clashes between commercial and defense-oriented engineers in Colorado Springs, Hewlett-Packard's Riggen noted, "Most of them are electrical engineers by training. Most have studied what the others are doing, and they're quite compatible."

Few other locational factors mattered in these siting decisions, including transportation costs. Costly products were easily shipped to market. Firms purchased most materials outside the region. Litton, for instance, conducts procurement at Van Nuys and ships parts to Colorado Springs for assembly.

Few pinpointed the incentives offered by Colorado Springs as an effective lure, although several did mention enjoying land deals, industrial revenue bonds, cheap and accessible water and electricity, and training aid (through CETA and its predecessors). But most other competing communities offered these features too.

By the mid-1980s, the people behind the QED effort claimed that they had recruited 150 companies and more than 17,000 employees. Ironically, during a decade when the nation was making a transition from a manufacturing to a service economy, Colorado Springs was moving in the opposite direction, from an economy heavily dependent on military facilities and tourism to one in which manufacturing was on the upswing. Manufacturing jobs climbed from 1,190 of the 1970 work force to 1,790 in 1985.[27] Colorado Springs' QED effort was an apparent success. "High tech was on the move," stated Jim Devine, "and we got there first." If the QED effort had not been undertaken, it is unlikely that Colorado Springs would have attracted anything other than purely defense-related high-tech activity.

But similar booster efforts in other interior cities did not produce the Springs' results. QED was a necessary, but not a sufficient condition for success. Firms are unlikely to relocate unless they can be assured of an ample supply of labor.[28] We have found something rather unique in this case—the simultaneous movement of both capital and labor to a relatively virgin location from disparate corners of the country.

Colorado Springs offered a unique blend of a tractable blue-collar work force and an environment sufficient to draw and hold professional and technical labor. The mix of military facilities played a central role in the dual structuring of this labor force. The Air Force Academy, NORAD, and related air defense activities provided an anchor for the broader technical community, while Fort Carson was the single most important element in building a regional blue-collar work force. The military presence was an essential factor in creating a distinctive labor force, with both unskilled and technical elements, which in turn was aggressively promoted by the QED program. Thus although defense markets were not the proximate cause of this industrial increment, the presence of defense facilities operated powerfully on the supply side to build an attractive work force and work environment.[29] With the military as a labor-supplying magnet, a modest-size agglomeration of technical branch plants evolved in Colorado Springs.

Building Space Mountain

By the early 1980s, the high-tech strategy cracked along its edges. Hard pressed by new international competition, the falling dollar, and the maturation of many of the electronics products produced in Colorado Springs, local business leaders once again turned their attention to the military, which was benefiting from the Reagan buildup. Playing up its position as the air defense communications center of the nation, the Springs sought SDI funds to expand its military facilities. Although Air Force officials disparage the notion that the booster effort was effective, the Springs won the Consolidated Space Operations Center (CSOC) in 1982, the unified United States Space Command, the new SDI National Test Bed facility, and the planned, although later canceled, Shuttle Operations and Planning Complex (SOPC). In the ensuing military buildup period, a number of major new defense-oriented labs launched and expanded operations in Colorado Springs, while many other contractors came to work on space defense communications in the area.

Winning the Space Defense Function

Colorado Springs owes its success as the "Space Capital of the Free World"— as it was dubbed by Chamber of Commerce president Freyschlag—to the outcome of debates about strategic policy and service functions, both within the military and in the larger foreign policy establishment. Fundamentally, our respondents agreed that it was the setting of national defense priorities that resulted in Colorado Springs obtaining these military operations; the effect of local economic-development efforts was negligible.

Of greatest importance was the strategic debate over mutually assured destruction (MAD) versus antiballistic missile defense systems in the late 1970s. One group believed that MAD would work, and continued to argue for experimentation, development, and stockpiling of strategic weapons to achieve military superiority. The opposition believed that the United States needed a ballistic missile defense system to render offensive weaponry obsolete and permit the capping of stockpiles. In tandem with Reagan's presidency, the latter group prevailed, and new appropriations went disproportionately for the design and development of a space-based defense system.

In Colorado Springs, this struggle was reflected first in the decline of the air defense function, and later in the development of the Consolidated Space Operations Center. The Springs complex, building on ADC and Cheyenne Mountain, had had its postwar heyday in the early 1960s, when it was chosen as the site for the first military-satellite-tracking system. With the mounting of missile-warning systems in the 1970s, its function had grown. It had also become the command center for aircraft and missiles.

But in the late 1970s, as offensive strategies prevailed, the Air Defense Command function came under fire. The Department of Defense spun off the air defense functions for fighting units to Tactical Air Command, in Langley, Virginia, and transferred missile warning and space surveillance to Strategic Air Command in Omaha. The Springs' Aerospace Defense Center, which operated the warning stations only, "had all but been completely emasculated," reported Colonel Szafranski of the United States Space Command. The Chidlaw building, the defense headquarters in the Springs, was nearly empty in 1981. Many people left, and houses emptied out.

Fortunately for the Springs, with the ascendancy of strategic defense within the Air Force, and President Reagan's embrace of its goals, space defense again won status as a separable function. Defense against missiles in space entailed operations beyond the "air-breathing" range of traditional aircraft. In a quick turnaround, which former Air Force officer Ed Warrell called "demise and resurrection," Colorado Springs began to recover its defense functions in the period between 1980 and 1984 by hosting the CSOC and the unified Space Command.

A second struggle that affected the future of Colorado Springs' space defense activities concerned the creation of the Air Force's own space command. The air-breathing air defense mission was diminishing, reflected General Robert Herres, commander-in-chief of the United States Space Command, but the space component was on the rise. Officers like Generals Herres, James Hartinger, and James Hill clashed with the Air Force's R&D and acquisitions groups over the lines of command—the operational end of the space business had not found a home. As Herres put it: "The space business grew up as an outgrowth of R&D activity. Going into space was a research adventure. But we tried to do useful things, as we went into space, and so we soon had R&D and operations overlapping."

Herres compared the evolving space function with aircraft, where R&D, development, acquisition, and deployment are conducted by a corresponding command or division. Not so in space, argued Herres, because space missions were so experimental and research-intensive that it was unthinkable to separate space defense operations and R&D. In Herres's words:

> It was all done in a white smock environment. The question was, when does the time come when the space operation activities are mature enough to peel off? There was a group here fighting to resurrect something out of the Aerospace Defense Center and they fought for an Air Force Space Command. But there was a group in Systems Command who believed that we didn't need it, because other groups—Space Division in Los Angeles and the R&D community of Air Force Systems Command—could continue to do these jobs. It was a natural role for them—they had been in the space business a long time and had a large infrastructure. And why would anybody in their right mind want to build a new staff, and a new headquarters, and a new everything?

Yet over several years, the Air Force top brass shifted their views in favor of a space command and expansion of space operations at Colorado Springs.

Dissension then arose between NASA, the agency long responsible for civilian U.S. space activity, and the Air Force. As military missions in space proliferated in the 1980s, the Air Force pushed for authorization to launch shuttles from Vandenberg Air Force Base and to build a new, duplicate center for military-defense-satellite monitoring. Owing in large part to the generosity of Ronald Reagan and Congress, the authorization for replicating the existing capacity of Houston and Sunnyvale at a third site was made, favoring once again the new space defense center at Colorado Springs.

Yet a fourth debate emerged among the services and their Pentagon managers over the necessity to consolidate operations. Throughout most of the postwar period, the Air Force, Army, and Navy had run their own commands. But in the context of modern cold warfare, especially with the movement into space, it became impossible to continue the decentralized triad. This was true across many functions of the services. General James Hill, commander-in-chief of NORAD at the time, was a leader in the move to consolidate space defense operations under the Air Force. He said, "Services don't operate forces—they plan, train, equip, and administer force. . . . I began to create a recognition that we needed to activate an AF Space Command, which would then be the nucleus for a unified space command."

Despite opposition from other groups in the Air Force, which feared that consolidation would reduce their personnel roster or their procurement budgets, the unified command position prevailed, and the Air Force became the lead service. As of 1985, the unified United States Space Command was 50 percent Air Force, 30 percent Navy and Marines, and 20 percent Army. For Colorado Springs, this meant twice as many uniformed personnel in the community.

The siting of space defense functions in Colorado Springs thus reflected several larger issues of strategic policy and four skirmishes within the defense bureaucracy. The military space complex was erected in Colorado Springs in several stages, often with long periods of gestation and much debate. The first and perhaps key element, the new Consolidated Space Operations Center, under discussion as early as 1975, was not officially announced until 1979. Construction began in 1982, and the facility opened in 1986.

According to General Hill, who originally proposed CSOC, the Air Force had decided that both its satellites and its planned shuttle flights should have their own planning, launch, control, and recovery facilities. Sunnyvale, the existing satellite-control facility, was outmoded and beset by security problems, owing to its congested urban location and position on earthquake faults. Since the Air Force was also proposing to launch and recover shuttles from Vandenberg, and felt that relying on NASA's Houston shuttle-control facility was dangerous (because of floods and hurricanes), it seemed judicious to consolidate its space operations in one place.

Hill strongly favored Colorado Springs at the time. He wanted CSOC close to the Space Defense Operations Center in Cheyenne Mountain, which he commanded, near our "Intelligence Data Handling System, our Indications and Warning Center and our Threat Assessment Center." The Air Force set up a standard site-selection process, with technical considerations its most important criteria, and whittled the choices down to Malmstrom Air Force Base in Great Falls, Montana; Kirtland Air Force Base near Albuquerque; and Colorado Springs.[30] General Herres reported a spirited struggle within the Air Force. All involved saw the location of CSOC as the stepping stone for winning the Air Force Space Command function. Kirtland, in particular, posed the toughest challenge. It was already an R&D center and had strong proponents in the Air Force. Its advocates argued that Albuquerque should be selected because among other reasons, the Springs' position under Pike's Peak cut down the line of sight to satellites. These efforts were of no avail: the decision was made in favor of Colorado Springs.

Did politics matter? At least one outside contractor, whose firm did a site-selection study for CSOC, claims that it did. Yet the political skirmishes did not begin until 1979, after the Springs site was announced. A CSOC historian argued that after the announcement was made, the New Mexico congressional delegation, led by Senator Harrison Schmitt, a former astronaut and staunch Reagan supporter, asked the Secretary of the Air Force to reconsider. Schmitt and his colleagues felt that lower labor costs and land availability made New Mexico a more economical choice than Colorado. Some New Mexicans claimed that Senator Gary Hart's chairmanship of the Senate subcommittee on military construction had influenced the choice of Colorado Springs. This controversy stalled the appropriations for construction until 1982, but eventually it went ahead as the Air Force had planned.[31] At least one high-placed military source argued that New Mexico, perhaps because of the congressional brouhaha, received its new Space Technology Center as a consolation prize for losing CSOC.[32]

CSOC and the United States Space Command propelled Colorado Springs into a unique position in the larger society. Within the span of a few years, these military facilities began to gather around them a new set of installations central to the emerging "space defense" of the nation—the physical manifestation of the American commitment to Star Wars. Because of CSOC, Colorado Springs had an inside track on the new SDI Test Bed facility, which will house supercomputers programmed to simulate and test Star Wars systems and to coordinate the C^3I functions associated with it. It also was the logical candidate for the Shuttle Operations and Planning Complex (SOPC). Together, this agglomeration of space defense facilities put Colorado Springs in an enviable position on the defense-contractor ladder. For the first time, in the mid-1980s, a significant amount of defense contracting began to take place in Colorado Springs, almost entirely drawn by newly generated opportunities in space defense.

Space Camp Followers

Colorado Springs has attracted an impressive set of private company branch offices, almost all of which work on C^3I. Through sensors, radars, and satellites, information from all over the world is piped into Cheyenne Mountain's Space Defense Operations Center to serve one paramount function: supplying the resident four-star general with enough information to advise the president of the United States of an attack by ICBMs, submarine-launched missiles, or aircraft.

C^3I requires an enormous amount of labor. The expensive hardware—computers and data-processing and display equipment—changes constantly with rapid technological advances and requires labor for installation, maintenance, evaluation, and upgrading. More labor is needed for writing software, integrating subsystems, and training personnel. For Space Command, and likewise for the SOPC and Test Bed facilities, the building costs are minuscule. And since literally none of the hardware is purchased in Colorado Springs, most local costs involve labor. As the TRW district manager put it: "This is a manpower-intensive operation. Mainly what we do is write software. We have hundreds of people who sit down everyday in front of a computer terminal and type out lines of code, because you have to make those computers work."

Three types of contractor activities gravitated toward Colorado Springs in the 1980s. One is the SETA (systems engineering and technical assistance) contractor, who must operate on or near a military installation. Another is the storefront operator, the on-site eyes and ears of the company, whose function is to detect emerging military requirements and market the firm's present and future capabilities. And in a few instances, defense contractors have taken the big step of setting up larger R&D/professional services branch plants in the Springs, portions of which are committed to CSOC and its progeny, but other portions of which serve the company's larger national mission.

The SETA Contractors

SETA operations arrived in Colorado Springs with the Air Defense Command, when Cheyenne Mountain was built. IBM, DEC, and Honeywell installed computers; Ford Aerospace wrote software; Hughes Aircraft worked with ADC on radar and fire-control systems. The cold war–instigated development of sophisticated weaponry, detection, and communications systems increased the share of defense dollars spent on design, testing, installation, and operations.

Yet it was not until CSOC that SETA contracting skyrocketed in Colorado Springs. With a potential cap on military employment, the Pentagon began turning to contractors to fulfill its needs. At the same time, a major renovation of Cheyenne Mountain was launched, requiring many contractors for upgrading and installing the latest equipment. By 1986, Space Command had thirty SETA contracts running out of Colorado Springs.

We interviewed representatives of a half-dozen SETA contractors, ranging in size from a nine-man leased office to a new company-owned office with several hundred employees. All were small branch offices. Typically, the firms maintained offices clustered around military users and procurement locations elsewhere, including Huntsville, Alabama, serving the Army's missile command there. Unlike the branch plants that arrived during the 1970s, they are classified as professional services organizations, not manufacturers. Their home offices, perhaps in Los Angeles or Washington, D.C., write proposals and produce or buy hardware or software, while the Springs office works on delivering and installing it. The Springs office usually becomes the prime contractor, although it may be teamed with other, even larger, subcontractors.

Many SETA contractors survive by cultivating a market niche, or as one of our respondents put it, by "working to be preeminent" in a certain service line.

These contractors came to Colorado Springs to benefit from the growth in activity associated with CSOC, Space Command, and the newer space defense functions. Mostly, they are there to advise the Air Force. One informant characterized his group's role as that of "test observers and critiquers." Another said that his firm's specialized in consulting for C^3 projects—defining equipment and matériel requirements, locating vendors, and assisting the Air Force in buying and installing equipment. Their employees sit at computer terminals, creating code or writing technical papers, or work with military clients on-site to advise or evaluate. It was a Springs SETA contractor who, in an interview, used the following vivid image: "Our primary weapon is pen and paper!"

An early SETA contractor was Science Applications International Corporation (SAIC), begun as a La Jolla spin-off in 1969 and now a 6,000-employee company. In the late 1970s, it anticipated that the new Air Force Space Command, in its first phases of development, would mean more space defense work for SAIC. Being there increased the information flow and the probability that SAIC would be favored in contract negotiations.

Being there also increased SAIC's chances to recruit the military personnel so badly needed for its work. The company's Colorado Springs office grew from six employees in 1978 to ninety-five in 1986, when it fulfilled about $500 million worth of contracts. "All, well almost all, of our technical staff are former military men," reported SAIC's Gary Willmart. Willmart himself joined the company after twenty-two years in the Air Force, including many tours in Cheyenne Mountain working on C^3I. On his last tour of duty, he was the chief enlisted man. Often, a request for proposal (RFP) for a SETA contract may specify the types of employees needed—by educational degrees and years of experience working on a particular military system—and employing former military people may help on this score. Since many military personnel who leave the services prefer to stay in Colorado Springs, companies like SAIC set up shop nearby. In many ways, SAIC is a product of the "overflow" phenomenon. As the military itself hits hiring ceilings, it increasingly contracts out the same functions, and not surprisingly, former military men end up staffing these positions and working with their former colleagues. Indeed, such arrangements may have quickened the exodus of younger officers from the Air Force, into the private sector.

Other SETA contractors, including some competitors, followed SAIC to the Springs. In the 1980s, Computer Sciences Corporation grew to a 135-person office, servicing CSOC and the proposed SOPC on telecommunications aspects. The minority-owned OAO Corporation, established in Greenbelt, Maryland, in 1973 as a spin-off of Grumman's operation at Goddard Space Flight Center and now a 1,300-person company nationwide, opened its Springs office in the early 1980s to advise CSOC on software, especially for command and control of the new global positioning satellite. OAO's strategy was a speculative one. "We came in with a contract, then expanded because we knew things would happen here," reported OAO's Ed Warrell, vice president for Air Force programs. "Now we have three bids in—if we win them, we will double in size."

BDM is yet another entrant to Colorado Springs. Originally set up in 1960 in El Paso by three Fordham physicists who landed an Army contract at White Sands, BDM had expanded by the mid-1980s into a 4,000-person corporation providing $330 million worth of professional services a year internationally. Drawn to the Pentagon, it moved its headquarters to Washington, D.C., in the 1970s, and later began branching out. With the establishment of CSOC and Air Force Space Command in Colorado Springs, BDM management opened a Springs office in 1986. BDM specializes in testing and evaluation (T&E) contracts and has been "the preferred contractor for Air Force [T&E] in particular" for more than a decade. In 1986, when we spoke to Bob Mollo, vice president for systems design, the office had twelve marketing prospects and boasted a success rate of 40 percent.[33] Particularly if the National Test Bed proceeds, BDM stands a good chance of dramatically increasing its Springs-based business. "Its a billion-dollar project," noted Mollo, "and that means a lot of jobs."

The "Permanizers"

At least two SETA contractors made a permanent move to Colorado Springs. Ford Aerospace and Communications Corporation, a subsidiary of Ford Motor Company, and TRW's Systems Engineering and Development Division. Each bought land for branch plants, built their own buildings, and began to serve larger national markets from their Springs base. Both came because of CSOC, Space Command, and the upgrading of Cheyenne Mountain, and are betting heavily on the future of the Springs as the "Space Capital of the Free World." But both have ambitions that range farther afield as well.

Ford Aerospace was headquartered until recently in Detroit, but 70 percent of its 13,000 employees work in California. The firm has thrived on the defense buildup, growing by 20 to 30 percent a year since 1981. Ford had been in the Springs in the early 1960s, when it developed software and bought equipment for Cheyenne Mountain's communications and missile-warning systems. Fifteen years later, Ford's Space Mission and Engineering Division heard the rumors that Space Command would be coming to the Springs and took the big step of buying 600 acres to set up a "pure defense" shop. By 1986, the "shop," which was primarily doing software development, had grown to a 1,200-person operation, with 50 defense contracts worth several hundred million dollars, including $15 million from SDI. Its largest contract was for installing in Cheyenne Mountain the new Space Defense Operations Center (SPADOC), a system that monitors and catalogs all objects in space. Unlike most of the smaller SETA contractors, Ford developed a national all-military customer base, and has a large contract to develop the Maneuver Control System for the Army, not a locally oriented project. Like the other

SETA contractors, Ford's Colorado Springs operation is officially classified as a "service-sector" facility, under computer-software services.

Bob Rankin, Ford's vice president in charge of the Colorado Springs operation, was precise about why Ford made the move: "sixty percent of our decision was market-driven, because of the future potential of the area and the user, and 40 percent supply side—the attractiveness of the area." Ford faced a choice between continuing to work out of Sunnyvale, California, or moving a contingent to the Springs. On the positive side, Colorado Springs had the infant space defense operations, which might one day yield great profits. On the negative side, Colorado Springs had poorer access to educational facilities, a less amenable transportation system, and more inclement weather.

The choice was difficult, particularly because a number of top Ford employees were reluctant to move. "Few people felt that a move from the Bay Area to Colorado Springs was an improvement in life style," said Rankin. "Having San Francisco available to you is a whole different world from having Denver available." Indeed, of the thirty people Ford moved to Colorado in 1980, some 80 percent returned to California. TRW also had difficulty relocating personnel. In 1986, TRW conducted only half of its Colorado Springs contract work locally; the rest remained in Los Angeles. The Springs share would have been lower had not the services in question required that 50 percent of the work be performed there.

Of all the contractors we interviewed, only Ford and TRW reported this type of resistance. But like other transplants to Colorado Springs, Ford now focuses on regional labor markets. "Now, we try to hire local people, those who are committed to the community," said Rankin. The Midwest again serves as a fertile recruiting ground. "You look at people from the Midwest—from Iowa, Kansas, Nebraska, Chicago, Texas. This is where they came to get out of the heat in the summertime. They think this is a resort—they love it here!" Ford has also aggressively recruited from the military: some 15 percent of its current total Springs employment consists of former military people. Generally, they are men and women the company already knows well from its contract work.

If attracting top-flight labor was a problem, Colorado Springs had another drawing card—cheap land. Ford sold 10 acres in Newport Beach, California, and bought 300 acres in Colorado Springs with the proceeds. But Ford faced one big problem: the parcels lay outside the city limits and thus were not entitled to city services. To aid Ford's entry, Colorado Springs officials turned to Frank O'Donnell, former head of the Economic Development Council for the Chamber of Commerce, to tackle the problem. O'Donnell knew how the wheels of government turned in the Springs, and rather quickly smoothed a path to bring the land into Colorado Springs. Although Ford ended up paying a lot of money to gain access to certain services, setting up a base in the area was still quite profitable for it.

Land, reported Rankin, is becoming increasingly important in his corporation's location decisions. Ford has its own land-development company, which recently teamed up with Ford Aerospace to buy two 300-acre parcels. But for Ford Aerospace, the point is not making money from land development; it is to use the acreage for expansion. "I'd rather fill up all 300 acres with our buildings than sell one of them," said Rankin. The land company, on the contrary, has drawn up plans for what it calls its "Ford Aerospace Technology Park." In 1981, Ford Microelectronics, a subsidiary of Ford Aerospace, took advantage of the land and built a $33 million building adjacent to Ford Aerospace.[34]

The Ford complex is on the north side of the city. To the east, closer to the airport, is TRW's new building, which houses about 300 employees on a twenty-seven acre site, giving the company a lot of room to grow. When the interviewer admired the view of Pike's Peak, TRW's chief, Dr. Ted Bettway, responded, "But in my mind's eye, we've got this other building out there, if there's enough work."

This TRW division, based in Los Angeles, also does almost exclusively military work in the professional services and software categories. The Springs site, built in 1983, currently contains about one-quarter of the division's $200 million in contracts. Its first local success, and the initial reason for its interest in the Springs, was a 1982 prime contract to do systems integration on CSOC,[35] followed shortly thereafter with a SPADOC software contract. "CSOC has a bunch of complex systems, built by IBM, Ford and others. Our responsibility is to bring all that stuff together and make it play," said Bettway. Doing that means overseeing installation, testing, systems, and developing software.

For TRW, Ford's presence was a critical factor when the two teamed up on Ford's SPADOC contract. Ford was already in the Springs and TRW was in Los Angeles, but "there is less risk in a software development job if your team is in close proximity to each other," reported Bettway. "There's a tremendous amount of interaction in how you build your systems." Bettway believes that the investment both TRW and Ford have made in the Springs will pay off in larger contract dollars. "On an upcoming contract, we're going to claim that there are only two companies who can do the job—Ford and TRW—because of our presence here."

Labor recruitment was somewhat different for TRW compared with Ford. Unlike Ford, TRW lives with a spatially split labor force, with about half of those working on Springs-based contracts still in California. And unlike Ford's Rankin, TRW's Bettway was not enthusiastic about military recruits. In his view, the twenty-year man was often not versatile enough and often had a hard time fitting in.[36] Bettway prefers developing his own managers, although he does hire retired military personnel with "unique capabilities." Along with other companies, including Ford, TRW is vigorously lobbying for improved Colorado engineering education and finds its chances significantly better among graduates within the region. And once in Colorado Springs, employees tend to stay put. Both Ford and TRW reported less turnover in this area than in other regions of the country.

Both TRW's Bettway and Ford's Rankin doubted that the Springs' promotional effort had much to do with their decisions to locate branches there.

"The defense pull is not based on them," stated Rankin, whose Colorado Springs experience dates back only to 1980. Furthermore, he claimed that companies like Ford have little interest in supporting the city's effort. He jokes about how he and some of his cohorts scheme "to keep these other guys out of town."

In many ways, Ford and TRW are harbingers of one possible future for Colorado Springs. Says Ford's Rankin, "If the Test Bed comes here [which it has], it will be the focal point for simulating and testing SDI. If we deploy the SDI, which is a big if, it could be a big deal. Especially if it has a huge ground-control element, we could benefit greatly as a community." Ford and TRW are speculators and pioneers with a big stake in that future.[37] Other operations are close on their heels, including the SETA contractors mentioned earlier, Ford Microelectronics with 300 employees in 1981, and Litton Mellonics with a 100-man office in 1984 to service contracts with NORAD and CSOC. Every other major aerospace firm has felt compelled to open up at least a storefront to test the waters.

The Storefronts

On the east side of Colorado Springs, on the apron of the airport, stand two postmodern buildings called the Atrium complex. This set of office towers houses the small marketing storefronts of defense contractors. Its directory reads like a list of top aerospace firms in the country: Lockheed, Boeing, Rockwell, TRW, Ball Aerospace, General Dynamics, Grumman, Hughes, Martin-Marietta, and McDonell-Douglas, to name a few. A representative from one firm can walk down a corridor and visit his counterparts without leaving the building. Informally, the Atrium has been dubbed "the commercial space operations center."[38]

Like the SETA contractors, this Colorado Springs storefront group has mushroomed since 1982, when CSOC and Space Command became a reality. Most firms act as "listening posts," keeping their eyes and ears tuned to Space Command headquarters. As Al Uhalt, local manager of Rockwell's Space Transportation Systems Division, put it:

> Why we are here can be summed up in two words, business opportunities. ... We're here to indicate to Unified Space Command, Air Force, as well as the Academy, Fort Carson, and Army and Navy Space Commands that Rockwell has products or can generate equipment and services that they need. To make a sale, go to the operating commands, which are here. Sell them a concept.

By the mid-1980s, every large corporation believed it ought to have such a "listening post" in the Springs, and in mid-1983, storefront operators formed the National Security Industrial Association, which now has seventy-six member companies, most of them in the Atrium complex. "We even have our meetings here," noted Bill Pollard, the head of Boeing's storefront. "There's a lot of teaming now on contracts," reported OAO's Warrell, "and if it's a big project, we can just walk down the hall."

Personnel with both engineering and military backgrounds run these offices. The technical background gives these "marketeers," as one contractor called them, the ability to understand the information they communicate back to home base and forward to military personnel. Their service backgrounds help them understand military culture. Rockwell's Uhalt is a former test pilot who spent twenty-eight years in the Air Force, retiring in 1979 as a colonel. Mick Anna, district office manager for TRW Defense Systems, was educated as an engineer and served in the Air Force for five years, working in the group that was responsible for rebuilding satellites.

Rockwell's ambitions in Colorado Springs demonstrate how storefronts may serve as incubators for expanded operations. The company, which bid on portions of both the SOPC and the National Test Bed,[39] manufactures the orbiter for the shuttle, does the payload integration, and is responsible for the overall design. Its storefront not only promotes its orbiter, but also smooths the way for initial SETA contracts and gleans information on future needs. Already Rockwell has nine engineers working in the Atrium building, executing two contracts to provide data and technical assistance to the Air Force in its initial efforts to replicate much of the Houston shuttle-control facility. This group is working to generate more business on the engineering requirements for the National Test Bed. If they win the contract, they will instantly be too large an operation for the Atrium and will have to buy or lease something else in the Springs area. "That building, the Atrium, is just kind of a frontrunner," says TRW's Bettway. "Rockwell is trying to build an office here; Space Communications Company has a building down on the south forty here; Litton has come here; BDM is trying to build here."

High-Tech Transformed

These new service activities have given the high-tech sector in Colorado Springs a face lift. New defense contracts ($190 million in 1986) have created a defense-services sector that employs 2,800 and is rapidly growing.[40] The high-tech manufacturing sector employs 14,000, down 27 percent from its peak in late 1984.[41] High-tech manufacturers sell 97 percent of their output outside the region, 53 percent to other divisions within their own corporations. In contrast, the professional-services sector delivers 38 percent of its "output" locally, to military installations, even though it is financed nationally, since 97 percent of its output is supported by defense contracts.

As commercial semiconductor sales slumped, the Springs branch plants turned to defense projects to survive. Both Texas Instruments and Litton, for example, have shifted their Colorado Springs operations to defense production.[42] In addition, as some high-tech firms close their doors, other more defense-oriented ones replace them. This is literally the case of Minneapolis-based Cray Computers, the world's leading supercomputer manufacturer, which announced in April 1988 that it would open a new branch plant in the

Springs to build its newest generation. It planned to take over a space vacated by Inmos, a 127,000-square-foot building completed in 1980, and to employ 300 people by 1989. Seymour Cray, the company's founder, said that the Inmos building was the main reason for choosing the Springs.[43]

One promoter made the rather farfetched argument that the new trend toward software and services was a natural outgrowth of Colorado Springs' high-tech manufacturing base. But the coming of the pure software and services operations like Ford and SAIC stems entirely from the presence of CSOC and Space Command. Most of the branch plant manufacturers are simply shifting to defense hardware from commercial ware, and are not entering the software market. There is little synergy among the firms, other than perhaps a shared labor market. Almost all the Colorado Springs high-tech firms, whether manufacturing or services, are still heavily tied to their corporate headquarters elsewhere.

One product of this leaner, more esoteric, and defense-dependent high-tech industry is that the demand for production workers has declined while that for engineers, scientists, and managers has continued to grow. This is even true for companies like Hewlett-Packard. "Managers and professionals made up only 22 percent of our Springs work for in 1966," reported Hewlett-Packard's Riggen. "Now they make up 52 percent. Our sales will grow 15 percent a year for the next few years without adding any people in the manufacturing areas." Often, blue-collar workers laid off from the routine high-technology jobs of the 1970s have a hard time finding a slot in the specialized economy of the 1980s.

Space Mountain Reconsidered

Has all the new military-oriented activity helped Colorado Springs grow? The answer is a resounding yes. Since 1980, writes a United Bank of Colorado analysis, "Colorado Springs has been the growth star of the state."[44] The local economy grew from 105,800 nonmilitary jobs in 1980 to 142,000 in 1985, an annual growth rate greater than 5 percent.[45]

This performance is even more impressive when one considers the surrounding state and national economies. Unlike most other communities, Colorado Springs has been relatively immune to adversity in the larger regional economy. Only 11 percent of Colorado Springs' export base is oriented toward the Rocky Mountain region.[46] While the rest of the state suffered from the energy burst and Colorado topped the nation in rates of business failure, the Springs continued to add jobs and population. Similarly, the community's dependence on the military dollar left it immune to heightened competition in the international arena, since only 6 percent of Springs' output goes abroad. Most of these are arms exports, one of the few U.S. export categories that continue to grow.[47]

While comfort is taken by some who believe that military bases act as shields against recession, it is also true that defense spending exhibits cycles

TABLE 8.3.   Top Colorado Springs Employers, 1987

	Top Colorado Springs Employers, 1987		*Top in Defense and High-Tech, 1987*	
1987 Rank	*Top Employer*	*1987 Employees*	*Top Employer*	*1987 Employees*
1	Fort Carson	24,808	Fort Carson	24,808
2	Peterson/NORAD/ Space Command	7,664	Peterson/NORAD/ Space Command	7,664
3	Air Force Academy	4,645	Air Force Academy	4,645
4	City Government	3,774	Digital Equipment Corp.	2,700
5	School District 11	2,930	Hewlett-Packard	2,400
6	Digital Equipment Corp.	2,700	Honeywell Inc.	1,425
7	Hewlett-Packard	2,400	Ford Aerospace	1,200
8	Penrose Hospital	1,480	TRW, Inc.	1,117
9	Honeywell Inc.	1,425	Ampex Corp.	1,000
10	Memorial Hospital	1,400	Kaman Corporation	750
11	County Government	1,375	Texas Instruments	700
12	U.S. Postal Service	1,245		
13	Broadmoor Hotel	1,200		
14	Ford Aerospace	1,200		
15	TRW Inc.	1,117		

Source: Colorado Springs *Gazette Telegraph*, February 22, 1987.

of its own.[48] And the Colorado Springs economy is now almost exclusively defense-dependent, increasing the area's vulnerability to changes in foreign policy and budgets. The U.S. government supports an enormous amount of local activity: in 1986, the three military bases were employers number 1, 2, and 3 (Table 8.3). Directly, the military employs 30 percent of the area's work force and has a payroll of $884 million. In addition to more than 30,000 military personnel stationed here, there are 36,000 dependents and 11,300 military retirees. If military construction and defense contracts are added, the military accounts for half of the Pikes Peak region's annual $4 billion economy.[49] Ironically, this town with a staunch free-market mentality owes its livelihood principally to the public purse, almost wholly secured in one-of-a-kind facilities that are dependent on the continuation of war threats.

Colorado Springs officials worry that the new defense-oriented high-tech is as fragile as the older high-tech branch plant economy, or even more so. Air Force budgets were halved from their original requests in 1987 and 1988, when the military-funding boom peaked.[50] Critics point to other deformities of defense-led growth, such as a highly bifurcated labor force, with a large number of relatively high-paid occupations and a plethora of low-wage jobs. At least one observer noted that the housing market reflected this strongly: "There's lots of housing in the under $80,000 range, and lots above $200,000, and less between than you'd think." Furthermore, such housing developments are spatially segregated, with much of the military "grunt" and minority housing south of the city toward Fort Carson, and posher developments, including retirement communities exclusively for the military, to the north.

Other complaints resound about the military presence and its local impact. Local merchants find themselves cut out by the commissaries, the BX/PX, on-base housing, medical facilities, and other services on military installations. Yet another problem is moonlighting—nearly 8 percent of the military population holds a second job, about 64 percent of which are in professional or skilled positions,[51] potentially squeezing out local job applicants.

With the coming of CSOC and its companion projects, much debate centered around the local economic effects of military-led growth. CSOC-related growth accounted for nearly 75 percent of all increases in El Paso County's population and jobs in 1988. "Without CSOC we would be in dire straits," stated economist Anthony Roso of the Pikes Peak Area Council of Governments, author of a major study on CSOC's impact. "When the local economy lost its healthy growth because of its growing reliance on international markets, CSOC came in and supported several thousand people with jobs."[52] Some are not bothered by this. Former Republican Congressman Ken Kramer, whose district included the Springs, crowed that "military space activity will become the dominant force in Colorado's economy."[53]

But others are skeptical of the military complexes' job-generating abilities. As Ford's Rankin put it, "How many private-sector jobs do you think CSOC created? Maybe 200 new military jobs here—that's what's really going on." Roso concurs with this pessimistic assessment. "CSOC is not a magnet for major firm location by aerospace and defense contractors not presently in the area," Roso writes." "Even prime contractors working on CSOC are . . . not choosing to relocate or house a local labor force as large as their contracts would imply."[54] While CSOC will directly employ 2,130, support another 1,000 private-sector contractor jobs, and generate 6,500 jobs by 1990, Roso concluded that CSOC and its accessories would add only 3 percent to the Springs' population, personal income, and work force over the next five years.[55]

Some enthusiasts reject Roso's analysis and predict that the designation of Colorado Springs as the centerpiece of SDI would double the Springs' population by the turn of the century. Not surprisingly, this view tended to be held by those with the greatest stake in growth. One was physician-turned-developer Martin List, a space promoter who hoped to build a 5,000-acre List Institute and Aerospace Center plus a 400-acre Space Age Tech Center office park on the western flank of CSOC. "The study [Roso's] should be discarded," complained List to the newspapers. "Are we comparing here the addition of 3,000 people to the economy, or are we comparing the creation of a one-in-the-world facility that is the centerpoint of everything relative to a whole new endeavor in space?"[56] Recent history reveals that List was overly optimistic. By mid–1988, he was out of business in the area.

Military leaders, while distancing themselves from such outlandish predictions, remain quietly optimistic. They base their assessment on what they see as the permanent investment going into the Springs' complex. General Herres, for instance, believes that Colorado Springs will be a growing center of gravity for the Air Force's space work. "This place orchestrates activities that take place all over the world. When SDI becomes a reality, its hard to believe that this won't become the center of activities." General James Abrahamson, director of the SDIO office in Washington, and General James Hill, the former NORAD commander-turned-developer, both echo this sentiment. Falcon will be the "brains" of the proposed space-based umbrella of defense against nuclear attack, said Abrahamson in an interview, and, in Hill's words, "Star Wars is gaining a lot of economic momentum, a life of its own. It's pretty hard to turn off the spigot once a program becomes institutionalized."[57]

Nor are the long-time economic developers worried. Despite the fact that their role is disputed by the private-sector firms involved, they continue to celebrate new gains, such as Cray, a possible Lockheed relocation, and the $508 million contract to Martin-Marietta to develop the National Test Bed network at Falcon. The boosters take credit for landing the United States Olympic Committee relocation from New York to Colorado Springs, with an estimated total economic impact of $15.8 million.[58] General Hill and his friend General Jack Forrest, former commander of Fort Carson, began the Space Foundation, another booster effort, in 1981. "We want to be a think tank for space," according to Forrest, and the foundation aims to promote interest and research in space through an ambitious program that includes educational efforts and a museum. Meanwhile, the Colorado Springs Chamber of Commerce has its normal contingent of projects, including promoting tourism and the Springs' free foreign trade zone, and pursuing the expansion of Colorado Springs' airport to hub status. Expansion of housing and commercial development in the area continue: one such project is the strategically named Chapel Hills Mall, on the north side of town near the Air Force Academy.

Development has become a hotly contested business in Colorado Springs. The spectacular growth of the 1980s has brought in moneyed speculators from Texas, Arizona, and farther afield. Some are cashing in, while others are going bankrupt. Many think the area is overbuilt. But the boosters believe the future is bright. In their view, they have irrevocably created a special place for the military in Colorado Springs. The Economic Development Council's director, Jim Devine, noted that eight out of twenty-three living four-star generals reside in Colorado Springs. The retired brass often assume positions of leadership in the local Chamber of Commerce or development community, or join one of the defense contractors, thereby boosting local economic-development efforts. General Hill, for example, became Chamber of Commerce President and then head of the Olive Development Company, while General Forrest, after his stint at the Space Foundation, accepted a position with Ford Aerospace.

The interpenetration of military, boosters, and defense-industry managers makes Colorado Springs a tough competitor when it comes to defense dollars or defense facilities. The Chamber's Freyschlag calls it,

> the networking of top people, of people you play golf with, people that you ski with, people that you served in the military with, like my predecessor here, General Hill. He knows the president of every aircraft company in the country on a first-name basis. He extolls the virtues of Colorado Springs because he's chosen to retire and live here himself.

When asked about the future, Freyschlag put it this way:

> Answer the question yourself by visualizing that by 2006, almost every officer in the Air Force will be graduated from the Air Force Academy. Well, once that happens, and particularly once all the Air Force generals are Air Force Academy generals, then they gotta come back here to the football games, [and to] what was once their fraternity scene.[59]

Given this direct Pentagon clout, Congress plays a less important role than it might elsewhere. Ken Kramer, until 1986 the district's Congressman, was an aggressive hawk, a new-right Republican, and an assiduous watchdog for Springs' military interests. But in many ways, he is a product rather than a creator of the Springs' relationship with the military. As noted earlier, the district he represented votes 70 percent Republican on average. Although he served on the Armed Services Committee, a natural choice for a Congressman from the Springs, rarely was Kramer cited by those interviewed as a major factor in the Springs' military success.

A community whose major growth impetus emanates from new defense facilities and the contracts associated with them is not likely to oppose new increments, regardless of questions about the national need for them or the general will of the nation. Colorado Springs is just one example of the new geopolitics created by the rise of the gunbelt—a town whose identity has been merged with Star Wars and the cold war, and whose residents have become staunch defenders of military budgets.

Conclusion

Colorado Springs' rich and eventful career is hard to summarize. It is a community that has won a great deal against formidable odds. Located in a remote place with few natural resources, it tried importing income and wealth, rather than generating it locally, and created a spatial niche for itself. It restyled itself successively at least a half-dozen times, as "Little London," "Newport of the Rockies," a tuberculosis miracle-recovery center, a mountain tourist attraction, a military encampment, a high-tech mecca, and, most recently, the "Space Capital of the Free World." In the postwar period, it has been more successful than ever, although its economic base remains precariously perched on the national-defense budget.

Of course, serendipity cannot be discounted. Had either General Palmer or the Tutts, or any of their millionaire counterparts gone broke, the original foundation for the Springs' success might never have been laid. Had David Packard's parents not gone to Colorado College and he not decided to drive through town during the months when Hewlett-Packard was searching for a new site, the high-tech contingent might never have arrived. In any town's history, some elements of luck and happenstance intrude—for most prairie places, the luck just seems to have gone the other way.

Three sets of actors took deliberate steps to stake out a place for Colorado Springs in the military–industrial complex. First, the boosters made an enormous contribution to shaping the town and its culture in ways that were to attract both the military and private-sector high-tech branch plants. Second, certain key military decision-makers in the Air Force and Army developed a strong preference for the Springs, both because of its strategic attributes and because of the community's positive attitude toward the military.

That the third set of actors, the private-sector companies, were "footloose" enough to come has much to do with changing business technology and philosophy. Beginning in the 1950s, but accelerating in the 1970s and spreading to more technical functions as well, large corporations began to spin off operations to locations far from company headquarters. Escalating costs of doing business in places like Los Angeles, Silicon Valley, and Boston heightened the attractiveness of cheap land and favorable living conditions in places like the Springs. Between the boosters' efforts and the advantages of the military presence, Colorado Springs became a major destination for such branching operations.

Ironically, as the military presence became permanently established and contractors began to gravitate toward the Springs, the latter became less and less willing to give credit to the local economic-development effort. Indeed, although as robust as ever, the economic-development operation does appear to have contributed relatively less to recent growth than it did in earlier decades.[60]

The Springs' story illustrates well our evolutionary theory of military-production centers. Era by era, increments of economic-base capacity were added, and the locational determinants of one helped to produce new features that become in turn the locational determinants of the next. Without the economic surplus and concentrated wealth generated in the frontier era, and without the boosters' strenuous effort, the Springs would not have become the home of the Air Force Academy or permanized the Air Defense Command and Fort Carson. Without these military installations, there would not have been a Kaman or a Hewlett-Packard, with all their high-tech counterparts. The military facilities endowed the Springs with several characteristics essential for the private sector to operate successfully: a critical minimum population size, a blue-collar work force, the prestige necessary to attract and satisfy an engineering and management staff, and the presence of a serious academic community.

In turn, without the high-tech entourage, the defense contractors would not have been willing to come, certainly not the larger facilities doing more than just SETA work. Again, the population and labor-force-enhancing contributions of the high-tech sector gave the city an edge it would not have had as a purely military encampment. It is likely, too, that the Springs would not have appeared as attractive to General Abrahamson and his SDI agency as the centerpiece for permanent Star Wars facilities had the high-tech contingent not expanded the sophistication of both the work force and the services available in town.

Today's Colorado Springs' economy is a product of more than forty years of planning and incremental capacity additions. It illustrates clearly, with its setbacks as well as successes, the developmental aspects of a gunbelt city. On the one hand, its evolution is totally contingent on foreign and military policy. None of it would be conceivable without the cold war and the rise of atmospheric warfare. On the other, it is also very much the creation of a dedicated set of boosters, an ambitious and forward-looking cadre within the military, and an energetic group of contract managers. Given development of the cold war, these activities had to be centered somewhere. That they ended up in such an improbable place is a story that can only be told as we have told it—in the words of the people who made it.

9

The Eavesdroppers:
SDI, Software, and Lobbying
in the Nation's Capital

In this millennial decade, there are two Washingtons. Which one you see depends on which side of the plane you occupy as you land at National Airport. On the right, across the Potomac, is the Washington everyone knows: the neoclassical Beaux-Arts landscape of Congress, Mall, and monuments. On the left is another landscape altogether. Behind Arlington National Cemetry and the Pentagon stretches an apparently endless landscape of low-density suburbs, into which have been injected islands of skyscrapers resembling mini-Dallases or mini-Atlantas. Much of this landscape is brand new, the product of the last few years. The most prominent skyscraper cluster of all, Tysons Corner, was a sleepy suburban shopping center and filling station a mere twenty years ago. And this new landscape stretches along the freeways, apparently as far as the eye can see—beyond the left wing tip, in the area between Interstate 66, leading westward to the Blue Ridge Mountains, and the Dulles Airport access road (Fig. 9.1).

For Americans and foreign visitors alike, the classical landscape of Washington has a rich symbolic value. It signifies the dignity of constitutional government, separation of powers, and equality under the law. Although many may not realize it, the other landscape is equally symbolic. It represents one of the most important, but not widely appreciated, facets of recent American history: the maturation of the military–industrial complex, now finally established in the very seat of government. It corresponds to a dramatic new phrase in the evolution of the entire complex, as revolutionary in its way as was the creation of the aerospace industry in the 1950s.

By the mid-1980s, the Washington–Baltimore metropolitan area ranked sixth in the United States in number of high-tech enterprises, after Los Angeles, San Francisco/San Jose, New York, Boston, and Chicago, with 1,100 plants and 120,000 workers. It was particularly strong in telecommunications (telephone, satellites, radar), biotechnology, and military electronics. Ten

211

FIGURE 9.1. Washington, D.C.: defense-industry firms.

percent of the Washington-region work force have high-tech jobs; 33 percent have at least one college degree, the highest proportions for any urban area in the United States.[1]

Military markets are the major driving force behind this high-tech growth. By the late 1970s, the Washington–Baltimore area was second only to Los Angeles in terms of federal R&D contracts.[2] All this is extraordinarily recent. The biggest firm here, Martin-Marietta, moved from New York to Bethesda in 1974. A conglomerate, it is specializing increasingly in military electronics, telecommunications, and space. Its major contracts include missiles, the tail of the B-1B bomber, and the module of the spacecraft. The firm has concentrated its R&D here, in close liaison with the Pentagon, NASA, and the FAA. Other large and relatively youthful defense-oriented companies include UNC Resources, Atlantic Research Corporation, BDM International, Syscon, Cerberonics, and Sutron.[3]

The Tertiarization of the Defense Industries

Defense firms in these Washington suburbs seldom occupy factories. They can be found in skyscraper offices or campus office parks. They make use of electronics, but—apart from a small IBM plant at Manassas—they do not make computers or computer components. Their products conform to the classic definition of the service industries: you cannot stub your toe on them. They are embedded in floppy disks, hard disks, hard disks, and tapes; but essentially the product, software, is pure knowledge. Eventually that knowledge will be used to navigate spacecraft, eavesdrop on conversations in distant places and record faraway events, anticipate and monitor attacks by hostile powers, and perhaps destroy missiles in space. It will thus be incorporated into expensive hardware, but that will happen in distant locations like Orange County or Utah. The product of the Washington suburbs is strictly intangible and immaterial.

These firms thus represent a new phase in the evolution of the advanced capitalist economy: a phase that geographers and urban economists have termed geographical specialization by function. Instead of the old pattern whereby regions and cities specialized in distinctive products—textiles in Lowell, steel in Pittsburgh, autos in Detroit—areas of the country now are distinguished by their functional position in the productive process. New York is the national-headquarters city; Atlanta and Minneapolis perform regional-headquarters functions; Highway 128 and Silicon Valley are R&D centers; routine production is increasingly pushed to low-wage peripheries in the rural South or the developing world. The defense industries, too, have followed this trend.

After World War II, military contractors became the first high-tech manufacturing industries. As seen in Chapters 5 and 6, the result was the development of new research and production complexes in California's Orange County and along Massachusetts' Route 128. But more recently, in the era of Star Wars, there is a new trend—the development of pure research complexes, without attendant manufacturing. We can best describe it by an ungainly word: the tertiarization of the defense industries. This process reaches its apogee, its quintessence, in the Maryland and Virginia suburbs of the national capital.

Because this is tertiary activity, standards and locational factors that apply to the manufacturing industry are irrelevant. In research, raw material consists of ideas. The product may leave over cable or via satellite; "transportation costs" are negligible. Theoretically, the industry could be located at the equator or at the North Pole; certainly it could be, and has been, located in places like California and Massachusetts. The intriguing question for our inquiry is why, in recent years, it should so suddenly and spectacularly have burgeoned in Washington, D.C.

In an earlier era of defense-industry building, military procurement followed the concentrations of existing expertise, whether in the laboratories of major technical universities like MIT and Caltech or in the manufacturing companies like the airframe firms or the electronics concerns that were willing and able to make the major entrepreneurial jump into aerospace. Now, these companies or their successors beat a path to the national capital.

There is no ready explanation for why this should be. Founding fathers, whose birthplaces or original locational choices proved so significant in the evolution of earlier defense-production centers, played little or no role here. After the disastrous pioneering aeronautical experiments of Samuel Pierpont Langley, the area had no founders of significance. Nor was it blessed with a concentration of federal research, procurement, or manufacturing agencies. True, Washington's Navy Yard, on the Anacostia River, was in place from the original L'Enfant plan, and from 1806 ships were built as well as repaired there. But it suffered from the silting of the river. In 1860, the Navy limited the yard's production role because it was so far from the sea, and it never achieved the importance of some other yards.[4] Later, early aeronautical research under the National Advisory Committee for Aeronautics (NACA), established by a congressional act of 1915 to "supervise and direct the scientific study of the problems of flight," was based at a remote site 100 miles to the south, at Hampton, Virginia. An attempt to move it to Bolling Field, in the District of Columbia, was beaten back by Congress, and the station, named for Langley, was subsequently ignored by both Army and Navy for their experimental work.[5]

Further, quite unlike that in southern California and Massachusetts, university research has played little part in the rise of this region. George Mason and George Washington universities have recently expanded their electronics programs, but this has occurred in response to demand, not the other way around. The same goes for state initiatives: in 1985, the governor of Virginia proposed a Center for Innovative Technology next to Dulles; almost simultaneously Maryland announced a Maryland Science and Technology Center, featuring a top-secret research center with fifth-generation computers under the sponsorship of the Institute for Defense Analysis.[6] But again, these are responses, designed to divert the manifestations of the high-tech wave to one side or the other of the Potomac. Its source has to be sought elsewhere.

The New Structure of Defense Procurement: Conflict at the Center

It is found in the changing structure of defense strategic formulation and procurement in the post–World War II era. In Chapter 2, we reviewed the huge battles during the 1920s and 1930s to forge a separate Air Force, finally resolved in 1947. But the reorganization of the armed services in that year, embodied in the historic National Security Act, was also about something else: the attempt to create a unified military organization, over and above the three armed services. That battle was lost. The 1947 act "established not a unified department or even a federation, but a confederation of three military departments presided over by a Secretary of Defense with carefully enumerated powers."[7] Subsequently, the position of the secretary was strengthened, and the three forces lost their status as executive departments. But it was not until 1961, with the arrival of Ford Motors' Robert McNamara as Secretary for Defense and of the RAND Corporation's Charles Hitch as his right-hand man, that the full powers of the Secretary of Defense to run the department on a unified basis were actually used.

What brought this about was the revolution in military technology during the 1950s, which created aerospace but also made necessary the central planning and direction of the military program. It was achieved through a new programming, planning, and budgeting function. "Now, for the first time," Hitch jubilantly wrote in 1965, "the largest business in the world has a comprehensive Defense Department–wide plan that extends more than one year into the future."[8] He could pronounce himself well satisfied that the new system was established and working smoothly.

Centralized planning was the salient feature of the system McNamara and Hitch designed, although McNamara, Hitch, and their top deputies stressed not centralization, but the new analytic tools for decision-making. But these implied centralization. Some have argued that McNamara used systems analysis in order to centralize, while others have maintained that his managerial philosophy would have meant centralization even without systems analysis. The fact was that from 1961 on, the Office of Systems Analysis (OSA) became the focal point of decision-making, and a target of growing service resentment. Initially it had only six members, by the spring of 1964 it had about 50, and by 1968 it had 200. This led to huge battles between the services—especially the Navy—and the civilian researchers in the OSA.[9]

However, McNamara and Hitch's reforms changed more in appearance than they did in reality. The Department of Defense, by far the most powerful Washington agency, remained the least manageable. Its budget-making process continued to be dominated by parochial behavior on the part of the services. Each service, within its established doctrine, continued to press for ever-more-advanced weapons and equipment—tanks, aircraft, carriers, and strategic bombers—incorporating the latest state-of-the-art technology. This was exacerbated by what one author has called "the bureaucratization of the military": a large force of Department of Defense employees who are not attached to military fighting units, but are involved with management, logistics, and weapons engineering.[10]

Compromising a number of powerful bureaucracies within the military–industrial complex and replacing soldiers as the main policy initiators, the bureaucrats and their clients succeeded in transforming internal Department of Defense incentives from their ostensible purpose, national security, to their real purpose, continued procurements. The weapons R&D offices within the three services have become powerful institutions because of their natural alliance with defense contractors and members of Congress, as witness the ultimately successful campaign for the B-1 bomber. The Undersecretary of Defense for Research and Engineering, usually a defense-industry career executive, has tended to support service demands, further complicating the job of the secretary. The Joint Chiefs of Staff further exacerbate these tendencies: four out of five represent service interests. James Schlesinger, a former Secretary of Defense, points out the ironic result: the civilian dominance of military matters, which was the last thing that the uniformed military wanted to see.[11]

The quintessence of this process was the Reagan presidency. The budget of January 30, 1981, involved a $32 billion defense hike for 1981 and 1982, in addition to $20 billion in real growth already in the Carter budget for these years. Reagan gave Caspar Weinberger, a lawyer, the defense portfolio, with a brief to get big dollars for defense. According to two Pentagon watchers, Richard A. Stubbing and Richard A. Mendel, the appointment took everyone, including the defense chiefs, by surprise. A longtime Weinberger acquaintance said that "the service chiefs simply run circles around Cap." They just went out and ordered everything. Nothing was done to limit interservice rivalry, and each service pursued its own agenda. "The Army and Air Force," Stubbing and Mendel wrote, "continue to field redundant systems for close air support and NATO air defense, while the Air Force and Navy are each building strategic missiles capable of destroying Soviet missile silos."[12] Reorganization of the Joint Chiefs of Staff structure, long thought overdue by experts, failed to happen

Reagan's March 1983 speech, introducing the idea of the Strategic Defense Initiative, was a brilliant political maneuver: by diverting attention from the escalation of costs, it allowed the package to escape virtually intact. Yet it offered nothing concrete in military terms for the next decade: the costs—$2.75 billion for 1986, $4.8 billion requested for 1987—represented merely "a small down payment on a missile defense system estimated to cost anywhere from several hundred billion up to a trillion dollars."[13] The Reagan 1985 defense budget exceeded allocations of the peak Vietnam year, and represented an unprecedented 50 percent increase in five years. One observer, *Atlantic* magazine columnist John Lemann, referred to it as the "first peacetime war."[14] Yet, ironically, it represented only a minimal increase in military force or weapons production: of the $330 billion increase, over half ($191 billion) was for modernization, including R&D and new weapon development, a 90 percent hike over the 1980 to 1985 period.

The net result of the entire process, which peaked in the last years of the Reagan presidency, was what might be called the civilianization of war. Instead of battles to be waged between real contestants, war became a highly esoteric and vastly expensive game, fought out in software laboratories and in committee rooms where scientific budgets were thrashed out. The logical location for that war was in the nation's capital. Proximity to the Pentagon, and to the myriad bureaucracies and sub-bureaucracies within and around it, became crucial. The contractors were tied into ever-closer relationships with the officials, whether uniformed or civilian, who wrote the specifications and argued the case for the cash. And increasing specialization meant more and closer relationships with other firms: the same kinds of contractual ties that earlier had characterized the emergence of industrial complexes in Orange County and along Route 128. And, insofar as the software would eventually be put into equipment that would be built or installed elsewhere, it also implied highly efficient communications with the rest of the United States and the world, through the region's airports.

The Three Capital Corridors

It was thus logical that the defense service industries should not only seek a home in the Washington, D.C., area, but also cluster within it, along the axis that joins the Pentagon and the two airports. Hence the emergence of the Pentagon–Dulles corridor. This east–west corridor, wholly on the Virginia side of the Potomac, runs from National Airport, via Crystal City and the Pentagon, to Rosslyn, Tysons Corner, Reston, Herndon, and Dulles International Airport; Manassas forms an outpost to the southwest.[15] Far less well known than Silicon Valley or Route 128, the Pentagon–Dulles corridor has joined them as one of the leading high-tech concentrations in the United States.

The first key to the development of this high-tech enclave is the location of National Airport itself; at Gravelly Point between the Fourteenth Street Bridge and Alexandria. Carefully chosen in 1940—after consideration of a number of alternatives—this site offered accessibility to the center city, and it could be easily developed by landfill. The decision was made under the pressure of impending war, and then only after presidential intervention. The airport was opened in the summer of 1941.[16]

Another, even more significant clue to Washington's emergence as a military–industrial center is the location of the Pentagon next door, on the Virginia side of the Potomac just south of Arlington National Cemetery. It resulted from a decision made under pressure. It was built at great speed, between 1941 and 1943. In 1941, the War Department was headquartered on Constitution Avenue, but it oversaw the activities of 24,000 people scattered in seventeen buildings throughout the D.C. area; this roster was expected to grow to 30,000 by the beginning of 1942. For years, the War Department had been slated to move to a new site in the Northwest Rectangle, west of the White House and north of the Lincoln Memorial. But it skillfully circumvented the opposition of both the Interior Department and the National Capital Park and Planning Commission, and obtained a $35 million congressional appropriation to start work on the Virginia site. The plan was bitterly opposed by the Commission of Fine Arts because of the proposed building invasion of the Arlington National Park area and its proximity to the national cemetery. The commission succeeded in diverting the War Department from its first locational choice at the Virginia end of the Arlington Memorial Bridge, but failed to stop the department's flight from the city. In April 1942, Frederic Delano, the distinguished chairman of the Park and Planning Commission, resigned on the ground that commissioners no longer performed any planning functions.[17]

Inevitably, once completed, the Pentagon exerted a huge influence on the development of the Virginia side of the Potomac. The building, designed for 30,000 workers, was virtually a self-contained city. It powerfully triggered the development of a multicentered regional city. The area's desirability as a place to live was enhanced by the increased accessibility to the Virginia shore provided by several key pieces of highway and bridge construction—some predating the Pentagon, like the Key Bridge of 1923 and the George Washington Memorial Parkway of the early 1930s; some coming later, like the Capital Beltway, first proposed in a regional plan of 1950 and completed in 1964.[18]

The first sign of the Pentagon's impact on land use on the west bank of the Potomac came only four years after the end of World War II and significantly, perhaps, at the outset of the cold war era. In 1949, the Arlington County Board varied its zoning regulations to allow the construction of Arlington Towers, a thirteen-story building at the Virginia end of the Key Bridge. The project was vigorously opposed by the Park and Planning Commission, but again it failed to stop its construction. Around it, during the late 1950s, Rosslyn, suburban Washington's first high-rise concentration, exploited a key strategic position at the Virginia end of the Key Bridge. A complex of over a dozen high-rise office buildings, luxury apartment buildings, hotels, and other commercial enterprises, it added significantly to Arlington County's tax base; predictably, large parts of it were federally leased. Later, Crystal City was developed just south of the Pentagon, following Arlington County plans that confined high-density development to the Jefferson Davis corridor. Soon, triggered by rapid suburban growth, other office complexes developed near the region's major thoroughfares, especially adjacent to the Capital Beltway after its completion in 1964, and at Tysons Corner.[19]

Tysons Corner, six miles northwest of Rosslyn, has become, since the mid-1970s, "a veritable peripheral CBD [central business district]." It has an estimated 20 million square feet of office space (more than the amount of space available in downtown Baltimore, Cleveland, Milwaukee, and Cincinnati), seven large department stores, 2.5 million square feet of retail space in two shopping centers, twelve full-size hotels, and major buildings designed by Skidmore, Owings and Merill, Burgee/Johnson, and many well-known local architects. Although it contains only about one-quarter of the office space in Washington proper, Tysons Corner is already the largest "downtown" in Virginia. It is a new phenomenon, described by critics Christopher B. Leinberger and Charles Lockwood as "urban villages", which they characterized as "mini-downtowns with maxi-gridlock in a new kind of low-density cityscape."[20] A fairly sleepy suburban shopping center twenty years ago, with a supermarket and a couple of filling stations, Tysons Corner, like Rosslyn, is now a mini-city of glistening new office towers, surrounded by endemic traffic congestion. Even outside the peak hours, it may take twenty minutes to drive a few blocks.

Still farther northwest in Virginia are the new town of Reston and the Dulles International Airport: both developed in the early 1960s, both ironically regarded originally as white elephants, both now booming. Dulles, long empty and echoing, has overcome the disadvantage of its twenty-three-mile distance to downtown Washington by the line of towns that has grown out to meet it. It is now hub to four airlines: Pan Am, United, New York Air, and Presidential Airways, a new cut-rate airline. The second-biggest American airport in physical terms after Dallas–Fort Worth, it will soon be connected to the capital by the Metro. Close by Herndon in Virginia is one of the most dynamic places in the United States in terms of job growth, with a projected increase of nearly 44,000, or 44 percent, between 1988 and 1993; most of the development now visible has occurred since 1984, as firms like Computer Sciences, C3 Inc., Telenet and CH2M Hill have come in.[21]

The so-called Dulles corridor is overwhelmingly the dominant location for the new defense-oriented firms, but there are two important secondary axes, both in Maryland. One lies along Interstate 270 toward the northwest (Bethesda, Rockville, Gaithersburg, Hagerstown) and features a preponderance of biotech firms. The other, still in the course of development in the late 1980s, wends north-northeast, connecting Greenbelt, Columbia, and Baltimore–Washington International Airport.[22] Connecting and bisecting all three corridors is the famous Washington Beltway, I-495, with its many small consultancy houses, long since stigmatized as the Beltway Bandits.

To some degree, the corridors have different economic foci. An analysis of federal contracts, made in the mid-1980s at the start of the defense buildup, shows that within the D.C. area, suburban Virginia—the site of the western corridor—was particularly well represented in defense, other R&D applications, and sophisticated electronic and communications equipment, together with professional, data-processing, and analytical services. Suburban Maryland, the location of the northwestern and northeastern corridors, had a technical bias toward federal agencies like NASA, the National Institutes of Health, and the Nuclear Regulatory Commission.[23]

The Rise of the Systems Houses

Nearly all the new activity here, our respondents told us, is in so-called systems houses: IBM, Martin-Marietta, SDC, Honeywell, and small (twenty-five to fifty employees) firms around the Beltway that specialize in writing systems procurement that the big companies then build. TRW, the California systems house, was the first firm to go into the Virginia suburbs, in 1964. The others followed over the years. IBM, one of the later arrivals, had bought its site dirt-cheap at Manassas, in the distant exurbs beyond Dulles Airport, after World War II, far in advance of need.

Systems houses are not a new phenomenon. We traced the rise of the first, TRW, to the birth of the missile era in the mid-1950s in Los Angeles. But their present prominence and their concentration in the D.C. area are quite recent. What is increasingly crucial is the design of the system, coupled with advice on what kinds of equipment and software the military contractors should buy. The premium on information flow also creates clusters of "storefronts" like those we saw in Colorado Springs—smaller operations that larger companies feel compelled to set up near the principal military commands, especially those with high-tech, cold war missions. "To be successful in competing later, you have to be involved as a contractor from the very front end of that requirements definition until the time they actually go on the street with the request for proposals," reported one of our sources. "If you aren't involved in it from the beginning, you might as well forget it because you have to understand what the Air Force really wants." Often, that may involve a shop near the operational bases. More and more, however, it also means a presence near the seat of high-level strategic thinking. This is a two-way process: the contractor and the military people will sit and interact. Thus storefronts both market ideas developed in the research lab in Los Angeles or Boston, and keep eyes and ears open to detect where the users themselves are going.

The best way to understand this process is by looking at the pure form of this industry, the software company/systems house, which clusters along the western corridor and is represented in our study by TRW. But because they developed earlier, we will first go out along the other two corridors, to consider two intermediate kinds of company that combine both service and manufacturing functions.

A Manufacturing–Service Combination: Fairchild

Fairchild Industries, the company we visited in April 1987, no longer exists. In 1989 it was taken over by the Banner Corporation, which sold its space and defense activities to the French firm of Matra. But under a new logo, the old company continues this part of its business as before.

The local facility of former Fairchild Industries is located in a campus office development at Germantown, set in the green landscape of the outer Maryland suburbs of Washington; it is about twenty miles from the Capitol along Interstate 270, the main highway that leads northwest to Frederick and the Civil War battlefields. Anyone returning to Washington after a relatively long absence would feel like Rip Van Winkle in traversing this, Washington's northwest high-tech corridor. For mile after mile, fields and farms have given way to an apparently endless succession of offices, laboratories, tract housing, chain hotels, and shopping centers, all the creation of the past fifteen years.

Like most other firms in this corridor and in the whole Greater D.C. area, Fairchild was not originally a local firm. It was founded in New York in 1920 by Sherman Mills Fairchild and his father, Congressman George Fairchild—later chair of CTR, first incarnation of IBM—to manufacture and market a vastly improved aerial camera. It proved a huge success, used by most of the world's air forces in the 1920s and 1930s. To provide a more stable platform for the camera and extend its civilian uses, Fairchild developed a small civil monoplane in 1926; it was highly successful, selling in quantity both to survey units and to airlines. The company had plants in Farmingdale on Long Island and in Hagerstown, Maryland; an Ontario branch served the buoyant market for survey aircraft in the Canadian north.

In 1936, Fairchild Aviation was split: cameras and aerial-survey instruments went to one corporation, aircraft and engines to another. The Fairchild Camera and Instrument Corporation stayed on Long Island, where it is now Fairchild Weston; it achieved lasting fame in 1956 when it acquired William Shockley's key staff, triggering the saga of Silicon Valley. The Fairchild Engine and Aircraft Corporation, after a series of redesignations, ultimately became Fairchild Industries, located at Farmingdale, Long Island,[24] and Germantown, Maryland; it produced more than 8,000 trainer aircraft and 11,000 engines during World War II, and reentered civil aviation in the 1950s while continuing to compete successfully in the military field. Progressively it acquired other companies, notably California-based Hiller Aircraft in 1963 and Republic Aviation, its Long Island neighbor, the following year.

Fairchild Industries got into space systems very early. In 1946, it bought a large tract of land in Germantown, opening its corporate headquarters and Space Systems Division there in 1948. Under the direction of Wernher von Braun, who became corporate vice president of engineering, it developed satellites for many NASA programs, notably the ATS–6 communications satellite. Thus Fairchild became a classic example of a firm that stayed with aircraft but diversified into sophisticated, top-secret avionics applications.

At Germantown, the complex of buildings progressively developed after Interstate 270 was built in the 1960s. The building in which we sat was only about two years old. Much later, in 1984 to 1985, Fairchild moved its headquarters to a location near Dulles Airport, because the chief executive wanted to be near international customers, especially the Swedish Saab company, with which Fairchild had links; its preference for Dulles over Baltimore International Airport is explained by the rapid growth of the northern Virginia suburbs.[25]

Since the company is heavily engaged in Department of Defense work, our interviewees explained, it is desirable to be closer to Washington to reach both military customers and politicians. The main military work is for the Air Force and Navy. There is a great deal of day-to-day contact with military people, but not necessarily at the Pentagon; this interaction takes place all over the country, primarily with Air Force base personnel, although a great deal is done locally at Goddard Space Flight Center at Greenbelt, a Maryland suburb just outside Washington that is readily accessible via I-270 and the Beltway. Fairchild has also diversified by buying other firms.[26] In this way, it has spread itself out across the gunbelt.

While Fairchild's preference is to be close to Washington, its competitors and partners are not necessarily in the area. The company's main competitors on larger projects are CONTEC, Ford Aerospace, Harris, RCA, Lear Siegler, and Westinghouse. It subcontracts to McDonnell-Douglas, Boeing, Hughes, and Rockwell, and bids on subcontracts to competing firms. Sixty percent of the work is subcontract; 40 percent, prime. The primes to which Fairchild subcontracts are all over the country, so proximity is not a factor.

Our interviewees told us that there is a lot of face-to-face contact during procurement, but very little afterward. This is a two-way street. Military people or other contractors may come to Fairchild in the early stages of a project to check out the firm's capacities, but Fairchild also goes out to demonstrate to clients in Boston, New York (IBM), St. Louis, Seattle, Los Angeles (Northrop), and Dallas (Grumman). Generally, it is easier for Fairchild clients to come to Washington, for they may have several visits to make in the D.C. area. Airport access is not a factor in local siting, although it played a large role in the decision to locate in the Washington area. Even at Hagerstown, the firm had access to a small airport.

Our interviewees confirmed that close links with Congress had helped Fairchild secure its contract for trainer planes (3,000 planes over twenty years). Congress is not important for the smaller contracts, however.

Nor is labor availability a major factor for Fairchild. Fairchild is a nonunion company. The labor force is balanced between males and females. As a government contractor, the company must be seen to be following affirmative action procedures. It tries to recruit locally in Maryland and Virginia, and has problems only during times of scarcity, although specific talents must be found by national search.

A Conglomerate Subsidiary: Amecon

The northeast corridor is also anchored by a defense-manufacturing-cum-research operation. Amecon, located inside the Beltway in the Maryland suburb of College Park, close to the University of Maryland, has been a subsidiary of Litton Industries since around 1950. It started as three separate companies, including a radio manufacturer and a machine shop, that came together at that time. It is one of a whole series of Litton electronic divisions, including one in Canada and another in California. Some are almost wholly in military business, as is this one; others almost wholly on the commercial side. There are few contacts between the divisions, apart from occasional meetings of professional engineers to discuss topics of interest or between engineers and headquarters. The facility in College Park combines administration, R&D, and manufacturing; the 1,650 employees include 400 professionals and administrative people, 500 in manufacturing.

For its professional staff, the company recruits mainly industrial engineers, both from agencies and from universities that mix industrial engineering and computer science. Amecon staff reported that it is difficult to keep an industrial engineer in a manufacturing environment, especially in an area where people follow the contracts from one small company to another around the Beltway, but things have begun to improve. The direct manufacturing labor is not unionized, which is fairly characteristic for the entire D.C. area. Women hold 25 percent of professional positions and account for a large proportion of the manufacturing jobs, most of which are repetitive tasks in electronic assembly that need skills, accuracy, and manual dexterity. The old machining work, which was dirty and hard and therefore went to men, has gone. Most of the work here is specialty products, in low volume.

Most of Amecon's R&D work is classified, so it is not contracted out. The firm has few links with the local universities; five people in the industrial engineering division, when we visited, were on programs at either the University of Maryland or Johns Hopkins. The company has had no trouble recruiting engineers from all over the country—Texas, New York, Florida, California. Six mechanical engineers had been recruited from the University of Maryland, but the school does not run an industrial engineering program.

Our respondent thought that Amecon's location in the Washington area affords the firm vital access to the Pentagon and to Congress. You can get in the car and exchange information with key Pentagon officials. This is particularly important because of BMP (Best Manufacturing Practices), the outline from the government of what it wants. If you do not conform to Navy practices, there is a black mark against you. The easy access to three major airports—National, Dulles, and Baltimore—is also a plus factor.

At this site, Amecon operations were scattered in a number of buildings constructed since the company outgrew its original structure. Because Amecon had twenty-five acres here, it could consolidate. At the time of our interview, the Metro was coming soon to a site near the Amecon building, a site that the company once owed, had sold to the Metro, and was now leasing back. But our interviewee did not expect a big impact: this was not the affluent side of town, and the company's employees commuted from all over the D.C. area, especially from outside the Beltway.

About 85 or 90 percent of Amecon's work is for the Navy, but the management ranked the Washington area good for contacts with all the services. The firm does considerable subcontracting work on naval aircraft for Grumman, which maintains one of its people there. Most of Amecon's main competitors—E Systems, Martin-Marietta, Gould, Westinghouse, and IBM—are not located in the area.

A Defense-Service Company: TRW

Sample companies from the two Maryland corridors enjoy their adjacency to Washington, but would not necessarily flounder without it. The primacy of proximity is quite different for those along the Pentagon–Dulles corridor. This is illustrated by the gravitation to the capital area of defense service firms like TRW, even from remote southern California. "If you're going to be a camp follower," as one of our respondents put it, you must "find the camp." TRW did.

As related in Chapter 5, TRW—Thompson-Ramo-Wooldridge—was established in Inglewood, California, in 1953 at the time of the gestation of the first intercontinental ballistic missile. At the beginning, TRW was an odd company. It was created as the first systems company and was precluded by law from manufacturing.[27] Thus it was the archetype of the tertiary service

company, thirty years in advance of its time. And it was entirely logical that
it should have pioneered the move to suburban Washington—specifically, to
the Dulles corridor.

The story goes back to 1964, when Admiral Charles Martell announced
that he wanted to commission high-level systems support for antisubmarine
warfare. A number of possible contenders—AT&T, Lockheed, McDonnell—
were excluded because of the conflict-of-interest provision that no contracting
manufacturing firm could undertake systems engineering. TRW did not have
that problem, so it came in. It was a case of the camp follower finding the
camp. In those days, TRW located wherever development took place.

The enormous distance between L.A. and D.C. was for a long time a
problem for the satellite office. The operation was called Washington Operations (the lowest recognizable operating unit) until 1983, when it became
a division (Systems and Applications Division). For a long time, the Washington staff found that it was out of the mainstream of TRW management.
Employees in the Los Angeles office joked that "you lost 20 points IQ" in
moving east. This prejudice broke down only very slowly.

Expansion brought administrative reorganization: TRW's Electronic and
Space Systems Group was split into three separate groups—Electronic Systems, Defense Systems, and Space and Technology Systems—in 1982.[28]
Shortly thereafter, with the expansion of SDI, the price of land and the cost
of living rose in Los Angeles. TRW conducted a demographic study of nine
or ten areas around the country, including Sunnyvale, Route 128, Research
Triangle, Huntsville, and northern Virginia. The last got a very high rating
on availability of the right kind of labor, lower cost of living, and nearness
to the customer. And TRW had a rapidly growing command and control
operation in the area, which helped justify the creation in 1986 of the Federal
Systems Group. Although growth provided the opportunity,[29] what really
inspired TRW was the desire of its military customers to "touch the whole
thing" on large projects.

To achieve this, the company bought 120 acres at the intersection of
Interstate 66 and Highway 50 (Fair Lake), where its Washington operations
will eventually be centered.[30] As a result, TRW now has 2,500 people working
in the area, in nineteen buildings, on contracts worth $400 million (the cor-
responding figures in 1980 were 600 people and $60 million). It also has 200
to 300 employees in Strategic Defense Command at Huntsville, engaged in
Army SDI-related activities, of which Huntsville is the acquisitions center.
When we interviewed the firm in 1987, pending consolidation at Fair Lake,
the relatively small Washington operations of the Electronic Systems Group
and the Defense Systems Group were located in an office complex in Arlington. The Federal Systems Group is at Tysons Corner.

Once a program gets started, it may be managed anywhere. The official
chain of command is a long one—the Pentagon to Air Force Systems Command at Andrews Air Force Base in Maryland, to Wright-Patterson in Dayton
or the parallel Space Systems Division in Los Angeles, to TRW at Space
Park. But on occasion, it is easier for the Pentagon to call TRW directly.

Our respondent told us that he spent about half his time communicating with Pentagon officials and the other half travelling to—or communicating with— the TRW operations in Los Angeles and San Diego. TRW has field people at Pentagon operations centers across the country, too, reporting to the director of the Electronic Systems Group in Washington.

Other TRW contracts in the D.C. area cover engineering services for the Navy and intelligence, including a particularly important element popularly known as "Rent an Engineer": providing office space and contracting out to military agencies (most within fifteen miles) that have reached their staff complement ceiling. The Command Support Division deals with security, communications, and C^3I, with an emphasis on fixed and mobile command centers embracing hardware and software. The work done here is mainly on prototype development involving a great deal of interaction between customer and contractor. The customer expects the vendor to be close, and that means Washington.

A different type of expertise is found in the military stationed in Washington, D.C., as compared to those housed in with large bases in California. Personnel on the West Coast operate equipment; Washington, D.C., personnel acquire equipment. Thus the Naval Air Systems Command—which contracts with Grumman and McDonnell-Douglas, not TRW—is much bigger than Moffett and is 70 to 80 percent concerned with acquisition. TRW and its competitors want what our interviewee called "plumbers": they had to configure the job with the customer in mind. Our respondent emphasized that there is now a new generation of military and civil servants, no longer content with management by objective, who want a hands-on share in developments that are no longer a black art to them, such as large-scale data-base operations. "The customer has become educated." These "customers" are headquarters managers who have designed a new system of co-development by themselves and with their systems contractors; they are not willing to travel 2,000 miles to meet their companies. They are in agencies like NASA, the CIA, and the DIA; at Air Force Systems Command and Andrews Air Force Base; at the Navy's Sea Systems Command and Naval Space and Warfare Systems Command; and in non–Department of Defense operations like Treasury, State, the FAA, the Department of Energy, the IRS, and Commerce, all of which are upgrading and developing their 1960s systems and are concerned with the need for secure systems.[31] While much work might still be developed in California and other places, top-secret operations favor the Beltway and its corridors.

Contracting for this kind of work involves complex negotiations. Your competitor on one project could be your partner (your prime contractor or subcontractor) on another a month later, and the same individuals could be involved at the top level. TRW is sometimes the prime contractor, sometimes the subcontractor. One TRW group, Electronic Systems, in Los Angeles, is primarily a subcontractor on other companies's major pieces of equipment, either hardware or software. It also receives subcontracts from other divisions of TRW.

Another important factor is the development of joint service programs, begun after congressional pressures twenty-five years ago. Even on these, 98 percent of the work could theoretically be done in California, Alabama, Texas, or elsewhere. Nevertheless, most programs of this type are centered in Washington. For instance, the Cruise Missile Program has an office, the Joint Cruise Missile Project Office (JCMPO), in the D.C. area. The Advanced Tactical Aircraft, due to become operational in about ten years, may also develop as an Air Force–Navy project. Undertakings of this sort involve complex interrelationships between services, and a Washington location can help overcome the communications problems and red tape inherent in cumbrous bureaucratic hierarchies.

Communications projects, in particular, often lend themselves to joint endeavors. A prototype is the new World Wide Military Communications System (WWMCS), which serves all branches of the military and so must conform to joint specifications. In general, software-related systems more readily lend themselves to concentration than did military-hardware products. Here the "products" are judgments, intelligence, and paper. Many complex projects, we were told, had to be designed right through, in one continuous process: they could not be fixed by trial and error. The D.C. area is an ideal location for this type of advanced engineering work.

The key locational feature now, according to TRW, is smart people. Even in choosing projects to pursue, TRW keeps its staff concerns foremost. Its chief concern is: Will this project appeal to our people? "Rack-and-stack" jobs–that is, mass production–is not something TRW would do. Instead, it matches projects to the right kind of qualified manpower, which cannot be found everywhere. Originally the skilled labor that TRW requires came primarily from California; the presence of the Pentagon was not then important. But Los Angeles labor is now very expensive, spurring TRW to begin operations in San Diego. More recently, TRW has discovered that Washington, D.C., has a choice supply of computer-literate military personnel who have degrees from Carnegie-Mellon's Software Engineering Institute (developed with federal aid, and now regarded as the best department nationally), George Mason University (where TRW endowed the Command and Control Chair in computer science), and the University of Maryland (which boasts the largest software department in the world). This labor also comes immediately after graduation from George Mason or the University of Maryland. TRW can recruit engineers from MIT or Georgetown University for $35,000 in Washington, much less than in Los Angeles. On the West Coast, engineers can easily move from one company to another, and often do so, spurring bidding wars that inflate the cost of labor. TRW's Washington groups recruit widely in New England, the South, the Mid-Atlantic states, and the Midwest. But they do not compete with TRW's West Coast operations although they may refer applicants to the other coast. As the second largest American software house, TRW finds it easy to recruit the right kind of people in the D.C. area.

States have made important efforts to upgrade education in this region. There are now "two Virginias" with a significant effect on Richmond politics.

Particularly, the state has built up George Mason University in nearby Fairfax. A community college some twenty years ago, it is now emerging as a major university and paying its professors very high salaries. This is important, since TRW recruits heavily in all the local universities. At George Mason, TRW and Virginia have collaborated, on a three to two basis, on a naval signal processor with a graphical syntax, allowing direct translation into programming language. According to TRW, they are getting "a hell of a bang for the buck."

Local graduates have their ties here—including housing, which makes it so much easier to recruit them. Particularly important is the large pool of military talent, important for some kinds of work (e.g. antisubmarine warfare). A significant number of TRW employees in Washington are former military personnel. They have at least a bachelor's degree and some twenty years' service experience. They are scientific types, not outdoor people.

Congress is an ever-present factor in defense, "the ultimate socialized industry," as one of our TRW correspondents termed it. The people on Capitol Hill have become increasingly involved in "micromanagement" of defense contracts in tandem with the Pentagon. This, in turn, has forced the latter to do a lot of work in Washington, rather than at the commands. Ten or fifteen years ago, all the procurement action, one of our respondents told us, was out of Dayton or Los Angeles. But now that programs and priorities are being determined in Washington, that is increasingly where TRW needs to be. Its staff spends a lot of time answering questions that are relayed through the Pentagon from Capitol Hill. TRW did not decide to build in Virginia on a whim, our respondent stressed; it did so to be near the center of government, and that includes Congress.

Lobbying is sometimes helpful—sometimes not—in the view of one of our TRW respondents. The Los Angeles–based groups maintain their small Rosslyn office for just this purpose. It is important because if two major companies are competing for a big contract, it would be foolish not to make presentations to the local senator, especially if the project would create jobs in a high-unemployment area. "With $3 to $4 million at stake, anyone would go to see the senator," our respondent said. TRW's groups do not deal directly with Congress. The company maintains lobbyists on Capitol Hill.

Conclusion: The New Locational Geography of Defense

The rise of the Washington complex represents a new stage in the geography of the American military–industrial complex. In the mid-1950s, when the aerospace era began, contractors believed that they had no option but to go to the manufacturers—which, at that time, meant the airframe manufacturers. But over the succeeding thirty years, with the process that we have called the tertiarization of the defense industries, this position has fundamentally changed. The process is analogous to that in the market sector of the economy. Just as headquarters offices and R&D tend to cluster in locations far distant from manufacturing facilities, this is the case here. The critical factor is the generation and exchange of valuable information, what the British geographer John Goddard has called unprogrammed information—that is, information most likely to be conveyed informally, by word of mouth.[32] But the imperative to cluster is heightened for these firms by the unique nature of the military contracting process, so imperfectly competitive and subject to enormous discretionary possibilities.

In the high-tech defense industries, proximity of supplier and customer is particularly crucial. In Britain, research shows that such industries are clustered in a tight crescent west of London so that industries can enjoy close day-to-day contact with the Government Research Establishments in the same area.[33] This arrangement developed because the GREs acted as procurement agencies for contracts that involved state-of-the-art prototypical technologies, which necessitated contact between agency and contractor. The increasing technological sophistication of the contractors and the shift into complex software have increased the need for this type of proximity.

Harder to research, yet obviously an element in the D.C. story, are the roles of influence peddling and outright corruption. The Reagan administration has been particularly noted for its contracting abuses, especially in the naval sector, the biggest gainer from the 1980s buildup. Bribes, kickbacks, and illegal padding of military bills have been a persistent problem in military expenditures over the postwar period, generating local economic activity in everything from the misconduct itself to watchdogging and auditing. Not surprisingly, during regimes more tolerant of such abuse, such as that of the 1980s, the level of such activity rises dramatically, accounting for a portion of the recent Washington boomlet.

Given these facts, Washington is almost a natural center of attraction. Agencies like the CIA and NSA have been located there from the beginning. So has the Navy, which—unlike the other services—has a long tradition of centralized purchasing. The Air Force Systems Command at Andrews Air Force Base is responsible for the acquisition of all Air Force systems and for all R&D. Following the McNamara reorganization of the 1960s, there was an increasing tendency to develop high-tech systems on an interservice basis. Naturally, this strengthened the advantage of a Washington location in comparison with distant sites—often chosen for historical reasons—that traditionally had been preferred by the separate services. Given all this, interservice rivalry may have caused the Army and the Air Force to believe that they had to establish a similarly strong presence in the capital. Finally, the Strategic Defense Initiative seems to have given a huge push to the development of the Washington complex, precisely because in this first stage it is essentially a systems-research program.

All this might not have had such a strong effect, in the view of some to whom we spoke, if it had not been for the impact of institutionalized lobbying. The micromanagement of defense projects through specialists on Capitol Hill, working closely with Pentagon officials, apparently helped spur a new level of activity in Washington, making it necessary for both Pentagon and contracting firms to relocate their top-level managers to the nation's capital. Opportunities for illicit influence may have further swollen the ranks.

The result has been the establishment of an information complex similar, in many ways, to the cluster of financial institutions on Wall Street or the concentration of industrial headquarters offices in midtown Manhattan. There are now two such clusters in the United States: one, the market cluster, in New York City; the other, the governmental procurement cluster, in Washington. In other nations, such as Great Britain, the two are combined in one capital city; in America, they are separated for historical reasons. This underlines the fact that they represent groups of firms that largely serve different, segregated markets. With the exception of a few of the airframe and electronics firms that originally made a successful transition into aerospace, the defense contractors are not greatly involved with the civilian-market sector. Still, it is significant that a company like IBM maintains a separate Washington operation for that part of its work.

The development of the Strategic Defense Initiative has given the Washington complex a massive boost since 1980, as evidenced by these firms' brand new offices. The termination or reduction of the program would provide an equally massive jolt. Yet no one should assume that sharp defense cutbacks will weaken the defense-services enterprises in the long run. What we have called the tertiarization of defense is a very long-term tendency that began with the development of the first electronic-information technologies around World War II, and has continued ever since. There may be large blips on the graph, but the Greater D.C. area will continue to loom large in the geography of American defense.

10

Why the Gunbelt?

Because of the size and singularity of the gunbelt, its rise ranks among the most powerful of changes in American settlement patterns in the postwar period, rivaling other momentous changes like the continued movement from central city to suburb. A whole new set of industries, arrayed around aerospace production and including electronics, communications equipment, and computing, and populated by a set of insurgent firms, has led to an extraordinary shift in the nation's industrial center of gravity away from the heartland. New communities and subcultures have been created, distinctive from those characterizing older, industrial cities from Buffalo to Milwaukee, Baltimore to Detroit.

The rise of the gunbelt was not accidental. Nor was it predetermined by inert features of geography like climate, terrain, and coastal access. It is the product of considerable human effort. Generals and colonels, early aircraft entrepreneurs and their corporate offspring, local business boosters, and key university personnel explicitly concerned themselves with the question of "where?" Because the nature of defense procurement offered them considerable discretion, their answers often contained a strong dose of personal preference. Certain places were favored over others; there, a new type of business culture emerged, one kinder to the priorities and status of military–industrial leaders.

The unique American gunbelt is a product first and foremost of the cold war. The cold war initiated a new era of industrial progress, nourished by government-financed, military-led research and development, with guaranteed government markets. The new dominant industries, arrayed around the aerospace complex, faced qualitatively new demands—to make small batches of experimental or innovative gear, with disproportionate numbers of scientists and engineers and dwindling numbers of blue-collar workers. With business practices strikingly different from the competitive cost-cutting and mass-marketing priorities of commercial firms, this new government-bred segment of American industry could, and did, set up camp in relatively virgin locations.

In this final chapter, we sum up our conclusions on this remarkable phenomenon. First, we recapitulate some of the most important of our findings, particularly about the combination of forces that has brought the gunbelt into being. Second, we go on more speculatively—and more contentiously—to discuss some of the implications of the rise of the gunbelt for the national economy and the national polity. Third, and even more conjecturally, we look at an alternative past and a possible future.

The Map of the Gunbelt

The Great Lakes and Mid-Atlantic regions were the industrial center of gravity of the United States from the late nineteenth century onward. They were the great war supplier, too. As late as World War II, ten states dominated prime contracts. All of them, with the exception of California, ranged in a row from Massachusetts to Illinois. The rise of the gunbelt changed all that irrevocably. By 1958, California passed New York and Michigan to rise to the top, with 21 percent of all contracts. By 1982, Illinois, Michigan, Indiana, and Pennsylvania had dropped out of the top ten, while Texas, Missouri, Florida, Virginia, and Maryland had joined this favored group.

The lopsided distribution of prime contracts drove manufacturing-job growth. By the late 1950s, industrial growth outside the heartland had begun to outpace that of the older centers. Aerospace and its related industries—electronics, computers, and communications equipment—were the key to this peripheral development. As commercially oriented industries faced tougher competition from international markets, these government-nurtured high-tech industries increased their comparative advantage, and they drew the gunbelt along in their wake. In the post–Vietnam War period, this divergence has been startling. From 1972 to 1986, manufacturing jobs fell by 22 percent in New York, by 27 percent in Pennsylvania, by 28 percent in Illinois, and by 18 percent in Ohio; they boomed by 34 percent in California, by 35 percent in Washington, by 30 percent in Texas, by 52 percent in Utah, and by 86 percent in Arizona.[1]

As a result, great cities like Milwaukee, Detroit, Cleveland, Pittsburgh, and Chicago have lost their cutting edge. Symbolic of the changing fortunes of their industrial hinterlands, Chicago and Los Angeles have changed places as the second- and third-ranked cities in the United States. In Illinois alone, more than 325,000 jobs were lost in the major heavy industries of metals and machinery between 1979 and the mid-1980s. Despite a historic lead in consumer electronics, military patronage of New England and California electronics firms has overwhelmed the Midwest's preeminence.

In glaring contrast stands California, the single biggest winner from cold war buildup. Since 1958, California's share of the nation's prime contracts has remained about 22 percent, except for a slight drop during the Vietnam War period, while its per capita share maintained itself at more than double the national average. It garners the lion's share of the research, development, testing, and evaluation (RDT&E) contracts that are so essential to long-term success. Without defense dollars, California's manufacturing-job growth would have been only about one-third what it was in the postwar period and the state's inmigration only about one-half its present level.[2]

California may be the new center of defense-manufacturing gravity, but other defense fulcrums have emerged too. Most remarkable is New England, where firms in older industries like radio, aero engines, and shipbuilding managed to make their mark in cold war supply and where a university-linked communications, electronics, and computing complex has been fostered by defense dollars. Small as they are, Massachusetts and Connecticut have consistently ranked in the top ten states for prime contracts, each with more than 5 percent of the nation's total: Massachusetts' per capita share is more than double, Connecticut's more than triple the national average. And Massachusetts' universities persistently account for an extraordinary share—more than one-quarter—of the nation's RDT&E contracts to educational institutions.

Of course, being on the receiving end of military largesse does not necessarily guarantee long-term prosperity. Massachusetts is a particularly revealing case of the unstable mechanics of a military–industrial region because its new military sectors evolved from an older industrial base without completely integrating that base into their activities. The Massachusetts economy has boomed during cold war buildups and slumped when the military-spending cycle starts on its downward slope. As the Reagan buildup drew to a close, the end of growth in military sales exposed the vulnerability of Massachusetts to the underlying difficulties of its civilian sectors and to the high costs of living and doing business, in large part a function of the defense-led boom. High-tech spin-offs in the region have not been sufficient to protect the state from the recession induced by real defense cuts. By 1990, the state faced rising unemployment, a budget crisis, and the loss of one seat in the House of Representatives.

This is true for other gunbelt locales, too. The benefits of being a major recipient of military contracts are the jobs, incomes, and high-tech spin-offs they generate. The costs include defense dependency and vulnerability to cutbacks. Since 1987, after a stunning buildup, defense appropriations in real terms began to fall by about 2 percent per year. In the early 1990s, barring renewal of cold war hostilities or continued Gulf-style conflict, the nation could achieve annual cuts much larger than that. Even moderate economists estimate that the budget could be cut from around $300 billion to about $160 billion in five to ten years. All of this spells difficulties for those places that have thrived on defense receipts in the past decade, particularly to the extent that their economies are highly specialized and dedicated to military weaponry and missions. These are the places that stud the gunbelt.

California and New England are the major poles of the gunbelt. In between them are dozens of other communities whose employment base is heavily dependent on cold war weaponry. We have highlighted several: Seattle with its one dominant company, Colorado Springs with its space-wars complex, and Washington, D.C., with its new defense-services compounds. There are many others that we could have included. Like Seattle, metropolitan areas such as San Diego, St. Louis, Wichita, Dallas–Fort Worth, and central Utah are beholden to one or two major companies with large aerospace procurement contracts; some smaller cities—Camden, Arkansas, and Marietta, Georgia—are even more dependent.[3] Like Colorado Springs, cities such as Huntsville, Alabama; Orlando and Melbourne, Florida; and Houston have major defense-user facilities that have drawn around them a mixed bag of SETA contractors and equipment-makers. Still others—San Diego; Norfolk; Honolulu; Arlington, Virginia; Cumberland, North Carolina; and Charleston, South Carolina—are heavily dependent on military payrolls.[4]

Gunbelt Specialties

Gunbelt cities and their surrounding regions are highly specialized. They are highly specialized by product, where the division of labor mirrors industrial traditions. Older industrial-era items, like tanks and ammunition, tend to be more heavily concentrated in older interior regions—tanks around the Great Lakes, and ammunition in the West North Central and East South Central regions. Aircraft manufacture, in contrast, is disproportionately concentrated: engines in New England and airframes in the Pacific states, although Kansas and Missouri are prominent too. Missiles are even more highly skewed toward the gunbelt: the New England, Pacific, and Mountain states overwhelmingly dominate. In weapons, including items such as nuclear warheads, New England and the Pacific lead. The same two regions also account for the largest, fastest growing share of electronics and communications-equipment contracts. Shipbuilding, of course, is largely a coastal activity. Ironically, New England is the most diversified of military–industrial centers. Its receipts exceed the national per capita norm, by more than 80 percent, in all military categories except ammunition.

Gunbelt cities are specialized by client, too. The Air Force is heavily gunbelt-oriented, especially toward the Southwest, Washington, Florida, and New England. As the ascendant service of the postwar period, it has played a very strong role in the redistribution of defense-industry capacity. During our interviews, the Air Force colonels, generals, and retirees left no doubt about their preferences for the West. They love the wide-open spaces, the proximity to air bases and communities they have lived in, and their "independence" from eastern bureaucracy and industry. The Navy has always had a coastal orientation, yet its purchases from the interior have further shrunk over the postwar period. The Army, the service of old-fashioned manned warfare, equips itself more ubiquitously than the others, and so continues to buy relatively more from the Midwest than do the others. But since the 1950s, even Army contracts have moved toward the South, West, and East. As the Navy and Army have struggled to compete with the new upstart Air Force, by becoming nuclear and airborne themselves, it seems that they too have been compelled to follow the Air Force toward the defense perimeter.

Military–industrial cities also differ in the roles they play in the production process. Places like Los Angeles, Seattle, Hartford, and Long Island host the assembly lines on which engines and airframes are actually made. They are also "flagships": each is host to major corporate headquarters of one or more defense companies. In these locations, military–industrial research and strategy take place. Other cities—like Wichita and Marietta, both dating from World War II—are branch-plant production centers. Such branch plants, we discovered, are surprisingly few, despite the concerted attempt by the government to decentralize employment in the 1940s and 1950s for strategic reasons. The forces favoring agglomeration in this highly innovation-oriented industry reinforce the preeminence of the original centers of planning and production.

Another set of defense-oriented cities performs secondary functions: making a particular subsystem or a specialized part. Some midwestern cities—such as Rockford, Illinois, and Cedar Rapids, Iowa—have managed to survive in the defense business in this way, because older industrial firms like Sundstrand and Woodward-Governor transformed themselves into defense contractors. Some of these smaller towns are thus heavily dependent on defense because they host one or two such plant operations, each with few other local linkages.

Some defense-industry cities do not manufacture anything at all; few actual weapons or items of equipment emanate from their "plants." These are the rapidly growing defense-service cities that sell advice, expertise, software, and systems design to the government. New, impressive high-rise office complexes have sprung up, clustered around key military facilities that range widely from cosmopolitan Washington to the barren high plains of Colorado Springs and the humid, Appalachian-flanked Huntsville, Alabama.

Los Angeles, of course, is the capital city of the military–industrial complex. It hosts an enormous contingent of defense-service activities as well as a major concentration of Pentagon personnel. It boasts the corporate headquarters or major concentrations of six of the top fifteen contractors in the nation (McDonnell-Douglas, Lockheed, Rockwell, Hughes, TRW, and Litton) and scores of other sizable defense-specialized companies. It does more airframe business than any other place, but it also is the leader in communications satellites, defense electronics, and software sales to the military. It is the truly diversified, one-stop shopping center for the military, performing all the functions that are more specialized in other gunbelt cities.

The Building of the Gunbelt

At first glance, the gunbelt appears to be a recent phenomenon. Certainly, this is suggested by all the alarms sounded in the 1980s about the unfair distribution of federal expenditures.[5] But in fact, the gunbelt is far beyond its infancy: it is at least middle-aged, perhaps even elderly. It might just be more evident now that the nondefense commercially oriented industries of the industrial heartland are sagging so badly. As we researched the origins of the gunbelt, we found we had to look further and still further back in time, to discover the key decisions that put military–industrial capacity in place.

Central to our locational story are the decades of the 1930s, 1950s, and 1980s, while World War II provided the scale that built small operations into big business. The 1930s were critical because they formed the era in which the commercial pioneers of early aircraft in the industrial heartland, like Ford, dropped out under Depression duress, while a few struggling new and relocated southern California airframe makers managed to survive on government orders. The futures of a number of key gunbelt firms—Lockheed, Douglas, North American, Grumman, and Boeing—were secured in this decade.

World War II was very important as well, because it added significantly to the ranks of the Los Angeles work force, enabled its small airplane makers to swell into gigantic corporations, and redistributed about 8 percent of American industrial capacity away from existing industrial centers. But if the war was the key event in shaping the *scale* of the industry, it was not as crucial as the other, quieter decades in terms of mapping the *location* of the industry. After all, most new temporary wartime plants were built in the industrial heartland itself, to make bombers and fighter planes and tanks on the massive scale required by the war. This mass-production nature of wartime work practically guaranteed that plants would be mothballed in the cold war period. From the atom bomb on, the demands on the industry would be quite different as man-powered war gave way to highly automated atmospheric warfare.

The dramatic escalation in the cold war during the 1950s was the most crucial causal factor in the rise of the gunbelt. After World War II, struggling aircraft firms with few other profitable markets relied on the Pentagon to funnel R&D contracts in their direction and to buy their output. As the cold war evolved, egged on by these same contractors, the airframe industry in particular positioned itself to become the leader in the emerging unmanned missile, defense electronics, and spacecraft arenas. A few other firms from communications and propulsion industries entered the fray as well. In this era, the preeminence of California and New England in defense was ensured, especially since midwestern industries were preoccupied with dismantling defense plants and meeting the huge pent-up demand for automobiles, appliances, and other consumer goods.

Surprisingly, not much on this gunbelt map changed from the 1950s to the 1980s. While technologies and industry structures have continued to evolve, the plants and companies that constitute the core of the defense–industrial complex today were largely in place by the close of the 1950s. They could be found in these new peripheral locations outside the older Rustbelt. Overall, the distribution of prime contracts has remained highly concentrated and remarkably inert since then, a prospect that is daunting to midwestern economic developers who have belatedly wondered how they might reap a larger share.

But the 1980s, the third critical decade, saw a more subtle shift. With the dramatic escalation of defense spending under the Reagan administration, above all after 1983, R&D and systems-analysis functions have proliferated and grown in importance. In consequence, the key actors in this emerging defense-services industry—the consultants, designers, coordinators, integrators, and advisers—have gravitated closer to the sites where the Pentagon and the services operate, while simultaneously reinforcing the original military–industrial headquarters centers. In tandem, new centers of military-oriented private-sector activity have blossomed in places like Huntsville, Melbourne, and Colorado Springs, as well as around the three poles of Boston, Los Angeles, and Washington, D.C. These are representatives of the military–industrial cities that are "at risk" in the 1990s.

The West as Military–Industrial Frontier

Why did the gunbelt sprout where it did, and why does it continue to be so obstinately rooted there? If the rise of a military–industrial perimeter is a uniquely American phenomenon, what is it about the American experience that might explain it? One answer lies in the fertile ground that the American frontier offered as an innovative milieu for aerospace.[6] The United States was, well into the twentieth century, a society with a rapid rate of technological innovation, a high percentage of immigration and internal movement, and an extraordinary acceptance of new ideas and new ways of doing things. Even after the closing of the agrarian frontier in 1890, the cities of the "new urban frontier" magnified the society's love of novelty and willingness to suspend disbelief in the face of new notions. The mania for flying became one such notion.

The expansive frontier presented the United States with opportunities that few other nations, with the singular exception of the Soviet Union, possessed. In other countries, strategic planning was constrained by the lack of open space and an abundance of borders with potential adversaries. These factors shaped those nations' military economic geography, concentrating military–industrial capacity in easily defended interior locations. In the United States, this situation was almost the opposite. After eliminating, often brutally, the claims of the Spanish, the Russians, the English, the French, and the Native Americans, the young nation had, by the twentieth century, few nearby enemies and vast tracts of open land, the latter handy for training bases and missile, jet, and nuclear-bomb testing. Furthermore, these immense, empty spaces had to be secured by settlement and development, a project that in the United States (as in the Soviet Union) was accomplished by national-government commitment rather than private-sector initative.

The western military–industrial cities, outside the traditional northeastern core and often in remote regions, were major beneficiaries of cheap federal-government land and infrastructure, and they often generated huge capital surpluses, available as a supply of local venture capital seeking new speculative outlets. As a result, emerging frontier cities developed aggressive traditions of civic boosterism. Both Los Angeles and Colorado Springs show this clearly. Their business elites stood to earn large speculative profits from urban land development. Over and over again, the western boosters successfully tapped federal spending programs for natural-resource development, such as water supply. During the New Deal and World War II, they were ready to exploit expanding federal spending. Feeding out of the federal trough became a convenient and lucrative habit.[7]

The relationship between the military and the frontier is also a special one in American history. The long siege carried on by the American forces against American Indians and Mexicans planted military bases in the empty but fast-growing and speculative regions on the nation's periphery. Young, ambitious officers were continually forced to adapt to new, often desert-like environments and to live in garrison societies. Not many years after Indian-fighting ceased, air-training bases sprang up in the same territory. The long but successful struggle of the Army Air Corps, western in its orientation from birth, to divorce itself from the Army enhanced the attractiveness of the West and nurtured a favoritism among its leadership for western locations. And because the Air Force, with its preference for contracting out to the private sector, outflanked the Army, which favored the arsenal system, the West became the locus for a new private empire selling to a generous public customer.

Thus the seeds of the new military-oriented western segment of modern American industry were planted early in the century. Nurtured by government contracts, promoted to a large-scale corporate status by World War II, the new aerospace firms forming the core of the postwar military–industrial complex clustered disproportionately in new centers like Los Angeles, Colorado Springs, and Washington, D.C. There they created around themselves, at the taxpayers' expense, the initial advantages of an innovative milieu that become progressively embedded in a permanent defense-dependent, research-intensive infrastructure.

The Rejection of the Heartland

Yet this massive geographical shift in American leading-edge industry cannot simply be attributed to the "cowboy" culture that lured many officers and early aircraft pioneers to the West. It also was caused by the failure of the industrial heartland to nurture the early aircraft pioneers who emerged out of its bicycle, auto, and machining industries. Although midwestern cities provided home bases for many of the earliest aircraft inventors and entrepreneurs—the Wright brothers, Alexander Graham Bell, Glenn Curtiss, and Henry Ford—all the commercial-aircraft ventures of these pioneers had perished by the 1950s. Dayton, Detroit, and Buffalo lost out to the newer airframe centers on the periphery. Profound differences in business culture, and unfortunate timing, explain a good part of the striking midwestern loss to the defense perimeter.

To be sure, pockets of defense–industrial base still exist in the heartland: Minneapolis, with its defense electronics and computers, and St. Louis, with its McDonnell-Douglas and General Dynamics contracts, are important instances. But New England is the stunning counterfactual case—an aging industrial region that successfully managed the transition into defense production and research. At the critical juncture, the 1950s, its human and physical resources were similar to those of the Midwest: excellent engineering schools, a strong machining tradition, heavily unionized and skilled blue-collar labor, and hotly contested partisan politics.[8] But in that critical decade, New England sported a different kind of business culture and faced dramatically different economic prospects from its Great Lakes neighbors to the west. Its factories were not flush with pent-up postwar demand. Many of its industrial mainstays—textiles, shoes, apparel—faced permanent low-cost competition from the South and overseas. By the 1950s, these industries had lost their market dominance. During that decade, volumes were written on the depressed New England economy. The recovery of the region became a public policy priority, and searching for new markets became a major preoccupation.[9]

In contrast, the midwestern industrial heartland faced tremendous postwar demand from consumers. During the war, the production of innumerable goods—automobiles, electric refrigerators, vacuum cleaners, sewing machines, electric ranges, washing machines, radios, and phonographs—had been prohibited. All were mainly midwestern products. After the war, households with forced savings clamored to make up the backlog.[10] Satisfying that demand required the total dedication of midwestern factories. Thus in the decade most critical for developing aerospace capacity, the Midwest had neither time nor incentive to go after government defense markets, while its northeasterly neighbors did.

Furthermore, the Midwest had developed a distinctly different economic mission. With its unusually egalitarian agricultural hinterland, the "third coast" had developed the mass-market and the mass-production technology to serve it, epitomized by Henry Ford's Model T and by Sears catalog sales. Efficient mass production required standardized commodities and enormous plants with relatively routinized labor. In contrast, New England remained a predominantly craft-oriented economy, with smaller plants and market niches in certain precision-machining sectors—characteristics that enabled a limited number of firms to move into the small-batch, innovative, and subsequently superprofitable product lines favored by the cold war economy.

Finally, the Midwest had a corporate culture that prejudiced its chances with the defense establishment. It was the region of big, powerful oligopolies—from the steel giants of Pittsburgh, through automobiles in Detroit, to farm machinery in Illinois.[11] These corporate giants controlled their markets, preoccupied themselves with fighting their unions, and eschewed risky investments in new technologies. Midwestern habits of making and selling were better suited to the car dealer and the housewife than to the Pentagon colonel. Selling to the military had been exasperating in World War II, and midwestern managers were glad to be done with it. In contrast, their New England counterparts had no choice but to learn the new customs associated with peddling to the military and defending their wares before Congress.[12] Supporting casts of universities and politicians busied themselves with defense-generated economic activity in New England, whereas in the Midwest they were too busy with the demands of agriculture and commercial industry. In retrospect, then, it is not hard to see why the more easterly portion of the nation's old industrial quadrant strove to revitalize itself through government largesse, while the then booming Midwest was indifferent, if not hostile.

Why the Winning Places?

Growing dichotomies between commercial and military sectors, plus vagaries of historical timing, thus explain the remarkable repulsion of military-oriented aerospace from the industrial heartland and its relocation elsewhere. Why, however, did certain places like Los Angeles, Seattle, and Washington, D.C., win out over other peripheral locations? Why did Los Angeles succeed in its intentional effort to make itself into an aircraft-manufacturing center while San Antonio, with the same vision, failed? Why did Colorado Springs beat out White Sands in its bid to become the nation's space defense colony?

One answer is vigorous boosterism. Southern and western cities consciously and assiduously courted defense-manufacturing industries. Boosters like Chandler in Los Angeles and Tutt and Reich in Colorado Springs drafted strategic plans for such industries, and with dollars from other speculative victories lobbied hard for the military funds to make it happen. Yet many western cities had military affairs committees from the turn of the century, and many southern cities sent congressional delegations to Washington, D.C., in an effort to open and retain military bases and related facilities in the region.[13] Why did some succeed where others failed?

Scholars often answer this question by describing the "factors" that appear to account for locational preference. Climate or a highly skilled labor force favored the southwestern corner of the nation; such is their argument. Yet we found that it is not the passive attributes of places that determine the location of defense-related activity in the economy, but the active involvement of many participants, each with distinctive motivations, choosing among a number of potential sites. Whether boosters, colonels, generals, firm managers, or elected representatives, selected groups have mattered a great deal in shaping America's military-production geography. In large part, this is because the peculiar making business of military weapons permits extraordinary discretion in the choice of sites for production and research. Shielded from normal commercial competition, actors in the defense business need not compute the simple "lowest-cost" location forced on most other firms. What did we find, then, that helps explain why certain cities won out?

The preferences of founding fathers must be given their due. Especially in the early years of the aircraft industry, with its remarkable relocation to southern California away from centers like Buffalo and Dayton, the lure of California for migrants like Kindelberger of North American was as powerful as it was for natives like the Lougheed brothers or returnees like Donald Douglas. Armed with contracts and the blessing of the services issuing them, these men chose to set up shop where the climate and culture maximized their chances of making it in the infant airplane industry.

Contemporary managers argued that securing a high-quality local labor supply was critical to the successful performance of their firms. Manager after manager claimed that the location where we were sitting was good for recruiting labor, because of existing pools or because of amenities the area offered. Yet it was impossible to arbitrate among the claims of firms in different regions. In Chicago, firms claimed that there was a surplus of engineering graduates from midwestern universities eager to stay in the region. Chicago firms get away with paying new employees less than they would earn on the coasts. In California, firms reported that local graduates were willing to accept the higher living costs, and hence somewhat lower real incomes, in return for staying in their home state. Similarly, managers differed enormously in their view of just what constitutes "amenities." Some emphasized surfing; others, skiing. Some motioned to nearby CBDs with opera and symphonies, while others pointed to Pikes Peak and the pristine, wide-open spaces. Engineers and scientists, evidently, have no monolithic set of preferences when it comes to environment.

More to the point, this retrospective emphasis is not consistent with the obvious fact that no such ample pools of skilled labor pre-dated the arrival of military–industrial activity. The remarkable feature of military–industrial labor is its extraordinary mobility. Labor pools have been built with ease around new emerging gunbelt cities. Remote and small-town Colorado Springs, or Washington, D.C., had few of the glamorous attributes of southern California, yet both were able to attract substantial new contingents of professional and technical labor. In other words, people followed jobs. Indeed, much of our place-by-place stories have to do with the way in which new firms, industries, and military facilities fashioned, often very deliberately, the labor market institutions that would generate an ongoing supply of labor. The Pentagon facilitates this lopsided recruitment, out of the heartland and into the gunbelt, by paying for the relocations of scientific and technical personnel as a part of the "cost of doing business." Unintentionally, this mechanism has financed one of the greatest selective and for-profit population resettlements in the nation's history.

A few key universities played a role in the construction of several leading military-production centers. But their significance was a strangely selective one. MIT's role in building the Greater Boston avionics complex, Caltech's in supporting Los Angeles aerospace, and Stanford's in the birth of Silicon Valley are outstanding cases. Yet many excellent midwestern engineering schools have failed to generate any local defense-contracting activity despite training generations of young people to fill such occupations. Instead, the majority of their graduates leave the region on graduation, a de facto national labor exchange or, from the midwestern point of view, a substantial brain drain. And Seattle, Colorado Springs, and Washington, D.C., succeeded in building major research and high-tech-based military–industrial complexes without a leading university role. The Springs lacked a graduate engineering program until local leaders forced the state to set one up. Rather, in these places, university involvement has followed the creation of the complex, not the other way around.

Originally, we thought that land speculation might be a major motivation for firms to locate on low-cost sites in places like Los Angeles in the 1930s or Colorado Springs in the 1970s. In this, we were dead wrong. Military–industrial managers turned out to be preoccupied with technological leadership and with getting the next contract. They sometimes saw that they could profit by advance speculation on land around their plants, but most contend that no spare funds are available for such subsidiary ventures.

City boosters have played a catalytic role, at critical turning points, in creating new military–industrial complexes. They marketed their cities, often with dubious claims regarding beauty, accessibility, and facilities. They assembled land and offered inducements of infrastructure and other city services. They sent delegations to Congress to try to channel installations and contracts their way. They assured the armed services and military-oriented firms, often themselves riddled with former military officers, that they and their kind would receive a warm and sustained welcome in the community. And they were rewarded by generous returns from military-induced land speculation.

Military end users also turn out to be important players in the defense locational game. In the 1930s and even the 1950s, certain military installations like flight-testing fields and naval bases anchored certain firms within regions. In the more recent cold war buildup, new factors—the growing complexity of weapons systems, their split-second capabilities, and the increasingly formidable task of coordinating the supporting communications and computing systems—have led to a new increment of contractors clustered around key military headquarters like Colorado Springs, Huntsville, and Washington, D.C. Working out of a phalanx of suburban office buildings, they advise the services and the Pentagon on what to buy and how to install and integrate systems, write software, train service personnel, and maintain and repair equipment.

Congress turns out to be less significant in the building of military cities than is widely believed. Its role does not boil down simply to that of pork-barreling, whereby members of Congress dole out bases and contracts at the taxpayers' expense for narrow electoral gains. Certainly, some congressional delegations do try to enhance their districts' share of the defense-budget pie, but others do not. In particular historical cases, this matters a great deal. Critics argue that Tip O'Neill had much to do with funneling defense contracts to his home state of Massachusetts, just as southerners like John Stennis, Jamie Whitten, and Mendel Rivers did for their districts. Yet despite decades of such efforts, prime contracts still show remarkable geographical concentration. And as the Colorado Springs case shows, congressional activity is more often a product of building military-production centers, in the sense that firms and boosters support political candidates who have their interests at heart. At best, Congress acts as a protector and reinforcer of existing military economies rather than as a causal force.

Officials within the Pentagon and the services, sometimes even in the White House, have often played a role in shaping the spatial distribution of defense-oriented facilities and contracts. In some cases, strategic concerns motivated them, but in others, interservice rivalries, conflicting philosophies, jockeying for position within a service branch, or sheer personal preference for community building, perhaps with an eye toward retirement, entered into their calculations. Colorado Springs is an outstanding example. There, the competition for primacy within the Air Force between groups invested in strategic bombing versus missiles and space defense, and between officers who personally preferred the Springs to the equally strategically attractive White Sands, New Mexico, had more to do with the outcome than did the verbal battles between New Mexico's and Colorado's congressional delegations.

So the question—why Los Angeles, and not San Antonio or Detroit or Buffalo?—turns out to have an elusive answer. Layers of actors including founding fathers, military personnel, and boosters interacted to create the milieu that made Los Angeles the aerospace capital of the United States. It could have happened in San Antonio, which had the climate, the topography, the Air Corps, and the boosters, although no coast and few founding fathers. It could have happened in Buffalo or Dayton, which had the topography and the founding fathers—the former with a coast of sorts and the latter with the Army Air Corps—but not the boosters or the climate. Each of the new military-production centers claims a rather unique set of features, which came together at pivotal moments in the larger dynamic of strategic competition and the changing technology of war.

Cold War and Military–Industrial Cities

Comparing Los Angeles with San Antonio or Buffalo often has the subtle consequence of suggesting that certain places became military–industrial cities because they possessed certain key features or harbored certain key actors. Cities become "winners" and "losers" in the competition for this increment of the American economy. Carried to its extreme by local economic developers, boosters often claim that jobs in their city were created by their superior marketing, land packaging, and having the right connections. Such claims, however, deflect attention away from the more fundamental structural forces that created the demand for global weaponry in the first place. Jobs at Rockwell or McDonnell-Douglas in Los Angeles or at Ford Aerospace or Kaman Sciences in Colorado Springs were not "created" by their respective cities' exuberant booster activity or even by founding fathers, but by the emergence of the cold war and its reliance on strategic warfare. Boosters, firm founders, generals, and members of Congress, for the most part, struggled over the siting of such jobs, but their very existence depends on deeper historical forces.

The landscape of American military–industrial cities is not simply the outcome of competition among various centers of self-started and self-fueled innovative complexes. It is primarily the product of the rise of strategic warfare in the 1930s and the onset of cold war in the 1950s. Without these developments, the industrial heartland centers of aircraft production would have had a better chance of surviving in a competitive environment governed by commercial rather than military concerns. As it was, the military, through its relationships with certain producers in the 1930s and 1940s, largely determined which infant aerospace companies would survive in the postwar period.

Without high-tech weaponry and the cold war, Los Angeles would still have an aircraft industry, but it would be one-third its present size, commercially oriented, and without contemporary missiles, communications, and defense-electronics progeny. Los Angeles would never have become the private economy's missile and space headquarters without the H-bomb, the ICBM, and yet newer generations of strategic bombers. Nor would it have flourished without the rise of cold war foreign policy, which justified in an otherwise isolationist America an enormous and permanent expenditure on strategic weapons. Without the cold war imperative to create ever-new generations of weapons, defensive machinery, and detection and communications devices, the clustering impulse that has come to characterize centers like Boston, Los Angeles, and, to a lesser extent, Washington, D.C., and Seattle would have been much weaker and production more dispersed. The cohesiveness and continued dynamism of such centers is not in the final instance a function of the synergy of a group of founding fathers, an indigenous creative milieu, or a mechanistic reproduction process—although all these played critical roles in the fortunes of each individual center—but of the peculiar demands of mid-twentieth-century American foreign policy, with its endogenously developed technology of war.

Yet this is not a wholly one-way process. While the new military–industrial centers have surely been the junior partners in this marriage of politics and the economy, it is inconceivable that there have been no forces running in the opposite direction. New military-production centers, growing far from traditional heartland cities, have exerted pressures in favor of enhanced military spending through their congressional representatives, who exert influence on key appropriations committees and who trade votes to get support for extra defense dollars. And this impact may extend beyond fights for extra defense dollars in a given year. It has wider implications, which we review below.

Postscript: The Gunbelt and the Nation

What does all of this mean? Is the emergence of a new locus for American defense-bred high-tech manufacturing a good or bad thing for the economy?

For the American people? Does it really matter what places the military–industrial complex calls home? Our answer to this last question is a resounding, yes! The gunbelt has been extraordinarily consumptive of national resources, while it has had complex impacts on regional-development patterns. It has played a lead role in fostering new high-tech industrial districts. It has contributed to the narrowing of the regional per capita income gap. Yet overall, it has heightened the segregation of Americans into disparate communities and, as a result, has had troubling geopolitical consequences. Leaving aside the question of the impact of the military–industrial complex on the economy as a whole—a topic for another book[14]—we explore in this concluding section the significance of gunbelt geography. How has this industrial shift colored the landscape of American politics and community life?

Gunbelt as Regional Policy

The first point to make about the rise of the gunbelt is that it has worked as a kind of underground regional policy. The United States has no regional policy comparable to that of most other developed nations of the world. Europeans have long been concerned with depressed regions. Extensive programs have been designed to bring new jobs and industry to agricultural backwaters or regions burdened with obsolete industry, and to discourage the overbuilding of major metropolitan industrial areas. With the exception of the Tennessee Valley Authority in the 1930s and the Appalachian Regional Commission of the 1960s, the American government has undertaken few explicit efforts to shape the regional distribution of economic activity.

One reason may be that policies engendering the incipient gunbelt performed this function, albeit imperfectly. Southern politicians, rather than working out a policy to redress low per capita incomes with government-sponsored and regionally targeted industrialization programs, turned instead to the Pentagon, for both the military bases that are disproportionately located in the South and the contracts for everything from uniforms to C-5A transport planes. Western politicians, with vulnerable resource-dependent economies, could woo new defense facilities and be guaranteed federally financed infrastructure to accompany them. Both regions could recruit a highly educated work force at the nation's expense, detouring the problems inherent in their below-average indigenous educational systems. Pentagon spending generated an enormous investment flood that poured into these regions, creating there a new economic base—new plants, amplified work force, new schools, roads, water, and sewer systems—all at the national taxpayers' expense.

Although the regional and urban programs of the Economic Development Administration and the Department of Housing and Urban Development foundered, the Pentagon quietly pursued the most geographically targeted program of any government agency.[15] While the nation as a whole has no coordinated response to communities hit by either abrupt boomtown growth or significant plant closings, the Department of Defense operates programs that do so for defense-related communities. Its impact-aid program helps pave the way for new defense activities, while its Office of Economic Adjustment responds to plant or base closings with substantial readjustment assistance to affected communities.

Of course, Pentagon-style regional policy proved to be highly selective. In particular, the traumas of inner-city displacement were difficult, if not impossible, to address this way. The attractiveness of defense dollars as a local economic-development stimulant may have hampered the efforts of big-city mayors to put together a successful coalition for an urban policy. Those cities well positioned to garner defense contracts had less of an incentive to fight for the survival of programs targeted for cuts by the Republicans, such as the Small Business Administration, the Economic Development Administration, and public housing.

Hard-hit regional economies could—and continue to—turn to the Pentagon as a source of revitalization aid. As already noticed, Tip O'Neill was widely credited with steering to his home state of Massachusetts the lion's share of contracts, spread across many sectors, that enabled it to weather its prolonged structural recession of the 1950s and rebound in successive decades. However, any effort to forge a more explicit regional policy, especially one not tied to military priorities, may be doomed. This is what the Northeast/Midwest Congressional Caucus found to its distress in its failed attempts in the 1970s to redistribute federal outlays, including what they dubbed "Pentagon tilt," more fairly among regions.[16]

Given that defense spending constituted a highly unorthodox regional policy, then, the question has to be how successful it was. Regional policies in other countries have variously sought to reduce income disparities between regions, to transfer industries to or promote new ones in lagging regions, to encourage infrastructure investments in backward regions, and to promote training and education policies in order to improve the quality of the regional work force. To what extent has defense policy done the same, and how successful has it been?

Gunbelt as National Equalizer

In the views of its makers, many of whom we interviewed, the gunbelt is a good thing. It has created new cities, life-styles, and real-estate markets that are highly praised by their partisans. The people who helped build the gunbelt feel strongly that it is a good place to live, work, and do business. But has the gunbelt yielded broader national dividends? One argument in its favor is that it seems over time to have contributed to the narrowing of disparity in American regional incomes. Since the 1940s, per capita incomes in the South and Southwest have risen from below 75 percent of the national average to close to the national norm, while per capita incomes in the Middle Atlantic and Great Lakes states have fallen from well above the national norm to levels much closer to the average.[17] As well-paying defense-industry jobs grew disproportionately in these outlying regions, they may have helped in particular to reverse the traditional cleavage between the industrial heartland and the Old South.

Doubts remain, however, about just how comprehensive this convergence has been and that it can be ascribed to defense spending. First of all, government largesse has helped per capita incomes in New England and the Far West to stay securely above the national average throughout this century. Military spending appears to have insulated these regions from the general downward pressure exerted by wage equalization and the movement of industry in other parts of the country. To a large extent, this military spending has rewarded regions with already high per capita income. A closer look at the distribution of jobs and incomes by city, suburb, and county shows that military procurement has had very uneven impacts, even in the regions garnering the lion's share.[18]

Of course, many other forces have affected regional-income patterns over the postwar decades. The convergence between the industrial heartland and the Old South is in large part a result of the migration northward of poor rural blacks and whites from the cotton belt and Appalachians. Displaced by mechanization from agriculture and coal mining, large numbers of relatively poor people were drawn in the 1940s and 1950s to the booming factories of Detroit, Chicago, and Cleveland, only to be displaced again by deindustrialization in subsequent decades. The funneling of military-procurement dollars away from the industrial heartland played a large role in this latter process. As aerospace-related industries supplanted consumer-oriented ones as the major manufacturing-job generators of the postwar period, the absence of those industries in the heartland compounded the dislocation problems of recent migrants. Meanwhile, a reverse migration of educated Northerners into southern defense-based communities—Oak Ridge, Huntsville, Titusville/Melbourne—helped to boost average southern per capita incomes, as did the retirement moves southward of higher-income Northerners.

Gunbelt as Roller Coaster

On top of this long-term trend lies another, more subtle, effect. The gunbelt consists of a series of highly specialized regional enclaves devoted to cold war armaments. Although Los Angeles, Seattle, and Boston do have other industrial segments (film, medical technology, commercial airlines, commercial computers) that help them ride out political cycles, their postwar economies have been quite vulnerable to defense cuts. Because these enclaves tend to be physically separate from commercially oriented urban industrial complexes, both types of communities are subject to more dramatic swings in local economic activity than would occur if the two industrial segments were more integrated and diversified across both defense and nondefense activities. Political cycles of defense buildup and contraction do not correspond very closely to business cycles as we know them. Indeed, there is some evidence that military-spending cycles are countercyclical. If defense-oriented industries were located in tandem with commercial ones, then we might expect some countervailing relief for unemployment problems created by a downturn in one or the other sector.

Historically, when the major military-supply industries were located in the industrial heartland, this convertibility worked rather well. The enormous diversion of resources into and out of defense production before and after World War II was handled quite easily, as Detroit retooled auto plants into bomber factories and Illinois retooled tractor plants into tank factories. But as defense production shifted away from the heartland, this flexibility was increasingly lost to regions at both ends. Seattle, as we saw in Chapter 7, has been highly vulnerable to defense swings. While alternative commercially oriented activity eventually took up the slack, Seattle suffered several years of wrenching displacement and outmigration: Los Angeles, too, has endured unsettling employment swings associated with defense-spending cycles, as have Dallas and Colorado Springs. While cutbacks have often bred entre-preneurship, it has never been sufficient to avoid local recession.

This is underlined by recent experience. In the past decade, the United States has experienced a remarkable divergence in regional-growth rates. From 1979 to 1986, when defense procurement rose rapidly, jobs in the New England, South Atlantic, Mountain, and Pacific regions grew in excess of 15 percent, while the Great Lakes states lost some 65,000 jobs.[19] There, in the early 1980s, a policy-induced recession was displacing workers from auto and steel plants, but no recession-proof aerospace jobs were available to take up the slack. Throughout the postwar period, the rise of the gunbelt has meant that regional economies are more apt to be plunged into idiosyncratic eco-nomic cycles that do not necessarily reflect national trends. This is exacerbated to the extent that certain regions specialize in certain technologies or weapons systems.

Gunbelt as Seedbed

A second case for the gunbelt—made strongly by its builders and boosters as well as by independent analysts—is its ability to generate diverse new industries. The locations where the high-tech defense dollars have been con-centrated—Greater Boston, Greater Los Angeles, Silicon Valley, Seattle, Minneapolis, Dallas–Fort Worth—are among those lauded for engendering high-tech industries in the postwar period. In almost all cases, from aerospace itself to electronics, communications equipment, and computers, Pentagon dollars were crucial to the founding of these industrial districts, either through direct R&D funding or by ensuring a market for sales. In Chapter 4, we chronicled the difficulty that certain entrepreneurs confronted in the older industrial heartland, where they found it difficult to sell their ideas to regional bankers and to compete in the shade of the large, established, oligopolistic, commercially oriented firms that then dominated both consumer- and capital-goods markets. Most accounts of Silicon Valley, Orange County, and resur-gent high-tech New England celebrate the development of new labor pools, the predominance of small, new firms, and the creation of new types of business services to serve youthful, innovative industries like computers and semiconductors.[20] Implicitly, their work suggests that without these virgin (or regenerated, in the case of New England) locations, the nation would not be as far advanced in the development of such technologies. In turn, Department of Defense patronage was essential in nurturing these infant firms in their new birthplaces.

This is a sophisticated and appealing argument. It is, of course, difficult to imagine what would have happened had such military spending not been geographically segregated from older industrial centers, although we attempt to speculate on this in the final section of this chapter. It does appear to be the case that the new computer-related and communications-related electronics found a more hospitable home in centers of defense preoccupation than they did in places like Illinois and New York, despite the early lead these states had in consumer and producer electronics. Industrial concentration at virgin sites might have been the best way to organize defense production, given its dissimilarities from commercial production and its requirements for a different kind of innovative milieu, a specialized set of agglomerative economies, and a military-oriented work force. But we have no definitive evidence for or against this speculation. Comparing the American military–industrial landscape with that of the Soviet Union and various European nations might be good test of this hypothesis, but we have not yet done so.

However, what happens in these new military–industrial districts is not a strictly homegrown, or "endogenous," process. It is heavily shaped by outside dollars and outside agencies. Most work written on the new industrial districts of Orange County, Silicon Valley, and Route 128 downplays or omits altogether the significance of government, with its peculiar demands, as market. The highly lauded "postindustrial" organization of manufacturing in these regions, with its flexible specialization and small-batch, custom-made product, is erroneously ascribed to the commercial sector, when in fact these attributes originated in their defense-based industries.

In any case, there is now much argument on a very important point: How far have defense-based firms and industries spun off commercial applications? Over the entire post–World War II period, some impressive commercial spin-offs have occurred—as witness semiconductors and personal computers in Silicon Valley, or minicomputers in Massachusetts. But there is also a strong emerging suggestion that this was an isolated windfall from technological advances of the 1950s, and that for many firms defense contracting has become a cozy alternative to the rough-and-tumble of the marketplace.[21]

Gunbelt as Investment Sink

Against the positive high-tech generative effects of Pentagon spending in the gunbelt must be set a fairly massive drawback: the discriminatory investment of billions of tax dollars in new, peripheral industrial centers, compounding the problems faced by industries in the older, commercially oriented regions.

These problems are of two kinds: a lack of basic investment in regional infrastructure, and a loss of vital creative talent.

It is undeniable that the new aerospace-oriented communities were erected far from the industrial heartland. And this has meant that considerable tax resources have gone into their construction and maintenance. While older plants in the Midwest have been shuttered and mothballed, new plants have been built in the South and West. Around them, cities and suburbs have sprouted, often with considerable taxpayer support in the form of money for sewers, water, highways, and other types of infrastructure. In many cases, the Pentagon pays "impact aid" to school districts and local governments, compensating for the tax base that is lost through government tax-exempt property.

Billions have been spent over the postwar period in such community building. Such a social investment would not pose a problem if it were true that infrastructure elsewhere was fully employed. But over the same period, older industrial regions have experienced industrial decline and dramatic out-migration, emptying plants, houses, and school districts and lowering infrastructure utilization rates to the point where receipts make it difficult to maintain or modernize the stock. To the extent that the new schools, plants, and utilities are paid for by taxpayers nationally, their closure or underusage in some parts of the country constitutes a net waste of societal resources. The funds spent on them could have been used to rebuild infrastructure in existing cities, to better house low-income people, or to cut taxes, lower deficits, or improve the quality of life in many different ways. If defense-related production had been more evenly distributed geographically, the nation could have saved a substantial amount of money.[22] It is interesting to ponder whether a portion of the current "competitiveness" problem in the United States can be ascribed to such wasteful duplication of infrastructure and to the opportunity costs it represents.

Gunbelt boosters, and some economists, would question this argument. They might argue that much of the infrastructural investment in the aging Rustbelt was fully amortized. Given that fact, the opportunity cost of replicating it in other places was relatively low. There might have been some transitional costs in shrinking the rustbelt cities and growing the gunbelt ones, but now that the process is over, the new geography is as efficient as the old one. There is no economic rule that it is more efficient to freeze economic patterns at a certain point in time. If that had been so, America would never have happened in the first place, and certainly the American West would never have been settled.

Some might go even farther, contesting that investing in underdeveloped areas with military dollars was a good thing, that it expanded the industrial territory of the nation westward. They might argue that while it is regrettable that a few cities like Buffalo and Detroit were neglected or left behind in the process, the contribution of California and other gunbelt states has more than made up for decline in the heartland and for the loss in that region's contribution to the national economy. We are not in a position to arbitrate these opposing claims. It is impossible to say whether the rise of the gunbelt was "efficient," despite the fact that it has clearly nurtured new centers of high-tech activity. It may have been an efficient way to provide national security. It may have even been an efficient way to engender new industrial sectors. Then again, it may not, because of its profligate consumption and replication of public infrastructure.

Gunbelt as People-Mover

American taxpayers have also financed one of the most impressive population redistributions in history. Generations of scientists and engineers have been recruited to gunbelt locations at the Pentagon's expense. When an engineer from Boeing in Seattle or a college graduate from the University of Illinois is recruited by Rockwell in Los Angeles, his or her moving expenses are paid for by the company and charged to the government on existing contracts. Estimates given us by contractors place the contemporary cost of such a move between $5,000 and $20,000, depending on the maturity of the recruit and the size of his or her family.

Over the postwar period, entirely new labor pools have been formed in this manner. Especially during initial growth spurts, as in Los Angeles during the 1950s, Titusville/Melbourne in the 1960s, and Colorado Springs in the 1980s, the share of new employees coming from universities and companies elsewhere is high. Over the years, midwestern engineering schools, many of them among the best in the nation, have routinely shipped a majority of their recent graduates out of state, predominantly to defense contractors. Although not designed as a population-resettlement program, this process has operated as one, paid for by American taxpayers. To the social tally for new infrastructure, then, must be added the cost of all defense-industry-related moves, a not inconsiderable sum that might have been spent more productively for the economy as a whole.

Already disadvantaged in the competition for government R&D and procurement dollars, the older industrial regions are further disabled by the geographical distance between them and the newer, more glamorous industries. The removal of large numbers of the most highly skilled and creative people from their regional economies, people who were educated with corporate and personal tax dollars from within the region, handicaps their ability to compete in increasingly competitive international markets. For it means an absence of cross-fertilizing ideas flowing through the regional business community. Undeniably, big firms in industries like auto, steel, consumer electronics, and machine tools are in large part responsible for their own disappointing performance—particularly through their oligopolistic preoccupation with dominating their markets. Nevertheless, their workers and host communities are doubly debilitated by the absence of high-tech alternatives nurtured in the new publicly supported defense-industry complexes.

Gunbelt as Segregator

This mass migration of talent to the gunbelt appears also to have contributed to the increasingly spatial segregation of America by class and race. For it has been a highly selective one. Defense-related industries are more apt to employ white, highly educated men than are other manufacturing industries.[23] Although during World War II, large numbers of blue-collar workers were also relocated, the need to do so has disappeared over time, leaving only the moves of more affluent employees to be taxpayer-financed. Furthermore, the share of blue-collar workers in the defense-related work force has dropped dramatically. Thus communities that have been built around defense plants and offices disproportionately consist of members of the white-collar, professional and technical social stratum and their families: what we call the gunbelt "Mippies," or military–industrial professionals.

The other side of the coin has been the creation of the urban "underclass." This is a recent phenomenon. It consists of labor pools of poor blacks, Hispanics, and whites from the South, Latin America, and Appalachia who migrated to northern cities as recently as the 1950s in search of good industrial jobs, which were then plentiful. But by the end of the 1950s, as the momentum in favor of peripheral gunbelt sites gathered speed and manufacturing jobs permanently shifted their centers of gravity, industrial plants in commercial markets closed, leaving behind dislocated workers and their children, often in inner-city ghettos.

Of course, the underclass was not wholly created by defense spending. But the gunbelt may have exacerbated the disparities between rich and poor. Copious Pentagon dollars have not inhibited the appearance of an underclass in Los Angeles, San Francisco Bay cities like Oakland and San Jose, and Washington, D.C., although the size of such groups may be smaller and their situation less severe than in Midwest cities. It may well be that the jobs generated in defense, wherever they located, would have required skills simply not possessed by the people who have fallen into long-term unemployment. In this sense, the high-tech defense industries are just harbingers of a general emerging structural change in the American economy, which is generating a mismatch between the demand for labor skills and the supplies of those skills. Were the unemployed of Detroit to migrate south and west, there is no guarantee that they would find jobs—although, statistically, they would be more likely to do so. Nor is there any guarantee that good, high-paying jobs would be offered to these people. Instead, a large body of evidence from Massachusetts suggests that the situation would be the reverse.[24]

Gunbelt as Political Realigner

The rise of the gunbelt has had dramatic geopolitical consequences, too. Over time, the center of gravity of American politics has shifted farther and farther south and west, paralleling the movement of leading-edge manufacturing capacity. Decade after decade, redistricting gives greater power in the electoral college and in Congress to voters from newer defense-dependent districts. The Northeast and Midwest are expected to lose fourteen seats in the 1990 redistricting, while a swath of states from the Pacific through the Southeast to Virginia will gain eighteen. Among states that benefit from defense dollars, only Kansas and Massachusetts are expected to lose a seat.

By and large, white-collar employees of defense industries vote much more strongly Republican than do their counterparts in the rest of the economy. Surely, it is no coincidence that southern California is a safe constituency for pro-military conservatism, or that Colorado Springs consistently elects hawks and votes 70 percent Republican. Over the postwar period, one of the more significant consequences of the shift of the military–industrial complex to the gunbelt is the simultaneous shift of political power toward regions that are markedly more conservative and Republican than those in the industrial heartland.[25] Similarly, the emergence of military–industrial centers in the Old South may have contributed to the recomposition of the southern electorate and its shift toward Republican presidential candidates, as these new centers attracted more well-educated white professionals while poor rural black Democrats left for the North.

Nowhere is this more apparent than in the presidential vote. Indeed, California, Texas, and Massachusetts—each of which has reaped a disproportionate share of the nation's defense contracts—account for no fewer than five of the nine postwar presidents. All the presidents elected in the postwar period hail from states outside the industrial heartland; only Gerald Ford, who was never elected, represented a heavily industrialized heartland state. Only Ford and Jimmy Carter came from states whose per capita shares of prime contracts were less than the nation's, although Georgia ranks exceptionally high in military facilities. In presidential races, the defense-dependent southern and western electorate in particular show greater preference for Republican candidates who promise a strong defense and are staunchly committed to major weapons systems. Congressional votes vary more by party, but when Democrats are elected from such districts, they tend to take promilitary stands.

Furthermore, as our study of the losing third coast demonstrates, the spatial segregation of defense-oriented aerospace from other industrial regions establishes an economic dualism that makes even distribution of defense contracts more difficult. Members of Congress from nondefense regions are less interested in defense matters and tend to shun committees that make the major decisions, preferring instead to serve on committees that deal with agriculture, the environment, labor, or social services. They surrender the playing field to their more concerned colleagues, who specialize in the intricacies of defense spending and are thus in a better position to funnel it to their home districts. Thus the rise of the gunbelt has created its own self-sustaining mechanism. By regionally differentiating participation in the procurement decision-making process, it has reinforced and expanded the imbalances that first emerged in the 1950s.

But there are even wider political implications. Because they have been such successful ensembles of creative talent, albeit underwritten almost entirely by the Pentagon, the major gunbelt cities have generated ever more stunning innovations in the power, accuracy, and speed of strategic weapons and their delivery systems. Each generation exacerbates the threat and sends the armed forces scurrying to secure appropriations for yet more research for arms to defend against these same systems and to develop the next offensive one. The clusters themselves, then, are part of the reproductive apparatus of strategic warfare.

Military-led innovation and government have created geographically concentrated cadres of scientists and engineers who believe fervently in the underlying military mission and in the future benefits to society that their military-oriented work will produce. Often, when we opened our interviews with contractors and turned on our tapes, we first were treated to a lecture about the seriousness of the Soviet threat, which set a rather intense tone to the ensuing discussion of efforts at product development. Not one interviewee ever expressed skepticism about Communist insurgency or offered his or her thoughts on how disarmament or negotiations might obviate the enormous defense expenditure. Offices decorated with Christmas cards proclaiming "Peace on Earth" housed contractors who were totally dedicated to waging war with paper and pen. In addition to community boosters, then, spatial concentration of defense activity creates clusters of professional experts who share a strong partisan view of our national interest. These views inevitably work their way into national debates about both foreign policy and government support of research.

The segregation of defense-based activities from commercial industrial centers, and the concentration of defense-dependent voters in new regions, may thus have had a strong positive-feedback effect on the level and geographic distribution of defense expenditure. Members of Congress from heavily defense-dependent districts can be expected to vote for appropriations on the basis of their employment and profit-generating potential, rather than on the grounds that the program is vital for American defense. There is ample evidence that the Pentagon has encouraged this behavior on the part of Congress.[26] But some senators and representatives have pushed for projects that were not even supported by the Department of Defense, to please the folks and firms back home. Many cases of "geographical constituency building" have been documented, the most famous of which was Rockwell's concerted effort to demonstrate that every state would benefit from B-1 bomber contracts.

Such actions are likely to lead to increases in defense budgets beyond the level that would be set by foreign policy and national political considerations alone. Overall, then, the gunbelt may operate as a mechanism that exacerbates the pressures for military spending and the continuation of cold war foreign policy. Military spending may, as in the stories of Pygmalion and Frankenstein, have fashioned places that increasingly control us, rather than vice versa.

A Nation Without a Gunbelt?

All these conclusions, we must again stress, are quite speculative. We have no way of measuring the degree to which the gunbelt has drained resources from other uses, bloated the size of the defense budget, quickened industrial decline elsewhere, exacerbated segregation by class, subjected host economies to worsening growth cycles, realigned votes, or substituted for a more even-handed regional policy. Gauging the extent of such consequences awaits further research. We can, however, end by speculating further: we can try to imagine what the map of the U.S. economy would look like if the rise of the gunbelt had never happened. Suppose that a military–industrial complex had existed, but that it had not become geographically distinct from the nation's traditional centers of industry. In other words, can we imagine what would have happened had defense spending in the United States followed the pattern it has in many other developed economies, gravitating toward existing industrial centers?

Without the cold war and its associated new aerospace enclaves, the population center of gravity in the United States today would most likely fall farther toward the Northeast than its current location near the Missouri–Kansas line. Although states like California and Texas would have robust manufacturing centers, including some aircraft and electronics activity, their size would not be as large and taxpayer-subsidized population migration would not have swollen their economies nearly as much. We might also expect that the older industrial regions of the country would be less depressed and distressed, and there would be greater emphasis on blending and equalizing commercial and military-oriented sectors, and greater success in sustaining seedbed functions. We might find that computers, electronics, and communications-equipment industries had evolved less rapidly, but we might find that other innovations with greater consumer orientation had flourished in their stead. More ominously, we might find, too, oligopolistic industries enjoying a continued stranglehold on regional resources, making technological advances more difficult in the heartland.

We can also anticipate that the composition of the federal budget might be quite different and its priorities more broadly placed. If fewer new geographical constituencies had pressured for higher defense budgets on nonstrategic grounds, the overall expenditure on military research and procurement might be significantly lower, freeing up resources for other industrial and infrastructural investments in the economy. National resources would also not have been diverted into the replication of infrastructure in newly developing regions and into the mass relocation of highly skilled scientists and engineers. Had the defense budget been correspondingly lower, and had public resources been devoted instead to existing commercially oriented sectors of the economy—those that make industrial equipment for factories, machinery for the farm and housing industries, automobiles, specialty steels, and so on—U.S. firms might have been all that much better equipped to compete with their counterparts in countries like Germany and Japan, where the limited defense spending has channeled investment resources and engineering talent into commercial industrial preeminence.

Such a vision contains quite a few "ifs," and it is beyond the capabilities of our current research effort to state definitively the magnitude of difference involved. Nevertheless, it is evident that the cold war has encompassed—and perhaps been fed by—a striking shift in the geography of American manufacturing and services. Had that shift not occurred, the composition and location of American industry would probably look quite different today. Perhaps it would resemble that of Japan, the one-time enemy upon which the United States imposed draconian restrictions on remilitarization, restrictions that in retrospect may have been a substantial gift. Instead of specializing in arms and in the products of defense-bred industries like aircraft, electronics, and computers, the American export portfolio might be much more diversified and regional economies, as a consequence, more robust. The fact that new high-tech military-serving plants have been disproportionately located outside the industrial heartland has contributed to uneven regional development and, at the same time, absorbed resources that might better have been deployed to strengthen the economy.

The Future of Gunbelt Cities

Finally, we turn from a possible past to a speculative future. The question at issue is the likely future of the gunbelt in the 1990s—a decade that, we can fairly confidently predict, will see a major shift in the strategic assumptions that have dominated American foreign policy and defense expenditures over the entire post–World War II period.

The first point to stress is that the American military–industrial frontier is now essentially closed. Pipe dreams about space ports and military bases on the moon aside, the geography of military procurement is more or less immobile. The industrial capacity built to make missiles, nuclear weapons, bombers, satellites, and their electronics and communications payloads was set in place by the late 1950s. Not much has changed since, with the exception of the new defense-services industries, clustered around strategic concentrations of military personnel like Washington, D.C., and Colorado Springs.

This is not particularly good news for Chicago, Cleveland, and scores of smaller cities where cold war military–industrial complexes never took root. Efforts to rewrite history, like the Illinois Defense Technology Association's belated bid for a military-research facility, appear to be doomed by inertia, military favoritism, and the continued impetus to geographical clustering that seems inseparable from cold war innovation. If high-tech weaponry continues to proliferate, new military-related private-sector jobs will go predominantly to the centers with an existing comparative advantage—especially those in southern California and New England.

But this is not necessarily good news for cities on the receiving end, either. Having a comparative advantage works only if demand for military–industrial output continues to grow. In the 1990s, several factors make this highly unlikely. New rivals in military production are emerging—especially Japan, with its new push into weapons production, and Europe, with its increasingly integrated economy. The continued debt crisis and stagnation of Third World countries makes them unlikely customers of new generations of weapons. The American budget-deficit problem is so intractable that despite previous presidential commitments to maintain current weapons-system initiatives (the MX missile, the Midgetman, the Stealth bomber, more nuclear-powered air-craft carriers, SDI), it is unlikely that the nation can avoid serious military-spending cuts. If Soviet–American relations continue to thaw, if NATO continues to move against new nuclear-weapon deployment in Western Europe, and if the Warsaw Pact continues to disintegrate, the arms race will slow drastically.

In the 1990s, the United States will thus most likely face major economic dislocations that will come from a contraction in defense spending. This will present the nation with a considerable challenge. Can the precious scientific, engineering, and entrepreneurial talents assembled for weapons making be redirected toward the difficult issues of industrial revitalization and nonmilitary innovation? Can these talents be applied to meet new global challenges: the AIDS epidemic, the greenhouse effect, the problem of solid-waste management, the huge projected growth in the old-age population, the threat of terrorism? Can a political consensus be reached to generate an attack on problems on a national scale: aging infrastructure, homelessness, the havoc wrought by crack cocaine, the need to develop competitive industrial technologies in computing, telecommunications, biotechnology, energy generation and transmission, and high-speed ground transportation? Can communities built around defense production restyle themselves as contributors to society in other ways? Can we ensure that military–industrial cities, the "veterans" of cold war, will not be treated as poorly as were returning Vietnam War veterans?

The nation has the resources, both human and financial, to attack successfully this adjustment and conversion problem. It will however require new forms of public–private partnership. There has been almost obsessive attention, in recent years, to the model of the Japanese "developmental state," wherein the government takes a lead in promoting and coordinating the efforts of competing firms in crucial high-technology applications.[27] What is sometimes forgotten is that ever since World War II, American defense policy has provided a home-grown example of such a policy; the only problem is that it has not been successful commercially. However, there is no doubt that the model exists—and that, ironically, the most politically conservative groups and regions are the biggest supporters of such large-scale government intervention. All that would be needed is to divert the entire program to fight peacetime enemies. To match workers and communities to this new agenda will be a major project—perhaps the major project—of the present decade.

Appendix

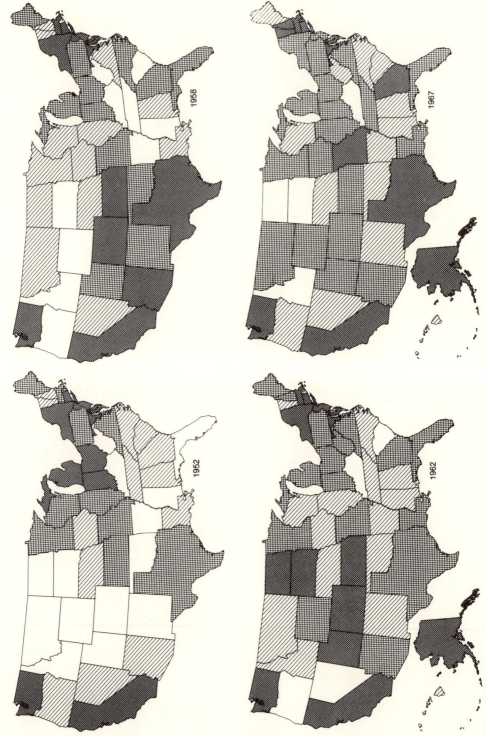

258

FIGURE A.1. Military prime contracts per capita, as percentage of U.S. average, by state, 1952–1984.

FIGURE A.2. Army, Navy, and Air Force prime contracts per capita, as percentage of U.S. average, by state, 1952–1982.

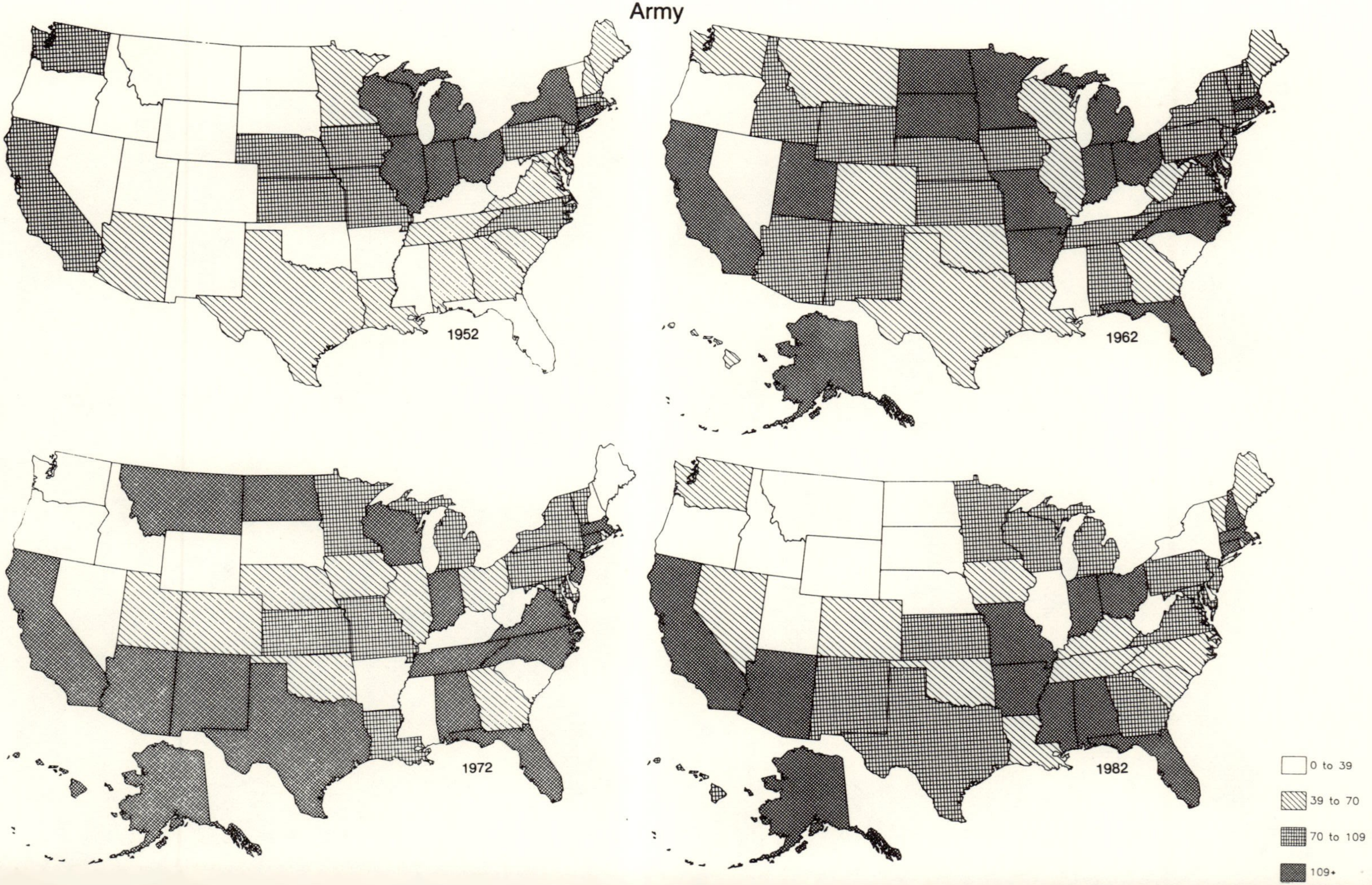

Navy

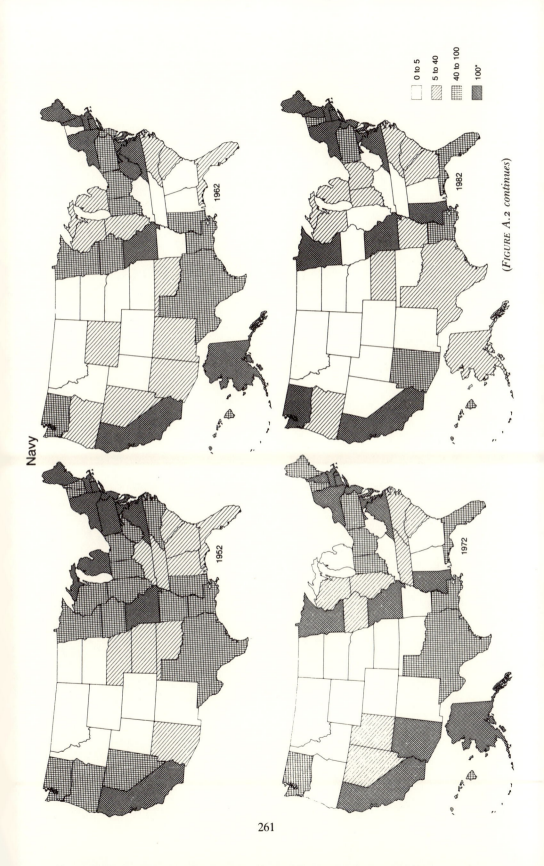

0 to 5
5 to 40
40 to 100
100*

1962

1982

1952

1972

(FIGURE A.2 continues)

261

Air Force

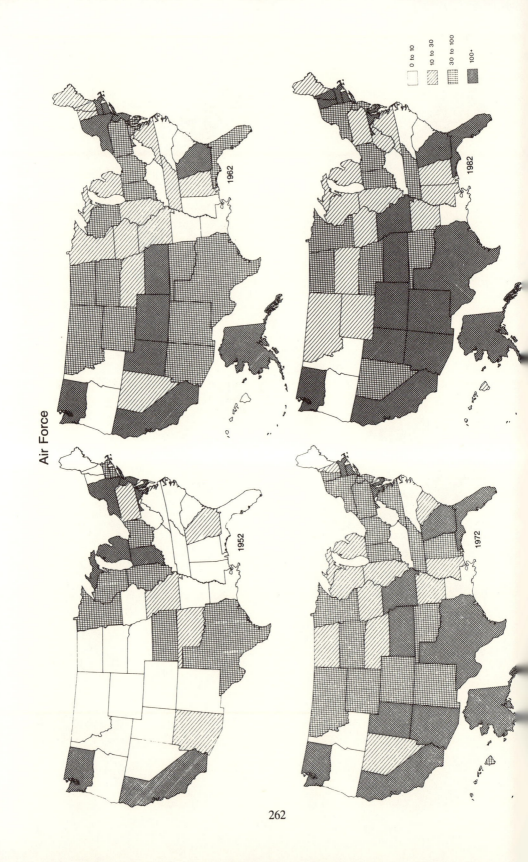

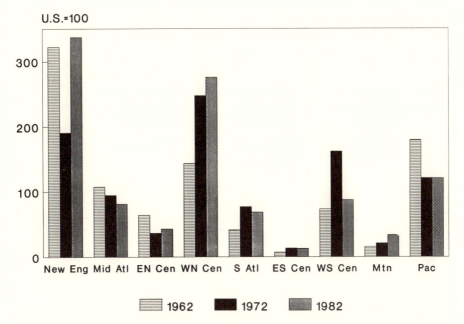

FIGURE A.3. Aircraft prime-contract awards per capita, by Census division, 1962, 1972, and 1982. (Department of Defense, prime-contract awards by region, annual)

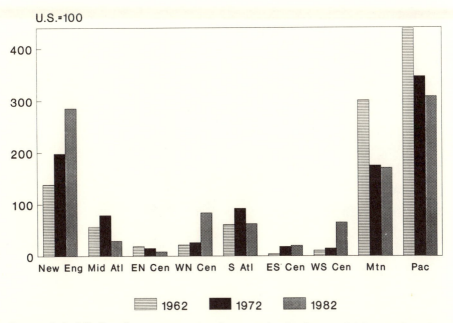

FIGURE A.4. Missile prime-contract awards per capita, by Census division, 1962, 1972, and 1982. (Department of Defense, prime-contract awards by region, annual)

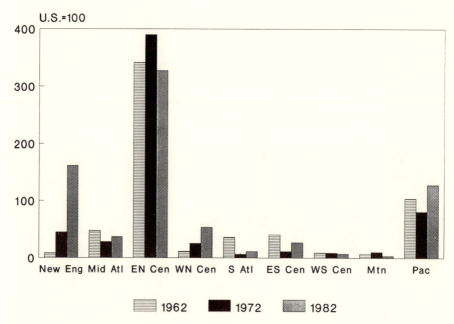

FIGURE A.5. Ship prime-contract awards per capita, by Census division, 1962, 1972, and 1982. (Department of Defense, prime-contract awards by region, annual)

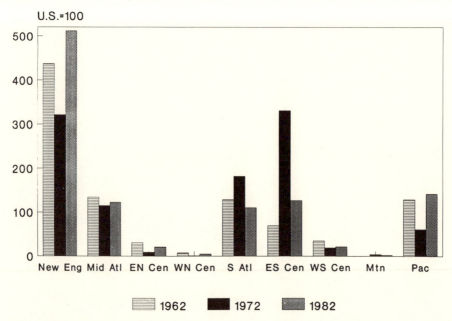

FIGURE A.6. Tank prime-contract awads per capita, by Census division, 1962, 1972, and 1982. (Department of Defense, prime-contract awards by region, annual)

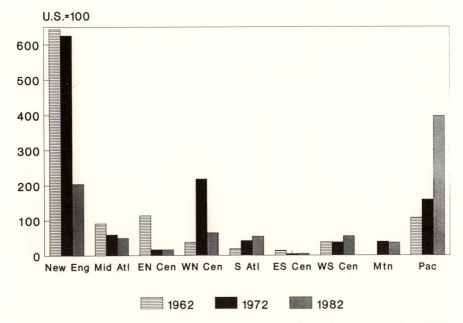

FIGURE A.7. Weapons prime-contract awards per capita, by Census division, 1962, 1972, and 1982. (Department of Defense, prime-contract awards by region, annual)

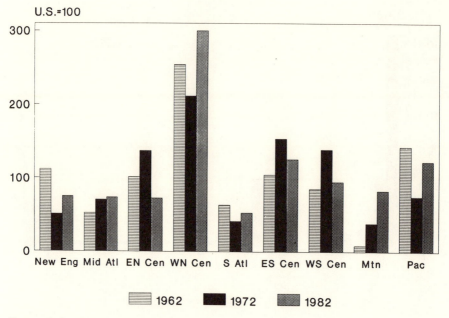

FIGURE A.8. Ammunition prime-contract awards per capita, by Census division, 1962, 1972, and 1982. (Department of Defense, prime-contract awards by region, annual)

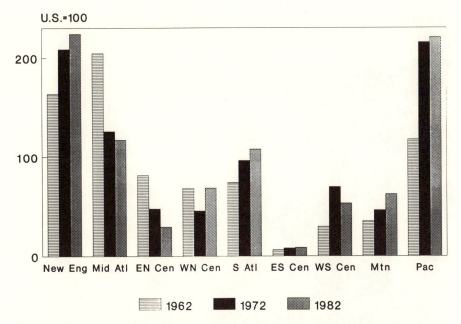

Figure A.9. Electronics- and communication-equipment prime-contract awards per capita, by Census division, 1962, 1972, and 1982. (Department of Defense, prime-contract awards by region, annual)

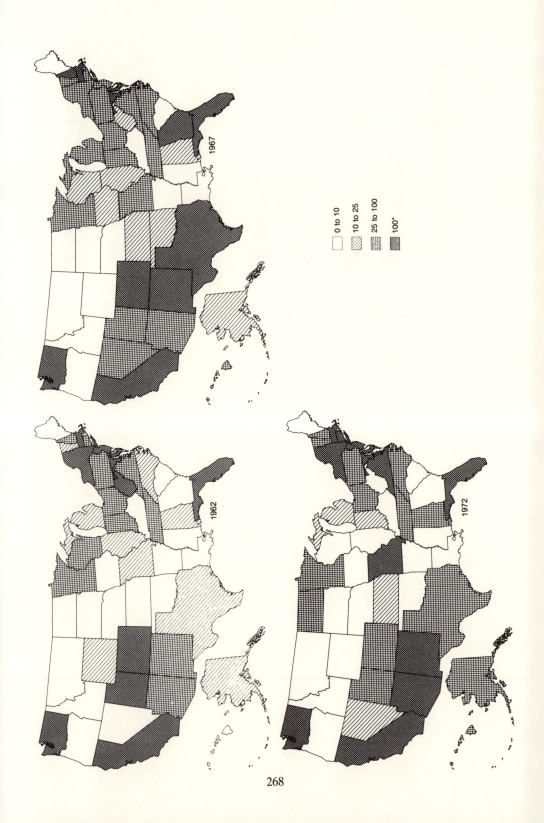

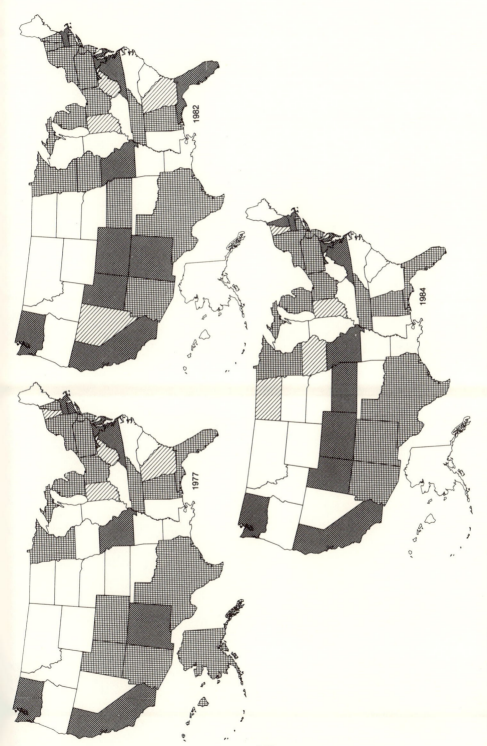

FIGURE A.10. Military contracts for research, development, test, and evaluation per capita, as percentage of U.S. average, by state, 1962–1984.

Notes

Chapter 2

1. Melman, 1974: 15–19; see also Gansler, 1980: 13.

2. Social scientists have long been interested in the role that military and defense spending plays in regional growth. See, for example, Bolton, 1966; Clayton, 1962; Isard and Schooler, 1964; Tiebout, 1966.

3. The Census divides the country by states into nine divisions: New England (Connecticut, Maine, Massachusetts, New Hampshire, Rhode Island, Vermont); Mid-Atlantic (New Jersey, New York, Pennsylvania); East North Central (Illinois, Indiana, Michigan, Ohio, Wisconsin); East South Central (Alabama, Kentucky, Mississippi, Tennessee); South Atlantic (Delaware, District of Columbia, Florida, Georgia, Maryland, North Carolina, South Carolina, Virginia, West Virginia); West North Central (Iowa, Kansas, Minnesota, Missouri, Nebraska, North Dakota, South Dakota); West South Central (Arkansas, Louisiana, Oklahoma, Texas); Mountain (Arizona, Colorado, Idaho, Montana, Nevada, New Mexico, Utah, Wyoming); and Pacific (Alaska, California, Hawaii, Oregon, Washington).

4. Throughout this chapter, per capita spending figures have been normalized to a U.S. average of 100 to present clear relative relationships for the reader.

5. For maps depicting these shifts, see the Appendix, Figure A.1. Because of the nature of prime contracting, where one firm may receive a large contract one year and none the following year, year-to-year variations may result. Overall, however, clear trends do emerge, and these are what the maps illustrate. See also Crump, 1989.

6. Bolton, 1966: 82–101.

7. Subcontracts are much more difficult to track than prime contracts, since reporting arrangements are not required in as much detail. We have looked at the two data sets on subcontracts, which we discuss later in the chapter. Neither is, however, adequate to present a full picture of a subcontracting geography. Indeed, our work suggests that serious inaccuracies have resulted from poor response rates in self-reported surveys. Nor are such data available to us over the broad historical period in which we are interested. For these reasons, the disbursements of prime contracts is our only recourse. We use them cautiously, as an approximation of industry incidence. Subcontracting accounts for about 50 percent of contract work, and although there is some disagreement about how concentrated or dispersed it is, it follows a geographic pattern not much different from that of prime contract work (Malecki, 1984; Rees, 1981; Karaska, 1967). However, our work shows a modest gain for the

Midwest, which in 1983 accounted for 9.5 percent of prime contract shipments and almost double that share of subcontract shipments. Still, even with subcontracts, states like Illinois remained far below the national average (Markusen and McCurdy, 1989: note 21). Subcontracting was not commonly used until after World War II, and initially only in response to government urging (Bright, 1978: 62).

8. Karaska, 1967: 122.

9. Of the remaining fifteen prime contract groups, only three—petroleum, construction, and services—regularly receive at least 3 percent of total prime contracts. Petroleum contracts are concentrated in Texas, Louisiana, and California. Both construction and service contracts are dispersed among states, following the location of military bases. See also Crump's (1989) analysis of weapons-related regional growth.

10. Bolton, 1966: 123.

11. Jonathan P. Hicks, "The Long Shipyard Slump," *New York Times,* November 15, 1985: D1.

12. Gansler, 1980: 101.

13. Clayton, 1970: 37.

14. Department of Commerce, 1965–83. These estimates, based on a sample of ninety-two industries, may be subject to sampling error.

15. Henry and Oliver, 1987.

16. Ibid.: 8

17. Ibid.

18. Ibid.

19. For a detailed study of this effect through the early 1960s, see Bolton, 1966. Markusen (1987b, chap. 6) includes a discussion of the per capita income convergence phenomenon.

20. Warren, 1989: 23.

21. "Coastal States Widen Economic Lead," *New York Times,* August 19, 1988.

Chapter 3

1. A lively debate concerns the formation of military and foreign policies and the extent to which each is influenced by economic interests. See the thoughtful reviews in Lovering, 1987.

2. Greer, 1955: 17–20; B. Davis, 1967: 173–76; Weigley, 1973: 230, 234, 236–37; Kelsey, 1982: 47; Douhet, 1983: 126; Shiner, 1983: 19–21; Sherry, 1987: 23–24, 36–37. After a Far East tour in 1923 and 1924, Mitchell astonishingly forecast that Japan would launch a surprise attack at Pearl Harbor.

3. McClendon, 1952: 127–32; Goldberg, 1957: 36–37; Kelsey, 1982: 32; Shiner, 1983: 25, 31; Ravenstein, 1986: 5.

4. McClendon, 1952: 175, 190–91, 215–24; Goldberg, 1957: 39–41, 95–96; Higham, 1972: 72; Hurley, 1975: 133–34; Shiner, 1983: 94.

5. Kelsey, 1982: 35, 43.

6. Glines, 1980: 143.

7. Holley, 1964: 26.

8. Ibid.: 38.

9. Greer, 1955: 110, 118; Goldberg, 1957: 43; Copp, 1980: 455; Sherry, 1987: 79–80.

10. Tobias et al., 1982: 50.

11. Kelsey, 1982: 15–16, 20–22.

12. Schoeneberger, 1984: 55–56.

13. Anderson, 1983: 26, 28, 31; Schoeneberger, 1984: 30–32, 50–51.

14. McClendon, 1952: 252–54; MacCloskey, 1968: 142.

15. U.S. Congress, House, 1959: 11; Futrell, 1974: 242–44; Bright, 1978: 41–42.

16. Tokaty, 1964: 280–82; Weighley, 1973: 400–3; Futrell, 1974: 213.

17. For an elaboration on this theme, see Markusen, 1990a, 1991.

18. York, 1970: 53; Futrell, 1974: 239, 256.

19. Schwiebert, 1965: 22, 69–72, 80, 217; Armacost, 1969: 58; Futrell, 1974: 244–45; von Braun and Ordway, 1975: 132–33; Hall, 1988: passim.

20. U.S. Congress, House, 1959; 23–25; Peck and Scherer, 1962: 230; Schwiebert, 1965: 113–14; Armacost, 1969: 59–60, 71, 86–87; von Braun and Ordway, 1975: 128, 131; Heims, 1980: 273; Bilstein, 1984: 209.

21. Hitch, 1965: passim.

22. Stekler, 1965: 18–22; Markusen, (1986e) shows how military R&D has risen from a small share of national R&D in the 1930s to about 50 percent in the mid-1980s. For a stunning comparison of modern rates of military innovation compared with historical rates, see Tobias, et al., 1982, chap. 1.

23. Markusen, Hall, and Glasmeier (1986: 18–19) show that missiles are the most high-tech of all industries, as measured by the share of engineers, scientists, and technicians in their occupational structure—41 percent compared with 22 percent in communications equipment, 19 percent in aircraft, and 13 percent in electronics. See also the studies of defense dependency of various occupations in Rutzick, 1970; Dempsey and Schmude, 1971; Oliver, 1971; DeGrasse, 1983; Reppy, 1985; U.S. Congress, Office of Technology Assessment, 1985; Hartung et al., 1985; Henry and Oliver, 1987.

24. Examples of each tradition are Schumpeter, 1939, 1961; Mandel, 1973, 1980; Rosenberg, 1972. Both Schumpeter and Kondratieff (1935, 1984) suggested the link between troughs in long waves and the bunching up of new innovations. The modern scholars of innovation, like Rosenberg, and Nelson, Peck, and Kalacheck (1967) tend to see it as technology-driven, where technology is an exogenous force; Schumpeter began with this view, but altered it later in life (Phillips, 1971: 4–6).

25. Stekler, 1965: 18–21.

26. See Cunningham, 1951: 25–26; Phillips, 1971: 119; Stekler, 1965: 3–6.

27. Gansler, 1980: 36–45, 128–44; Adams, 1981: 33–41; Baldwin, 1967: 62–78, Marfels, 1978; Bluestone, Jordan, and Sullivan, 1981: 55. There is some debate about the extent to which Defense Department patronage has also prevented even greater monopolization in the industry (Phillips, 1971: 1–3).

28. For a number of reasons, these estimates are unduly low. They include only Department of Defense expenditures, not foreign military sales, the Department of Energy's nuclear warheads, or NASA's space defense activities. See the discussion in Markusen, 1986b: 109–11. Regrettably, these figures also exclude service industries, some of which, like computer software, have large defense components. We use the term "industry" in the broader sense, including service activities.

29. Gansler (1982: 39–41) shows the sensitivity of military orientation to political cycles. In 1958, at the end of the initial cold war decade, the top twenty-five contractors had 40 percent of their business in defense. By 1975, this had fallen to 10 percent, but most of this apparent diversification was achieved through acquisitions. The defense division of these companies, and certainly individual plants within them, remained almost exclusively defense-dependent.

30. An excellent, although somewhat dated, literature exists in the industrial organizational tradition on the structure of defense markets. See Peck and Scherer, 1962; Baldwin, 1967; Gansler, 1980; Adams and Adams, 1982.

31. Cunningham, 1951: 17. He also noted that by the late 1930s, 90 percent of aircraft labor was either skilled or semiskilled, although this share declined somewhat during the heavy production runs of World War II (p. 21).

32. This was less the case with mechanical and electrical machinery. Some segments of the precision-machining industry and radio industries were able to make the transition into aircraft engines and radar.

33. Cunningham (1951: 29–31) argues that the infant airframe industry gravitated toward the clear, predictable weather of the Southwest, which permitted more flying days and more frequent testing, lowered the risk of missing delivery dates, and minimized heating and storage costs for space-extensive assembly. Topography, too, he claims, favored coastal plains like those on Long Island, around Lake Erie, and in the Los Angeles Basin. In the final section of this chapter, we argue that these factors may have been overstated in the literature and offer evidence of cases where aircraft manufacture endured, despite climatic and topographical disadvantages.

34. For a review of the literature on the tendency of innovative industries to cluster in initial superprofit stages, see Markusen, 1985b.

35. For this reason, we suspect that some scholars' efforts to proclaim the industrial era over and to celebrate the advent of flexible specialization and innovative industrial districts miss underlying causal relationships. Interestingly, the better scholars in this field are often generalizing from their observations in their own regional economies, which are among the most military-dependent in the nation: Scott, 1982, 1983a, 1983b, 1984a, 1984b, 1985, 1986a, 1986b, 1986c, 1987; Scott and Angel, 1987; Scott and Storper (1986b) in the Orange County/Los Angeles area; Piore and Sabel (1984) in New England. The aerospace industry, as of 1964, consumed 38 percent of the nation's R&D funds, most of it from government coffers and most of it concentrated in New England and southern California (Bluestone, Jordan, and Sullivan, 1981: 159).

36. This argument about oligopolistic clustering is reviewed at length in Markusen, 1985b.

37. Starting with Pirenne's (1914: 259) reflections on how existing capitalists are displaced by "new men, bold, entrepreneurial, who allow themselves audaciously to be driven by the wind," continuing through Schumpeter's (1939) "new men," and reaching to modern analysts like Andersson (1985a, 1985b) and Andersson and Strömquist (1988), a lively literature exists on entrepreneurship, including its locational attributes. For an overview of the literature on founding fathers, see Chapters 4–7 of this book.

38. In such instances, a prior question is why military facilities and procurement offices are located where they are. This we have not been able to explore thoroughly, although in our case studies we do inquire into the origins of certain key military installations when they become important lures for private-sector activity.

39. On the military's response to this status problem, see Janowitz, 1960. On the military profession generally, see also Huntington, 1957.

40. For an exposition of these differences, see Fallows, 1981: 107–14. Japanese labor relations are much closer to the military model.

41. The arsenal vs. contractor debate, documented earlier, reaches back to efforts by both the Army and the Navy to build their own aircraft in factories in Dayton and Philadelphia, respectively. It also, as we will show, has a contemporary counterpart in the current struggle over who will build booster rockets for space missions.

42. See, for instance, J. Anderson, 1983; Mazza and Wilkinson, 1980.

43. For a review and comparison of a raft of studies by political scientists on this question, see Rundquist, 1983.

44. It is important to note that some districts heavily favored by defense spending are represented in Congress by men and women who are staunch doves. In the mid-1980s, for instance, George Brown in southern California and Ron Dellums and Barbara Boxer in northern California all strongly supported significant defense cutbacks. See the extended discussion in Markusen, 1990b.

45. Lotchin (1984) describes this competition and suggests, among other things, that the unity of San Diego–area local governments, compared with the internal squabbling among the Bay Area cities of Oakland, Vallejo, and San Francisco, helped swing the base toward that southernmost port.

46. A number of urban historians have documented the prominent role of boosters in the West. See Abbott, 1981; Glabb and Brown, 1976; Boorstin, 1965; Reps, 1979; McWilliams, 1946. For a conceptual model of locally tied interests, see Markusen, 1987b, chap. 7.

47. We have not included here others whose actions may heighten or damage a place's chances of becoming a military-production center, specifically labor unions, peace groups, and professional and technical employees of defense firms. We do cite instances in the chapters that follow, particularly negative ones. But we are not convinced that any of these groups are important enough as decision-makers to have had a significant impact on the generalized pattern of military production that has evolved across the nation. Business culture has been increasingly viewed as an important determinant of location, particularly in the sitting of new innovative activity. See Stowsky, 1989.

48. Scott and Angel (1987) argue, "The seeds of many of these growth sectors seem to have been planted at particular locations in what amounts to a set of highly contingent circumstances. . . . The main analytical issue here, however, is not so much how these centers came to be precisely where they are, but how they subsequently grew quite systematically as a function of their own internal dynamic . . . " (p. 878). They then proceed to examine new regional high-tech complexes in and of themselves, without comparative reference to other candidate regions. We try here to reinsert this comparative sensitivity, because it is particularly important in fashioning policy recommendations.

49. In its early orientation to commercial industrial location, this body of theory assumed perfectly competitive markets and a fixed panoply of differentially endowed regions. It then derived the profit-maximizing locations of individual firms and sectors (Weber, 1929), the optimal pattern of land uses (von Thünen, 1966), and a set of central places with functional hierarchies for the total urban system (Christaller, 1966; Lösch, 1954). It is possible to relax many of the constraining assumptions of the original formulations to encompass, for instance, imperfect competition, knowledge as an input, and even simultaneous movements of labor and capital, to modernize the theory.

50. Cunningham, 1951: 25, 29–30; Stekler, 1965: 2–4. Before the early 1930s, airframe companies paid for their own construction facilities. By 1934, 45 percent of new capacity was financed by government advances and payments under contracts. This rose to 67 percent in 1939 and 92 percent during World War II. Aircraft-engine makers, on the other hand, had substantial government patronage from a much earlier date.

51. Cunningham, 1951: 20; Stekler, 1965: 2.

52. See, for instance, the account of why Detroit was a logical center for auto

production, and thus why Henry Ford and others might have succeeded there where their New England counterparts failed (Markusen, 1985b: 168–69). See also Koestler's account (1975: 121–124) of how Gutenberg invented the printing press by combining three disparate technologies—wood-block engraving, raised letters, and the wine press—all practiced in his wine-growing region of Mainz.

53. See, for instance, Rees and Stafford, 1983; Joint Economic Committee, 1982.

54. Sometimes this has been a wholesale process. In 1948, when Chance Voight moved from San Diego to Dallas, at the government's urging, the Pentagon paid to move 1,500 families (Cunningham, 1951: 23).

55. Long (1976); Bluestone, Jordan, and Sullivan (1981) found that 12 percent of the new hires of New England aircraft firms came from the military in the period from 1964 to 1967. Some states deliberately foster this presence. Florida's Department of Education has a computer program listing the skills and availability of 13,000 military retirees in the state for the use of company recruiters ("Florida's Business Climate Attracting New Industry," *Aviation Week and Space Technology,* February 21, 1983: 63).

56. Markusen, Hall, and Glasmeier (1986) found that the incidence of educational options—the number of postsecondary educational programs in a metropolitan area— was significantly and positively related to high-tech growth and distribution in the 1970s.

57. Bluestone, Jordon, and Sullivan, 1981: 140–48.

58. Cunningham, 1951: 22–23; Bluestone, Jordan, and Sullivan, 1981: 107, 153. In the postwar period, a number of important moves appear to have been made to escape unions, including Pratt & Whitney's move to Maine, General Electric's moves to Vermont and Kentucky, and Litton's construction of its Passagoula, Mississippi, shipyards. Many aircraft and related companies reluctantly permitted unionization during World War II, as part of the deal for a no-strike pledge, but have chafed under them ever since. However, Markusen, Hall, and Glasmeier (1986: 155) found no significant inverse relationship between rates of unionization and metropolitan high-tech activity. Indeed, they found a positive relationship between the two in explaining high-tech job and plant distribution in 1977.

59. Malecki, 1981a.

60. For a review of research parks in the United States, see Goldstein and Luger, 1988.

61. Dorfman, 1982, 1983; Saxenian, 1985a, 1985b; Segal Quince Wicksteed, 1985.

62. In a national study of university research-and-development spending across all 277 metropolitan areas, we found a negative relationship between such spending and high-tech location and growth. (Markusen, Hall, and Glasmeier, 1986: chap. 9)

63. Others, like shuttles or communications satellites, may require costly strapping on 747s to deliver them to Cape Canaveral.

64. Several scholars, building on an established tradition in regional science and in the industrial restructuring literature, have recently worked on the ideas of "production complexes" (Scott, 1982, 1983a, 1985, 1986b, 1986c); industrial enclaves (Markusen, 1988); and industrial districts (Piore and Sabel, 1984). These extend pioneering studies of new industrial places by Perloff et al. (1960) and Duncan and Dickerson (1970).

65. Some, notably Scott and Angel (Scott, 1986a; Scott and Angel, 1987), have argued that the question of proximate causation is neither important nor interesting. They reject the notion of a privileged "independent variable" that anchors the entire locational process (Scott, 1984: 25) and concentrate instead on the dynamic process

in which conditions of growth are reproduced. While their contributions to the explication of the clustering process are significant, we think that their indifference to proximate causes leads them in some cases to misinterpret and overstate the endogeneity of development. In their analysis of Orange County, for instance, they miss the crucial connection between new "innovative" defense subcontractors and SETA firms, whose location and apparent "disintegration" have explanatory roots in the military–industrial complex and cold war dynamics described above. When Scott (1986a) characterized Orange County as "a major growth center in the classical sense of the term . . . characterized by a core of dynamic propulsive (high technology) industries around which a penumbra of dependent input suppliers has grown up" (p. 21), he credits the Orange County complex with a degree of autonomy that is belied by its Pentagon client and its origins in and ongoing ties with the Los Angeles aerospace industry.

66. Scott (1984a: 25) makes this point well; yet this argument easily leads to the artificial detachment of a local or regional inquiry from the larger structural forces that gave it its start. This is the central dilemma in modern regional geography, articulated powerfully by Massey and her colleagues in their original papers on industrial restructuring as a derivative of capitalist dynamics (Massey and Meegan, 1978) and their more recent emphatic claim that "geography matters!" (Massey, 1984; Massey and Allen, 1984).

67. See Perroux, 1961: 152, 168. Many contemporary scholars have combined the older mechanics of agglomeration with an emphasis on innovation. See, for instance, the creative milieu (Aydalot, 1986b, 1988; Aydalot and Keeble, 1988b), creative drift (Jacobs, 1984: 230), the creative city (Andersson, 1985a, 1985b; Andersson and Strömquist, 1988), and creative economic regions (Johansson, 1987; Johansson and Westin, 1987).

68. See Vance, 1970: 103–52; Jacobs, 1984: 141–48, 230.

69. The seedbed function has been developed by Thompson (1965, 1975), Hägerstrand (1967), Pred (1977), and others pondering the stability of the hierarchy of cities. See the lengthier discussion of this literature in Chapter 4 of this book.

70. For the original work on spatially differentiated activities within a single corporate entity, see Hymer, 1973.

Chapter 4

1. Other entrepreneurs who hailed from the heartland, or at least spent time there, did not stay. A short-lived Martin–Wright merger was initiated in New Jersey in 1916. On its dissolution one year later, California native Glenn Martin set up shop in Cleveland to produce bombers; Martin moved in 1929 to Baltimore. Both Donald Douglas and Dutch Kindelberger worked for Martin in Cleveland. Another Californian, Victor Lougheed, spent time in a Chicago airplane plant early on. Consolidated was originally a Buffalo firm before it moved to San Diego in 1934.

2. Although Chanute had suggested San Diego or the Florida coast, both of which he had used, the Wrights chose to experiment at Kitty Hawk for several months each year in 1900 to 1903 because the U.S. Weather Service assured them that it had the ideal moderate and steady winds. However, after 1903 they returned permanently to Simms Station, in a pasture a few miles east of Dayton. The Wrights opened up a flying school in 1910 in Montgomery, Alabama, but they also started one in Dayton in the same year (Kelly, 1951: 374). Curtiss worked in the New York City area for

some years and pioneered pilot-training operations in San Diego, but set up his Aerial Experiment Association, bankrolled by Alexander Graham Bell and his wife, at Hammondsport, near Buffalo, and that remained his production headquarters (Chandler and Lahm, 1943: 259).

3. Howard, 1987: 141.

4. Ibid.: 137; Beringer, 1955: 10–11; Smith, 1972: 13–14, 17, 27, 30; Kelly, 1943: 39, 92, 93, 114, 117; 1951: 7, 51, 107.

5. McFarland, 1978: 24; Kelly, 1943: 37; Howard, 1987: 54; McMahon, 1930: 76; Hallion, 1978b:xi; 1978c: 66; Crouch, 1981: 9, 11, 229–30, 295.

6. McFarland, 1978: 25.

7. Crouch, 1978: 18–19; 1981: 78–103, 130–31, 262–63, 290–92; Vaeth, 1966: 86–91; Howard, 1987: 123, 125, 131–32.

8. Kelly, 1951: 130, 216, 255; Howard, 1987: 149, 182.

9. Kelly, 1951: 354, 375; Howard, 1987: 352, 404.

10. Howard, 1987: 410.

11. Ibid.: 411.

12. Ibid.: 413–14; Cunningham, 1943: 79–80; Moore, 1958: 54.

13. Howard, 1987: 413; Coffey, 1982: 117.

14. Fernandez, 1983: 9–11; Ravenstein, 1986: 5, 13; Walker and Wickam, 1986: 3, 23, 25, 51, 79–82, 87–91, 105–14, 154, 458.

15. Walker and Wickam, 1986: 134, 301, 458.

16. Wilson, 1965: 23; Futrell, 1974: 238; Coffey, 1982: 117.

17. Futrell, 1974: 238; Fernandez, 1983: 22–38. Columbus, Ohio, has a sizeable Rockwell-North American plant. It was originally a Curtiss-Wright facility hastily erected in 1941 to employ 25,000. The plant changed hands several times before North American took it over in the early 1950s, and has produced aircraft parts there ever since, including sections of the B-1 bomber in the 1980s.

18. Roseberry, 1972: 2, 4, 10, 16, 36, 42–43, 49–50.

19. Ibid.: 71, 78, 151, 257, 361; Howard, 1987: 405.

20. Rubenstein and Goldman, 1974: 33, 57.

21. Goldman, 1983: 216; Rubenstein and Goldman, 1974: 27, 33, 65, 133. Curtiss-Wright also entered the small-airplane market, but the glut of war-surplus machines from World War I and the intense competition kept its efforts modest. Curtiss-Wright also manufactured a Condor transport in the 1930s, which later was sold as a military transport during World War II. Meanwhile, the Navy, desirous of producing its own aircraft, began to manufacture the Curtiss machine at its own aircraft factory in Philadelphia.

22. Holley, 1953: 125–26; Rubenstein and Goldman, 1974: 53–54.

23. Rubenstein and Goldman, 1974: 121–23. The firm lost bids to Grumann, Martin, Douglas, and Boeing. It survived on contracts from China, Thailand, Argentina, the Netherlands, and France.

24. Rubenstein and Goldman, 1974: 162.

25. Faneuf, 1958: 10; Howard, 1987: 405.

26. Faneuf, 1958: 8–13.

27. Ibid.: 12–14.

28. Ibid.: 14; Rubenstein and Goldman, 1974: 166. A new Curtiss-Wright plant was also built at Columbus, Ohio, and the St. Louis plant was expanded. The biggest expansion was in Buffalo itself, where 1.2 million square feet were added in plant 2 at government expense. Pursuit planes were the major product, but the Buffalo plant also built 1,039 transports for the Air Corps.

29. Adams, 1951: 7–9, 86; Goldman, 1983: 233. Besides the aircraft plants, Buffalo's steel mills, motor-vehicle plants, foundries, and other factories supplied the matériel for war, from steel armor for ships to machine guns, chemical-warfare equipment, bomb racks, howitzer shells, and many other items. About half the $5.3 billion was estimated to have been subcontracted out of the region. Quote is from Adams, 1951: 86.

30. Rubenstein and Goldman, 1974: 174, 193–94. A double blow for Buffalo was the failure, too, of Bell's pursuit plane to withstand the coastal competition.

31. Rubenstein and Goldman, 1974: 196–98. In a final effort in the early 1960s to produce helicopters for the Army, the crew was killed in a test flight and Curtiss-Wright lost out to Lockheed. That Curtiss-Wright was permitted to drop out contradicts the follow-on imperative hypothesis, whereby the military rotates contract awards to keep existing suppliers in business (Kurth, 1973). Perhaps the Pentagon's concern to keep firms afloat did not evolve until a later period.

32. Goldman, 1983: 267–68. The Buffalo economy did well in the Vietnam period, due to demand for steel and mass-produced goods. But with the passing of Curtiss-Wright, the city lost its chance to cash in on the cold war economy.

33. Western New York has several other aerospace operations: Irving Air Chute in Fort Erie, Toras Instruments, Moog Servo-Controls, Sierra Research, and Scott Aviation ("Air Museum Will Honor Area's Contributions to Flight," *Buffalo News,* October 29, 1988: C1).

34. Faneuf, 1958: 18–21, 23, 25–27.

35. Perry, 1987a; Goldman, 1983: 216–17. Dillaway (1988) argues that the drying up of local reinvestment and inaction on the part of Buffalo's elite were responsible for the city's inability to respond to downward-spiralling economic decline.

36. Burgess-Wise, 1987: 1–2; Nevins and Hill, 1954: 64. In contrast, recall that more than twenty years later, FDR's proposal for 50,000 airplanes from the entire U.S. industry was considered exceedingly ambitious.

37. The Packard story is very similar to that of Ford. Aggressively pioneering an aircraft engine in 1914, the company also preoccupied itself with standardized designs and mass production (Grayson, 1978).

38. Nevins and Hill, 1954: 65–67; Burgess-Wise, 1987: 3.

39. An indefatigable inventor, Stout had worked both for Packard and for the airplane equipment division of the Army. A genius of structural design, his strategy was to "simplicate and add more lightness." He invented the all-metal airplane (Burgess-Wise, 1987: 10, 16, 23, 28, 33; Nevins and Hill, 1954: 238–39).

40. Ford, 1926: 204–5.

41. Ford's expertise and innovative abilities were highly respected. Colonel Henderson of the Air Mail Service predicted that "if Ford develops a Tri-Motor, it will dominate aircraft manufacturing in the United States." The Ford product was indeed impressive. Ford hosted what was to become an annual contest—the National Air Reliability Tour—in which competing cargo designs raced 1,900 miles to thirteen cities. Ford's Tri-Motor consistently won (Burgess-Wise, 1987: 33–35, 44, 46–47; Nevins and Hill, 1954: 170, 240–42; Bombard, 1958: 19–20; Ingells, 1968: 85–87)

42. Sciever, Horvath, and Bessmer, 1980: 6–7; Nevins and Hill, 1954: 243–45; 1962: 170. Charles Lindbergh believed the Tri-Motor was the best available commercial airplane.

43. Bombard, 1958: 19–20.

44. Ibid.: 35; Nevins and Hill, 1954: 245–46; Bombard, 1958: 20. Stout tried to revive the Tri-Motor after World War II. He built a prototype in 1957, but died shortly

thereafter. Although his company, Hayden Aircraft, continued to work on the plane, testing it in 1966, it never could catch up with the industry leaders (Ingells, 1968: 87–90).

45. Ford, 1926: 205.

46. Nevins and Hill, 1954: 245–46; interview with Bob Isom, director, Corporate History Office, and Walter Hayes, vice president, Ford Motor Company, October 12, 1988.

47. For a discussion of the reasons why Detroit became the center of auto production in the United States, see Markusen, 1985b: chap. 10.

48. Ford, like many midwestern businessmen, was an isolationist before both world wars. By the late 1930s, this was further complicated by Ford's British and German operations, which he feared would be greatly threatened by the outbreak of war, and by his close personal ties with the Third Reich. Ford refused to make Rolls Royce aircraft engines for the British in 1940, although Ford–Britain did. Indeed, the United Auto Workers' union was much more bullish on war than was Ford. In December 1940, Walter Reuther offered a plan to convert unutilized auto capacity to military-airplane production. Ford actually profited by selling to both sides before and during the war, as did many other multinationals (Nevins and Hill, 1962: 155–75, 181–82; Clark, 1942).

49. Lacey, 1986: 387; Nevins and Hill, 1962: 174–78.

50. Nevins and Hill, 1962: 185.

51. Quoted in Lacey, 1986: 390–92. Ironically, Ford made no attempt to organize a total civilian war-production complex, the way Kaiser did during the war. Ford seems to have been adamantly opposed to such "socialism." The company made no allowances for housing, built no model towns, even though the School of Architecture at the University of Michigan designed one and offered it to the company. As a result, commutes and living conditions were terrible (Carr and Stermer, 1952: 320–21.)

52. Nevins and Hill, 1962: 179, 190.

53. Lacey, 1986: 393.

54. Quoted in Lacey, 1986: 393.

55. Nevins and Hill, 1962: 191–92; see Chapter 6 for the Grumman discussion.

56. The Packard story in World War II is very similar to Ford's. Packard produced the Rolls Royce Merlin engine, employing 14,000 workers to make 55,000 engines by the war's end. It, too, was feverishly dedicated to mass production performance. Packard tried to succeed with jet-engine design after the war, but its contract was canceled by the Air Force in 1949. A later effort to produce GE's J-47 Turbojet for Korea also failed to give Packard a permanent role in military engines, and in 1954 the facility became an auto-parts, engine, and transmission facility. Meanwhile, management was struggling to compete in the fierce world of stylized autos, failing altogether in 1956 (Hamilton and Heinmuller, 1978; telephone interview with Michael Kollins, Detroit, November 1988).

57. Lacey, 1986: 390. As measured by expansion in facilities, DuPont was first, GM second, Ford eighth, and Chrysler ninth (Nevins and Hill, 1962: 226).

58. Correspondence with Mark Baldwin, United Auto Workers union, Research Department, May 1988.

59. Detroit-area aircraft plants were shut down rapidly—Willow Run was sold first to Kaiser-Fraser, and then in 1955 to GM, which still makes cars there. For a time, due in large part to the Korean conflict, Ford manufactured Pratt & Whitney–designed aircraft engines in its Chicago plant (Sloan, 1964: 206).

60. U.S. Congress, House, 1959: 251; von Braun, 1964: 108–10; von Braun and Ordway, 1975: 127; Bilstein, 1984: 206–7.

61. Peck and Scherer, 1962: 228–29; Armacost, 1969: 89n, 137, 155–56.

62. Bright, 1978, 184–85.

63. Ford sent his lieutenants, Lynch and Breech, to California to look around. Both men, unlike old Henry Ford, loved airplanes more than cars. In the early 1950s, they bought up a group of twenty scientists who had just left Lockheed en masse to form a small company. With the Ford "whiz kids" of 1946 in mind, they dreamed of building into an aircraft business bigger than Boeing. Henry II then tried to buy the Martin company, to graft it on this innovative base, but the price was too high. Bitterly disappointed, Ford grabbed the next thing that came along, a consumer appliance business named Philco, which Ford wanted in order to diversify its consumer markets. Almost by accident, Ford also acquired Philco's small defense electronics operations, which it merged with the division formed by the Lockheed émigrés (Lacey, 1986: 393).

64. Interview with Bob Isom, director, corporate History Office, and Walter Hayes, vice president, Ford Motor Company, October 12, 1988.

65. Ford Aerospace, undated memorandum, Arlington, Virginia, 1988.

66. Crouch, 1981: 78–100, 223; Young and Callahan, 1981: 11–15; Howard 1987: 160, 167.

67. Young and Callahan, 1981: 6–8, 23–26, 50, 56. Other Chicago aircraft pioneers did, however, sell airplanes in the early decades. Horace Wild started his international Aircraft Company in 1911, building a plane powered by a Curtiss motorcycle engine. When Wild was arrested for impersonating an Army captain in a stock-sales scheme in 1917 and again in 1920 for receiving stolen property, his firm foundered with his reputation. Another firm, Heath Aerial Vehicle Company, made airplanes until 1931, when it succumbed to the Depression.

68. For detailed documentation of Chicago's high-tech occupational offerings and research-and development labs, see Testa and Geise, 1987a, 1987b.

69. See Markusen, Hall, and Glasmeier, 1986: 104–29. They show that the Chicago Standard Metropolitan Statistical Area (SMSA) gained only 1 percent in high-tech employment in the period from 1972 to 1977, when the nation's high-tech employment was 8 percent. In comparison, Boston's high-tech job growth was 12 percent and San Jose's was 86 percent in the same period. Illinois claimed 360,000 high-tech jobs in 1977, second only to California, but was not "high tech-intensive"—the share of the state work force in high-tech industries was not appreciably different form the national average (Glasmeier, 1986).

70. Rubinstein and Brewer, 1962: 9–16. See also "Midwest Finds Itself Guilty," *Business Week*, October 21, 1961; "NEC Finds Illinois R&D Scanty," *Electronics*, March 30, 1962.

71. Rubinstein and Brewer, 1962: 19.

72. The link between high-tech development and defense spending is well established in the literature (Tirman, 1984; Stowsky, 1986). Bolton (1966) demonstrates the connection between defense spending and regional income-growth differentials in the first decades of the postwar period in the United States. Barff and Knight (1987) document the connection between military spending, high-tech, and the timing of the New England turnaround. Rees (1982) and Markusen (1986) offer conceptual arguments for the link. OhUallachain (1987) and Markusen, Hall, and Glasmeier (1986) confirm empirically that high-tech and manufacturing-job shifts are locationally tied to defense-spending differentials.

73. Erdevig (1984) shows that the Midwest has received progressively lower shares of the federal government's research budget, principally because of the shift toward defense. See also Batteau and Meyer, 1986.

74. Over the years, Illinois has ranked first in a number of categories—construction equipment, with $128 million in sales in 1984, 51 percent of the national total; photographic equipment and supplies, with $38 million and 23 percent of the defense market; and materials-handling equipment, with $55 million and 35 percent of the market. It has occasionally ranked in the top five states in the country in several others: petroleum, military building supplies, and subsistence (chiefly food), but never garnering more than 10 percent of the total defense demand. Data are from Department of Defense, *Prime Contracts by Region and State,* selected years.

75. Rubinstein and Brewer, 1962: 9.

76. Ideally, we would have liked to review three types of firms: those that had successfully moved into high-tech defense contracting in the Chicago area; those that had relocated to some other site outside the area for their defense work; and those that had remained there but had chosen not to pursue defense markets. We chose to concentrate on the first group. Some insights into the second group have been culled from our interviews elsewhere. Observations about the final group were gleaned directly from the one manager interviewed whose firm had more or less dropped out of defense work, and indirectly by asking other interviewees about their more exclusively commercially oriented counterparts. However, our findings may be biased by the absence of direct responses from the latter.

77. The state of Illinois received a total of $1.5 billion in prime contracts in 1983, of which the city of Chicago won $219 million and the six-county Chicago SMSA $823 million. The majority of the state's awards are concentrated in northeastern Illinois, almost entirely in the Chicago suburbs and in the nearby cities of Joliet and Rockford. For further details on the research methodology, see Markusen and McCurdy, 1989.

78. The problem with the prime-contract data is that it does not track the myriad subcontracts, some quite substantial, that work back into the Midwest from the aerospace and shipbuilding centers of the country. This is particularly critical for understanding Chicago, for Chicago does relatively better as a subcontractor than it does in primes. Some of the subsystems, parts, and machinery going into the new generations of fighter planes, missiles, communications satellites, and nuclear submarines are still manufactured in the Midwest. OhUallachain (1986) uses military shipments data from the Census of Manufacturers to show this effect.

79. Three significant national defense contractors are headquartered in the Chicago area—Motorola, FMC, and Morton-Thiokol—but none of them does a significant share of its defense-oriented work in the Greater Chicago area. We chose not to interview them for this reason. A spokesman for the Chicago-based Morton Salt company, which acquired Utah-based Thiokol, the only unit that does significant defense work, confirmed that all of Thiokol's operations and location decisions continue to be made from Utah. FMC, a farm-machinery maker that successfully moved into the production of tanks and related equipment for the military, moved its headquarters to Chicago in 1972, but it continues to concentrate most of its defense operations in California. Schaumburg-based Motorola does some defense work in the Chicago suburbs, but its major research-intensive electronics activities were relocated to Phoenix in 1949 when Dan Noble, vice-president for military electronics, decided to build an R&D lab there, partly because he suffered from asthma and partly because he wanted to escape the stifling environment of Chicago and corporate headquarters. In our interview, a Motorola spokesman noted that Scottsdale had rolled out the red carpet and had members of Congress who seemed eager to lobby on Motorola's behalf. Over the years, most of Motorola's defense-related activities have been shifted to the Arizona facilities, which employ more than 22,000 people. See also Glasmeier, 1986.

80. The two exceptions are branch plants whose headquarters are not in Illinois. However, the exceptions prove the rule. In one case, a company acquired the branch plant but let it stay in the Midwest because its top executives lived there. In the other firm, a small branch plant was established in the Chicago area because its technical adviser lived in that area. In addition, we found that if the head office of any of these companies had to be moved, a new location would be chosen according to the preference of the current chief executive officer.

81. The major pioneering work in this area was done by Thompson, 1965, 1975. On the face-to-face contact in innovative industries and the tendency for industries to disperse, see Vernon, 1960, 1966. Friedman (1972) argued that this innovative dynamic would reinforce polarized development.

82. Rees and Stafford, 1983: 97–107, Joint Economic Committee, 1982.

83. Norton and Rees (1979) conclude that seedbeds of innovation have shifted toward the Southwest. Markusen, Hall, and Glasmeier, (1986: 130) found that new centers of high-tech agglomeration have evolved and that with a few important exceptions (e.g., Boston), their cores are not coterminant with older centers of innovation.

84. Malecki (1980) argues this and shows that government-sponsored research, in particular, is distributed quite differently than is corporate research.

85. Glasmeier (1986) develops the notion of the technical branch plant and shows some outstanding examples, such as Motorola's huge semiconductor research and production facility in Phoenix.

86. Taylor (1975) argues that a majority of new firms sprout in the founders' hometown. Saxenian (1985a) traces the role of Frederick Terman in building up the Stanford-based complex. There are dissenting voices, however. Feller (1975) shows that there is no necessary connection between the location of inventive activity and the site of its successful commercialization.

87. Checkland (1975) calls this the "upas tree" effect, a reference to a poisonous tree which prevents any other living thing from growing beneath it. For elaborations on the role of oligopoly in urban and regional development, see Chinitz, 1960; Markusen, 1985b.

88. See, for instance, Markusen, Hall, and Glasmeier, 1986; Schlottman and Herzog, 1990. Even these two studies do not completely agree on the relative significance of various hypothesized factors influencing recent high-tech location.

89. The ideal test of the seedbed function would pool time-series and cross-sectional data in a regression of cities' high-tech performance on a set of independent variables capturing the hypothesized causal relationships. However, the absence of good time-series data, particularly on the independent variables, makes this nearly impossible to achieve.

90. We found that the number of successful defense contractors in northwestern Illinois were few. Of forty-eight Fortune 500 firms headquartered in Illinois, only a handful are major defense contractors. Between our two data sources, we found fewer than fifty firms that might be considered appropriate candidates for interviews. This is a stunningly small number for an economy of Illinois' size and resources.

91. We are grateful to Jim Shanahan of the University of Akron for this example.

92. Certainly the Ford story, which epitomizes this strategy, demonstrates technological brilliance (Halberstam, 1986: 77–82)

93. For a exposition of these features of midwestern industry, see Markusen and Carlson, 1989.

94. Nash, 1985: 164–5; Smith, 1965; Powaski, 1987: 17–18; Ackland, 1984. Mid-

western locales are still strong centers for peace initiatives, although so are the states of California and Massachusetts (Cutter, Holcomb, and Shatin, 1986).

95. See, for instance, the congressional testimony of Congressman Ralph Church of Illinois (*Congressional Record,* 1939, 84, pt. 7: 6949–8032).

96. The same conclusion is stated in Warren, 1989: 22.

97. Arsenal-21 Project, "The Joliet Arsenal in the 21st Century: A Proposal for the Development of a Portion of the Joliet Army Ammunition Plant Site as a Defense R&D Center," August 11, 1987. (draft prepared by the Arsenal-21 Committee of the Illinois Defense Technology Association; see also Merrill Goozner, "High Caliber Plan for Joliet Arsenal," *Chicago Tribune,* September 28, 1987: B1. The Joliet plant contains two facilities, both built during World War II to manufacture munitions and TNT. Currently, both Uniroyal and Honeywell have modest contracts to maintain facilities and, in the case of Honeywell, to manufacture small-caliber munitions and anti-tank rockets on the site. Uniroyal receives contracts of $17 million a year and employs 150. The Army also has a staff of nine people on the site. The Arsenal-21 Project has prepared an entire site plan to buttress its proposal and has presented it to the technical director of the U.S. Army Laboratory Command. The IDTA lists eleven areas of expertise which such a center might concentrate. These include parallel-computing hardware and software, expert systems, electromagnetic launch, directed energy weapons, superconductivity, advanced fuel-cell systems, space reactor power systems, advanced-materials research, crew–vehicle interface, electronic surveillance, and optical and electron target recognition. The depth of Chicago-area contractors in many of these areas is questionable—many of them are activities now conducted solely by Argonne or by one or another contractor. Furthermore, there are many other centers of expertise in the country where such defense research might be carried out.

98. Nimroody, 1987; Council on Economic Priorities, 1987.

99. For a detailed breakdown of the composition of the midwestern professional and technical work force and a comparison with the national average, see Testa and Geise, 1987a.

100. For a review of these policies, see Markusen and Carlson, 1989.

Chapter 5

1. U.S. Department of Defense, 1983: passim.

2. Lockwood and Leinberger, 1988: 35.

3. Johnson, 1961: 66–75; Schoneberger, 1984: 20.

4. Faneuf, 1958: 10; Rae, 1968: 5.

5. Cunningham, 1943: 107.

6. Ibid.: 198; Schoneberger, 1984: 30–32, 50–51; Rae, 1968: 8–9.

7. Anderson, 1983: 13–14, 16–19, 21, 24–26, 28, 31; Schoneberger, 1984: 32–34.

8. Schoneberger, 1984: 55–56; interview with J. Leland Atwood, 1987; cf. Atwood, 1970: passim.

9. Cunningham, 1943: 198–201; 1951: 44.

10. Barlett and Steele, 1979: 62–63, 78–79, 105–56, 171–72.

11. Ibid.: 173.

12. "North American comes to Los Angeles": 1935: n.p.

13. Ainsworth, 1959: passim; Hart, 1981: 61; Berges, 1984: 35.

14. Cunningham, 1943: 142–43; Ainsworth, 1959: 22; Nadeau, 1960: 197; Gottlieb and Wolt, 1977: 155–56; Berges, 1984: 42.

15. Bonelli, 1954: 103; Hatfield, 1973: 201; Gottlieb and Wolt, 1977: 157; Friedman, 1978: 18–20, 23–24; Rolle, 1981: 53; Berges, 1984: 35.

16. Nadeau, 1960: 201.

17. Friedman, 1978: 33–36, 42; Cunningham, 1943: 211. For the aircraft industry, see also Scott, 1989: 11–14; Scott and Mattingly, 1989: passim.

18. Weiss, 1987: passim.

19. Hallion, 1977: 27, 46–50; Schoneberger, 1984: 81. Previously, there were only five American university aeronautical engineering programs: MIT (the first, in 1914), California Institute of Technology, University of Michigan, University of Washington, and Stanford University.

20. Hanle, 1982: 93.

21. von Kármán, 1967: 147; Hallion, 1977: 50–51.

22. Malina, 1964: 46–53, 60–61; Hallion, 1977: 188.

23. Pendray, 1964: 20–23; von Kármán, 1967: 242. Belatedly, the Navy supported Goddard's work until his death.

24. Coffey, 1982: 148–50.

25. Copp, 1980: 118; Arnold, 1949: 139.

26. Coffey, 1982: 208; Hanle, 1982: 136; Koppes, 1982: 2–3, 8–9, 11–14, 21–21; Malina, 1964: 60; von Kármán, 1967: 235–39, 243–44, 253. Von Kármán, always "receptive to ideas that struck others as bizarre," was approached by Frank Malina, his graduate assistant, and two highly unconventional undergraduates, John Parsons and Ed Forman, for support in their work on rockets. Their work won unexpected support from Arnold, who paid a surprise visit in 1938 and who was responsible for a purported $1,000 grant in 1939; field trials began in 1942. For the expansion of science at Caltech, and in the American West generally during World War II, see Nash, 1985: 153–58.

27. von Kármán, 1967: 243–44. This skepticism was shared by Arnold's assistant, Major General Chidlaw, then vice president of TRW, and later commanding general of Air Matériel Command. Arnold proved right, and the others wrong. The $1,000 grant led within three years to the first tests of rocket-assisted takeoff at Muroc Field (now Edwards Air Force Base) and to the $3 million Jet Propulsion Laboratory established at Caltech in 1944 to develop research on guided missiles.

28. von Kármán, 1967: 299.

29. Ibid.: 256–58.

30. Arnold, 1949: 532.

31. von Kármán, 1967: 271.

32. Ibid.

33. Rand, 1967: 80–85.

34. Cunningham, 1951: 37, 39, 42, 52–53, 59–60, 67–70. Consolidated was the product of a merger between Vultee of Glendale, California, and Reuben Fleet's Consolidated Aircraft Company of Rhode Island. Fleet, who had received a huge order for naval flying boats in 1934, moved the company to San Diego, which offered boat-testing facilities that were more amenable than frozen Lake Erie (Rae, 1968: 91; Schweibert, 1965: 58, 92, 117; York, 1970: 93).

35. Cunningham, 1951: 99, 109, 119, 124, 148–50, 164–66.

36. Ibid.: 18–23, 28–32.

37. This story is told more fully in Hall, 1988.

38. Janowitz, 1960: 164–65.

39. Manno, 1984: 24–25; Beard, 1976: 157, 164; Schwiebert, 1965: 22, 69–72, 80, 217; Armacost, 1969: 58; Futrell, 1974: 244–45; von Braun and Ordway, 1975: 132–33.

40. Armacost, 1969: 39, 46.

41. von Braun and Ordway, 1975: 120.

42. Heims, 1980: 274.

43. Witze, 1965: 171; U.S. Congress, House, 1959: 7, 12; Beard, 1976: 170, 178.

44. Beard, 1976: 169.

45. U.S. Congress, House, 1959: passim; Schwiebert, 1965: 80–84, 219; Armacost, 1969: 160–62; Futrell, 1974: 245.

46. U.S. Congress, House, 1959: 223.

47. Rand, 1967: 74–75; Barlett and Steele, 1979: 171–72, 190–92; Mettler, 1982: 16.

48. Armacost, 1969: 89n, 137,154, 159–60, 223, 245; Dornberger, 1964: 29–37; Peck and Scherer, 1962: 228–29.

49. Armacost, 1969: 156.

50. Ibid.: 89, 155–56; Schwiebert, 1965: 58, 92, 117; Yarmolinsky, 1971: 56–57; York, 1970: 93.

51. von Braun and Ordway, 1975: 133; Simonson, 1968a: 231–33.

52. Stekler, 1965: 118, 121.

53. Simonson, 1968a: 232–33, 237–41.

54. Rand, 1967: 76.

55. Higham, 1972: 5. For the rise of avionics, see also Scott and Drayse, 1990: passim.

56. Ball, 1962: 87.

57. Aydalot, 1986a: passim; Aydalot and Keeble, 1988a: passim.

58. McWilliams, 1946: 369.

59. Hall and Preston, 1988: chaps. 8 and 13.

60. See Cunningham, 1951; Bloch, 1987: 75–76.

61. Lockwood and Leinberger, 1988: 35–36.

62. Ibid.: 48.

63. For a description of Orange County aviation, see Smith, 1974.

64. As Scott (1986a: 21, 41) has shown, Orange County became a classical example of a growth center, characterized by a core of dynamic propulsive industries and a penumbra of dependent input suppliers, with extreme vertical disintegration of production processes and economies of agglomeration.

65. Soja (1986: 261) has commented on the distribution of aerospace engineers in the beach communities of Greater Los Angeles, with special concentration on the Palos Verdes Peninsula.

66. Ball (1962) provides a thorough history of Edwards.

67. The Northrop strategic bomber contract was later canceled in favor of Consolidated Vultee's B-36 design, which was a bitter defeat for Jack Northrop's pet project (Schoneberger, 1984: 70).

68. In later moves to Colorado Springs and Washington, D.C., as Chapters 8 and 9 will show, TRW was attracted to the site of its prime customer.

69. Schoneberger, 1984: 67.

70. North American already operated a large facility in Columbus, Ohio. Northrop saw problems both in Seattle and in Silicon Valley. Yet other firms contradicted this, suggesting that the presence of other firms in the area would attract new entrants to

the labor force. Another advantage of being near other companies is the ability to keep an eye on what the competitor is doing.

71. Markusen, 1985b.

Chapter 6

1. This was the name we gave to the area in our earlier study (Markusen, Hall, and Glasmeier, 1986).

2. Frankel and Howell, 1988: 296.

3. Warsh, 1988: 322.

4. Most of New York State outside the eastern seaboard belongs to the industrial heartland and shares its difficulties: "The state's major defense prime contracts are heavily concentrated on Long Island, along the southern tier and in a few other parts of the state. The economically troubled regions of western New York and the outer boroughs of New York City receive relatively few prime contracts" (Gurwitz, Auda, and Greer, 1984: iii, 8–11).

5. Hall and Preston, 1988: 255–256.

6. Rossano, 1984: 76–78.

7. Smits, 1974: 79, 80, 82, 84, 89–91, 102–3; Rossano, 1984: 66–67.

8. Thruelsen, 1976: 18–19; Smits, 1974: 91, 109.

9. Hughes, 1971: xiv, 2–3, 18–19, 24, 42–44, 53, 61, 65–67, 70, 103–6, 110, 112, 120, 129–30, 136, 143, 151, 153–57, 240. Sperry had already established his reputation in a variety of enterprises before his arrival in New York at the age of forty-five in 1905. Born near Cortland village in upstate New York in 1860, Sperry was Thomas Edison's chief rival in the history of American technological innovation, with 350 patents to his name. First in his native village, then in Chicago and Cleveland, he had developed important inventions, successively in electric lighting and generation, electric traction, automobiles, batteries, and industrial chemistry.

10. Hughes, 1971: 164, 173, 177, 178, 181, 186, 201, 203, 210, 234–35, 263–74.

11. Davenport, 1978: 139, 142–43, 189, 285–91. Lawrence drove a hard bargain with his father, insisting on taking a profit from all sales of apparatus they had patented and those on which they had worked together. All twenty-four of these dealt with airplanes, two-thirds of them with control devices. It is possible that Grover Loening, a close friend, aided and abetted Lawrence's bid to break free. Then, in 1919, Lawrence obtained an exclusive license to manufacture and sell the "aerial torpedo," or flying bomb, that he had already tested.

12. Rossano, 1984: 68; Smits, 1974: 109–10.

13. Smits, 1974: 110–13; Rossano, 1984: 72–74.

14. Thruelsen, 1976: 21.

15. Ibid.: 17–19, 29, 42, 54–55, 69–70, 74, 89.

16. Ibid.: 33, 57, 63–64, 91, 106.

17. Ibid.: 116, 138, 148, 235, 335.

18. Ibid.: 155.

19. Ibid.: 359.

20. In New York, they depend greatly on both Kennedy, and La Guardia airports for the very extensive movements of their staff at just below senior level.

21. Philip Gutis, "Grumman Says It Will Reduce 2300 L. I. Jobs," *New York Times,* March 1, 1988: 1; James Bernstein, "600 Layoffs at Grumman: Another 1700

LI Jobs to Be Eliminated Later This Year," *Newsday,* March 10, 1988: 1; Charles Stevens, "Grumman Role as Combat Plane Maker Periled by Pentagon Budget Proposals," *Wall Street Journal,* April 21, 1989: A7A.

22. Eric Schmitt, "Grumman's Loss of Jet Work Hurts Hundreds of Companies," *New York Times,* April 13, 1989: 14.

23. James Bernstein, "When Houston Came A-Courtin' on Long Island," *Newsday,* May 16, 1988: 11.

24. Cunningham, 1943: 69, 88–89; 1951: 37, 39, 42, 52–53, 59–60, 67–70; Boulet, 1982: 90–96, 154, 164.

25. Niven, Canby, and Welsh, 1960: 59, 61; Morris, 1966: 50–52, 61, 67, 89; Goodwin, 1985: 26, 27, 29, 33–36.

26. Goodwin, 1985: 33, 43, 45–47; Morris, 1966: 92, 96, 100, 107, 111–12; Franklin, 1986: 21, 25.

27. Morris, 1966: 113, 116, 124; Niven, Canby, and Welsh, 1960: 78, 83; Franklin, 1986: 27–28.

28. Franklin, 1986: 31, 39, 43; Niven, Canby, and Welsh, 1960: 101; Goodwin, 1985: 75.

29. Franklin, 1986: 57, 87, 90–91, 94.

30. Niven, Canby, and Welsh, 1960: 337; Franklin, 1986: 127.

31. Niven, Canby, and Welsh, 1960: 337; Franklin, 1986: 136, 127–29, 137, 143–44, 150.

32. Sikorsky went to Stratford for family reasons; Norden established a bombsight-making facility in the Norwalk area during World War II.

33. Roe, 1916: 54–55, 128–29, 137–38, 166–70, 177–79; Smith, 1977: 29–33.

34. Estall, 1966: 158; Bluestone, Jordan, and Sullivan, 1981: 19–20.

35. Horner, 1958: 11–12; Pratt & Whitney, 1950: 15–18, 21, 25–27, 29, 35.

36. Pratt & Whitney, 1950: 22, 39; Fernandez, 1983: 22.

37. Pratt & Whitney, 1950: 33, 36–41; Horner, 1958: 13.

38. Pratt & Whitney, 1950: 45, 49, 59, 99; Horner, 1958: 13–14.

39. Pratt & Whitney, 1950: 105.

40. Horner, 1958: 18.

41. Horner, 1958: 15; Pratt & Whitney, 1950: 40, 101.

42. Pratt & Whitney, 1950: 143; Bluestone, Jordan, and Sullivan, 1981: 39.

43. The North Berwick site, which manufactures blades and vanes and disks, had an existing factory that was retrofitted for UTC's needs. The Columbus plant, a highly automated operation for robotics opened in 1984, also seems to have owed something to congressional politics in the final decision. Another plant in West Palm Beach, Florida, with 5,000 to 6,000 workers, was originally the site of super-secret operations involving engine test cells. This project was meeting environmental opposition on noise grounds, and the site was wet and difficult to develop. The company may eventually be forced to shut it, but not immediately.

44. There is one crucial exception: the decision to locate very expensive engine test cells—essentially, huge concrete bunkers with attendant cranes—elsewhere, because of the environmental implications, which has resulted in a policy of dispersal around the country, four to six on each site. And management is often concerned about the dangers of concentration because of the risks from war, a natural disaster, or a major strike.

45. Bean et al., 1986: 123–24; Thomas Lueck, "Connecticut Growth Makes Its Economy One of Best in U.S.," *New York Times,* September 11, 1984: 1.

46. Bean et al., 1986: 129–30; Lueck, "Connecticut Growth Makes Its Economy One of Best in U.S.": 11.

47. MacLaren, 1943: 121–24; Bright, 1949: 82, 94; Passer, 1953: 26–27, 324.

48. Prout, 1921: 208–9; Estall, 1966: 162.

49. Estall, 1966: 162; Miller and Sawers, 1970: 161; Bluestone, Jordan, and Sullivan, 1981: 39, 100, 112.

50. Noble, 1977: 136–40; Wildes and Lindgren, 1985: passim; Scott, 1974: 7–8, 21–25, 36–48, 74, 96; Warner, 1984: 184–94.

51. Scott, 1974: 107–8, 112–13, 162, 184–85, 198, 215; Warner, 1984: 198–99; Warsh, 1988: 322. After the war, MIT created the Research Laboratory in Electronics to continue the wartime work of the Radiation Laboratory; and the Whirlwind project under Jay Forrester, supported by the Navy, produced one of the most advanced computers of its time in 1951. Raytheon, making an early decision to go into microwave cookers, found that its concern for quality and disregard for price were a decided disadvantage in the civilian world

52. GE's research laboratories at Schenectady, New York, founded in 1900 and headed by former MIT professor Willis R. Whitney, struck a brilliant balance between fundamental research and commercial application (Wise, 1985: 81, 139, 173–77, 210; Reich, 1985: 86–87).

53. Fishman, 1981: 212; Dorfman, 1982: 56; 1983: 302, 309–10, 312–14; Warner, 1984: 180–208; Wildes and Lindgren, 1985: 199; Saxenian, 1985a, 1985b: passim.

54. Rubenstein, 1958: 20–25, 52.

55. Ibid., 22–24.

56. Brock, 1975: 10; Flamm, 1988: 29–60; Warsh, 1988: passim.

57. Fagen, 1978: 359, 370–71, 505–7, 618–19; Smits, 1985: 49.

58. Fishman, 1981: 212; Dorfman, 1982: 56; 1983: 302, 309–10, 312–14; Warner, 1984: 180–208; Wildes and Lindgren, 1985: 199; Saxenian, 1985a, 1985b: passim.

59. Dorfman, 1983: 301.

60. Browne, 1988: 17. Draper Lab, started in 1930 as part of MIT's engineering constellation and later named for a professor who achieved fame for the development of gunsights on naval vessels during World War II, has—like the Lincoln Laboratory—remained dedicated to defense work. In July 1973, it was separated from the university as an independent nonprofit corporation but continues to contract with MIT. As TRW does for the Air Force, Draper Lab acts as the Navy's "design agent," producing designs for integrating subsystems, helping the Navy identify suppliers, evaluating competitive bids, and transferring the designs to contractors. It recruits 25 percent of its staff from MIT, another 15 to 20 percent from other New England universities, and the rest from Ivy League schools. Although it does not encourage spin-offs, there have been no fewer than fifty-four identifiable ones, virtually all in computer applications, in the Boston area.

61. Murdock, 1974: 23–25; Herken, 1985: 61–63, 105.

62. Hekman and Strong, 1981: 40–44; Fishman, 1981: 212; Dorfman, 1982: 56; 1983: 302, 309–10, 312; Wildes and Lindgren, 1985: 199.

63. Scott, 1974: 238, 240, 249, 251.

64. Fishman, 1981; Dorfman, 1982, 1983; Wildes and Lindgren, 1985; Loria, 1984; Saxenian, 1985a.

65. This was a result of the Textron acquisition, which otherwise had had no effect on their work.

66. Avco has an expansion option at Tewkesbury, only ten minutes' distant on

Interstate 495, but will not give up its Route 128 site. Labor, traditionally drawn from the 128–495 belt, is now commuting from a wide area beyond I-495, and housing prices along the Massachusetts Turnpike have escalated. To the north, Highway 93 in New Hampshire now has unpredictable traffic jams. When we visited the area, the Communication System section of GTE Government Systems was moving some of its workers from Needham to Taunton, thirty-seven miles south, in search of labor supply and, it was suggested, because this was a nonunion area. Raytheon was considering a takeover of the old Digital plant at Norwood close to Route 128.

67. Harrison and Kluver, 1989.

68. Scott, 1974: 152, 174–76, 226–37.

69. For a review of northeastern regional economic and political organizing, see Markusen, 1987b: 161–71.

70. Barff and Knight, 1988: 162.

71. Browne and Gavian, 1981.

72. Ibid.: A5–A6.

73. Eric Schmitt, "The Area's Economy Feels the Austerity at the Pentagon," *New York Times*, April 16, 1989.

74. *Wall Street Journal*, May 19, 1989; *New York Times*, May 21, 1989.

75. Gordon McKibben, "Peace Breaks Out All Over," *Boston Sunday Globe*, November 19, 1989: A101; Nick Ravo, "The High Cost of Peace Jolts a Connecticut Factory Town," *New York Times*, April 26, 1990: B1; Machine Action Project, 1990; Department of Employment and Training, 1989; Economic Security Subcommittee, 1986.

Chapter 7

1. Holland and Wandschneider, 1989.

2. Sale, 1976: 51, 78.

3. The company history of Boeing was written by Mansfield, 1956.

4. Sale, 1976: 136–37.

5. Wilson, 1950: 172.

6. Mansfield, 1956: 106; Schoeneberger, 1984: 50.

7. Wilson, 1950: 182.

8. Mansfield, 1956: 137.

9. *New York Times*, October 30, 1985. In the war years, William Allen, Boeing's legal council and later president, resolved some of these problems by developing contracts that required payment of the cost of the project plus a fixed fee. This "cost-plus" structure became a model for future contracts in the industry.

10. Collison, 1945: 3, 116.

11. Mansfield, 1956: 271–72.

12. Sale, 1976: 181–83.

13. Ibid.: 181–82.

14. Mansfield, 1956: 261.

15. During the war, Boeing had begun developing the XC-97 transport plane, loosely based on the B-29, which first flew in November 1944. The company's management believed that the design could also be adopted to commercial transport. It led to the Stratocruiser several years later, although this was not a commercial success. Boeing also began work on a jet-powered bomber in 1943. This project, the B-47 Stratojet, had a slow start compared with European jet technology; yet it eventually provided Boeing with a crucial head start in the U.S. military- and

commercial-jet market. The firm also won the design competition in 1946 for the large B-52 jet bomber.

16. Mansfield, 1956: 316–25. As yet there was no demand yet in the United States for a civilian jetliner, and competition from overseas firms was looming. The British government had sponsored the development of the jet-powered Comet in a bold attempt to capture the world market. A similar government-sponsored commercial-jet program went to Congress in 1949, but the prototype bill got nowhere.

17. Mansfield, 1956: 358–66. The Air Force initially balked; Boeing took on the $15 million joint tanker/commercial liner venture without military orders. But in 1954, the Air Force decided to purchase the plane, known as the KC-135 Stratotanker, and commercial orders from Pan Am came in late 1955. Before Boeing received permission to use the government-owned Renton facility for commercial 707 Stratoliner production, it had to assure a skeptical Air Force that commercial production would not delay tanker deliveries.

18. Sale, 1976: 188.

19. Kuter, 1973: 118; *The Economist,* May 3, 1986; Prochnau, 1972: 247. However, some Seattle observers felt that the SST cancellation was a blessing in disguise because Boeing already had a vast inventory of unsold 747s and was facing a bleak commercial-jet market (see Ognibene, 1975: 109).

20. Nelson, 1977: 39; Boeing Co., *Portfolio of Opportunities;* Rainey et al., 1973: 24–27. Most of these cuts came on the commercial side, where employment plummeted from 68,200 to 12,000 between 1969 and 1972; military and space employment actually increased marginally, from 11,800 to 13,600.

21. Rainey et al., 1973: v, 8.

22. Sale, 1976: 233.

23. *Fortune,* September 28, 1987.

24. *The Economist,* May 3, 1986.

25. Ibid.

26. For excellent discussions of this argument, see Stubbing and Mendel, 1986: 184–90; Kurth, 1973. Boeing's bad luck on the TFX contract award to General Dynamics may also be due to inadequate political clout stemming from a peripheral location. We return to this issue below.

27. *Business Week,* September 23, 1985; *Seattle Times,* November 19, 1985.

28. *Seattle Times,* November 19, 1985.

29. Kuter, 1973: 6; Stubbing and Mendel, 1986: 33–39.

30. *Wall Street Journal,* May 13, 1986.

31. Although its purchase of Hughes was thwarted by General Motors' counterbid, in 1985 Boeing created the Seattle-based Boeing Electronics Company, serving military and civilian programs; this was merged with the company's aerospace division in 1989 to form Boeing Aerospace and Electronics. In 1986, Boeing bought ARGO Systems and established the Electronics High Technology Center in the Seattle area.

32. Campbell, 1986.

33. Bonnelycke and Sieverts, 1985.

34. *Journal of Commerce,* August 20, 1982.

35. Nelson, 1977: 42.

36. *Wall Street Journal,* April 28, 1982.

37. Sale, 1976: 185.

38. For the adoption of Canadian staples theory to the Pacific Northwest, see North, 1955.

39. Sale, 1976: 182.

40. Ibid.: 236; see also Holland and Wandschneider, 1989.

41. Sale, 1976: 188–89.

42. Chinitz (1961) observed this pattern in his classic study of Pittsburgh.

43. *Plowshare Press* (Winter 1986); *Journal of Commerce,* August 20, 1982.

44. *Puget Sound Business Journal,* October 17, 1988.

45. Art, 1968; Prochnau, 1972: 252.

46. Art, 1968.

47. Ognibene, 1975: 74; Prochnau, 1972: 239.

48. Stubbing and Mendel, 1986: 33–36.

49. *Forbes,* June 21, 1982; Stubbing and Mendel, 1986: 37–39.

50. John White, "Would a Lasting Peace Be Devastating to Area?" *Valley Daily News*, March 13, 1989; Patz, 1989; Shield, 1989.

51. Nelson, 1977: 32.

52. Krumme and Hayter, 1975: 349.

53. Cleveland, 1942: 162.

54. Hallion, 1977: 221–23; Cleveland, 1942: 164.

55. Boeing's Seattle corporate headquarters generally does all the recruiting for its remote sites. Huntsville is one exception; it does its own recruiting. The corporate recruiting office tries to steer potential employees regionally. Thus hopefuls from the Plains states get steered to Wichita.

56. *Journal of Commerce,* October 7, 1986.

57. *Miami Herald,* October 14, 1986.

58. *Washington Post,* January 29, 1984; *People's Daily World,* May 23, 1981.

59. *People's Daily World,* July 3, 1987; *The Weekly* (Seattle), April 8, 1987.

60. Mansfield, 1956: 183.

61. Collison, 1945: 63.

62. Mansfield, 1956: 263–64.

63. Quoted in Mansfield, 1956: 314–15.

64. A key player in this "decoastalization" debate was Louis W. Johnson. As assistant secretary of war in 1938, he had urged that all military installations be moved "inside the mountains." In 1949, as Secretary of Defense, he was feared to be in a powerful enough position of power to implement his decoastalization policy (*Seattle Times,* August 21, 1949).

65. *Seattle Times,* August 21, 1949.

66. *Seattle Times,* August 22, 1949.

67. *Seattle Times,* August 23, 1949.

68. Mansfield, 1956: 342.

69. *Seattle Times,* April 23, 1981.

70. *Journal of Commerce,* March 6, 1987; *New York Times,* December 8, 1979; *Seattle Daily Journal of Commerce,* December 28, 1979.

71. *Aviation Week and Space Technology,* August 2, 1982; *Metals Weekly,* December 28, 1987.

72. Pete Dakin, Boeing spokesman, quoted in *Seattle Times,* September 1, 1987.

73. *Seattle Times,* November 15, 1984. Boeing has been in Huntsville since the early 1960s. Its first program there was the Saturn S-1C booster, and then the lunar roving vehicle. Employment has fluctuated widely, from a peak of over 5,500 to a low of fewer than 50.

74. *Seattle Times,* November 30, 1988; *Seattle Daily Journal of Commerce,* December 1, 1988.

75. *Journal of Commerce,* June 17, 1986.
76. *San Francisco Examiner,* June 1, 1987; *Journal of Commerce,* June 3, 1987.

Chapter 8

1. This compares with a civilian labor force (in 1985) of 142,000.

2. For histories of Colorado Springs, see Sprague, 1971; Ellis, 1975.

3. Sprague, 1971: 310–12. This and the account that follows draws heavily on interviews with Joseph Reich, K. Freyschlag, General Robert Herres, and others in Colorado Springs.

4. That boosterism was a necessary but not sufficient condition for winning wartime dollars can be illustrated by reflecting on the Springs' neighbors to the north. In the same era that the Springs' committee was wooing bases, Denver's war-related growth was stunted by the caution and conservatism of its banking and business elite, who stymied Henry Kaiser's grandiose plans for military–industrial development. On the other hand, aggressive efforts by North Dakota boosters, who formed the North Dakota War Resources Committee in 1941, and by similar groups in Wyoming were stunningly unsuccessful. See also "Relationship of Military, City Reviewed," *Gazette Telegraph* (Colorado Springs), April 11, 1981: 12.

5. "Nation's Air Defense Needs Rest on Springs' Headquarters," *Gazette Telegraph* December 17, 1950.

6. Ibid.

7. The Air Force in these years held a "strategic concept that if present tension with Russia would erupt into World War III, the gravest danger of aerial blows against the United States would focus on the northwest 'gateway.' " The westward shift of the Air Force is attributed to this strategic concern by some (see "Safety, Central Location Reasons Springs to be Air Defense Capital," *Gazette Telegraph,* November 13, 1950). Tom Fuller and Larry Brandeis, staff historians at NORAD, helped summarize this history for us.

8. "Air Force Survey Team Will Study Facilities Here Monday," *Gazette Telegraph,* November 11, 1950.

9. Interviews with K. Freyschlag and Joseph Reich, December 1986.

10. "Nine-Man Air Force Team Inspects Region's Facilities," *Gazette Telegraph,* November 13, 1950; "Air Defense Command Moves Headquarters to Springs," *Gazette Telegraph,* November 16, 1950; "Defense Area Designation, Building Spurt Seen for City," *Gazette Telegraph,* January 1, 1951; "Military Housing Offices Are Moved Back to Chamber," *Gazette Telegraph,* February 9, 1951; "Rental Unit Programs Await Action on Housing Measure," *Gazette Telegraph,* May 25, 1951.

11. On the status of the military in U.S. society, see Janowitz, 1960.

12. Fort Carson, 1986: 38–39.

13. The 1950s generally was a time when industrial recruitment became a general local development activity.

14. For an analysis of the technical branch plant and its locational tendencies, see Glasmeier, 1986.

15. It is likely that Kaman's military client strongly urged it to locate away from the major defense industrial complexes, in concert with its general policy of favoring interior sites for strategic reasons. Kaman Sciences in 1986 remains 94 percent DOD-dependent, working simultaneously on more than 200 contracts.

16. Hewlett-Packard reported that size mattered a lot. Hewlett-Packard's growth

in Loveland created problems, it was reported, because it was too small. Within a couple years of its birth, the branch plant needs for water and electricity were anticipated to exceed the entire city of Loveland's needs in five or six years.

17. In addition to Hewlett-Packard and Kaman, the Springs attracted branch plants of Ampex and Litton in the 1960s. The latter closed down and reopened later.

18. Fort Carson, 1986: 37–38.

19. Committee for Community Quality Economic Development, 1971: 1–3.

20. The committee also noted that "the constant fundraising problems of our most beneficial cultural and charitable endeavors, and the underemployment of our skilled, well-educated and highly productive work force." The concern with the relatively low incomes of community residents is interesting and suggests that the development industry had a conscious stake in attracting higher-paying jobs, which would translate into higher housing prices, higher taxes for infrastructure, and general community cultural improvement.

21. Committee for Community Quality Economic Development, 1971.

22. One fascinating aspect of the Springs' economic-development effort is that it has always been almost exclusively a private-sector activity. The Chamber of Commerce, reported one interviewee, "is the city's strongest intra-community organization. It serves so many groups—the military, the cultural community, the economy." It does appear to have been a very effective and relatively unique organization, perhaps because of the scale of the community and the relative unity of goals among most major actors. Even in the 1980s, the economic-development agency for the city was privately funded and operated out of the Chamber of Commerce. The chamber directs the activities of 20 employees and 500 volunteers on a budget of $500,000, with no public funds beyond interim contributions of $50,000 each from the city and county budgets.

23. For the evolution of western environmentalism and its political manifestations in Colorado, see Markusen, 1987b: chap. 9. On the anatomy of local growth control, see Greenberg, 1986.

24. These are drawn from a more extensive list supplied by the Economic Development Council, entitled "Companies Locating Initially or Expanding in Colorado Springs, 1975–1986." There are several dozen non-high-tech firms also listed, spanning simple manufacturing and services. However, the high-tech companies in Table 8.2 account for the bulk of new jobs created—over 60 percent of the growth claimed by the EDC, not counting Kaman or Hewlett-Packard.

25. Surveyed in the mid-1980s, Springs' high-tech firms reported that 53 percent of their sales were dedicated to the plant's parent company (Roso, 1987: 11). Inmos, Litton, and Digital reported that a fair amount of their product turned up in equipment purchased by the government for defense. Inmos, for instance, make a pilot line of semiconductors in Colorado Springs and does some new product development, which it sells as components for F-16 fighters, the space shuttle, and guidance systems, as well as in computers and automobiles. Only about 25 percent of the high-tech manufacturing done in Colorado Springs is directly defense-related.

26. Litton noted that military managers sometimes have difficulty adjusting. They are used to rigid hierarchy, more formality, and certain perks like reserved parking, which commercial companies and their employees find difficult to stomach.

27. United Bank of Colorado, 1986: 6.

28. For an explanation of the relationship between the role of labor and the theory of location, see Storper and Walker, 1983.

29. As Tom Fuller, staff historian for the Space Command complex, put it: "High-

tech companies may believe that high tech is autonomous in Colorado Springs, but I don't think they would be here without the military stuff."

30. Hill reported that the advantages of the connection with Cheyenne Mountain were almost lost when it was discovered that Fort Carson land on which CSOC was planned could not be used, since it was too close to the mountain to permit observance of satellites. "But I didn't want to eliminate Colorado Springs," said Hill. "I thought the proximity still outweighed other factors. So we found a site to the east, which was state-owned and available." That kept Colorado Springs in the running.

31. Memo from Tom Fuller, historian at CSOC headquarters in Colorado Springs.

32. It is still unclear whether Hart's committee membership played a role in the Air Force's choice. It could be that the Air Force needed Hart's support for the appropriation and therefore leaned toward the Springs. However, it may be that Hart worked his way onto that subcommittee precisely because of this Air Force constituency within his jurisdiction. This is one more instance of the complex interconnections between Congress and the Pentagon drawn in Chapter 3. However, almost to a man, past and present key military decision-makers pooh-poohed the notion that politics matters in siting decisions.

33. BDM was purchased by Ford Aerospace in July 1988. Eventually, its Colorado Springs operations will be merged with the Ford complex.

34. Nancy John, "Ford Ready to Produce New Circuit," *Gazette Telegraph,* February 23, 1986: EE22.

35. Interestingly, TRW and Bettway, himself, had been working on CSOC since 1975, in its earlier planning phases. TRW supported a site-selection study for the Air Force, surveying possible sites and settling on the two that did emerge as the final competitors—Colorado Springs and White Sands, New Mexico.

36. Perhaps the difference lies in the two managers' own backgrounds. Bettway came to his job via a Ph.D. in engineering and a stint at Hughes before TRW. Rankin joined Army ROTC while getting his B.S. in engineering, and subsequently served three years.

37. Ford, for instance, has financed a $1 million simulation facility as part of its effort to win a major role in SDI battle management and systems integration work. Ford calls it the prototype Strategic Defense Initiative command center, and plans to use it for experiments on human intervention in battle management–C^3 functions of a future strategic defense system (*Aviation and Space Weekly,* November 9, 1987: 27).

38. Raschke, 1986: 37. The Atrium was built on spec by Van-Tex operations in the mid-1980s. Its location was central—three miles from Peterson Air Force Base, three miles from the Chitlaw Building (where Space Command is located), and not much farther from Cheyenne Mountain.

39. Nationally, Rockwell has about $600 million in SDI contracts.

40. See Roso, 1987: 19. He distinguishes between R&D labs and other services. However, his category "R&D labs" is a misnomer. Roso worked with ES202 data, where apparently most SETA contractors were so classified. In our view, most of them should be in the computer-software, data-processing, or professional-services categories. For a discussion of SIC classification problems, see Roso, 1986: 5–6.

41. United Bank of Colorado, 1986: 8. In 1986, 1,300 employees were laid off in Springs' electronics firms, following 800 in 1985 (Economic Development Council, 1986: 19). The 1986 cuts included 450 at Inmos, 202 at Hewlett-Packard, 423 at TRW, 105 at Ampex, 75 at Honeywell, and 40 at Brown Disc.

42. See Nancy John, "Litton Ends Decade in City with Expansion of Facility," *Gazettte Telegraph,* February 23, 1986; Brad Johnson, "Litton Awaiting Contract,"

Gazette Telegraph, January 15, 1987. In other instances, Honeywell opened a new Colorado Springs very-high-speed integrated circuit (VHSIC) facility in 1985. Much of the product of this facility ends up in military gear. United Technologies Corporation's presence was bolstered in 1986 when it was awarded a $1.8 million contract to evaluate and test software for the Department of Defense.

43. Also, plentiful labor was a factor. Cray's three-person search team looked primarily at Colorado, Arizona, Texas, New Mexico, and Utah. California was dismissed as saturated with high-tech firms. Cray did not seek any financial incentives from Inmos or the city (see Jeff Thomas, "New Supercomputer to Be Built in the Springs," *Gazette Telegraph*, April 1, 1988: 1–3).

44. United Bank of Colorado, 1986: 6.

45. Colorado, Department of Labor and Employment, 1986. This Springs' growth presaged a statewide boom in which DOD spending was expected to grow from $2.6 billion a year to $4 billion by 1990.

46. Roso, 1986: ii. Fifty percent is tied to the remainder of the United States and 6 percent to foreign markets; the rest is chiefly military.

47. Litton, for instance, manufactures an F-15 fighter jet command and control system which is sold to Japan.

48. See "Military Bases: Shields Against Recession," *U.S. News & World Report*, September 27, 1982. To some extent, the town's economy is diversified among defense functions, so that if Star Wars becomes less fashionable, the maintenance of conventional forces at Fort Carson will counterbalance Space Command–related cuts. And, of course, the academy is completely acyclical. Nevertheless, cutbacks in Star Wars would have serious repercussions for Colorado Springs.

49. Roso, 1987; United Bank of Colorado, 1986: 7.

50. United Bank of Colorado, 1986: 7.

51. Ibid.: 33. Miernyk (1967), in an early study of the impact of space activity on the nearby Boulder economy, found a relatively low output multiplier also, on the order of 1.72.

52. Cited in Wayne Hellman, "CSOC Will Not Bring County Economic Bliss, Study Says," *Gazette Telegraph*, January 9, 1986.

53. Joan Lowy, "State's Future Rockets," *Rocky Mountain News*, January 9, 1986: 1.

54. See Roso, 1987: iii.

55. Roso, 1986. His estimates, based on a rigorous methodology and assuming the most optimistic outcomes, fall far below the military's own estimate of 5.3 percent. See Colonel James Menees, Comptroller, U.S. Air Force, "Total Estimated Economic Impact of the New Space Command Programs on the Colorado Springs' Areas," May 19, 1983 (mimeo).

56. Raschke, 1986: 38; Dick Foster, "Economist Doubts Space Center's Impact," *Rocky Mountain News*, January 9, 1986: 40. Several consultants have produced more optimistic assessments than Roso's. See Sue McMillin, "$508-Million SDI Contract is Awarded," *Gazette Telegraph*, January 23, 1988.

57. Cited in Kris Newcomer, "Star Wars Test Site to Cost $89 Million, Employ 2500," *Rocky Mountain News*, June 26, 1986: 6. Training activities for space control will expand activities at the Springs facilities. By 1988, the Air Force planned to train 1,500 to 1,600 people a year in space operations. See Susan Leonard, "Springs Becomes Training Center," *Gazette Telegraph*, February 16, 1986: B1.

58. Ancel Martinez, "Olympic Center Draws Thousands," *Gazette Telegraph*, February 22, 1987. The Chamber of Commerce put together an attractive package

for the committee, including the donation of old Ent Air Force base facilities, offers of use of Air Force Academy recreational facilities, and guarantees of volunteer coaching by academy and military personnel. In its presentation to the committee, the chamber emphasized its long track record in "providing task forces to attract and help build" Fort Carson, Peterson Field, Ent Air Force Base, NORAD, UCCS, the unified Space Command, and the Air Force Academy: "Colorado Springs is proud of all these fine institutions, their staffs and their participants and the collosal [*sic*] impacts they have on this community from a cultural, social and economic standpoint" (letter from K. Freyschlag to Robert Helmick, president of the United States Olympic Committee, February 26, 1986).

59. Captain Larivee of the Air Force Academy disagrees with this forecast. He believes that Air Force Academy graduates are and will always be a minority in the Air Force.

60. Among other things, the Colorado Springs effort is no longer as unique as it once was. Most medium-size communities, and larger, have similar economic-development offices and most make more or less the same pitch.

Chapter 9

1. Boquet, 1986: 218–19.
2. Abbott, 1987: 19, quoting Malecki, 1981: 19–35.
3. Boquet, 1986: 218–19.
4. Green, 1962: 4, 36, 192; Gutheim, 1977: 27, 57.
5. Anderton, 1978: introduction; Hansen 1987, 11, 20–21, 233, 241–42.
6. Boquet, 1986: 225.
7. Hitch, 1965: 15–17.
8. Ibid.: 23, 28–29, 39.
9. Ibid.: 63, 67; Murdock, 1974: 47, 75–76, 83–84, 86, 92–93.
10. Stubbing and Mendel, 1986: 70, 109, 111.
11. Ibid.: 79, 111–16, 135; Schlesinger, 1985: 257.
12. Stubbing and Mendel, 1986: 375–76, 393.
13. Ibid.: 45–46.
14. Ibid.: 30, 43, 51.
15. Boquet, 1986: 222.
16. Gutheim, 1977: 221; Green, 1963: 446, 470.
17. Gurney, 1964: 2–3, Gutheim, 1977: 204, 224–25; Green, 1963: 470.
18. Gurney, 1964: 5; Gutheim, 1977: 198, 223, 263, 276–77, 281.
19. Gutheim, 1977: 245, 263, 281–82, 309. The House Subcommittee on Military Installations has been investigating the lucrative leases charged for this space and is considering outright purchase or construction as an alternative. Although we did not have time to investigate such links, we believe that real-estate interests may have been in cahoots with Pentagon personnel over the terms of leasing of such space.
20. Miller, 1987: 79; Boquet, 1986: 222.
21. Boquet, 1986: 225; Bernard Wysocki, Jr., "The New Boom Towns," *Wall Street Journal,* March 27, 1989: B1; Jeffrey A. Tannenbaum, "In Herndon, Va., Growth Elicits Some Mixed Feelings," *Wall Street Journal,* March 30, 1989: B1.
22. Boquet, 1986: 222, 224.
23. Fuller, 1984: 21–23.

24. The Farmingdale facility was closed in 1987, and the site is to be sold by Banner, the new owners.

25. Boquet, 1986: 222.

26. Thus it purchased INSAT, a North Carolina company that manufactures large-scale integrated circuits and micro-devices, renaming it Spectrum Microdevices and moving it to Frederick as an in-house submanufacturer. It also bought a satellite company to own satellites and rent them to long-distance users, but sold it after five years. It took over a Long Island company (CONTEC Data Products Division), renamed it Fairchild Data Products, and relocated in Scottsdale, Arizona. This facility houses the company's nonmilitary, commercial operations. Many stem from a small company originally located in Frederick, and chiefly concerned with manufacturing earth stations for satellite communications; this has been relocated in Scottsdale and the expert labor taken to Arizona. The Frederick facility is still used for manufacturing and repairing. The company has also bought facilities in Florida and Arizona, but found it easier simply to leave them there.

27. Later it diversified into civilian activities where it manufactured auto parts.

28. These groups together constitute the electronics and defense (later space and defense) sector.

29. TRW had a major operation on security, and the customer insisted on an East Coast location because this was a joint development operation. WIMEX, a large classified program, was big enough to justify a new division.

30. Expansion brought administrative reorganization. TRW's Electronic and Defense Systems Group was split into separate groups in 1982. Pending consolidation at Fair Lake, the Electronic Systems Group and the Defense Systems Group are presently located in a major office complex at Rosslyn. The Federal Systems Group, which was separated only in 1986, is at Tyson's Corner a little farther out along the corridor, at the intersection of Highways 122 and 123. Other groups—Space and Technology, and Operations and Support—also deal with defense. The Electronic Systems Group does a great deal of work for the Pentagon. Air Force work is the biggest, followed by the intelligence agencies, the Navy, and NASA. The Space Technology Group has about the same division of work; Defense Systems has a more even split, while the Federal Systems Group is anywhere and everywhere.

31. Major commands also had headquarters organizations outside Washington, but none as big as here, and, besides, co-development is done here.

32. Goddard, 1973; Goddard and Morris, 1975.

33. Hall et al., 1987.

Chapter 10

1. Markusen and Carlson, 1989: Table 6; Shapira, 1986.

2. Clayton, 1970: 34, 80; Tiebout, 1966.

3. Camden on General Dynamics, Marietta on Lockheed.

4. Scarce resources prevented us from interviewing contractors and other relevant parties in key places like Florida, Huntsville, Wichita, San Diego, and other defense–industrial cities. For a sampling of studies on these regions see Schlesenger, Gaventa, and Merrifield (1983) on the upper South; Zlatkovich (1978) on Wichita Falls; Levy (1972) on San Diego; Tansik and Billings (1971) on Arizona; Clayton (1967) on central Utah; Bowen (1971) on Alaska; Mulhern (1981) and Glickman (1977) on Philadelphia; Siegel (1983) on Huntsville; Kahley (1982) and "Space Age Boom Is Bringing a

Revolution to the Southeast," *New York Times*, August 23, 1963, on the Southeast; Johnson (1978) and Osterbind (1967) on Florida; Maki et al. (1989) on Minnesota; and the chapters on various cities in Lotchin (1984).

5. See, for instance, Anderson, 1983; Anderson, Frisch, and Oden, 1986.

6. Particularly, Vance (1970) and Jacobs (1984) on new urban frontiers; Aydalot (1988, 1986b) and Aydalot and Keeble (1988b) on the creative milieu; Andersson (1985a, 1985b) and Andersson and Strömquist (1988) on the creative city; and Scott (1982, 1983a, 1985, 1986b, 1986c) on the concept of the productive complex.

7. Nash, 1985; Gottlieb and Wiley, 1982; Mollenkopf, 1983.

8. Mollenkopf (1983) argues that, in general, conflictual city-level politics has been an inducement to Sunbelt-oriented migration on the part of private-sector firms. But for defense activity, it appears not to be true in the aggregate, especially for New England.

9. For a summary of studies on New England from the 1950s, see Markusen, 1987b: 117–20.

10. For a discussion of wartime prohibition, see Rosenberg (forthcoming): chap. 2.

11. See Chinitz, 1960; Markusen, 1985b.

12. Barff and Knight (1987) show that the timing of New England's employment turnaround is closely associated with defense buildups. See also Harrison and Kluver (1989) for a discussion of New England's defense industries.

13. See also the articles in Lotchin (1984), especially those on California (Schiesl) and San Antonio (Johnson), and Lotchin's (1979, 1982) studies of competition among California cities.

14. One of us is just completing such a study (Markusen, 1991).

15. For a discussion of ways in which military spending has operated as an informal urban policy, see Bolton, 1979.

16. For a discussion of the caucus's efforts to redirect more federal spending, including defense dollars, into the industrial heartland, see Markusen, 1987b: chap. 8.

17. Markusen, 1987b: 136. Support for the relationship between defense expenditure and regional growth through the 1960s can be found in Bolton, 1966.

18. For an exposition of how unevenly Sunbelt growth has visited the South, see Glickman and Glasmeier, 1989. Harrison and Kluver (1989) show that the Greater Boston area accounts for almost all of Massachusetts' income gains in the last decade.

19. Markusen and Carlson, 1988: Table 1.

20. See, for instance, Saxenian, 1985a; Scott, 1986b; the contributions in Lampe, 1988.

21. For an eloquent statement, see Stowsky, 1986a, 1986b.

22. For a fuller exposition of this argument about the social costs of uneven development, see Markusen, 1977.

23. On the socioeconomic makeup of defense workers, see Markusen, 1987a, 1989.

24. For evidence, see Barry Bluestone and Bennett Harrison, "The Grim Truth About the Job 'Miracle,' " *New York Times,* February 1, 1987: D2.

25. Not all regions that have shared in the military buildup vote consistently conservatively—New England is an example. But New England has not experienced a major population increase; indeed, it has suffered net population outmigration over the entire postwar period, and, even in the 1980s, the defense buildup was associated with lower population-growth rates than the nation's and continued outmigration.

Thus the buildup in New England has not stemmed the geopolitical shift to the South, although it has prevented New England from losing as many congressional districts as the Great Lakes states (Northeast Midwest Institute, 1990).

26. See, for example, the comments of Congressman Jamie Whitten, Democrat of Mississippi, in the 1960s on the way in which the Pentagon explicitly arrayed military-spending requests by congressional districts (quoted in Lens, 1970: 44).

27. Johnson (1982) is the standard source for the "developmental state."

References

Abbott, Carl. 1981. *Boosters and Businessmen: Popular Economic Thought and Urban Growth in the Antebellum Middle West.* Westport, Conn.: Greenwood Press.

Abbott, Carl. 1987. *The New Urban America: Growth and Politics in Sunbelt Cities.* Chapel Hill: University of North Carolina Press.

Ackland, Len. 1984. "Fighting for Time: How a Small Band of Scientists is Struggling to Tame the Nuclear Monster." *Chicago Tribune Magazine* (March 11): A7.

Adams, Gordon. 1981. *The Iron Triangle: The Politics of Defense Contracting.* New York: Council on Economic Priorities.

Adams, Leonard. 1951. *Wartime Manpower Mobilization: A Study of World War II Experience in the Buffalo–Niagara Area.* Cornell Studies in Industrial and Labor Relations, vol. 1. Ithaca, N.Y.: Cornell University Press.

Adams, Walter, and William James Adams. 1982. "The Military–Industrial Complex: A Market Structure Analysis." *Papers and Proceedings* (American Economic Association) 62: 279–87.

Ainsworth, Edward M. 1959. *Memories in the City of Dreams: A Tribute to Harry Chandler, Gran Benefactor de la Ciudad.* Los Angeles: Privately printed.

Allardice, Corbin, and Ernest R. Trapnell. 1974. *The Atomic Energy Commission.* New York: Praeger.

Allen, Thomas Lee. 1972. "Aerospace Cutbacks: Impact on the Companies and Engineering Employment in Southern California." Ph.D. diss., Massachusetts Institute of Technology.

Anderson, James. 1983. *Bankrupting American Cities: The Tax Burden and Expenditures of the Pentagon by Metropolitan Area.* Lansing, Mich.: Employment Research Associates.

Anderson, Marion, Michael Frisch, and Michael Oden. 1986. *The Empty Pork Barrel: The Employment Cost of the Military Buildup, 1981–85.* Lansing, Mich.: Employment Research Associates.

Anderson, Roy A. 1983. *A Look at Lockheed.* New York: Newcomen Society in North America.

Andersson, Åke E. 1985a. "Creativity and Regional Development." *Papers of the Regional Science Association* 56: 5–20.

Andersson, Åke E. 1985b. *Kreativitet: StorStadens Framtid.* Stockholm: Prisma.

Andersson, Åke E., and Ulf Strömquist. 1988. *K—Samhällets Framtid.* Stockholm: Prisma.

Anderton, David A. 1978. *Sixty Years of Aeronautical Research 1917–1977.* Washington, D.C.: National Aeronautics and Space Administration.

Armacost, Michael H. 1969. *The Politics of Weapons Innovation: The Thor–Jupiter Controversy*. New York: Columbia University Press.

Armitage, M. J., and R. A. Mason. 1983. *Air Power in the Nuclear Age*. Urbana: University of Illinois Press.

Arnold, Henry H. 1949. *Global Mission*. New York: Harper and Brothers.

Arrington, Leonard, and George Jensen. 1964. "The Defense Industry of Utah." Department of Economics, Utah State University, Utah State Planning Program, Economic and Population Studies.

Arrington, Leonard J., and Jon G. Perry. 1962. "Utah's Spectacular Missiles Industry: Its History and Impact." *Utah Historical Quarterly* 30: 3–39.

Art, Robert J. 1968. *The TFX Decision: McNamara and the Military*. Boston: Little, Brown.

Art, Robert J., Vincent Davis, and Samuel P. Huntington, eds. 1985. *Reorganizing America's Defense: Leadership in War and Peace*. Washington, D.C.: Pergamon-Brassey's.

Atwood, J. Leland. 1970. *North American Rockwell: Storehouse of High Technology*. New York: Newcomen Society in North America.

Aydalot, Philippe, ed. 1986a. *Milieux innovateurs en Europe*. Paris: GREMI (privately printed).

Aydalot, Philippe. 1986b. "Trajectoires technologiques et milieux innovateurs." In *Milieux innovateurs en Europe,* ed. Philippe Aydalot. Paris: GREMI (privately printed).

Aydalot, Philippe. 1988. "Technological Trajectories and Regional Innovation in Europe." In *High Technology Industry and Innovative Environments: The European Experience,* ed. Philippe Aydalot and David Keeble. London: Routledge and Kegan Paul.

Aydalot, Philippe, and David Keeble, eds. 1988a. *High Technology Industry and Innovative Environments: The European Experience*. London: Routledge and Kegan Paul.

Aydalot, Philippe, and David Keeble. 1988b. "High Technology Industry and Innovative Environments in Europe: An Overview." In *High Technology Industry and Innovative Environments: The European Experience,* ed. Philippe Aydalot and David Keeble. London: Routledge and Kegan Paul.

Bain, Trevor. 1973. "Labor Market Experience for Engineers During Periods of Changing Demand." Final report. Office of Research and Development, Manpower Administration, Department of Labor, Washington, D.C.

Baldwin, William L. 1967. *The Structure of the Defense Market, 1955–1964*. Durham, N.C.: Duke University Press.

Ball, John D. 1962. *Edwards: Flight Test Center of the U.S.A.F.* New York: Duell, Sloan & Pearce.

Barff, Richard A., and Prentice L. Knight III. 1987. "Military Spending, High Technology Industry, and the Timing of the New England Employment Turnaround." Working paper. Department of Geography, Dartmouth College, Hanover, New Hampshire.

Barff, Richard A., and Prentice L. Knight III. 1988. "The Role of Federal Military Spending in the Timing of the New England Employment Turnaround." *Papers of the Regional Science Association,* 65: 151–66.

Barnes, C. Taylor. 1987. "Military Installations as Determinants of Military Retirement Migration." Paper presented at the twenty-sixth annual meeting of the Western Regional Science Association, Kona, Hawaii (February).

Barnes, C. Taylor, and Curtis C. Roseman. 1981. "The Effect of Military Retirement on Population Redistribution." *Texas Business Review* 55: 100–4.

Bartlett, Donald L., and James B. Steele. 1979. *Empire: The Life, Legend, and Madness of Howard Hughes*. New York: Norton.

Batteau, Allen W., and Michelle S. Meyer. 1986. *Federal Spending: An Illinois Handbook*. Washington, D.C.: Institute for Illinois.

Bean, Kevin, Kevin Cassidy, Marta Daniels, Edward Deak, and Philip Lane. 1986. "Hitting Home: The Nuclear Freeze and the Defense-Dependent Economy of Connecticut." *Social Science Journal* 23: 123–34.

Beard, Edmund. 1976. *Developing the ICBM: A Study in Bureaucratic Politics*. New York: Columbia University Press.

Berges, Marshall. 1984. *The Life and Times of Los Angeles: A Newspaper, a Family, and a City*. New York: Atheneum.

Beringer, Sara M. 1955. *Dayton Industries*. Dayton: Privately printed.

Bezdek, R. 1975. "The 1980 Impact—Regional and Occupational—of Compensated Shifts in Defense Spending." *Journal of Regional Science* 15.

Biederman, Harry R. 1985. "The Aerospace Outlook for the U.S. and California." In *Proceedings of the UCLA Business Forecasting Conference*. Los Angeles: UCLA Business Forecasting Project, Graduate School of Management.

Bilstein, Roger E. 1984. *Flight in America, 1900–1983: From the Wrights to the Astronauts*. Baltimore: Johns Hopkins University Press.

Bland, William M. 1964. "Project Mercury." In *The History of Rocket Technology: Essays on Research, Development, and Utility*, ed. Eugene M. Emme. Detroit: Wayne State University Press.

Bloch, Robin. 1987. "Studies in the Development of the United States Aerospace Industry." Working paper (D-875). School of Architecture and Urban Planning, University of California, Los Angeles.

Bluestone, Barry, and Bennett Harrison. 1982. *The Deindustrialization of America: Plant Closings, Community Abandonment, and the Dismantling of Basic Industry*. New York: Basic Books.

Bluestone, Barry, Peter Jordan, and Mark Sullivan. 1981. *Aircraft Industry Dynamics: An Analysis of Competition, Capital, and Labor*. Boston: Auburn House.

Boddy, Martin, John Lovering, and Keith Bassett. 1986. *Sunbelt City: A Study of Economic Change in Britian's M4 Growth Corridor*. Oxford: Oxford University Press.

Boeing Company. n.d. *Portfolio of Opportunities*.

Boeing Company. *Boeing News* (various issues).

Boeing Company. 1977. *Pedigree of Champions. Boeing Since 1916*. 4th ed.

Boeing Company. 1986. *Annual Report*.

Boeing Company. 1987. *Directory of Buyers: Small and Disadvantaged Business Programs*.

Bolton, R. 1966. *Defense Purchases and Regional Growth*. Washington, D.C.: Brookings Institute.

Bolton, Roger. 1979. "Impacts of Defense Spending on Urban Areas." In *The Urban Impact of Federal Policies*, ed. Norman Glickman. Baltimore: Johns Hopkins University Press.

Bombard, Owen. 1958. "The Tin Goose." *Dearborn Historical Quarterly* 8.

Bonelli, William G. 1954. *Billion Dollar Blackjack*. Beverly Hills, Calif.: Civic Research Press.

Bonnelycke, Nina J., and Michael C. Sieverts. 1985. "The Greater Seattle Area:

Center of Commerce for the Pacific Northwest." Unpublished paper. Department of City and Regional Planning, University of California, Berkeley.

Boorstin, Daniel J. 1965. *The Americans.* Vol. 2: *The National Experience.* New York: Random House.

Boquet, Yves. 1986. "Les Entreprises à technologie avancée dans la région de Washington D.C." *Bulletin de l'Association de Geographes Français* 63: 217–26.

Borrus, Michael, James Millstein, and John Zysman. 1982. "U.S.–Japanese Competition in the Semiconductor Industry: A Study in International Trade and Technological Development." *Policy Papers in International Affairs,* no. 17. Institute of International Studies, University of California, Berkeley.

Bosak, Steve. 1988. "High Tech Future Requires Brains But Also Big Capital Ideas." *Chicago Enterprise* 1: 7–9.

Boston Study Group. 1982. *The Price of Defense.* San Francisco: Freeman.

Boudeville, J.R. 1966. *Problems of Regional Economic Planning.* Edinburgh: Edinburgh University Press.

Boulet, Jean. 1982. *L'Histoire de l'helicoptère: racontée par ses pionniers, 1907–1956.* Paris: Editions France-Empire.

Bowen, B. 1971. "Defense Spending in Alaska." *Review of Business and Economic Conditions,* (University of Alaska, Institute of Social, Economic and Governmental Research) 8: 1–16.

Bowers, Peter M. 1966. *Boeing Aircraft Since 1916.* Fallbrook, Calif.: Aero Publishers.

Braun, Ernest, and Stuart Macdonald. 1978. *Revolution in Miniature: The History and Impact of Semiconductor Electronics.* Cambridge: Cambridge University Press.

Breheny, Michael, and Ronald McQuaid, eds. 1987. *The Development of High Technology Industries: An International Survey.* London: Croom Helm.

Bremner, Brian. 1986a. "Defense Spending Zooms in Cook, McHenry Counties." *Crain's Chicago Business* (April 14).

Bremner, Brian. 1986b. "Why Defense Buildup Won't Aid Illinois." *Crain's Chicago Business* (June 16): 23–26.

Bright, Arthur A. 1949. *The Electric Lamp Industry: Technological Change and Economic Development from 1800 to 1947.* New York: Macmillan.

Bright, Charles D. 1978. *The Jet Makers: The Aerospace Industry from 1945 to 1972.* Lawrence: Regents Press of Kansas.

Brock, Gerald W. 1975. *The U.S. Computer Industry: A Study of Market Power.* Cambridge, Mass.: Ballinger.

Brooks, John. 1976. *Telephone: The First Hundred Years.* New York: Harper & Row.

Brotchie, John F., Peter Hall, and Peter W. Newton, eds. 1987. *The Spatial Impact of Technological Change.* London: Croom Helm.

Browett, John. 1984. "On the Necessity and Inevitability of Uneven Spatial Development Under Capitalism." *International Journal of Urban and Regional Research* 8: 155–76.

Brown, Joseph M. 1976. *Helicopter Directory.* Newton Abbot, Eng.: David and Charles.

Browne, Lynne E. 1988. "Defense Spending and High Technology Development: National and State Issues." *New England Economic Review* (September–October): 3–22.

Browne, Lynne E., and S. Gavian, 1981. "The Importance of Defense to New England." *New England Economic Indicators* (Federal Reserve Bank of Boston) (October): A3–A6.

Brusco, Sebastiano. 1982. "The Emilian Model: Productive Decentralisation and Social Integration." *Cambridge Journal of Economics* 6: 167–84.

Burgess-Wise, David. 1987. *Ford in the Air*. Essex, Eng.: Corporate History Office, Ford Motor Company.

California. Legislature. 1972. "California Aerospace Industry: The Unemployed Aerospace Worker." Hearing Before the Joint Committee on Atomic Development and Space (January 28).

California. Office of Economic Policy, Planning, and Research. 1982. *The Effect of Increased Military Spending in California*. Sacramento: Department of Economic and Business Development.

Campbell, Scott. 1986. "The Transformation of the San Francisco Bay Area Shipping Industry and Its Regional Impacts." Working paper. Institute of Urban and Regional Development, University of California, Berkeley.

Campbell, Scott. 1990. "National Defense Migration: Labor Migration in the United States During the Second World War." *Annals of Regional Science*. Forthcoming.

Carr, Lowell Juilliard, and James Edson Stermer. 1952. *Willow Run: A Study of Industrialization and Cultural Inadequacy*. New York: Harper and Brothers.

Castells, Manuel, ed. 1985. *High Technology, Space, and Society*. Urban Affairs Annual Reviews, no. 28. Beverly Hills, Calif.: Sage.

Chandler, Charles de Forest, and Frank Lahm. 1943. *How Our Army Grew Wings*. New York: Ronald Press.

Checkland, S. 1975. *The Upas Tree*. Glasgow: Glasgow University Press.

Chinitz, Benjamin. 1961. "Contrasts in Agglomeration: New York and Pittsburgh." *Papers and Proceedings* (American Economic Association): 279–89.

Christaller, Walter. [1933] 1966. *Central Places in Southern Germany*. Translated by C. W. Baskin. Englewood Cliffs, N.J.: Prentice-Hall.

Clark, D. 1981. *Los Angeles: A City Apart*. Woodland Hills, Calif.: Windsor.

Clark, George. 1942. "The Strange Story of the Reuther Plant." *Harper's Magazine* (May).

Clayton, James. 1962. "Defense Spending: Key to California's Growth." *Western Political Quarterly* 15: 280–93.

Clayton, James. 1967. "The Impact of the Cold War on the Economies of California and Utah, 1946–1965." *Pacific Historical Review* 36: 449–73.

Clayton, James, ed. 1970. *The Economic Impact of the Cold War: Sources and Readings*. New York: Harcourt, Brace & World.

Cleveland, Reginald M. 1942. *America Fledges Wings: The History of the Daniel Guggenheim Fund for the Promotion of Aeronautics*. New York: Pitman.

Coffey, Thomas M. 1982. *HAP: The Story of the U.S. Air Force and the Man Who Built It, General Henry H. "HAP" Arnold*. New York: Viking Press.

Collison, Thomas. 1945. *The Superfortress Is Born: The Story of the Boeing B-29*. New York: Duell, Sloan & Pearce.

Colorado. Department of Labor and Employment, Division of Employment and Training. 1986. *Colorado Labor Force Summary: Data Supplement*. Denver: State of Colorado.

Committee for Community Quality Economic Development. 1971. "A Program for Quality Economic Development." Colorado Springs. Mimeo.

Commonwealth Club of California. 1946. *The Population of California*. San Francisco: Parker.

Congressional Budget Office. 1987. *Defense Spending and the Economy*. Washington, D.C.: Government Printing Office.

Cook, Fred T. 1962. *The Warfare State*. New York: Macmillan.

Coons, Arthur Gardiner. 1941. *Defense Industries and Southern California's Economy*. Los Angeles.

Copp, Dewitt S. 1980. *A Few Great Captains: The Men and Events that Shaped the Development of U.S. Air Power*. Garden City, N.Y.: Doubleday.

Corn, Joseph J. 1983. *The Winged Gospel: America's Romance with Aviation, 1900–1950*. New York: Oxford University Press.

Council on Economic Priorities. 1987. *Star Wars: The Economic Fallout*. New York: Ballinger.

Crouch, Tom. 1981. *A Dream of Wings: Americans and the Airplane, 1975–1905*. New York: Norton.

Crump, Jeffrey. 1989. "The Spatial Distribution of Military Spending in the United States, 1941–85." *Growth and Change* 20: 50–62.

Cumberland, J. 1973. "Dimensions of the Impact of Reduced Military Expenditures on Industries, Regions, and Communities." In *Economic Consequence of Reduced Military Spending*, ed. B. Udis. Lexington, Mass.: Lexington Books.

Cunningham, Frank. 1943. *Sky Master: The Story of Donald Douglas*. Philadelphia: Dorrance.

Cunningham, William G. 1951. *The Aircraft Industry: A Study in Industrial Location*. Los Angeles: Morrison.

Cutter, Susan, H. Briavel Holcolm, and Dianne Shatin. 1986. "Spatial Patterns of Support for a Nuclear Weapons Freeze." *Professional Geographer* 18: 42–52.

Cypher, James. 1981. "The Basic Economics of Re-arming America." *Monthly Review* (November).

Danelian, Norbar R. 1939. *AT&T: The Story of Industrial Conquest*. New York: Vanguard Press.

Davenport, William W. 1978. *Gyro! The Life and Times of Lawrence Sperry*. New York: Scribner.

Davis, Burke. 1967. *The Billy Mitchell Affair*. New York: Random House.

Davis, Vincent. 1967. *The Admiral's Lobby*. Chapel Hill: University of North Carolina Press.

Davis, Vincent. 1985. *The Evolution of Central U.S. Defense Management. Reorganizing America's Defense: Leadership in War and Peace,* ed. Robert J. Art, Vincent Davis, and Samuel P. Huntington. Washington, D.C.: Pergamon-Brassey's.

de Camp, Lyon S. 1961. *The Heroic Age of American Invention*. Garden City, N.Y.: Doubleday.

Decoster, Elisabeth, and Muriel Tabariés. 1986. "L'Innovation dans un pôle scientifique et technologique, le cas de la Cité Scientifique Ile de France Sud." In *Milieux innovateurs en Europe,* ed. Philippe Aydalot. Paris: GREMI (privately printed).

"Defense Shift Favors Region." 1981. *New England Business* (May 4): 12–17.

DeGrasse, Robert, Jr. 1983. *Military Expansion, Economic Decline: The Impact of Military Spending on U.S. Economic Performance*. New York: Sharpe.

Deitrick, Sabina. 1984. "Military Spending and Migration into California." Unpublished paper. Department of City and Regional Planning, University of California, Berkeley.

Dempsey, Richard, and Douglas Schmude. 1971. "Occupational Impact of Defense Expenditures." *Monthly Labor Review* (December): 12–15.

Dillaway, Diana. 1988. "Political Leadership and Economic Restructuring in a Declining City: Buffalo, New York." Master's thesis, Department of City and Regional Planning, University of California, Berkeley.

Dorfman, Nancy S. 1982. *Massachusetts' High Technology Boom in Perspective: An Investigation of Its Dimensions, Causes, and of the Role of New Firms.* Cambridge, Mass.: MIT, Center for Policy Alternatives.

Dorfman, Nancy S. 1983. "Route 128: The Development of a Regional High Technology Economy." *Research Policy* 12: 299–316.

Dornberger, Walter R. 1964. "The German V-2." In *The History of Rocket Technology: Essays on Research, Development, and Utility,* ed. Eugene M. Emme. Detroit: Wayne State University Press.

Douhet, Giulio. 1983. *The Command of the Air.* USAF Warrior Studies. Translated by D. Ferrari. Washington, D.C.: United States Air Force, Office of Air Force History.

Dumas, Lloyd. 1986. *The Overburdened Economy.* Berkeley: University of California Press.

Duncan, Beverly, and Stanley Fieberson. 1970. *Metropolis and Region in Transition.* Beverly Hills, Calif.: Sage.

Dunlap, Carol. 1982. *California People.* Salt Lake City: Peregrine Smith.

Dutton, William S. 1942. *Du Pont: One Hundred and Forty Years.* New York: Scribner.

Economic Development Council. 1986. *Annual Report 1985/1986.* Colorado Springs: Economic Development Council.

Economic Security Committee. 1986. *The Cambridge Case for Diversification Planning Towards Stability in an R & D Economy.* Cambridge, Mass.: Cambridge Peace Commission, City of Cambridge.

Ellis, Amanda. 1975. *The Colorado Springs Story.* 9th rev. ed. Colorado Springs: House of San Juan.

Emme, Eugene M., ed. 1964. *The History of Rocket Technology: Essays on Research, Development, and Utility.* Detroit: Wayne State University Press.

Erdevig, Eleanor. 1984. "The Bucks Stop Elsewhere: The Midwest's Share of Federal R&D." *Chicago Economic Perspectives* 7: 13–23.

Estall, Robert C. 1966. *New England: A Study in Industrial Adjustment.* London: Bell.

Fagen, M. D., ed. 1975. *A History of Science and Engineering in the Bell System: The Early Years (1925–1975).* Murray Hill, N.J.: Bell Telephone Laboratories.

Fagen, M.D., ed. 1978. *A History of Science and Engineering in the Bell System: National Service in War and Peace (1925–1975).* Murray Hill, N.J.: Bell Telephone Laboratories.

Fallows, James. 1981. *National Defense.* New York: Random House.

Faneuf, Leston. 1958. *Lawrence D. Bell: A Man and His Company, "Bell Aircraft."* New York: Newcomen Society in North America.

Feller, Irwin. 1975. "Invention, Diffusion, and Industrial Location." In *Locational Dynamics of Manufacturing Activity,* ed. L. Collins and D. Walker. London: Wiley.

Fernandez, Ronald. 1983. *Excess Profits: The Rise of United Technologies.* Reading, Mass.: Addison-Wesley.

Fishman, Katharine D. 1981. *The Computer Establishment.* New York: McGraw-Hill.

Ford, Henry, with Samuel Crowther. 1926. *Today and Tomorrow.* Garden City, N.Y.: Doubleday, Page.

Fort Carson, Public Affairs Office. 1986. *A Tradition of Victory.* Fort Carson, Colo.: Public Affairs Office.

Fox, J. Ronald. 1974. *Arming America: How the U.S. Buys Weapons.* Boston: Harvard University, Graduate School of Business Administration.

Frankel, Linda D., and James M. Howell. 1988. *Economic Revitalization and Job Creation in America's Oldest Industrialized Region.* In *The Massachusetts Miracle,* ed. David Lampe. Cambridge, Mass.: MIT Press.

Franklin, Roger. 1986. *The Defender: The Story of General Dynamics.* New York: Harper & Row.

Friedmann, John. 1972. "A General Theory of Polarized Development." In *Growth Centers in Regional Economic Development,* ed. Niles Hansen. New York: Free Press.

Friedman, Paul D. 1978. "Fear of Flying: The Development of the Los Angeles International Airport and the Rise of Public Protest over Jet Aircraft Noise." Master's thesis, University of California, Santa Barbara.

Fuller, Stephen S. 1984. *Federal Purchases in the Washington Metropolitan Area.* Washington, D.C.: Greater Washington Research Center.

Futrell, Robert F. 1974. *Ideas, Concepts, Doctrine: A History of Basic Thinking in the United States Air Force, 1907–1964.* Maxwell, Ala.: Air Force University. Reprint. New York: Arno Press, 1980.

Gaffard, Jean-Luc. 1986. "Restructuration de l'espace économique et trajectoires technologiques." In *Milieux innovateurs en Europe,* ed. Philippe Aydalot. Paris: GREMI (privately printed).

Gansler, Jacques S. 1980. *The Defense Industry.* Cambridge, Mass.: MIT Press.

Gansler, Jacques S. 1985. "How to Improve the Acquisition of Weapons." In *Reorganizing America's Defense: Leadership in War and Peace,* ed. Robert J. Art, Vincent Davis, and Samuel P. Huntington. Washington, D.C.: Pergamon-Brassey's.

Gavin, James H. 1958. *War and Peace in the Space Age.* New York: Harper and Brothers.

Glabb, Charles N., and A. Theodore Brown. 1976. *A History of Urban America.* 2nd ed. New York: Macmillan.

Glasmeier, Amy. 1986. "The Structure, Location, and Role of High Technology Industries in United States Regional Development." Ph.D. diss., University of California, Berkeley.

Glickman, Norman. 1977. *Regional Econometric Analysis.* New York: Academic Press.

Glickman, Norman, and Amy Glasmeier. 1989. "The International Economy and the American Sunbelt." In *Deindustrialization in the U.S.: Lessons for Japan,* ed. Lloyd Rodwin and Hidehiko Sazanami. London: Unwin Hyman.

Glines, Carroll G. 1980. *The Compact History of the United States Air Force.* 2nd rev. ed. New York: Arno Press.

Goddard, John B. 1973. "Office Linkages and Location." *Progress in Planning* 1: part 2.

Goddard, John B., and Diana Morris. 1975. *The Communications Factor in Office Decentralization.* Oxford: Pergamon Press.

Goldberg, Alfred, ed. 1957. *A History of the United States Air Force 1907–1957.* Princeton, N.J.: Van Nostrand.

Goldman, Mark. 1983. *High Hopes: The Rise and Decline of Buffalo.* Albany: State University of New York Press.

Goldstein, Harvey, and Michael Juger. 1988. "Science/Technology Parks and Regional Economic Development" Paper presented at the European Community PR Joint Sessions, Bologna, Italy.

Goodwin, Jacob. 1985. *Brotherhood of Arms: General Dynamics and the Business of Defending America.* New York: Times Books.

Gordon, Richard, and Linda Kimball. 1987. "The Impact of Industrial Structure on Global High Technology Industry." In *The Spatial Impact of Technological Change,* ed. John F. Brotchie, Peter Hall, and Peter W. Newton. London: Croom Helm.

Gottlieb, Robert, and Peter Wiley. 1982. *Empires in the Sun: The Rise of the New American West.* New York: Putnam.

Gottlieb, Robert, and Irene Wolt. 1977. *Thinking Big: The Story of the "Los Angeles Times," Its Publishers, and Their Influence on Southern California.* New York: Putnam.

Grayson, Stan. 1978. "In the Cause of Liberty: Packard in World War I." In *Packard: A History of the Motor Car and the Company,* ed. Beverly Rae Kimes. Princeton, N.J.: Princeton University Press.

Green, Constance McL. 1962. *Washington: Village and Capital, 1800–1878.* Princeton, N.J.: Princeton University Press.

Green, Constance McL. 1963. *Washington: Capital City 1879–1950.* Princeton, N.J.: Princeton University Press.

Greenberg, Douglas. 1986. "Growth and Conflict at the Urban Fringe." Ph.D. diss., University of California, Berkeley.

Greenwood, Michael, Gary Hunt, and Ellen Pfalzgraff. 1987. "The Economic Effects of Space Activities on Colorado and the Western United States." *Annals of Regional Science* 21: 21–44.

Greer, Thomas H. 1955. *The Development of Air Doctrine in the Army Air Arm, 1917–1941.* Maxwell, Ala.: Air Force University, Research Studies Institute. Reprint. Washington, D.C.: United States Air Force, Office of Air Force History, 1985.

Gurney, Gene. 1964. *The Pentagon.* New York: Crown.

Gurwitz, Aaron, Kathleen Auda, and William Greer. 1984. *Federal R & D and Defense Outlays in New York State.* Regional Economic Studies, Occasional Papers on the Economy of the Second Federal Reserve District. New York: Regional Economics Staff, Federal Reserve Bank of New York.

Gutheim, Frederick. 1977. *Worthy of the Nation: The History of Planning for the Nation's Capital.* Washington D.C.: Smithsonian Institution.

Haber, Ludwig F. 1958. *The Chemical Industry During the Nineteenth Century: A Study of the Economic Aspect of Applied Chemistry in Europe and North America.* Oxford: Oxford University Press.

Haber, Ludwig F. 1971. *The Chemical Industry 1900–1930: International Growth and Technological Change.* Oxford: Oxford University Press.

Hagen, John P. 1964. "The Viking and the Vanguard." In *The History of Rocket Technology: Essays on Research, Development, and Utility,* ed. Eugene M. Emme. Detroit: Wayne State University Press.

Hägerstrand, Torsten. 1967. *Innovation Diffusion as a Spatial Process.* Chicago: University of Chicago Press.

Halberstam, David. 1986. *The Reckoning.* New York: Morrow.

Hall, Peter. 1988. "The Creation of the American Aerospace Complex, 1955–65: A Study in Industrial Inertia." In *Defence Expenditure and Regional Development,* ed. Michael Breheny. London: Mansell.

Hall, Peter, Michael Breheny, Ronald McQuaid, and Douglas Hart. 1987. *Western Sunrise: The Genesis and Growth of Britain's Major High Tech Corridor*. London: Allen and Unwin.

Hall, Peter, and Ann R. Markusen, eds. 1985. *Silicon Landscapes*. Boston: Allen and Unwin.

Hall, Peter, Ann R. Markusen, Richard Osborne, and Barbara Wachsman. 1983. "The American Computer Software Industry: Economic Development Prospects." *Built Environment* 9: 29–39.

Hall, Peter, and Paschal Preston. 1988. *The Carrier Wave: New Information Technology and the Geography of Innovation, 1846–2003*. London: Unwin Hyman.

Hallion, Richard P. 1977. *Legacy of Flight: The Guggenheim Contribution to American Aviation*. Seattle: University of Washington Press.

Hallion, Richard P., ed. 1978a. *The Wright Brothers: Heirs of Prometheus*. Washington, D.C.: Smithsonian Institution.

Hallion, Richard P. 1978b. "Introduction." In *The Wright Brothers: Heirs of Prometheus,* ed. Richard P. Hallion. Washington, D.C.: Smithsonian Institution.

Hallion, Richard P. 1978c. "The Wright Brothers: A Photographic Essay." In *The Wright Brothers: Heirs of Prometheus,* ed. Richard P. Hallion. Washington, D.C.: Smithsonian Institution.

Hamilton, George, and Dwight Heinmuller. 1978. "In the Nation's Defense: Packard in World War II." In *Packard: A History of the Motor Car and the Company,* ed. Beverly Rae Kimes. Princeton, N.J.: Princeton University Press.

Hanle, Paul A. 1982. *Bringing Aerodynamics to America*. Cambridge, Mass.: MIT Press.

Hansen, James R. 1987. *Engineer in Charge: A History of the Langley Aeronautical Laboratory, 1917–1958*. Washington, D.C.: National Aeronautics and Space Administration.

Harrison, Bennett, and Jean Kluver. 1989. "Re-assessing the 'Massachusetts Miracle': The Sources and Patterns of Employment and Economic Growth in the Revitalization of a 'Mature' Region." In *Deindustrialization in the U.S.: Lessons for Japan,* ed. Lloyd Rodwin and Hidehiko Sazanami. London: Unwin Hyman.

Hart, Jack R. 1981. *The Information Empire: The Rise of the "Los Angeles Times" and the Times Mirror Corporation*. Washington, D.C.: University Press of America.

Hartung, William, et al. 1985. *The Strategic Defense Initiative: Costs, Contractors, and Consequences*. New York: Council on Economic Priorities.

Hatfield, D. D. 1973. *Los Angeles Aeronautics 1920–1929*. Inglewood, Calif.: Northrop Institute of Technology.

Haynes, Williams. 1949. *American Chemical Industry*. Vol. 1: *Background and Beginnings*. New York: Norstrand.

Haynes, Williams. 1954. *American Chemical Industry*. Vol. 6: *The Chemical Companies*. New York: Norstrand.

Heims, Steve J. 1980. *John von Neumann and Norbert Wiener: From Mathematics to the Technologies of Life and Death*. Cambridge, Mass.: MIT Press.

Heise, J. A. 1969. *The Brass Factories: A Frank Appraisal of West Point, Annapolis, and the Air Force Academy*. Washington, D.C.: Public Affairs Press.

Hekman, John S. 1978. "An Analysis of the Changing Location of Iron and Steel Production in the Twentieth Century." *American Economic Review* 68: 123–33.

Hekman, John S., and John S. Strong. 1981. "The Evolution of New England Industry." *New England Economic Review* (March–April): 35–46.

Henderson, Jeffrey, and Allen J. Scott. 1987. "The Growth and Internationalization of the American Semiconductor Industry: Labour Processes and the Changing Spatial Organization of Production." In *The Development of High Technology Industries: An International Survey,* ed. Michael Breheny and Ronald McQuaid. London: Croom Helm.

Henry, David, and Richard Oliver. 1987. "The Defense Buildup, 1977–85: Effects on Production and Employment." *Monthly Labor Review* (August): 3–11.

Henstell, Bruce. 1981. "A Sky-Minded City." In *Los Angeles, 1781–1981,* ed. L. L. Meyer. San Francisco: California Historical Society.

Herken, Gregg. 1985. *Counsels of War.* New York: Knopf.

Herrera, Philip. 1967. "Megalopolis Comes to the Northeast." *Fortune* (December): 57–58.

Hewlett, Richard G., and Oscar E. Anderson, Jr. 1962. *The New World, 1939/1946.* Vol. 1 of *A History of the United States Atomic Energy Commission.* University Park: Pennsylvania State University Press.

Hewlett, Richard G., and Francis Duncan. 1969. *Atomic Shield, 1947/1952.* Vol. 2 of *A History of the United States Atomic Energy Commission.* University Park: Pennsylvania State University Press.

Higman, Robin. 1972. *Air Power: A Concise History.* New York: St. Martin's Press.

Hitch, Charles J. 1965. *Decision-Making for Defense.* Berkeley: University of California Press.

Holland, David, and Philip Wandschneider. 1989. "U.S. Military Expenditures: Their Impact on the Washington Economy." Preliminary report. Department of Agricultural Economics, Washington State University, Pullman.

Holley, Irving B. 1953. *Ideas and Weapons: Exploitation of the Aerial Weapon by the United States During World War I—Study in the Relationship of Technological Advance, Military Doctrine, and the Development of Weapons.* Hew Haven, Conn.: Yale University Press.

Holley, Irving B. 1964. *Buying Aircraft: Matériel Procurement for the Army Air Forces.* Washington, D.C.: Department of the Army, Office of the Chief of Military History.

Horgan, James J. 1964. *City of Flight: The History of Aviation in St. Louis.* Gerald, Mo.: Patrice Press.

Horner, Horace M. 1958. *The United Aircraft Story.* New York: Newcomen Society in North America.

Howard, Fred. 1987. *Wilbur and Orville: A Biography of the Wright Brothers.* New York: Knopf.

Hughes, Thomas P. 1964. *The Development of Modern Technology Since 1500.* New York: Macmillian.

Hughes, Thomas P. 1971. *Elmer Sperry: Inventor and Engineer.* Baltimore: Johns Hopkins University Press.

Huie, William B. 1942. *The Fight for Air Power.* New York: Fischer.

Huntington, Samuel P. 1957. *The Soldier and the State: The Theory and Politics of Civil/Military Relations.* Cambridge, Mass.: Belknap Press.

Huntington, Samuel P. 1985. "Organization and Strategy." In *Reorganizing America's Defense: Leadership in War and Peace,* ed. Robert J. Art, Vincent Davis, and Samuel P. Huntingdon. Washington, D.C.: Pergamon-Brassey's.

Huntington, Samuel P., ed. 1962. *Changing Patterns of Military Politics.* New York: Free Press.

Hurley, Alfred F. 1975. *Billy Mitchell: Crusader for Air Power.* Bloomington: Indiana University Press.

Hymer, Stephen. 1973. "The Multinational Corporation and the Law of Uneven

Development." In *Economic and World Order*, ed. J. W. Baghwati. New York: Macmillan.

Ingells, Douglas. 1968. *The Tin Goose: The Fabulous Ford Tri-Motor*. Fallbrook, Calif.: Aero Publishers.

Isard, Walter. 1956. *Location and Space Economy*. New York: Wiley.

Isard, Walter, and Eugene W. Schooler. 1964. "An Economic Analysis of Local and Regional Impacts of Military Expenditures." *Peace Research Society Papers*, l: 15–44.

Isikoff, Michael. 1968. "NASA's Plan for Its Own Rocket Plant Sets Off a Fiery Battle." *Washington Post National Weekly* (March 21–27): 31–32.

Jacobs, Jane. 1964. *Cities and the Wealth of Nations: Principles of Economic Life*. New York: Random House.

Janowitz, Morris. 1960. *The Professional Soldier: A Social and Political Portrait*. New York: Free Press.

Johansson, Börje. 1987. "Information Technology and the Viability of Spatial Networks." *Papers of the Regional Science Association* 61: 51–64.

Johannsson, Börje, and Lars Westin. 1987. "Technical Change, Location, and Trade." *Papers of the Regional Science Association* 62: 13–25.

Johnson, Brian. 1981. *Fly Navy: The History of Naval Aviation*. New York: Morrow.

Johnson, Chalmers A. 1982. *MITI and the Japanese Miracle: The Growth of Industrial Policy, 1925–1975*. Stanford, Calif.: Stanford University Press.

Johnson, David. 1984. "The Failed Experiment: Military Aviation and Urban Development in San Antonio, 1910–40." In *The Martial Metropolis: U.S. Cities in War and Peace*, ed. Roger W. Lotchin. New York: Praeger.

Johnson, Kenneth M. 1961. *Aerial California: An Account of Early Flight in Northern and Southern California, 1849 to World War I*. Los Angeles: Dawson's Book Shop.

Johnson, R. 1978. "America's Military Might Is Also Bastion of the Florida Economy." *Florida Trends* (July): 30–39.

Joint Economic Committee. 1982. *Location of High Technology Firms and Regional Economic Development*. Washington, D.C.: Government Printing Office.

Kahley, W. 1982. "Southern Fireworks: Will Defense Spending Light Up the South?" *Federal Reserve Bank of Atlanta Economic Review* (December): 21–31.

Kaldor, Mary. 1981. *The Baroque Arsenal*. New York: Hill and Wang.

Karaska, Gerald. 1967. "The Spatial Impacts of Defense-Space Procurement: An Analysis of Subcontracting Patterns in the United States." *Peace Research Society Papers* 8: 108–22.

Karlson, Stephen. 1983. "Modeling Location and Production: An Application to U.S. Fully-Integrated Steel Plants." *Review of Economics and Statistics* 65: 41–50.

Keeble, David. 1988. "High Technology Industry and Local Environments in the United Kingdom." In *High Technology Industry and Innovative Environments: The European Experience*, ed. Philippe Aydalot and David Keeble. London: Routledge and Kegan Paul.

Kelly, Fred. C. 1943. *The Wright Brothers: A Biography Authorized by Orville Wright*. New York: Harcourt, Brace.

Kelly, Fred C., ed. 1951. *Miracle at Kitty Hawk: The Letters of Wilbur and Orville Wright*. New York: Farrar, Straus, and Young.

Kelsey, Benjamin S. 1982. *The Dragon's Teeth: The Creation of United States Air Power for World War II*. Washington, D.C.: Smithsonian Institution.

Kennedy, Gavin. 1983. *Defense Economics*. London: Duckworth.

Kinder, Frank L., and Philip Neff. 1945. *An Economic Survey of the Los Angeles Area*. Los Angeles: Haynes Foundation.

Kleinknecht, Kenneth S. 1964. "The Rocket Research Airplanes." In *The History of Rocket Technology: Essays on Research, Development, and Utility,* ed. Eugene M. Emme. Detroit: Wayne State University Press.

Koestler, Arthur. 1975. *The Act of Creation*. London: Picador.

Koistinen, Paul A. C. 1980. *The Military–Industrial Complex: An Historical Perspective*. New York: Praeger.

Kondratieff, Nikolai D. 1935. "The Long Waves in Economic Life." *Review of Economic Statistics* 17: 105–15.

Kondratieff, Nikolai D. 1984. *The Long Wave Cycle*. New York: Richardson and Snyder.

Koppes, Clayton R. 1982. *JPL and the American Space Program: A History of the Jet Propulsion Laboratory*. New Haven, Conn.: Yale University Press.

Kort, John Richard Beemiller, and Cary Harmon. 1986. "Defense Procurement and State Economic Growth." Paper presented at the meetings of the Southern Regional Science Association, New Orleans (March 6–8).

Krumme, Gunter, and Roger Hayter. 1975. "Implications of Corporate Strategies and Product Cycle Adjustments for Regional Employment Changes." In *Locational Dynamics of Manufacturing Activity,* ed. L. Collins and D. Walker. London: Wiley.

Kurth, James R. 1973. "Aerospace Production Lines and American Defense Spending." In *Testing the Theory of the Military–Industrial Complex*, ed. Steven Rosen. Lexington, Mass.: Heath.

Kuter, Laurence S. 1973. *The Great Gamble: The Boeing 747*. Huntsville: University of Alabama Press.

Lacey, Robert. 1986. *Ford: The Men and the Machine*. Boston: Little, Brown.

Lampe, David., ed. 1988. *The Massachusetts Miracle*. Cambridge, Mass.: MIT Press.

Lee, Jim, and Linda McDaniel. 1985. "The U.S. Defense Market." In *Proceedings of the UCLA Business Forecasting Conference*. Los Angeles: UCLA Business Forecasting Project, Graduate School of Management.

Leighton, Richard M. 1969. "The American Arsenal Policy in World War II: A Retrospective View." In *Some Pathways in Twentieth Century History,* ed. D. R. Beaver. Detroit: Wayne State University Press.

Lens, Sidney. 1970. *The Military–Industrial Complex*. Philadelphia: Pilgrim Press.

Leontief, W., A Morgan, K. Polenske, D. Simpson, and E. Tower. 1965. "The Economic Impact—Industrial and Regional—of an Arms Cut." *Review of Economics and Statistics* 47: 147–64.

Levin, Richard C. 1982. "The Semiconductor Industry." In *Government and Technical Progress: A Cross-Industry Analysis,* ed. Richard R. Nelson. New York: Pergamon Press.

Levy Y. 1972. "On San Diego Bay." *Federal Reserve Bank of San Francisco Monthly Review* (September): 3–9.

Lockwood, Charles, and Christopher Leinberger. 1988. "Los Angeles Comes of Age." *Atlantic Monthly* (January): 31–56.

Long, Franklin A., and Judith Reppy. 1980. *The Genesis of New Weapons: Decision Making for Military R&D*. New York: Pergamon Press.

Long, John F. 1976. "Interstate Migration of the Armed Forces." Paper presented at the annual meeting of the Southern Sociological Society, Miami (April).

Loomba, R. P. 1967. "A Study of the Re-employment and Unemployment Experiences of Scientists and Engineers Laid off from 62 Aerospace and Electronics Firms in the San Francisco Bay Area During 1963–65." Manpower Research Group, Center for Interdisciplinary Studies, San Jose State College (February).

Loria, Joan. 1984. "Die Massachusetts Institute of Technology und die Entwicklung der Region Boston." In *Die Zukunft der Metropolen: Paris, London, New York, Berlin: Katlog zur Ausstellung*, ed. Karl Schwarz. Berlin: Technische Universität.

Los Angeles. 1976. "Aerospace and Industrial Development in Los Angeles." In *The Economic Development of Southern California, 1920–1976*. Vol. 1. Los Angeles: Office of the Mayor.

Los Angeles. Chamber of Commerce. Aviation Committee. 1940. *Summary of a Report on the Master Plan of Airports for the Los Angeles County Regional Planning District*. Los Angeles: Chamber of Commerce.

Los Angeles County. Regional Planning Commission. 1967. *Industrial Location Factors Survey*. Los Angeles: The Commission.

Lösch, August. [1944] 1954. *The Economics of Location*. Translated by W. H. Woglom. New Haven, Conn.: Yale University Press.

Lotchin, Roger W. 1979. "The Metropolitan/Military Complex in Comparative Perspective: San Francisco, Los Angeles, and San Diego, 1919–1941." In *The Urban West*, ed. Gerald D. Nash. Manhattan, Kans.: Sunflower University Press.

Lotchin, Roger W. 1982. "The City and the Sword in Metropolitan California, 1919–1941." *Urbanism Past and Present* 14: 1–16.

Lotchin, Roger W., ed. 1984. *The Martial Metropolis: U.S. Cities in War and Peace*. New York: Praeger.

Lovering, John. 1987. "Militarism, Capitalism, and the Nation-State: Toward a Realist Synthesis." *Environment and Planning, D: Society and Space* 5: 283–302.

MacClosky, Monro. 1968. *From Gasbags to Spaceships: The Story of the U.S. Air Force*. New York: Richards Rosen.

Machine Action Project. 1987. *The Hampden County Metalworking Industry: Structure, Products, Possibilities*. Springfield, Mass.: Machine Action Project.

MacLaren, Malcolm. 1943. *The Rise of the Electrical Industry During the Nineteenth Century*. Princeton, N.J.: Princeton University Press.

Maclaurin, W. Rupert. 1949. *Invention and Innovation in the Radio Industry*. New York: Macmillan.

Maitland, Lester. 1929. *Knights of the Air*. Garden City, N.Y.: Doubleday, Doran.

Maki, Wilbur, David Bogenschultz, Christine Evans, and Michael Senese. 1989. *Military Production and the Minnesota Economy*. St. Paul: State of Minnesota, Department of Jobs and Training.

Malecki, Edward J. 1980a. "Corporate Organization of R&D and the Location of Technological Activities." *Regional Studies* 14: 219–34.

Malecki, Edward J. 1980b. "Science and Technology in the American Urban System." In *The American Metropolitan System: Past and Future,* ed. S. D. Brunn and J. O. Wheeler. London: Edward Arnold.

Malecki, Edward J. 1980c. "Technological Change: British and American Research Themes." *Area* 12: 253–60.

Malecki, Edward J. 1981a. "Government-Funded R&D: Some Regional Economic Implications." *Professional Geographer* 33: 72–82.

Malecki, Edward J. 1981b. "Public and Private Sector Interrelationships, Technological Change, and Regional Development." *Papers of the Regional Science Association* 47: 121–37.

Malecki, Edward J. 1981c. "Recent Trends in the Location of Industrial R&D in the

United States." In *Industrial Location and Regional Systems: Spatial Organization in the Economic Sector,* ed. John Rees, Geoffrey Hewings, and Howard A. Stafford. London: Croom Helm.

Malecki, Edward J. 1984. "Military Spending and the U.S. Defense Industry: Regional Patterns of Military Contracts and Subcontracts." *Environment and Planning C: Government and Policy* 2: 31–44.

Malina, Frank J. 1964. "Origins and First Decade of the Jet Propulsion Laboratory." In *The History of Rocket Technology: Essays on Research, Development, and Utility,* ed. Eugene M. Emme. Detroit: Wayne State University Press.

Mandel, Ernest. 1973. *Late Capitalism.* Atlantic Highlands, N.J.: Humanities Press.

Mandel, Ernest. 1980. *Long Waves of Capitalist Development.* Cambridge: Cambridge University Press.

Manno, Jack. 1984. *Arming the Heavens: The Hidden Military Agenda for Space, 1945–1995.* New York: Dodd, Mead.

Mansfield, Harold. 1956. *Vision: A Saga of the Sky.* New York: Duell, Sloan & Pearce.

Marfels, Christian. 1978. "The Structure of the Military–Industrial Complex in the United States and Its Impact on Industrial Concentration." *Kyklos* 31: 409–23.

Markusen, Ann. 1977. "Federal Budget Simplication: Preventive Programs vs. Palliatives for Local Government with Booming, Stable and Declining Economies." *National Tax Journal* 30.

Markusen, Ann R., et al. 1985a. "Military Spending and Urban Development in California." *Berkeley Planning Journal* 1: 54–68.

Markusen, Ann R. 1985b. *Profit Cycles, Oligopoly, and Regional Development.* Cambridge, Mass.: MIT Press.

Markusen, Ann R. 1986a. "Defense Spending: A Successful Industrial Policy?" *International Journal of Urban and Regional Research* 10: 105–22.

Markusen, Ann R. 1986b. "Defense Spending and the Geography of High Tech Industries." In *Technology Regions and Policy,* ed. John Rees. New York: Praeger.

Markusen, Ann R. 1986c. "The Economic and Regional Consequences of Military-led Innovation." In *Strategic Computing: Defense Research and High Technology,* ed. Paul Edwards and Richard Gordon. New York: Columbia University Press.

Markusen, Ann R. 1986d. "The Militarized Economy: Deforming U.S. Growth and Productivity." *World Policy Journal* 3: 495–516.

Markusen, Ann R. 1986e. "The Military Remapping of the United States." *Built Environment* 11: 171–80.

Markusen, Ann R. 1987a. "America's Militarized Economy." *Best of Business* 9: 39–46.

Markusen, Ann R. 1987b. *Regions: The Economics and Politics of Territory.* Totowa, N.J.: Rowman and Littlefield.

Markusen, Ann R. 1988. "Industrial Restructuring and Regional Politics." In *Spatial Variations: Community, Politics and Industry in the Postwar United States,* ed. Robert Beauregard. Newbury Park, Calif.: Sage.

Markusen, Ann R. 1990a. "The Economic, Industrial and Regional Consequences of Defense-led Innovation." In *Technology, Innovation, and Society,* ed. Åke Andersson. Forthcoming.

Markusen, Ann R. 1990b. "Government as Market: Industrial Location in the U.S. Defense Industry." In *Industrial Location and Public Policy,* ed. Henry Herzog and Allan Schlottman. Knoxville: University of Tennessee Press.

Markusen, Ann R. 1991. *The Cold War Economy*. New York: Basic Books. Forthcoming.

Markusen, Ann R., and Robin Bloch. 1984. "Defensive Cities: Military Spending, High Technology, and Human Settlements." In *High Technology, Space, and Society,* ed. Manuel Castells. Urban Affairs Annual Reviews, no. 28. Beverly Hills, Calif.: Sage.

Markusen, Ann R., and Virginia Carlson. 1989. "Deindustrialization in the American Midwest: Causes and Responses." In *Deindustrialization in the U.S.: Lessons for Japan,* ed. Lloyd Rodwin and Hidehiko Sazanami. London: Unwin Hyman.

Markusen, Ann R., Peter Hall, and Amy Glasmeier. 1986. *High Tech America: The What, How, Where, and Why of the Sunrise Industries*. Boston: Allen & Unwin.

Markusen, Ann R., and Karen McCurdy. 1989. "Chicago's Defense-Based High Technology: A Case Study of the 'Seedbeds of Innovation' Hypothesis." *Economic Development Quarterly* 3: 15–31.

Mason, Herbert M. 1976. *The United States Air Force: A Turbulent History*. New York: Mason/Charter.

Massachusetts. Department of Employment and Training. 1989. *Adjusting to Change in Defense Spending: A Report to the Legislature*. Boston: State of Massachusetts, Department of Employment and Training, Field Research Service.

Massey, Doreen. 1984. *Spatial Divisions of Labor: Social Structures and the Geography of Production*. New York: Methuen.

Massey, Doreen, and John Allen, eds. 1984. *Geography Matters: A Reader*. Cambridge: Cambridge University Press.

Massey, Doreen, and Richard Meegan. 1978. "Industrial Restructuring Versus the Cities." *Urban Studies* 15: 273–88.

Massey, Doreen, and Richard Meegan. 1982. *The Anatomy of Job Loss: The How, Why, and Where of Employment Decline*. London: Methuen.

Mayers, Jackson. 1975. *Burbank History*. Burbank, Calif.: Anderson.

Mazza, Jacqueline, and Dale E. Wilkinson. 1980. *The Unprotected Flank: Regional and Strategic Imbalances in Defense Spending Patterns*. Washington, D.C.: Northeast-Midwest Institute.

McClendon, R. Earl. 1952. *The Question of Autonomy for the United States Air Arm, 1907–1945*. Maxwell, Ala.: Air Force University, Research Studies Institute, Documents Research Division.

McFarland, Marvin W. 1978. "Wilbur and Orville Wright: Seventy-five Years after." In *The Wright Brothers: Heirs of Prometheus,* ed. Richard P. Hallion. Washington, D.C.: Smithsonian Institution.

McLaughlin, Constance McL. 1962. *Washington: Village and Capital, 1800–1878*. Princeton, N.J.: Princeton University Press.

McLaughlin, Constance McL. 1963. *Washington: Capital City, 1879–1950*. Princeton, N.J.: Princeton University Press.

McMahon, John R. 1930. *The Wright Brothers: Fathers of Flight*. Boston: Little, Brown.

McWilliams, Carey. 1946. *Southern California Country: An Island on the Land*. New York: Duell, Sloan & Pearce.

Melman, Seymour. 1970. *Pentagon Capitalism: The Political Economy of War*. New York: McGraw-Hill.

Melman, Seymour. 1974. *The Permanent War Economy: American Capitalism in Decline*. New York: Simon and Schuster.

Melman, Seymour. 1983. *Profits Without Production*. New York: Knopf.

Melman, Seymour, ed. 1971. *The War Economy of the United States: Readings on Military Industry and Economy.* New York: St. Martin's Press.

Mettler, Ruben F. 1982. *The Little Brown Hen that Could: The Growth Story of TRW Inc.* New York: Newcomen Society in North America.

Metzger, H. Peter. 1972. *The Atomic Establishment.* New York: Simon and Schuster.

Miernyk, William. 1967. *Impact of the Space Program on a Local Economy: An Input–Output Analysis.* Morgantown: West Virginia University Library.

Miller, Robert L. 1987. "The New American Downtown: Tyson's Corner as a Case Study." *Architectural Record* 175: 79–83.

Miller, Ronald, and David Sawers. 1970. *The Technical Development of Modern Aviation.* New York: Praeger.

Mingos, Howard. 1930. *The Birth of an Industry.* New York: Privately printed.

Mollenkopf, John. 1983. *The Contested City.* Princeton, N.J.: Princeton University Press.

Molotch, Harvey, and John Logan. 1987. *Urban Fortunes: The Political Economy of Place.* Berkeley: University of California Press.

Moore, Samuel T. 1958. *U.S. Airpower: Story of American Fighting Planes and Missiles from Hydrogen Bags to Hydrogen Warheads.* New York: Greenberg.

Morris, Richard K. 1966. *John P. Holland, 1841–1914: Inventor of the Modern Submarine.* Annapolis: United States Naval Institute.

Mulhern, J. 1981. "The Defense Sector: A Source of Strength for Philadelphia's Economy." *Federal Reserve Bank of Philadelphia Business Review* (July–August): 3–14.

Munson, Kenneth. 1968. *Helicopters and Other Rotorcraft Since 1907.* New York: Macmillan.

Murdock, Clark A. 1974. *Defense Policy Formation: A Comparative Analysis of the McNamara Era.* Albany: State University of New York Press.

Nadeau, Remi. 1960. *Los Angeles: From Mission to Modern City.* New York: Longman.

Nash, Gerald D. 1985. *The American West Transformed: The Impact of the Second World War.* Bloomington: Indiana University Press.

Nelson, Gerald B. 1977. *Seattle: The Life and Times of an American City.* New York: Knopf.

Nelson, Richard R., Merton J. Peck, and Edward D. Kalachek. 1967. *Technology, Economic Growth and Public Policy.* Washington, D.C.: Brookings Institution.

Nevins, Allan, and Frank Ernest Hill. 1954. *Ford: Expansion and Challenge, 1915–1933.* New York: Scribner.

Nevins, Allan, and Frank Ernest Hill. 1962. *Ford: Decline and Rebirth, 1933–62.* New York: Scribner.

Nimroody, Rosy. 1987. "SDI Costs: Some Win, Some Lose." *Council on Economic Priorities Newsletter* (June): 1–5.

Niven, John, Courtlandt Canby, and Vernon Welsh. 1960. *Dynamic America: A History of General Dynamics Corporation and Its Predecessor Companies.* New York: General Dynamics Corporation and Doubleday.

Noble, David F. 1977. *America by Design: Science, Technology, and the Rise of Corporate Capitalism.* New York: Knopf.

North, Douglass C. 1955 "Location Theory and Regional Economic Growth." *Journal of Political Economy* 63: 243–58.

"North American Comes to Los Angeles." 1935. Press release, *Los Angeles Chamber of Commerce* (July 28).

Northeast-Midwest Institute. 1990. "The Northeast-Midwest Groups Set Their Agenda for the New Year." *Northeast-Midwest Economic Review* (January 22): 5–15.

Norton, R. D., and John Rees. 1979. "The Product Cycle and the Spatial Decentralization of American Manufacturing." *Regional Studies* 13: 141–51.

Nutter, Ervin J. 1982. *The Elano Story: An Engineer's Free Enterprise Dream.* New York: Newcomen Society in North America.

Ognibene, Peter J. 1975. *Scoop: The Life and Politics of Henry M. Jackson.* New York: Stein and Day.

O'Hare, Kenneth. 1986. "Nation's Military Buildup Hurts Chicago Economy." *Crains Chicago Business* (February 17): 11.

OhUallachain, Brendan. 1987. "Regional and Technological Implications of the Recent Growth in American Defense Spending." *Annals of the Association of American Geographers* 72: 208–23.

Oliver, Richard P. 1970. "Increase in Defense-Related Employment During Viet Nam Buildup." *Monthly Labor Review* (February): 3–10.

Oliver, Richard P. 1971. "Employment Effects of Reduced Defense Spending." *Monthly Labor Review* (December): 3–11.

Osterbind, Carter C. 1967. "The Impact of Aerospace and Defense Programs on the Florida Economy." *Business and Economic Dimensions* 3: 1–8.

Parzen, Julia. 1981. *The Aerospace Industry in California.* San Francisco: State of California, Office of Economic Policy, Planning, and Research.

Passer, Harold C. 1953. *The Electrical Manufacturers 1875–1900: A Study in Competition, Entrepreneurship, Technical Change, and Economic Growth.* Cambridge, Mass.: Harvard University Press.

Patz, William. 1989. "Northwest Conversion Planning." *Plowshares Press* (Spring): 8.

Peck, Merton J., and Frederick W. Scherer. 1962. *The Weapons Acquisition Process.* Boston: Harvard University, Graduate School of Business Administration.

Pendray, G. Edward. 1964. "Pioneer Rocket Development in the United States." In *The History of Rocket Technology: Essays on Research, Development, and Utility,* ed. Eugene M. Emme. Detroit: Wayne State University Press.

Perrin, Jean-Claude. 1988. "New Technologies, Local Synergies, and Regional Policies in Europe." In *High Technology Industry and Innovative Environments: The European Experience,* ed. Philippe Aydalot and David Keeble. London: Routledge and Kegan Paul.

Perloff, Harvey, Edgar Dunn, Jr., Eric Lampard, and Richard Muth. 1960. *Regions, Resources and Economic Growth.* Baltimore: Johns Hopkins University Press.

Perroux, François. 1961. *L'Economie du XX siècle.* Paris: Presses Universitaires de France.

Perroux, François. 1965. *La Pensée économique de Joseph Schumpeter: les dynamiques du capitalisme.* Geneva: Droz.

Perry, David. 1987a. "The Politics of Dependency in Deindustrializing America: The Case of Buffalo, New York." In *The Capitalist City: Global Restructuring and Community Politics,* ed. Michael Smith and Joseph Feagin. Oxford: Basil Blackwell.

Perry, Edward C. 1987b. *Burbank: An Illustrated History.* Northridge, Calif.: Windsor.

Perry, Robert L. 1964. "The Atlas, Thor, Titan, and Minuteman." In *The History of Rocket Technology: Essays on Research, Development, and Utility,* ed. Eugene M. Emme. Detroit: Wayne State University Press.

Peterson, Paul. 1981. *City Limits.* Chicago: University of Chicago Press.

Phillips, Almarin. 1971. *Technology and Market Structure: A Study of the Aircraft Industry.* Lexington, Mass.: Lexington Books.

Piore, Michael J., and Charles F. Sabel. 1984. *The Second Industrial Divide: Possibilities for Prosperity.* New York: Basic Books.

Pirenne, Henri. 1914. "Les Périodes de l'histoire sociale du capitalisme." *Bulletin de l'Académie Royale de Belgique* 5: 258–99.

Polmar, Norman. 1963. *Atomic Submarines.* Princeton; N.J.: Van Nostrand.

Polmar, Norman. 1975. *Strategic Weapons: An Introduction.* New York: Crane, Russack for the National Strategy Information Center.

Powaksi, Ronald. 1987. *March to Armageddon: The United States and the Nuclear Arms Race, 1939 to the Present.* New York: Oxford University Press.

Pratt & Whitney Division of United Aircraft Company. 1950. *The Pratt & Whitney Aircraft Story.* [New Haven, Conn.:] Pratt & Whitney Aircraft.

Pred, Allan. 1977. *City-Systems in Advanced Economies: Past Growth, Present Processes, and Future Development Options.* London: Hutchinson.

Prochnau, William M., and Richard W. Larsen. 1972. *A Certain Democrat: Senator Henry M. Jackson, A Political Biography.* Englewood Cliffs, N.J.: Prentice-Hall.

Prout, Henry G. 1921. *A Life of George Westinghouse.* New York: American Society of Mechanical Engineers.

Rae, John B. 1968. *Climb to Greatness: The American Aircraft Industry, 1920–1960.* Cambridge, Mass.: MIT Press.

Rainey, Richard B., et. al. 1973. *Seattle's Adaptation to Recession.* Santa Monica, Calif.: RAND.

Rand, Christopher. 1967. *Los Angeles: The Ultimate City.* New York: Oxford University Press.

Raschke, Carl. 1986. "Space Capital, U.S.A.: Boosters vs. Skeptics." *Colorado Business* (March): 38–9.

Ravenstein, Charles A. 1986. *The Organization and Lineage of the United States Air Force.* Washington, D.C.: United States Air Force, Office of Air Force History.

Redmond, Kent C., and Thomas M. Smith. 1980. *Project Whirlwind: The History of a Pioneer Computer.* Bedford, Mass.: Digital Press.

Rees, John. 1981. "The Impact of Defense Spending on Regional Industrial Change in the United States." In *Federalism and Regional Development,* ed. G. W. Hoffman. Austin: University of Texas Press.

Rees, John. 1982. "Defense Spending and Regional Industrial Change." *Texas Business Review* (January–February): 40–44.

Rees, John, Geoffrey Hewings, and Howard A. Stafford, eds. 1981. *Industrial Location and Regional Systems: Spatial Organization in the Economic Sector.* London: Croom Helm.

Rees, John, and Howard A. Stafford. 1983. *A Review of Regional Growth and Industrial Location Theory: Toward Understanding the Development of High Technology Complexes in the United States.* Washington, D.C.: Office of Technology Assessment.

Reich, Leonard. 1985. *The Making of American Industrial Research: Science and Business at GE and Bell, 1876–1926.* Cambridge: Cambridge University Press.

Reppy, Judith. 1985. "Military R&D and the Civilian Economy." *Bulletin of the Atomic Scientists* 41: 3–7.

Reps, John William. 1979. *Cities of the American West: A History of Frontier Urban Planning*. Princeton, N.J.: Princeton University Press.

Riefler, R., and P. Downing. 1968. "Regional Effect of Defense Effort on Employment." *Monthly Labor Review* 91: 1–8

Rodell, Michael J., ed. 1971. "The Palmdale Intercontinental Airport and Urban Development in the Antelope Valley: Selected Issues and Policies." Working paper. School of Architecture and Urban Planning, University of California, Los Angeles.

Roe, Joseph W. 1916. *English and American Tool Makers*. New Haven, Conn.: Yale University Press.

Rolle, Andrew F. 1981. *Los Angeles: From Pueblo to City of the Future*. San Francisco: Boyd and Fraser.

Roseberry, C. R. 1966. *The Challenging Skies: The Colorful Story of Aviation's Most Exciting Years, 1919–1939*. Garden City, N.Y.: Doubleday.

Roseberry, C. R. 1972. *Glenn Curtiss: Pioneer of Flight*. Garden City, N.Y.: Doubleday.

Rosen, Steven, ed. 1973. *Testing the Theory of the Military–Industrial Complex*. Lexington, Mass.: Heath.

Rosenberg, Nathan. 1972. *Technology and American Economic Growth*. New York: Harper & Row.

Rosenberg, Sam. 1991. *American Economic Development Since 1945*. London: Macmillan.

Roso, Anthony, Jr. 1986. *Consolidated Space Operation Center: Economic Impact Analysis, El Paso County*. Colorado Springs: Pikes Peak Area Council of Government, Department of the Air Force, Consolidated Space Operations Center.

Roso, Anthony, Jr. 1987. *Defense Contract Spending and Local Economic Development Potential in El Paso County, Colorado*. Colorado Springs: Pikes Peak Area Council of Government, Department of the Air Force, Consolidated Space Operations Center.

Ross, Jean, and Gary Fields. 1984. "Defense Spending and the Economy of Los Angeles County." Unpublished paper. Department of City and Regional Planning, University of California, Berkeley.

Rossano, Geoffrey. 1984. "Suburbia Armed: Nassau County Development and the Rise of the Aerospace Industry, 1909–60." In *The Martial Metropolis: U.S. Cities in War and Peace*, ed. Roger W. Lotchin. New York: Praeger.

Rubenstein, Albert. 1958. "Problems of Financing and Managing New Research-Based Enterprises in New England." Department of Industrial Management, Massachusetts Institute of Technology. Mimeo.

Rubenstein, Albert, and Dawson Brewer. 1962. *Research and Development in the Chicago Area Electronics Industry*. Evanston, Ill.: Northwestern University.

Rubenstein, Murray, and Richard Goldman. 1974. *To Join with the Eagles: Curtiss-Wright Aircraft, 1903–1965*. Garden City, N.Y.: Doubleday.

Rundquist, Barry. 1983. "Politics' Benefits and Public Policy: Interpretation of Recent U.S. Studies." *Environment and Planning C: Government and Policy* 1:401–12.

Rutzick, Max A. 1970. "Skills and Location of Defense-Related Workers." *Monthly Labor Review* (February): 11–16.

Sale, Roger. 1976. *Seattle: Past to Present*. Seattle: University of Washington Press.

Sarkesian, Sam C., ed. 1971. *The Military–Industrial Complex: A Reassessment*. Beverly Hills, Calif.: Sage.

Saxenian, AnnaLee. 1980. "Silicon Chips and Spatial Structure: The Spatial Basis of Urbanization in Santa Clara County, California." Working paper, no. 345. Institute of Urban and Regional Development, University of California, Berkeley.

Saxenian, AnnaLee. 1983. "The Genesis of Silicon Valley." *Built Environment* 9: 7–17.

Saxenian, AnnaLee. 1985a. "The Genesis of Silicon Valley." In *Silicon Landscapes,* ed. Peter Hall and Ann R. Markusen. Boston: Allen and Unwin.

Saxenian, AnnaLee. 1985b. "Innovative Manufacturing Industries: Spatial Incidence in the United States." In *High Technology, Space, and Society,* ed. Manuel Castells. Urban Affairs Annual Reviews, no. 28. Beverly Hills, Calif.: Sage.

Saxenian, AnnaLee. 1988. "The Cheshire Cat's Grin: Innovation and Regional Development in England." *Technology Review* 91: 67–75.

Scherer, Frederick M. 1984. *Innovation and Growth: Schumpeterian Perspectives.* Cambridge Mass.: MIT Press.

Schiesl, Martin. 1984. "Airplanes to Aerospace: Defense Spending and Economic Growth in the Los Angeles Region, 1940–1960." In *The Martial Metropolis: U.S. Cities in War and Peace,* ed. Roger W. Lotchin. New York: Praeger.

Schlesinger, James. 1985. "The Office of the Secretary of Defense." In *Reorganizing America's Defense: Leadership in War and Peace,* ed. Robert J. Art, Vincent Davis, and Samuel P. Huntington. Washington, D.C.: Pergamon-Brassey's.

Schlesinger, Tom, John Gaventa, and Juliet Merrifield. 1983. *Our Own Worst Enemy: The Impact of Military Production on the Upper South.* New Market, Tenn.: Highlander Research and Education Center.

Schlottman, Alan, and Henry Herzog. 1990. *Industrial Location and Public Policy.* Knoxville: University of Tennessee Press.

Schoneberger, William A. 1984. *California Wings: A History of Aviation in the Golden State.* Woodland Hills, Calif.: Windsor.

Schumpeter, Joseph A. 1939. *Business Cycles.* New York: McGraw-Hill.

Schumpeter, Joseph A. [1911] 1961. *The Theory of Economic Development.* Cambridge, Mass.: Harvard University Press.

Schwiebert, Ernest G., ed. 1965. *A History of the U.S. Air Force Ballistic Missiles.* New York: Praeger.

Sciever, Thomas, Alma Horvath, and T. Bessmer. 1980. *History of Ford Air Transportation Department: 1901–1979.* St. Louis: VIP Printing.

Scott, Allen J. 1982. "Locational Patterns and Dynamics of Industrial Activity in the Modern Metropolis." *Urban Studies* 19: 114–42.

Scott, Allen J. 1983a. "Industrial Organization and the Logic of Intra-Metropolitan Location: I. Theoretical Considerations. *Economic Geography* 59: 233–50.

Scott, Allen J. 1983b. "Industrial Organization and the Logic of Intra-Metropolitan Location: II. A Case Study of the Printed Circuits Industry in the Greater Los Angeles Region." *Economic Geography* 59: 343–67.

Scott, Allen J. 1984a. "Industrial Organization and the Logic of Intra-Metropolitan Location: III. A Case Study of the Women's Dress Industry in the Greater Los Angeles Region." *Economic Geography* 60: 3–27.

Scott, Allen J. 1984b. "Territorial Reproduction and Transformation in a Local Labor Market: The Animated Film Workers of Los Angeles." *Environment and Planning D: Society and Space* 2: 277–307.

Scott, Allen J. 1985. "Industrialization and Urbanization: A Geographical Agenda." *Annals of the Association of American Geographers* 76: 25–37.

Scott, Allen J. 1986a. "High Technology Industry and Territorial Development: The Rise of the Orange County Complex, 1955–1984." *Urban Geography* 7: 3–45.

Scott, Allen J. 1986b. "Industrial Organization and Location: Division of Labor, the Firm, and Spatial Process." *Economic Geography* 62: 215–231.

Scott, Allen J. 1986c. "Location Processes, Urbanization, and Territorial Development: An Exploratory Essay." *Environment and Planning A* 17: 479–501.

Scott, Allen J. 1987. "The Semiconductor Industry in Southeast Asia: Organization, Location, and the International Division of Labour." *Regional Studies* 21: 143–60.

Scott, Allen J. 1989. *The Technopoles of Southern California.* UCLA Research Papers in Economic and Urban Geography, no. 1. Los Angeles: UCLA, Department of Geography.

Scott, Allen J., and David P. Angel. 1987. "The U.S. Semiconductor Industry: A Locational Analysis." *Environment and Planning, A* 19: 875–912.

Scott, Allen J., and M. Drayse. 1991. "The Geography of High Technology in Southern California, II: Growth and Development of the Electronics Sector, 1945–1989." *Economic Geography.* Forthcoming.

Scott, Allen J., and D. J. Mattingly. 1989. "The Geography of High Technology in Southern California, I: Aircraft and Parts Manufacturing from the Inter-War Years to the 1990s." *Economic Geography* 65, 48–71.

Scott, Allen J., and Michael Storper, eds. 1986a. *Production, Work, Territory: The Geographical Anatomy of Industrial Capitalism.* Boston: Allen and Unwin.

Scott, Allen J., and Michael Storper. 1986b. "Industrial Change and Territorial Organization: A Summing Up." In *Production, Work, Territory: The Geographical Anatomy of Industrial Capitalism,* ed. Allen J. Scott and Michael Storper. Boston: Allen and Unwin.

Scott, Otto J. 1974. *The Creative Ordeal: The Story of Raytheon.* New York: Atheneum.

Segal Quince Wicksteed. 1985. *The Cambridge Phenomenon: The Growth of High Technology Industry in a University Town.* Cambridge: Segal Quince Wicksteed.

Segal Quince Wicksteed. 1988. *Universities, Enterprise and Local Economic Development: An Exploration of Links, Based on Experience from Studies in Britain and Elsewhere.* A Report to the Manpower Services Commission. London: HMSO.

Shapira, Philip. 1986. *"Industry and Jobs in Transition: A Study of Industrial Restructuring and Worker Displacement in California."* Ph.D. diss., Department of City and Regional Planning, University of California, Berkeley.

Sherry, Michael S. 1987. *The Rise of American Air Power: The Creation of Armageddon.* New Haven, Conn.: Yale University Press.

Shield, Margaret. 1989. "Citizen Lobbyists Urge Economic Diversification." *Washington State SANE/FREEZE Citizen* (May–June):3.

Shiner, John F. 1983. *Foulois and the U.S. Army Air Corps, 1931–1935.* Washington, D.C.: United States Air Force, Office of Air Force History.

Siegel, B. 1983. "High Tech Revives Town but Prosperity Has Limits: Few Blue-Collar Jobs in Huntsville." *Los Angeles Times* (April 26): 1.

Silk, Leonard S. 1968. "Outer Space: The Impact on the American Economy." In *The History of the American Aircraft Industry: An Anthology,* ed. Gene R. Simonson. Cambridge, Mass.: MIT Press.

Simonson, Gene R., ed. 1968a. *The History of the American Aircraft Industry: An Anthology.* Cambridge, Mass.: MIT Press.

Simonson, Gene R. 1968b. "Missiles and Creative Destruction in the American Aircraft Industry, 1956–61." In *The History of the American Aircraft Industry: An Anthology,* ed. Gene R. Simonson. Cambridge, Mass.: MIT Press.

Skoro, Charles. 1988. "Rankings of State Business Climates: An Evaluation of Their Usefulness in Forecasting." *Economic Development Quarterly* 2: 138–52.

Slater, Jerome, and Terry Nardin. 1973. "The Concept of a Military-Industrial Complex." In *Testing the Theory of the Military–Industrial Complex,* ed. Steven Rosen. Lexington, Mass.: Heath.

Sloan, Alfred Q. 1964. *My Years with General Motors.* New York: Doubleday.

Slowick, Judith. 1980. *Defense Dependency in Connecticut.* Hartford: Economic Development Planning, Connecticut Department of Economic Development.

Smith, Alice Kimball. 1965. *A Peril and a Hope: The Scientists' Movement in America: 1945–47.* Chicago: University of Chicago Press.

Smith, Dan, and Ron Smith. 1983. *The Economics of Militarism.* London: Pluto.

Smith, Merritt R. 1977. "Military Arsenals and Industry Before World War I." On *War, Business and American Society: Historical Perspectives on the Military–Industrial Complex,* ed. Benjamin F. Cooling. Port Washington, N.Y.: Kennikat Press.

Smith, Michael, and Joseph Feagan, eds. 1987. *The Capitalist City: Global Restructuring and Community Politics.* Oxford: Basil Blackwell.

Smith, Neil. 1986. "On the Necessity of Uneven Development." *International Journal of Urban and Regional Research* 10: 87–104.

Smith, Robert A. 1972. *A Social History of the Bicycle: Its Early Life and Times in America.* New York: American Heritage Press.

Smith, V. 1974. *From Jennies to Jets: The Aviation History of Orange County.* Fullerton, Calif.: Sultana Press.

Smits, Edward J. 1974. *Nassau: Suburbia U.S.A.: The First Seventy-five Years of Nassau County, New York, 1899 to 1974.* Syosset, N.Y.: Friends of the Nassau County Museum.

Smits, F. M., ed. 1985. *A History of Science and Engineering in the Bell System: Electronics Technology (1925–1976).* Murray Hill, N.J.: AT&T Bell Laboratories.

Soja, Edward W. 1986. "Taking Los Angeles Apart: Some Fragments of a Critical Human Geography." *Environment and Planning, D: Society and Space* 4: 255–72.

Soja, Edward W., Rebecca Morales, and Goetz Wolff. 1983. "Urban Restructuring: An Analysis of Social and Spatial Change in Los Angeles." *Economic Geography* 59: 195–230.

Sprague, Marshall. 1971. *Newport in the Rockies.* Chicago: Swallow Press.

Stanford Research Institute. 1964. *An Exploratory Study of the Structure and Dynamics of the R&D Industry.* Menlo Park, Calif: SRI.

Stares, Paul. 1985. *The Militarization of Space.* Ithaca, N.Y.: Cornell University Press.

Starr, K. 1985. *Inventing the Dream: California Through the Progressive Era.* New York: Oxford University Press.

Steiner, George A. 1961. *National Defense and Southern California, 1961–1970.* Los Angeles: Committee for Economic Development.

Stekler, Herman O. 1965. *The Structure and Performance of the Aerospace Industry.* Berkeley: University of California Press.

Stöhr, Walter B. 1986. "Territorial Innovation Complexes." In *Milieux innovateurs en Europe,* ed. Philippe Aydalot. Paris: GREMI (privately printed).

Storper, Michael, and Allen J. Scott. 1986. "Production, Work, Territory: Contemporary Realities and Theoretical Tasks." In *Production, Work, Territory: The*

Geographical Anatomy of Industrial Capitalism, ed. Allen J. Scott and Michael Storper. Boston: Allen and Unwin.

Storper, Michael, and Richard Walker. 1983. "The Theory of Labour and the Theory of Location." *International Journal of Urban and Regional Research* 7:1–41.

Stowsky, Jay. 1986a. "Beating Our Plowshares into Double-Edged Swords: Assessing the Impact of Pentagon Policies on the Commercialization of Advanced Technologies." Working paper. Berkeley Roundtable on the International Economy, University of California, Berkeley.

Stowsky, Jay. 1986b. "Competing with the Pentagon." *World Policy Journal* 3:697–721.

Stowsky, Jay. 1989. "Regional Histories and the Cycle of Industrial Innovation: A Review of Some Recent Literature." *Berkeley Planning Journal* 4:114–24.

Stubbing, Richard A., and Richard A. Mendell. 1986. *The Defense Game: An Insider Explores the Astonishing Realities of America's Defense Establishment.* New York: Harper & Row.

Tansik, D., and R. B. Billings. 1971. "Current Impact of Military–Industrial Spending in Arizona." *Arizona Review* 20:8–9.

Taylor, M. J. 1975. "Organizational Growth, Spatial Interaction, and Locational Decisionmaking." *Regional Studies* 9:313–23.

Taylor, Michael J. H. 1982. *Boeing.* London: Jane's.

Testa, William, and Alenka Geise. 1987a. "Measuring Regional High Tech Activity with Occupational Data." Regional working paper. Federal Reserve Bank of Chicago (January).

Testa, William, and Alenka Geise. 1987b. "Industrial R&D: An Analysis of the Chicago Area." Regional working paper. Federal Reserve Bank of Chicago (June).

Thompson, Chris. 1988. "High Technology, Development, and Recession: The Local Experience in the United States, 1980–1982." *Economic Development Quarterly* 2:153–67.

Thompson, Wilbur. 1965. *A Preface to Urban Economics.* Baltimore: Johns Hopkins University Press.

Thompson, Wilbur. 1969. "The Economic Base of Urban Problems." In *Contemporary Economic Issues,* ed. Neil Chamberlain. Homewood, Ill.: Richard Irwin.

Thompson, Wilbur. 1975. "Internal and External Factors in Urban Economies." In *Regional Development and Planning: A Reader,* ed. John Friedmann and William Alonso. Cambridge, Mass.: MIT Press.

Thruelsen, Richard. 1976. *The Grumman Story.* New York: Praeger.

Thurow, Lester. 1986. "Economic Case Against Star Wars." *Plowshares Press* (Spring): 1.

Tiebout, Charles. 1966. "The Regional Impact of Defense Expenditures: Its Measurement and Problems of Adjustment." In *Defense and Disarmament,* ed. Roger Bolton. Englewood Cliffs, N.J.: Prentice-Hall.

Tilton, John E. 1971. *International Diffusion of Technology: The Case of Semiconductors.* Washington, D.C.: Brookings Institution.

Tipton, Richard S. N.d. *They Filled the Skies.* Fort Worth: Bell Helicopter Textron, Office of Public Affairs.

Tirman, John, ed. 1984. *The Militarization of High Technology.* Cambridge, Mass.: Ballinger.

Tobias, Sheila, Peter Goredinoff, Stefan Leader, and Shelah Leader. 1982. *What Kind of Guns Are They Buying for Your Butter?* New York: Morrow.

Tokaty, G. A. 1964. "Soviet Rocket Technology." In *The History of Rocket Technology: Essays on Research, Development, and Utility,* ed. Eugene M. Emme. Detroit: Wayne State University Press.

Trescott, Martha M. 1981. *The Rise of the American Electrochemicals Industry, 1880–1910: Studies in the American Technological Environment.* Westport, Conn.: Greenwood Press.

Treyz, George, Benjamin Stevens, David Ehrlich, Marion Anderson, Michael Frisch, and Michael Oden. 1987. "Using a Multiregional Forecasting and Simulation Model to Estimate the Effects of the Military Buildup from 1981–1985 on State Economies." Paper. Regional Economic Models, Inc., Amherst, Mass.

United Bank of Colorado. 1986. "Southern Regional Forecast." Denver. Mimeo.

United States Arms Control and Disarmament Agency. 1965. *A Case Study of the Effects of the Dyna-Soar Contract Cancellation upon Employees of the Boeing Company in Seattle, Washington.* Washington, D.C.: Government Printing Office.

U.S. Congress. House of Representatives. Select Committee Investigating National Defense Migration Pursuant to House Resolution 113. 1940–1942. *Hearings* (34 parts). 77th Cong., 2nd sess. Washington, D.C.: Government Printing Office.

U.S. Congress. House of Representatives. 1959. *Organization and Management of Missile Programs: Hearings Before a Subcommittee of the Committee on Government Operations.* 86th Cong. 1st sess. Washington, D.C.: Government Printing Office.

U.S. Congress. Office of Technology Assessment. 1985. *Demographic Trends and the Scientific and Engineering Work Force: A Technical Memorandum.* Washington, D.C.: Office of Technology Assessment.

U.S. Congress. Senate. Subcommittee of the Committee on Military Affairs. 1944. *Hearings on Labor Shortage in the Pacific Coast and Rocky Mountain States.* 78th Cong., 1st sess. Washington, D.C.: Government Printing Office.

U.S. Congress. Senate. Committee on Government Operations. Permanent Subcommittee on Investigations. 1963–1964. *TFX Contract Investigation. Hearings.* 88th Cong., 1st sess. Washington, D.C.: Government Printing Office.

U.S. Congress. Senate. Committee on Government Operations. Permanent Subcommittee on Investigations. 1970. *TFX Contract Investigation. (Second Series) Hearings.* 91st Cong., 2nd sess. Washington, D.C.: Government Printing Office.

U.S. Department of Defense. 1983. *Prime Contract Awards over $25,000 by State, County, Contractor and Place, Fiscal Year 1983.* Washington, D.C.: Government Printing Office.

U.S. Federal Trade Commission. 1980. *The Impact of Department of Defense Procurement on Competition in Commercial Markets: Case Studies of the Electronics and Helicopter Industries.* Washington, D.C.: Federal Trade Commission.

U.S. War Department. 1943. *You're Going to Employ Women.* Washington, D.C.: Government Printing Office.

Uselding, Paul. 1980. "Business History and the History of Technology." *Business History Review* 54: 443–52.

Utterback, James, and Albert Murray. 1977. *The Influence of Defense Procurement and Sponsorship of Research and Development on the Development of the Civilian Electronics Industry.* Final Report of U.S. National Bureau of Standards, Experimental Technology Incentives Program. Cambridge, Mass.: MIT, Center for Policy Alternatives.

Vaeth, J. Gordon. 1966. *Langley: Man of Science and Flight.* New York: Ronald Press.

Vagtborg, Harold. 1976. *Research and Industrial Development: A Bicentennial Look at the Contributions of Applied R&D*. New York: Pergamon Press.

Vance, James E. 1970. *The Merchant's World: The Geography of Wholesaling*. Englewood Cliffs, N.J.: Prentice-Hall.

Vernon, Raymond. 1960. *Metropolis 1985: An Interpretation of the Findings of the New York Metropolitan Region Study*. Cambridge, Mass.: Harvard University Press.

Vernon, Raymond. 1966. "International Investment and International Trade in the Product Cycle." *Quarterly Journal of Economics* 80: 190–207.

Virginia. 1983. "The Report of the Governor's Task Force on Science and Technology in Virginia." Vol. 2.

von Braun, Wernher. 1964. "The Redstone, Jupiter, and Juno." In *The History of Rocket Technology: Essays on Research, Development, and Utility*, ed. Eugene M. Emme. Detroit: Wayne State University Press.

von Braun, Wernher, and Frederick I. Ordway. 1975. *History of Rocketry and Space Travel*. 3rd ed. New York: Crowell.

von Kármán, Theodore. 1967. *The Wind and Beyond: Theodore von Kármán, Pioneer in Aviation and Pathfinder in Space*. Boston: Little, Brown.

von Thünen, Johann H. [1826] 1966. *von Thünen's Isolated State*. Edited by P. Hall, translated by C. M. Wartenberg. Oxford: Pergamon Press.

Wagner, William. 1976. *Reuben Fleet and the Story of Consolidated Aircraft*. Fallbrook, Calif.: Aero Publishers.

Walker, Lois E., and Shelby E. Wickam. 1986. *From Huffman Prairie to the Moon: The History of Wright-Patterson Air Base*. Washington, D.C.: Government Printing Office.

Walker, Richard. 1978. "Two Sources of Uneven Development Under Advanced Capitalism: Spatial Differentiation and Capital Mobility." *Review of Radical Political Economics* 10: 28–37.

Warner, Sam B. 1984. *Province of Reason*. Cambridge, Mass.: Harvard University Press.

Warner, Sam B. 1987. "The Evolution of High Technology in the Boston Region." Paper presented at the RICE Symposium, University of Karlstad, Sweden (June).

Warren, William. 1989. "The Influence of Defense Spending on the Rustbelt Syndrome: The Impact of the Reagan Revolution." Paper presented at the annual meeting of the Western Social Science Association, Albuquerque, New Mexico (April 29).

Warsh, David L. 1988. "War Stories: Defense Spending and the Growth of the Massachusetts Economy." In *The Massachusetts Miracle*, ed. David Lampe. Cambridge, Mass.: MIT Press.

Washington. Department of Commerce and Economic Development. 1965a. *Aerospace Industry in the State of Washington. Aircraft and Parts Industry* (SIC 372).

Washington. Department of Commerce and Economic Development. 1965b. *Transportation Equipment Industry in the State of Washington* (SIC 37).

Weber, Alfred. [1909] 1929. *Alfred Weber's Theory of the Location of Industries*. Translated by C. J. Friedrich. Chicago: University of Chicago Press.

Weigley, Russell F. 1973. *The American Way of War: A History of United States Military Strategy and Policy*. New York: Macmillan.

Weiss, Marc A. 1987. *The Rise of the Community Builders: The American Real Estate Industry and Urban Land Planning*. New York: Columbia University Press.

Weiss, Marc A. 1988. "Community Builders and the Growth of Los Angeles and

Southern California: An Historical View." Unpublished paper. Lincoln Institute of Land Policy, Cambridge, Mass.

Whitestone, Nicholas. 1973. *The Submarine: The Ultimate Weapon*. London: Davis-Poynter.

Wildes, Karl L., and Nilo A. Lindgren. 1985. *A Century of Electrical Engineering and Computer Science at MIT, 1882–1982*. Cambridge, Mass.: MIT Press.

Wilson, Alan G. 1981. *Catastrophe Theory and Bifurcation: Applications to Urban and Regional Systems*. Berkeley: University of California Press.

Wilson, Eugene. 1950. *Slipstream: The Autobiography of an Air Craftsman*. New York: McGraw-Hill.

Wilson, Eugene. 1965. *Slipstream: The Autobiography of an Air Craftsman*. 2nd ed. New York: McGraw-Hill.

Wise, George. 1985. *Willis R. Whitney, General Electric, and the Origins of U.S. Industrial Research*. New York: Columbia University Press

Witherow, Phil. 1987. "Springs Team at Core of SDI." *Gazette Telegraph* (Colorado Springs) (December 26).

Witze, Claude. 1965. "The USAF Missile Program: A Management Milestone." In *A History of U.S. Air Force Ballistic Missiles*, ed. Ernest G. Schwiebert. New York: Praeger.

Wright, Frank. 1969. "How Colorado Landed the Air Academy." *Denver Post, Empire Magazine* (June 22): 15–18.

Yarmolinsky, Adam. 1971. *The Military Establishment: Its Impacts on American Society*. New York: Harper & Row.

York, Herbert F. 1970. *Race to Oblivion: A Participant's View of the Arms Race*. New York: Simon and Schuster.

Young, David, and Neal Callahan. 1981. *Fill the Heavens with Commerce: Chicago Aviation, 1855–1926*. Chicago: Chicago Review Press.

Zegveld, Walter, and Christien Enzing. 1987. *SDI and Industrial Technology Policy: Threat or Opportunity?* London: Frances Pinter.

Zlatkovich, C. 1978. "Wichita Falls: An Emerging Manufacturing Center." *Texas Business Review* (November): 228–30.

Index